Rules, norms, and decisions

CAMBRIDGE STUDIES IN INTERNATIONAL RELATIONS: 2

Cambridge Studies in International Relations is a joint initiative of
Cambridge University Press and the British International Studies
Association (BISA). The series will include a wide range of material,
from undergraduate textbooks and surveys to research-based
monographs and collaborative volumes. The aim of the series is to
publish the best new scholarship in International Studies from Europe,
North America and the rest of the world.

D0839886

Cambridge Studies in International Relations

RULES, NORMS, AND DECISIONS

On the conditions of practical
and legal reasoning
in international relations and
domestic affairs

FRIEDRICH V. KRATOCHWIL
University of Pennsylvania

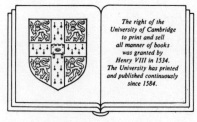

The right of the
University of Cambridge
to print and sell
all manner of books
was granted by
Henry VIII in 1534.
The University has printed
and published continuously
since 1584.

CAMBRIDGE UNIVERSITY PRESS

Cambridge

New York   Port Chester   Melbourne   Sydney

Published by the Press Syndicate of the University of Cambridge
The Pitt Building, Trumpington Street, Cambridge CB2 1RP
40 West 20th Street, New York, NY 10011–4211, USA
10 Stamford Road, Oakleigh, Melbourne 3166, Australia

First published 1989
Reprinted 1990
First paperback edition 1991

Printed in Great Britain at the University Press, Cambridge

British Library cataloguing in publication data

Kratochwil, Friedrich
  Rules, norms, and decisions: on the conditions of practical
  and legal reasoning in international relations and domestic
  affairs. – (Cambridge studies in international relations; 2).
  1. Jurisprudence
  I. Title
  340'.1

Library of Congress cataloguing in publication data

Kratochwil, Friedrich V.
  Rules, norms, and decisions: on the conditions of practical
  and legal reasoning in international relations and domestic
  affairs / Friedrich Kratochwil.
      p.   cm. – (Cambridge studies in international relations)
  Bibliography.
  Includes index.
  ISBN 0 521 35398 X
1. International law – Philosophy.   2. International relations –
Philosophy.   3. Law – Philosophy.   I. Title.   II. Series.
JX1245.K67 1989
341'. 01–dc19   88–23471   CIP

ISBN 0 521 35398 X hardback
ISBN 0 521 40971 3 paperback

To my friends

ἐκ τῶν φοβερῶν τῶνδε προσώπων
μέγα κέρδος ὁρῶ τοῖσδε πολίταις·
τάσδε γὰρ εὔφρονας εὔφρονες ἀεὶ
μέγα τιμῶντες καὶ γῆν καὶ πόλιν
ὀρθοδίκαιον
πρέψετε πάντως διάγοντες.

Great gain for Athens shall arise
From these grim forms and threatening eyes.
Then worship them with friendly heart,
For theirs is friendly. Let your State
Hold justice as her chiefest prize;
And land and city shall be great
And glorious in every part.

Aeschylus, *Eumenides* 990–995

CONTENTS

ACKNOWLEDGEMENTS

This research was furthered by a grant from the Alexander von Humboldt Foundation which made it possible for me to spend a year as a guest at the Geschwister Scholl Institut of the University of Munich. My sincerest thanks to the foundation and to Prof. Nikolaus von Lobkowicz, who was my academic host in Germany. I am also grateful to Columbia University, whose faculty development leave enabled me to finish the typescript.

Beyond the most immediate support I am indebted to many other people who helped me over the years. Although my days of a graduate student at Princeton have long passed many of the ideas in this book are the result of the influence my two mentors Richard Falk and Robert Gilpin had on my thinking during these formative years. Ralf and Angela Brückner gave much-needed encouragement at crucial moments. Simone Chambers proved to be an invaluable critic. My research assistants Kathrine Sikkink and Larry Reina contributed by tackling their assignments with imagination and diligence. Michael Barkun, Terry Nardin, Nicholas Onuf, and John Ruggie carefully read previous versions of this book and offered many helpful suggestions. Thomas Franck, both an eminent lawyer and social scientist, saved me from many errors by sharing his thoughts with me.

In addition, I profited greatly from the discussions with Nicole Fermon, Harvey Goldman, Helen Millner, Deborah Larson, and Jack Snyder, who were exemplary colleagues and friends at the seventh-floor "Bantustan" of Columbia's International Affairs Building. I also owe a debt of gratitude to Karen Boiko, who was kind enough to help with the proof-reading, and to Anita Mercier, Jennifer Thorn, and the staff of the War and Peace Institute of Columbia, who took care of the word-processing chores of seemingly interminable drafts.

Finally, since several of the sections of this book have appeared in slightly different versions, I gratefully acknowledge the help I received from various editors of journals, including Peter Katzenstein of *International Organization*, Gerhard Sprenger of the *Archiv für Rechts-*

und Sozialphilosophie, Kenneth Oye of *World Politics*, and many other reviewers who have helped me to re-think and reformulate my ideas. Errors of fact and judgment are, as always, exclusively mine.

Reprint permission has been granted for the following articles, which appear in (slightly) different form as chapters or sections of this book:

"On the Notion of 'Interest' in International Relations," *International Organization*, vol. 36, no. 1 (1982), 1–30.

"Is International Law 'proper' Law?", *Archiv für Rechts- und Sozialphilosophie*, vol. 69, *Heft* 1 (1983), 13–46.

"Thrasymachos Revisited: On the Relevance of Norms and the Study of Law for International Relations," *Journal of International Affairs*, vol. 37, no. 2 (1984), 343–356.

"Errors have their Advantage," *International Organization*, vol. 38, no. 2 (1984), 305–320.

"The Force of Prescriptions," *International Organization*, vol. 38, no. 4 (1984), 685–708.

"The Role of Domestic Courts as Agencies of the International Legal Order," in Richard Falk, Friedrich Kratochwil, and Saul Mendlovitz (eds.), *International Law, A Contemporary Perspective* (Boulder, Colo.: Westview Press, 1985), cht. 13.

"International Organization: A State of the Art on an Art of the State" (together with John Ruggie), *International Organization*, vol. 40, no. 4 (1986), 753–775.

"Of Systems, Boundaries and Territoriality," *World Politics*, vol. 34, no. 1 (1986), 27–52, by permission of Princeton University Press.

"Rules, Norms, and the Limits of 'Rationality,'" *Archiv für Rechts- und Sozialphilosophie*, vol. 73, *Heft* 3 (1987), 301–329.

"Norms and Values: Rethinking the Domestic Analogy.'" *Ethics and International Affairs*, vol. 1 (1987), 135–160.

"Diritto e Principi di Natura: Pufendorf e le leggi di natura come condizioni transcendentali di un discorso sulle controversie," *Teoria Politica*, vol. 4, no. 1 (1988), 3–27.

"Regimes, Interpretation and the 'Science' of Politics," *Millennium*, vol. 17, no. 2 (1988), 263–284.

INTRODUCTION:
THE RESORT TO NORMS

I HISTORICAL RECOLLECTION AND THE ESTABLISHMENT OF "FIELDS"

This book examines the role of norms in international life. To the extent that the focus is on interactions in the international arena, it is a book about international relations. To the extent that the investigation is interested in legal norms it is a book on legal theory. Insofar as issues of "interpretation," "precedent," and "sources of law" will be discussed, it is in a way a treatise on jurisprudence. To the extent that rules and norms are viewed as means to maintain social order, it is a book on social theory. Finally, to the extent that the analysis is occasioned by the re-reading of some of the classics of international law and political theory, it is – at least indirectly and without wanting to claim comprehensiveness or completeness – a study of political thought.

Locating the inquiry at the boundary or intersection of various established fields has obvious dangers because it may satisfy none of the respective specialists and draw the ire of all of them. Nevertheless, interdisciplinary works, when successful, have their own rewards. Two justifications can be tendered in support of such an enterprise. First, an interdisciplinary approach can pose new and theoretically interesting questions. It can show important conceptual and empirical links which are lost in the more specialized inquiries that take a well-defined "field of study" for granted. Second, although the present regime discussion in international relations[1] has sparked renewed interest in the investigation of the role of norms in the international arena and thus has legitimated new types of inquiry, its treatment of norms suffers from a variety of epistemological shortcomings.[2]

Thus, while even the most promising approaches in political science are of limited help in illuminating the workings of norms in domestic and international affairs, traditional conceptualizations of law do not fare much better. They either depict law as a static system[3] of norms or as a normative order which becomes "legal" through its sanctioning character.[4] Powerful attacks against either of these conceptualizations have been launched during the past few decades. Nevertheless, a new consensus has now emerged and law as process, exemplified, for instance, by the prolific writings of the McDouglian "New Haven School,"[5] contrasts sharply with the more traditional approaches predominant on the Continent or in Latin America. In addition, there are some norm-types which do not clearly fall into the traditional Procrustean scheme and which have therefore to be characterized largely in terms of negative analogies. A case in point is the conceptualization of "soft law"[6] exemplified by the I.M.F. exchange agreements (gentlemen's agreements) or by the Helsinki Accords, which do not qualify as either law in the strict sense or as mere political statements with no legal consequences. Thus, the concept of law itself has become increasingly problematic.[7]

These two justifications suggest that perhaps something has gone fundamentally wrong in the conventional divisions of fields which provide the perimeters of our normal investigations. I suspect that it is our reliance on the unquestioned dichotomy between a "domestic order" and the international "anarchy" which is to blame for the continuing theoretical embarrassments.[8] By making social order dependent upon law and law, in turn, upon the existence of certain institutions – be they the existence of a sovereign or central sanctioning mechanisms – we understand the international arena largely negatively, i.e., in terms of the "lack" of binding legal norms, of central institutions, of a sovereign will, etc. As inappropriate as this "domestic analogy"[9] may be for understanding *international relations*, the conceptual links between order, law, and special institutions remain largely unexamined even for domestic affairs.

Given the increasing incoherence, it might be useful to rethink the whole set of problems. Two strategies offer themselves for this purpose. One would be to start anew with certain assumptions concerning the role of norms and deductively trace their implications. The other approach is largely embedded in a historical recollection. It raises new issues by attempting to rid us of the amnesia of what usually we take for granted and by rearticulating the unstated assumptions of our practices and theoretical understandings. As Charles Taylor reminds us:

> If one tries to identify the reasons for (the) differential placing of the onus of proof from age to age; why certain views have to fight for credence, how they can only acquire plausibility through creative re-

2

description while others are so to speak credible from the start, the answer is to be found in the background of practices, scientific, technological, practical, and the nature of their organizing principles . . . the dominant interpretations and practices may be so linked with a given model that this is, as it were, constantly projected for the members as the way things obviously are . . . Freeing oneself from the model cannot be done just by showing an alternative. What we need to do is to get over the presumption of the unique conceivability of the embedded picture. But to do this, we have to take a new stance towards our practices. Instead of just living in them and taking their implicit construal of things as the way things are, we have to understand how they have come to be, how they came to embed a certain view of things.[10]

In this context Hobbes's creation of a paradigm of international relations is particularly instructive. It has always been noted that one of the apparent great inconsistencies in Hobbesian thinking was its failure to espouse a Super-Leviathan above the states, a solution to which the logic of the model necessarily leads. Actually, it was only the "idealists," the world government advocates, who drew this logical conclusion.[11] Hobbes, on the other hand, having invoked international relations as a justification for the construction of the ahistorical state of nature,[12] himself cast doubt upon the appropriateness of his analogy. To that extent, Hobbes never committed the mistakes which much of theorizing in international relations made when it started from the domestic analogy. A further brief discussion seems required.

How do the two arenas of domestic and international politics differ, or rather, given the radical individualism of the construct, how do the different incentive-structures prevalent in these arenas influence the actors' choices? In the case of the Leviathan among individuals, all persons have a negative as well as positive incentive to leave the state of nature, i.e., the fear of violent death and the prospects of "commodious living." Hobbes realized, however, that neither of those incentives is strong enough to motivate *states* to leave the state of nature. Most of the benefits from a division of labor (i.e., the positive incentive) can be realized through the establishment of a commonwealth. In addition, states are also able to overcome the negative incentive, i.e., the fear of violent death. They do not share the infirmities of individuals, which prevent the latter from securing their own survival. While even the strongest man has to sleep sometime, and, therefore, can be overpowered, communities can institute shifts in guarding the safety of their members. Consequently, the reality of international life is quite different from the state of "war of all against all."[13]

3

But if this argument is correct then the international arena is far different from, and not so terrible as, the situation in which man is like a wolf to his fellow man ("homo homini lupus"). Thus, although Hobbes adduced international politics[14] to give some plausibility to his construct, his own arguments disclose the questionable nature of the analogy. Since the laws of nature are always obliging in the individual conscience ("in foro interno," as Hobbes says), but not in actual conduct until institutional safeguards are provided,[15] it follows that as soon as international reality can be shown to differ from the state of nature, these "natural laws" provide a set of rudimentary understandings for regulating interactions among "persons of sovereign authority." It was precisely this conclusion which legal theorists such as Pufendorf[16] and Christian Wolf[17] drew from some of the Hobbesian premises and it is more the ignorance and amnesia of our contemporary specialists which make out of these theorists advocates of some type of mysterious "natural law."

Our initial efforts to counteract the "genesis amnesia"[18] by reconstructing the original Hobbesian argument turn out to have not only historical interest but also tremendous theoretical implications. It is not merely important to realize that we have misinterpreted Hobbes – although this is certainly true. After all, the charge of misinterpretation could easily be countered by pointing out that what Hobbes originally meant is irrelevant; what matters now is how *we* presently perceive the international arena, and to that extent the present neo-realist interpretation is what people believe to be "reality."[19] Nevertheless, it is our present reality which is, through the drifts and fundamental changes, out of tune with our models and understandings. In this context material factors such as the changes in the technology of destruction have to be noted, as have the changes in our ideas concerning issues of legitimacy, sovereignty, governmental powers, etc. Recovering the original is, therefore, not an idle undertaking.

But understanding the "original" is only a first, although indispensable, step. The second step entails going beyond the conventional conceptual divisions and their constitutive assumptions, and casting a fresh and unobstructed look of how – in the case of my research – norms and rules "work," i.e., what role they play in molding decisions. For that reason, I consider it useful not to select too prematurely a concept of law and then decide by more or less explicit verbal definitions whether the status of norms in international relations satisfies the criteria of a given concept of law. Precisely because the concept of law is itelf ambiguous, I propose to investigate the role of rules and norms in choice-situations *in general*. At a later point I

4

introduce distinguishing characteristics which allow us to separate legal from other types of norms. Furthermore, I intend to examine in a second step the respective roles norms play in the domestic and international arena. In casting the net much wider than is traditional, I am following a type of inquiry which once gave rise to "international law" as a special discipline. None of the original founders of the "law of, and among nations" (*ius gentium, ius inter gentes*) limited his investigation to narrow legal issues in international life, and for good reasons. From Grotius[20] to Vattel[21] and Triepel,[22] treatises on international law were always inquiries about law in general, and they concerned a wide variety of historical, political, and philosophical issues.

The revival of this kind of philosophical inquiry seems timely since the classic international lawyer writing and teaching public international law is more and more superseded by several specialists. This trend has serious implications for our understanding of international reality. While the lawyer-bureaucrat, attached to the policy-making machinery, may influence the creation of legal norms through (state-) practice by proposing and accepting new "standard solutions," such impact is no longer mediated through the development of a conceptual framework which is in tune with the changes of international reality.[23] The specialists in tax law, in corporation law, in the conflict of laws, etc., can win cases without a general understanding of international relations. Similarly, the scholar of the international political economy focuses on an equally specialized set of problems,[24] and "security studies" develop largely by following the "logic" of new weapons technologies. By reviving a more philosophically oriented discussion which attempts to assess the role of norms in decision-making, if all goes well we not only counteract such an unwarranted narrowing of focus in regard to international relations, but also gain a better picture of why actors in the international as well as in the domestic arena *have to resort to norms*.

The last question is of decisive importance for the substance of this investigation as well as for the choice of my methodology. In particular, I shall argue that our conventional understanding of social action and of the norms governing them is defective because of a fundamental misunderstanding of the function of language in social interaction, and because of a positivist epistemology that treats norms as "causes." Communication is therefore reduced to issues of describing "facts" properly, i.e. to the "match" of concepts and objects, and to the ascertainment of nomological regularities. Important aspects of *social* action such as advising, demanding, apologizing, asserting, promis-

5

ing, etc., cannot be adequately understood thereby. Although the philosophy of ordinary language has abandoned the "mirror" image of language since the later Wittgenstein, the research programs developed within the confines of logical positivism are, nevertheless, still indebted to the old conception. I shall argue in this book that only a fundamental reorientation of the research program is likely to overcome these difficulties. However, before we can hope to develop a more appropriate approach we have to understand how the social world is intrinsically linked to language and how language, because it is a rule-governed activity, can provide us with a point of departure for our inquiry into the functions of norms in social life.

II THE RESORT TO NORMS

Since human beings possess only weak instincts it has been a tenet in political analysis, at least from Aristotle on, that the human world is one of artifice.[25] Precisely because actors are seldom impelled by a stimulus, they have to make choices. In this context Aristotle points to the decisive importance of language.[26] Although some communication is possible by means of signals ("voice," as Aristotle calls it), language is significantly different from the signaling systems available to animals such as bees or wolves. Signals depend for their success in communication upon situation-specific, appropriate interpretations. Warning yells are called forth by the appearance of an enemy, and exclamations such as "ouch!" communicate quickly and without the intercession of words or reasons. Language, on the other hand, utilizes symbols whose communicative function is separate from the sounds used in signaling. Thus, the sound of a long "o" as in "hope" no longer has anything to do with the transmission of astonishment for which "oh" is used within the signaling system.

Language therefore not only enhances our ability to communicate through the use of abstract concepts, but also frees us from the here and now and thus makes remembrance and planning possible. Furthermore, through language we can learn from others not merely through imitation (*mimesis*) but through following their suggestions which encapsule their experiences. For example, the instruction "do not use anything less than a 2 × 12 in spanning a distance of more than 10 feet in any weight-bearing part of a construction" incorporates an important experience based on the causal texture of the world. We are thereby enabled to pursue our goals by simply following the instruction-type rule. Doing so, we can be confident that our efforts will not be frustrated and we need not re-invent the wheel every time.

6

Many communications, however, concern even more complicated matters. In pursuing our goals we are likely to interfere with each other. Unless we immediately give up attempts to communicate with the other, and prefer an exchange of blows, we utilize a variety of communicative acts.[27] We demand, warn, threaten, claim, criticize, assert, consent, suggest, apologize, pressure, persuade, praise, grade, promise, forbid, appoint, authorize, contract, or even bet, in order to further our goals. The list of these types of action-words seems very large, and Austin[28] has suggested that there are more than one thousand of them in English. Their function can be analyzed through "speech-act" theory.

But what is speech-act theory, and how does it help us to understand these actions and their underlying logic better? The first thing we notice in the above examples is that they represent action words of a peculiar kind. While, for example, the word "riding" stands for an action, it functions differently from promising or claiming, in that riding is an activity which takes place independently of referring to it by language. Fishing, hammering, washing, etc., are similarly action words of the latter category. But when I bet, claim, promise, etc., I am not only referring to an action, I am "doing" it, i.e., I perform the action itself.

The second important point is that all the action words of the latter category have a *normative* component. This can be seen most clearly when we authorize or appoint, forbid, grade, or praise, since such actions would not make much sense if there were no underlying norms which provided the meaning for these actions. Similarly, when I make a contract, or promise, I (at least obliquely) have to refer to the rules and norms. Only with reference to the rules and norms constitutive of a practice does, for instance, the utterance of "I do" in a marriage ceremony mean that I have committed myself. In other words, rules and norms constitute a practice within which certain acts or utterances "count" as something.

Finally, speech-act theory and the theory of communicative action[29] allow us to analyze the problem of the conditions of effective communication in a new and illuminating way. Conventional analysis focused solely on the propositional content of an utterance and its reference. It held that effective communication takes place when the propositional content of the message matched empirical reality. All other messages were either metaphysical or nonsense. Consequently, since normative statements containing such words as "ought," "must," etc., provided no match with objects of the outer world, they could only refer to certain mental or emotional states of the speaker, such as to his/her preference or values. On this basis language could be neatly divided into two mutually exclusive sets of "is" and "ought" statements. Debates about normative concerns outside of the goal–means context of instrumental rationality, therefore, had to be considered useless because of their lack of "reference."

This conceptual framework created numerous puzzles in the theory of reference and meaning which need not further concern us here.[30] For our purposes it is only important to note that problems of obligation could not be analyzed within that framework. Consider in this context the "I promise" mentioned above. It is neither a statement about facts nor one about values and thus it fits neither category. Furthermore, to construe this sentence as a statement about the speaker's state of mind is also missing the point; since insincere promises are "obligatory," we cannot reduce the deontic component of a statement to an indication of the psychological state of the speaker. It is here that speech-act theory provides us with more appropriate tools. It distinguishes between the *locutionary* dimension of an utterance (saying something), the *illocutionary* force of the utterance (doing something by saying something such as, for example, making an assertion, promise, etc.) and the *perlocutionary* effects of a statement (i.e., the impact it has on the hearers). These distinctions provide a framework for specifying the conditions under which communication becomes effective.

However, these remarks have implications far beyond the scope of the traditional concept of "obligation." One of the examples above included "threatening" as a speech act and thereby suggested that threatening is a norm-governed activity. Threats seem to be particularly characteristic of international relations, and their link to coercion and violence makes it appear that threats stand in opposition to norms, law, and order. Promises and threats, however, might actually have much more in common than is assumed in this conventional dichotomy. The effectiveness of both might depend on certain common normative understandings. I do not want to push this point too far at present (since it will be taken up in chapter 2); it is sufficient to notice that even in our common-sense understandings we sometimes conceive of threats as "negative promises." While such an analysis leaves much to be desired,[31] it nevertheless points to a commonality which the traditional dichotomy obscures. Furthermore, we seem to be able to add emphasis to our resolve by adding to a threat an additional "this I promise you," even if such a use is somewhat at odds with our normal conventions. When Vito, an enforcer for the Cosa Nostra, "suggests" that "If you do '*x*' I'll break your legs, this I promise you," it

8

is quite clear what is meant. What is less clear, and what needs further elaboration, is why such an addition reinforces the message. In addition, since threats, unlike promises, need not be cast in verbal form, the similarities and differences between these two speech acts give rise to some interesting problems, such as "tacit understandings" and "unspoken rules" which rely on signaling and unilateral imputations.[32]

The upshot of this argument is that there does not seem to be a *prima facie* contradiction in claiming that the making of threats is rule-governed (like that of promises), while at the same time holding that any particular threat itself might violate fundamental norms. The first set of norms or rules concerns the conditions under which communication is effective; the second set deals with the issue whether the utilization of the practice of threats or promises, etc., is allowed or enjoined by a normative order. Mixing up these two issues, i.e., the conditions of the validity of a speech act with those of securing social order through particular normative arrangements, has led to the well-known confusion in the regime debate concerning the (in)appropriateness of the regime approach to security issues. From the fact that unauthorized threats are not permitted but quite common in international politics, it was inferred that norms do not exist, or play no role in making threats, or that threats cannot result in expectations which have some type of normative standing as, for instance, in the case of "rules of the game."[33]

Actors also have to resort to norms when they want to air their grievances and establish the various obligations that result from general prescriptions and the utilization of certain speech acts. Thus, when Bill promises Jane to look after her terrier, "Professor Higgins," in her absence, he has an obligation. It can be overridden only by exceptional circumstances. Bill's serious injury will serve as an excuse, as might the sickness of Bill's mother, which makes Bill's leaving town necessary. His claim that he changed his mind will simply not do. Similarly, when Antigone and Portia plead with Creon and Shylock respectively, they do not doubt the existence of certain legal obligations, but rather they adduce "reasons" which could provide defeating circumstances for their obligations. In order to arrive at decisions which are not only based on idiosyncratic grounds but which command assent, such pleas will have to satisfy some formal criteria and certain substantive norms which are widely held in the society. The *formal* criteria in such a discourse on grievances and obligations largely concern conditions of equality in the claiming process, as well as the acceptance of the no-harm principle as a baseline from which we

9

argue. The more *substantive* understandings enter our arguments when we have to decide what is, for example, due care, what is an adequate compensation, what represents the proper functioning of an institution (which allows for the assessment of whether and why certain activities fall within its authority), or which duty or right overrides others.

At this point, a definitional clarification as well as an explicit statement of the three assumptions underlying my inquiry is in order. The *clarification* concerns the usage of the terms "rules," "norms," "principles," and "directives." Since, for the moment, I am mainly concerned with the action-guiding function of these devices, I will use the terms "rules," "norms," and "principles" more or less inter-changeably until the task of distinguishing among different norm-types in chapters 3 and 4 warrants further distinctions. For now, I shall simply note that while all norms are directives, not all directives function like norms, and while all rules are norms, not all norms exhibit rule-like characteristics. Furthermore, the term "prescriptions" is here used as a summarizing concept that encompasses all types of rules and norms, with the exception of direct commands.

My three *assumptions* concern the grounds for choosing a particular research strategy as well as my substantive commitment concerning the "nature of the beast" I intend to study. The *first* underlying assumption in regard to my research strategy is that it is useful to study the role of norms in shaping decisions from the baseline of an abstract initial situation which is defined, more or less, in public-choice terms. Thus, I begin with the analysis of a world in which self-interested actors with non-identical preferences have to make choices in the face of scarcity and with the prospects that they have to interact again with each other in future rounds. I maintain that one of the most important functions of rules and norms in such a world is the reduction in the complexity of the choice-situations in which the actors find them-selves. Rules and norms are therefore guidance devices which are designed to simplify choices and impart "rationality" to situations by delineating the factors that a decision-maker has to take into account. Although it will soon become obvious from my second and third assumption that my approach differs in significant respects from the public-choice approach,[34] I find it useful to take such an initial situation as a point of departure. Furthermore, as in the public-choice literature, the term "actor" refers in my discussion variously to individuals and collectivities, and often inferences are made from individual to collec-tive-actor behavior without explicit attention being paid to the prob-lems that occur on various levels of analysis. While neither I nor anybody else can deny significant differences between individual choices and those filtered through group or organizational channels, the simplifying assumption here is that the initial metaphor is heuristically fruitful and that it leads us to the discovery of important new insights. In addition, I maintain that it is flexible enough to allow for the construction of more isomorphic models or "thicker" descriptions later when the explication of complicating factors warrants a more detailed examination.

My *second* assumption is that human action in general is "rule-governed," which means that – with the exception of pure reflexes or unthinking conditioned behavior – it becomes understandable against the background of norms embodied in conventions and rules which give meaning to an action. Thus, not only must an actor refer to rules and norms when he/she wants to make a choice, but the observer, as well, must understand the normative structure underlying the action in order to interpret and appraise choices. Norms are therefore not only "guidance devices," but also the means which allow people to pursue goals, share meanings, communicate with each other, criticize assertions, and justify actions.

These are heady claims, and I will attempt to make good on them in the first chapter, in which I deal with the epistemological foundations of this approach. For the moment let me simply state that such a claim *does not* suggest that no other types of (competing) explanations are possible, or even useful, given certain circumstances. To "explain" certain actions, such as eating when someone is hungry, or to invoke self-interest as an explanatory variable in a particular choice-situation, need not make reference to norms. But even here, much depends upon the context. Different aspects of the situation might make it necessary to invoke norms. Table manners, dietary laws, and general rules of courtesy will be important when we want to explain not only *that* someone is eating but why he/she behaves in a certain way and chooses certain foods (such as taking the smaller piece or avoiding canapes with ham).

This leads me to my *third* assumption. Since rules and norms influence choices through the *reasoning process*, the processes of deliberation and interpretation deserve further attention. While various choice models have attempted to give a coherent account of certain aspects of choosing, such as specifying rational action as a maximizing choice under certainty, risk, or even certain conditions of interdependence, these models are of limited help in understanding the reasoning procedures we use when we argue about our grievances. In that case the reasonableness, fairness, or appropriateness of our valuations and their attendant claims to priority are at issue. Here rational-choice models are of little help precisely because the criteria of traditional rationality presuppose the independent and fixed valuations of the actors. However, most of our arguments concerning policy or rights are not so much about the determination of the likely result, *given* a certain distribution of "preferences," as they are debates over which preferences deserve priority over others, which ones ought to be changed, and which judgments deserve our assent. Here the overall persuasive "weight" of claims rather than their logical necessity or aggregation is at issue.

The crucial question, therefore, is simply this: how do we reason with rules and norms when no logically compelling solution seems possible, yet when certain decisions and their supporting reasons are more persuasive than others? In spite of a great deal of indeterminacy in our reasoning, our arguments are usually not simply arbitrary statements of personal preferences. The "logic" of arguing requires that our claims satisfy certain criteria, and that means that they cannot be based on purely idiosyncratic grounds. Were this not the case, not only would no one assent to anyone else's decision, but it also would be impossible to give a coherent account of the obligatory character of other-regarding choices. It is here that the classical teachings on practical reasoning become relevant. Practical reasoning not only deals with issues of action but also investigates the formal properties of arguments which satisfy neither the conditions of induction nor those of deduction, and in which value-considerations figure prominently beyond the ends–means nexus of instrumental rationality.[35]

The relevance of these brief remarks for legal arguments becomes obvious when we realize that legal reasoning too does not follow either a purely deductive or inductive style, although both inductive generalizations and deductions may be part of an argument. In spite of this "deficiency" of legal arguments – when measured by the standard forms of logic – there is a certain rigor which this reasoning with rules and norms exhibits, and practitioners are usually in agreement about what represents "good" legal reasoning, even if they disagree about a particular decision.

III THE PLAN OF THIS BOOK

Now that the scope of the book has been described it might be useful to outline the content of the individual chapters. In the first chapter, I begin with a short justification of the assumptions made above, i.e., the rule-governed character of human action, and of rule-

and norm-use in different contexts. Thus, while making a threat is a norm-governed action, as the brief discussion above showed, it is not part of our conventional understanding of reasoning with norms for which legal pleadings seem to provide the paradigm. However, instead of accepting the traditional boundaries, I want to expand the inquiry precisely for the reasons indicated in the first section above. As long as we take the application of norms by a third party as our only, or even as the most, decisive model of reasoning with rules, some of the most interesting social phenomena remain unexamined. Following the suggestion of Thomas Franck,[36] I therefore introduce three contexts in which norms and rules are used. In a second step, I attempt to identify the modes of reasoning corresponding to these three contexts.

In a *first-party* mode of reasoning only the interest of one actor counts. The success of the norm-guided action is then largely circumscribed by the conditions of effective speech acts, such as threats, warnings, etc., and the imposition of "solutions" without explicit reference to the interest of other affected parties. The second-party mode concerns the role of norms in bargaining processes. While norm-guidance can be important in this context, it is often subsidiary to attempts to break the other's will, and thus does not rule out coercive moves. Finally, the third-party mode is characterized by the emergence of a "moral point of view," i.e., impartiality and equality as to the claims and interests of the contending parties, and the commonly accepted forbearance of breaking the other's will.

In chapter 2, the present regime debate in international relations serves as my point of departure. By placing my discussion within the present debate about the role of regimes in international life I want to achieve two objectives. On the one hand, I want to avoid too legalistic an analysis by profiting from the wider set of questions which regime-analysis has placed on the agenda. On the other hand, I also want to improve on this approach, which was conceived by political scientists in order to account for two puzzles: the decline of the U.S.'s hegemonic position in the post-war era, and the strains which changing political conditions had put on post-war arrangements of international cooperation. The fact that states did not proceed in terms of a "beggar thy neighbor" approach represented an anomaly which neither systemic factors nor formal institutional constraints could adequately explain.[37] Regimes, therefore, seemed to provide the necessary "intervening variable" which explained the constraint on state action.

The research program of conventional regime-analysis, however, is limited by several important shortcomings. In particular, the indiscriminate aggregation of the most disparate phenomena, such as

13

expectations, informal understandings, explicit rules, higher-level norms, decision-making procedures, etc., obscures rather than clarifies the impact of norms on decision-making. In this context, it is somewhat strange that the present regime discussion profited neither from the discussion in international law concerning the emergence of customary rules and their decline (desuetude) nor from the more recent controversy concerning the issues of "soft law."[38] Furthermore, the premature fascination with regime *change* has failed to develop criteria by which regime adaptation (modification) can be distinguished from regime change itself or from regime decline. Finally, the predominance of "tacit" rather than "explicit" rules in strategic relations explains a great deal of the difficulty for viewing security issues as part of regime analysis; consequently, the fruitfulness of the approach appears to be limited to economic transactions.[39] However, such an interpretation inhibits a more detailed investigation of the *role of norms* in the strategic domain. Whether the existing rules and norms and their impact satisfy the conditions of a well-formed regime can safely be held in abeyance for the moment.

In bringing the discussion of tacit rules and of "soft law" to bear upon regime analysis, I hope to clarify some of the conceptual puzzles that have plagued this approach. In particular, the problem of boundaries of a regime appears in a new light if we allow for distinctions among different modes of regime change. Although I cannot claim to have solved the problem of the "fuzzy" boundaries of regimes by providing a clear demarcation once and for all, I suggest that such clear demarcations are only possible under very exceptional circumstances. Only when a "consensual knowledge" in a particular issue area has developed and agreement exists as to the links between goals and means can the boundaries of a regime be considered to be unequivocal. Since such a widespread and virtually unchallenged consensus existed in the post-war era in respect to (Keynesian) economics, it comes as no surprise that the regime approach appeared most appropriate for explaining economic issues.[40] Nevertheless, even in economic matters, such agreement is exceptional and regimes do remain, like most other concepts in the social sciences, "contestable."[41]

The third chapter proposes an alternative approach for assessing the role of rules and norms in social life. I begin with an examination of the generic features of all norms, i.e., their problem-solving character. Rules and norms simplify choices for actors with non-identical preferences facing each other in a world characterized by scarcity. I then show how tacit understandings develop and under what circum-

14

stances these rules can remain tacit but nevertheless fulfill their function as "wholesale advance-coordination devices."[42] Although in a way all rules and norms have a coordinating function, they vary in significant respects. A brief discussion outlining the conceptual distinctions among different types of rules and norms follows. Beginning with the simplest norm-type, i.e., instruction-type rules, I next examine coordination-norms proper. In that class I distinguish further: conventions, decrees, and rights. In that context, several problems in the conventional treatment of "custom" are also pointed out.

The analysis of other types of norms proceeds along the following lines. First, a game-theoretical analysis characterizes typically recurring choice-situations in social life. Second, different types of norms are distinguished according to a conceptual analysis. Finally, I try to show that certain norm-types are designed to overcome the choice problems of specific recurrent social situations, i.e., that there is a contingent relationship between the *types of situation* and *the types of norms*. I maintain further that the prescriptive force of practice-type rules and precepts, designed to overcome the difficulties of PD situations, cannot be explained by instrumental reasoning, either in its act- or rule-utilitarian version.[43]

Chapter 4 focuses on the issue of how different rules attain prescriptive status. Although my approach here is largely based on ordinary language philosophy, my analysis proceeds by means of an interpretation of three theories of obligation. I examine Hobbes's, Hume's, and Durkheim's theories of the status of norms in social life. These theories are roughly identifiable with the realist, rule-utilitarian and idealist positions, respectively. I want to argue that while each of these theories contributes to our understanding of the function of norms – and the inclusion of Freud's observations solves some of Durkheim's puzzles – each approach, nevertheless, has certain blind spots. The reason for these distortions is that each approach was developed by means of examples taken largely from only one norm-type. Consequently, each theory mistakes rule-following in the case of a *particular type of rule* with rule-following *in general*. However, all three theories can be understood as special cases of a theory of "communicative action." In the latter approach, "reasons" specific to a given rule-type provide the necessary justification for the authoritative status of the prescription.

My critique of the utilitarian positions involves two steps. First, I show the shortcomings of the Hobbesian construction, which takes as its paradigmatic case the dilemma arising out of the sequential performance of contractual obligations. In a second step, I introduce fifteen cases taken from contract law and demonstrate that the complexities of these cases cannot be resolved by focusing merely on the "enforcement" problem, or on the "shadow of the future." What is needed is a different approach that investigates more closely the process by which people can adjust their differences without resorting immediately to violence. I maintain that the theory of communicative action is helpful in this respect. Within a normatively secured framework of communication, actors can air grievances and debate value-choices, even if such debates are no longer limited to instrumental questions only.

Chapter 5 is devoted to a more thorough examination of the suggestion made above that social conflicts become susceptible to a nonviolent and norm-guided solution through the emergence of a "moral point of view" within a framework of communicative action. The first problem is to provide criteria for a "moral point of view" which can be used in deciding our grievances. Three proposals for specifying such criteria are then examined in greater detail: the "generalization principle," which is basic to rule-based arguments, second, Kant's "categorical imperative," and finally, Pufendorf's "laws of nature." Having shown that the categorical imperative often fares no better than the *ad hominem* argument of the generalization principle in providing criteria for deciding cases of conflicting duties or grievances, I attempt to argue that the main reason for this failure lies in the formal character as well as in the autonomy-requirement of the categorical imperative. In the second step, I argue, therefore, that some *substantive* principles are required in order to overcome at least some of these difficulties. In discussing Pufendorf's absolute and hypothetical laws of nature, I demonstrate the importance of some "naturalist" principles in giving structure and plausibility to intersubjectively valid arguments within a discourse on grievances. In this context, I conclude that not only are "natural laws" so conceived, i.e., as constitutive principles of a discourse, compatible with positive law, but that even the most positivistically inclined jurists will have to invoke these principles in making choices satisfying the criteria of justice. Furthermore, the constitutive nature of these "laws of nature" explains their norm-generative capacity in the process of adjudication. Consequently, these laws or principles are of great significance in understanding judicial law-making and the nature of judicial discretion.

I conclude from the above arguments that attempts to separate rigidly moral and legal considerations in deciding cases and controversies have to fail (although I do not want to suggest that "law" and "morals" are coextensive, and/or that a law can be true law only when

16

it is just).[44] Precisely because important legal institutions are parasitic upon moral precepts, as well as on the substantive "no harm principle" (*neminem laedere*), judges often have to interpret rules in such a way that decisions are made *praeter legem* or sometimes even *contra legem*, if the moral point of view strongly suggests such deviations.

Chapter 6 deals with the notion of "right" in a historical as well as analytical fashion. The investigation begins with an examination of various uses of the word "right" and develops the basic notion of rights as a socially protected claims. Rights are used, however, not only to add emphasis, or insistence, to claims but also to limit possible objections to the exercise of one's discretion. Furthermore, rights are used in order to specify clearly the range of duty-bearers against whom I, as a right-holder, may make a valid claim. In this light, the conferral of rights upon artificial persons and groups is discussed. The issue of whether states as such have rights, or whether these rights are only those of individuals, is examined on the basis of several cases taken from international law.

Analytically, various distinctions among rights are then introduced, such as the notion of positive, negative, and basic rights, and their historical grounding in a specific understanding of individual action is shown. This understanding is traced in its historical shifts from a "natural law" to a "natural rights" discourse in the seventeenth century, in which the notion of "right" emancipated itself from the older notion that "right" denotes what *is* right. Fundamental to the new concept of a right is therefore the assertion of a claim by the right-holder. Here speech-act theory proves helpful in showing that even legal orders which do not have a name for a right, such as ancient Greek law, nevertheless knew the "concept" of rights. The institutionalization of a formal process of claiming, captured in the "status" teachings of the ancient rhetoricians, proves this. In this process, which heavily emphasizes the pleas of the contending parties, claims could be asserted and discussed according to special procedural rules and limitations on relevant proofs.

The logic of the rights discourse is further explored through an inquiry into certain types of rights, which attained paramount importance in the political theories of the eighteenth century and through the development of constitutionalism. Liberties, powers, and inalienable rights show important discontinuities with the paradigmatic cases of rights as rights *in rem*, or *in personam*. Based on these considerations, the issue of basic rights is taken up, and the question of whether human rights are only "manifesto claims," or rights proper, is

17

broached. Finally, given the fact that the notion of right figures prominently in the moral, political, and legal discourse, the dynamic character of right-claims is shown, and countermoves by courts are discussed, which limit right-based claims through exacting "standing requirements" or through a variety of "avoidance techniques."

The last problem indicates already the need for a more extensive discussion of "judicial discretion," which is taken up in chapter 8. However, since a treatment of the discretion of judges presupposes a clarification of the distinction between the legal character of a norm and other forms of prescriptions, chapter 7 is devoted to the "demarcation criterion" of law. In reviewing the theories of Kelsen, Hart, and McDougal, I contrast two families of approaches: law as a "system of norms," and law as a "process."

The difficulties with the systemic conception largely have to do with the inappropriate static representation of norms as logical hierarchies that leaves out the process of interpretation and judicial law-making. The McDouglian "law-as process" approach, however, fails to distinguish adequately law from "policy" and exhibits too instrumental a view concerning the function of legal norms in the decision-making process. A brief discussion of the pitfalls of instrumentalism is intended to clarify the distinctions between merely instrumentally rational actions and those rule-guided decisions which satisfy the criteria of justice. It is this emphasis on the distinctive style of reasoning which justifies the interpretation of law as a particular branch of practical reasoning.

"The law," I argue, can be understood neither as a static system of norms nor as a set of rules which all share some common characteristic such as sanctions; in the same vein as it is, in my view, mistaken to depict law simply as a process in which claims and counterclaims are made. Rather law is a choice-process characterized by the principled nature of the *norm-use* in arriving at a decision through reasoning. What the law *is* cannot therefore be decided by a quick look at statutes, treaties, or codes (although their importance is thereby not diminished), but can only be ascertained through the *performance* of rule-application to a controversy and the appraisal of the reasons offered in defense of a decision.

Chapter 8 attempts then to illuminate the structures of legal arguments by examining the persuasiveness of the conclusions at which courts (or other lawyers) arrive when they reason with rules in the "third-party" mode. Starting from the conventional position that legal reasoning consists in the subsumption of a given factual situation under the applicable norm, I try to show why such a position is untenable. In discussing alternative views concerning legal inferences, I examine in particular the quasi-logical procedures such as the *argumentum a simili, e contrario, ad absurdum*, etc., which modern "rhetorical" theorists concerned with the process of juridical inference have studied.[45]

This investigation of the "rhetorical" features of legal arguments then provides the background for a more extensive discussion of the topical structure of legal reasoning, particularly in the initial phrasing of a controversy (pleas) and in the area of legal proofs. Finally, by examining the judicial pronouncements of the courts in the international arena, in particular the International Court of Justice, I show that the conception of legal reasoning as a particular "style" of practical reasoning can be relevant to international law. In spite of different cultural backgrounds and differing role-conceptions, judges in the international courts exhibit a reasoning style which not only resembles that of reasoning with rules in the domestic arena, but which also satisfies the same criteria. Thus, the nature of international law as "proper" law can be established (which is not to say that the legal process serves the same function in international relations as in the domestic arena).

The conclusion focuses in greater detail on the nature of legal orders often (mis)represented as systems and on the alleged primitive nature of the international legal order. While there is no contention with the lack of effectiveness of international law in certain areas, the primitive law analogy fails to explain this weakness for two interrelated reasons. First, against the systemic conception of law I argue that even mature legal orders show only a much weaker ordering than the systemic approach suggests. This does not exclude certain partial orderings, such as we find in private law, where the autonomy of private persons by implication leads to certain consequences for the law of contracts, remedies, the protection of good faith, etc. Nevertheless, none of the various areas within a legal order can be bolted together into one deductive system of norms, not even in civil law systems. Second, the primitive systems analogy of law is more misleading than helpful as it fails to do justice to the features that are *sui generis* in the international legal order. Unlike primitive orders that usually do not differentiate between religious ideas, morals, and laws and between public and private domains, international law is precisely constituted by these important conceptual distinctions.

Finally, the implications of law for the present anarchy debate in international relations is broached. A more discursive inquiry like the one of this book not only seems helpful in providing a corrective for the genesis amnesia mentioned above, but serves a critical function in still another way: it directly challenges the traditional conceptualization of international relations.[46] It remains to be seen, however, to what extent such an alternative vision enables us to reflect more critically upon our practices and, therefore, to understand better our shared task in constructing our human and, it is hoped, more humane world.

1 RULES, NORMS, AND ACTIONS: LAYING THE CONCEPTUAL FOUNDATIONS

I ACTION AND MEANING

How do we understand human action, and what role do norms play in this process? The answers to these questions obviously depend upon our concept of knowledge, and this concept, in turn, is constituted by our ideas about the world we live in and which we experience as reality. One way of approaching this problem is, therefore, to reconstruct images of possible worlds and show their epistemological presuppositions. Such a procedure might enable us to see in turn the limitations of certain concepts of knowledge, based on certain world-images.

In this section I want to follow this procedure and investigate three world-images and their corresponding concepts of knowledge. These worlds are: one, the world of observational facts; two, the world of mental facts; and three, the world of institutional facts. While these world-images are not incommensurable, they do establish different "referents" and emphasize different concepts of knowledge. Consequently, they not only give rise to different epistemological puzzles, but they are also only partially translatable into each other. On the other hand, precisely because certain aspects *are* translatable, concrete phenomena can often be explained by, or be understood from, the presuppositions of a different concept of knowledge.

The world of observational facts

On the most naive level the world of brute facts consists of "givens" that any theory has to analyze. Scientific progress depends upon an exhaustive description of these facts and upon the establishment of certain regularities among them: so goes at least the inductivist fervor à la Bentham or the positivism of Comte.[1] A more sophisticated version of this argument recognizes that phenomena are classifiable

21

only against a background of a theoretical problem. In this case a hypothesis has to be formulated which must, at least in principle, be testable. Facts are no longer simply "there" but are to a certain extent theory-dependent. A common "unproblematic background knowledge"[2] of measurement not only mediates between various theories, but also allows for accuracy, a certain conclusiveness in experimental design, and the establishment of proofs (or corroborations).[3] Measurement is of decisive importance in this world since only through accurate measurements of the crucial theoretical terms can the theory provide numerous deductions and thus guide the discovery of novel facts. Only if the "data" are in the form of numbers and maintain their properties as numbers can "the powerful transformations of algebra, calculus and matrix algebra . . . be carried out upon them."[4] As long as we have only ordinal measurements of our theoretical terms we cannot use certain operations such as additions and multiplications. The importance of multiplications for theory-building can, however, be seen by Newton's derivation of the concept of force from the other three already measured concepts of mass, distance, and time. By means of a simple equation he could show that

$$F = ma$$

i.e., that the amount of force could be derived from the amount of motion (acceleration – which in turn is a measure derived from distance and time) it produced in a given amount of mass. "Causes" in this world are therefore – at least ideally – expressable in mathematical functions.[5]

These last remarks have important implications for the social sciences since attempts at arriving at scientific explanations have often focused on the general lack of measurement. Consequently, the remedy for such a shortcoming seemed to lie in the establishment of operational definitions and in the design of measurement procedures. Two operations are required for such purposes. The first is one of *comparison*, which imposes an order restriction on the assignment of numbers so that the relations "larger than" or "equal to" $(> =)$ between these objects (x_i) and (x_j) satisfy the criterion of the same relations between real numbers, i.e.,

$$m(x_i) > m (x_j) \text{ or } m(x_i) = m(x_j).$$

The second operation, a combination of objects x_i and x_j, transforms a property which orders the objects into one which makes the assignment of a quantity or metric measure possible. In other words,

$$m(x_i \text{ comb } x_j) = m(x_i) + m(x_j).$$

It is here that most measurement procedures in the social sciences fail. While the first procedure specifies an ordinal scale, the wide freedom in assigning numbers (as long as the criteria of > = are satisfied) means that the operations of addition and multiplication cannot be carried out in order to make further derivations. However, it is precisely these deductions that we need for a powerful theory. Only in this way are equivalences established by weighing; mass and acceleration can then account for "force." What is important to note is that it is *not the observing scientist* who decides that a particular numerical value can be assigned, as long as he/she can get some co-researchers to agree with his/her estimates. Rather, it is the *behavior* of the objects themselves *in the measuring procedure* which determines the numerical values.

Although investigators in the social sciences were usually very careful in validating their comparisons and combination operations, there is nevertheless a decisive flaw in such consensual validation procedures. As Coleman points out:

> More generally, the whole movement of "operationism," with its insistence on operational definition of concepts, has overlooked this one most crucial point. It is not up to the whim of the investigator to determine what operation is to be used to establish a definition; the operation must constitute action on the part of the objects of the theory, and it must be the same action that the theory is about. Otherwise, it is to no avail to establish a cardinal measure, by even the most rigid adherence to Campbell's criteria of measurement. The measure will exist, to be sure, but it will be of no use.[6]

Thus the problem in the social sciences is less that we do not have enough quantified data but rather that usually we do not know what the data mean even if they come in quantified form.

The world of intention and meaning

The last remarks echo already some of the critical observations Weber made in his methodological writings. For him the knowledge appropriate to social phenomena does not consist in the amassing of statistical data or even law-like regularities or generalizations. The world of intention and meaning is no longer one of measurement but rather one in which the reconstruction of the parameters of action is at issue. Within such a horizon an actor's choice and his/her subjective intentions and motives can be understood:

> The various sociological generalizations which it is customary to identify as "scientific laws," as for example Gresham's law, are in fact typical probabilities confirmed by observation. The assumption is

23

> that under certain given conditions a projected course of action will occur which will be intelligible in terms of typical motives and the typical subjective intentions of those engaged in a certain behavior. These generalizations are both understandable and definitive to the highest degree insofar as the typically observed course of behavior can be understood in terms of the purely rational pursuit of a goal . . .[7]

Thus, the appropriate model of knowledge is one in which the reconstruction of a subjective interpretation of a coherent (rational) course of action discloses the motive which "appears to the individual involved, or to the observer, to be a sufficient reason for his conduct."[8] *Social* action, in turn, is a subcategory of meaningful action requiring that an "individual's conduct is meaningfully oriented toward that of others."[9] For example, a collision of two cyclists is

> merely an isolated event comparable to a natural catastrophe. On the other hand, any attempt by any one of them to avoid hitting the other, with ensuing insults, a brawl or even a peaceful discussion would constitute a form of social behavior.[10]

The differences to the world of observational facts and its corresponding knowledge become obvious. It not only contains mental terms, such as intention, wishing, and wanting, but the *interactions* among the social subjects are norm-governed. The rules of the road will be as relevant to a discussion of the bicyclists after a collision as they are to them when they are attempting to avoid an accident. Such a difference can also be seen quite clearly in the changed meaning of the term "cause." In an action-perspective, we need "mental" terms not only because we lack information about the neuro-physiological processes, as some positivists argue, but because *causal explanations within the action-perspective are fundamentally different from the causes of nature.*

This creates difficulties in explaining human actions, if done purely in physicalist terms. Thus, describing the opening of a door by means of physical movements and physiological processes does not tell us whether what happened was a random action, was done in order to let fresh air into the room, was a gesture of politeness, or was intended as a signal for another person to leave the room. Meaningful action is created by placing an action within an intersubjectively understood context, even if such imputations are problematic or even "wrong" in terms of their predictive capacity. To have "explained" an action often means to have made intelligible the goals for which it was undertaken. In this sense our explanations appear "causal" even in the positivist sense since, by definition, motives are always prior to the action and

24

thus can be considered its antecedent conditions. Nevertheless, there is a crucial difference between causal explanations in the world of observational facts and that of intentions. In the case of natural phenomena (that is, in a physicalist framework), cause and effect have to be determined *independently* from each other through neutral measurements. But the same is *not* true in the case of motivational accounts, where "causal" motives can only be imputed by the observer *after* a goal is assumed to be controlling. (The imputation can be based on the actor's direct reports about objectives, but need not be; this is Weber's famous argument against "empathy.")

It should be clear that such finalistic explanation schemes create serious difficulties for the refutability of an explanation and, by implication, for the argument that prediction and explanation have the same logical form.[11] Indeed, it would be odd to say that a person who missed his/her train thereby "refuted" the explanation that he/she intended to catch it.[12] Instead, we preserve the proffered motivational account and elaborate on it. Explaining means elaborating, justifying, or possibly excusing the action rather than simply "refuting" the hypothesis. Similarly, when we explain an action in terms of an underlying norm, a counterfactual observation will usually not impel us to consider the norm invalid, analogously to the refuted general law in scientific explanations. Thus, causal explanations via antecedent conditions and motivational accounts are two *different* ways in which we understand reality. For certain purposes, explanations resembling physicalist accounts might be appropriate; in other circumstances (when, for instance, we assess responsibility), only the intentional framework will do.

The world of institutional facts

There remains an important set of "facts" that are not well explained either by the theory of meaningful action or by theories relying on observational facts. Thus, when Ms. Smith marries Mr. Jones, when George promises Bill to give him a ride, when the President receives a foreign diplomat and accepts his letter of accreditation, or when Congress passes a bill, there seems to be no "simple set of statements about physical or psychological properties to which the statements of fact such as these are reducible."[13] Furthermore, even the language of intention does not seem to be appropriate to capture some of the essential features. Consider in this context the difference between two activities which both seem to be intentional, for instance, "fishing" and "promising." Both allow for mistakes and even strategic behavior, but there is a decisive difference between the institutional practice, or speech act, of promising, and the practice of fishing. As Searle reminds us:

> In the case of fishing the ends–means relations, i.e., the relations that facilitate or enable me to reach my goal, are matters of natural facts; such facts, for example, as that fish sometimes bite at worms but very seldom at empty hooks . . . Now there are, indeed, techniques, procedures and even strategies that successful fisherman follow, and no doubt in some sense all these involve regulative rules. But that under such and such conditions one catches fish is not a matter of convention . . . In the case of speech acts performed within a language, on the other hand, it is a matter of convention – as opposed to strategy, technique, procedure, or natural fact – that the utterance of such and such expressions under certain conditions counts as the making of a promise.[14]

These remarks show not only that rules are intrinsically involved in speech acts but that their character is quite different from that of regulative rules, which serve as our usual model of rules. Regulative rules such as "Thou shall not kill" are constraining in that they order us to adopt a certain behavior. Usually they can be expressed as imperatives, and it is this fact that gave rise to the Austinian mistake of conceptualizing law as a "command of the sovereign."[15] If imperative regulations are our paradigm of rules, constitutive rules which specify, i.e., what counts as a checkmate, a treaty, a vote, etc., strike us as somewhat curious. Therefore, there is an understandable tendency to amalgamate constitutive (or "enabling" rules, as Hart[16] has called some of them), with the paradigm of constraining or regulative rules.[17] Nevertheless, there exist important differences between regulative and institutional rules, differences which have decisive epistemological implications.

Assume there is a regulative rule such as a provision of Art. 2.4, of the U.N. Charter not to use force. Thus, if someone resorts to force the specification of the action can be given without explicit reference to the existing regulation. In other words, "when a rule is purely regulative, behavior which is in accordance with the rule could be given the same description or specification (the same answer to the question 'what did he do') whether or not the rule existed."[18] The problem is, however, significantly different in the case of an institutional rule, constitutive of a practice. Threatening the king in a chess game by announcing "check" means something *only* with reference to the underlying rules of the game. Thus, the meaning of the move and its explanation crucially depend upon the knowledge of the rule-structure.

26

The difference between a world of institutional facts and that of brute or observational facts is well brought out by imagining how we would have to "explain" a football game in the language of observational facts alone. We could keep a statistical record of how many clusters we observed, how the periodic circular clustering is always followed by a linear ordering and wild running over the field, and the pulling or pushing down of the persons clad in a different outfit:

> But no matter how much data of this sort we imagine our observers to collect and no matter how many inductive generalizations we imagine them to make from the data, they still have not described American football. What is missing from their description? What is missing are all those concepts such as touchdown, offside, game points, time out, etc., and consequently what is missing are all the true statements one can make about a football game using those concepts . . . The other descriptions, the descriptions of brute facts, can be explained in terms of the institutional facts. But the institutional facts can only be explained in terms of the constitutive rules which underlie them.[19]

The upshot of this argument is that even descriptive terms such as "offside," "checkmate," "home run," etc., are not simply labels for a state of affairs but attain their meaning by pointing to further consequences within the game-structure, such as choosing a move, making a point, having to pay a penalty, etc. While these remarks show that the language of observational or brute facts is not rich enough to capture the peculiarities of institutional rules, the language of intention is also insufficient. Neither the model of instrumental rationality nor that of empathy, reconstructing the purposes of the actor, adequately explains a practice such as promising.

To elaborate on the latter point, i.e., intentionality of the action, it is sufficient to remember that we need not necessarily mean what we say. A person who intends to promise something in Spanish but says instead of "prometo" or "de acuerdo" "mucho gusto," has not promised anything even if he/she intended to. The meaning of the act – or the illocutionary force of the utterance – "is more than a matter of mere intention; it is at least sometimes a matter of convention and a correct analysis will have to capture both the intentional as well as the conventional aspects of such a speech act."[20]

These conceptual distinctions are of interest not only for purely academic purposes, as the following examples will show. One of the main issues in present contract law concerns the question whether contract should be understood as an institution by itself, or whether it should be subsumed under the general principles of tort law.[21] But if my analysis is correct, then contracting cannot be simply reduced to questions of tort. The binding character of contracts, as mutual promises, depends for its validity not on the "reliance" which one of the contracting parties might have placed on the promise of the other, but on the institution of contract itself. Not the *perlocutionary* effect but the *illocutionary* force of the mutual promises establishes the binding character of contracts.

Similarly, Waltz's main argument for the need of a systemic theory is based on the observable gap between intentions and the systemic meaning of acts. He therefore argues against a "reductionist" mode of explanation and for a derivation of the system-properties from a distribution of capabilities.[22] However, the inference from the gap between intention and meaning to the argument that only a physicalist account – cast in the form of observational facts – can explain is patently false, and our analysis shows why this is so. While it is obvious that unintended consequences can no longer be accounted for within the *intentional* framework, it seems that we have to take one step up to the world of institutional facts rather than step down to the world of observational fact. In other words, we have to understand international relations as a "game" rather than as an "observation" of heaps of capabilities. This suspicion is confirmed by Waltz's own argument that the decision-makers have to be "socialized" into the system, i.e., have to understand their interaction as one governed by certain rules which make assessments possible.[23] Furthermore, insofar as the system is based on alliances and strategic calculations, the moves have to be conceptualized even more so within the framework of a game rather than within that of observational facts. Since promising and contracting are part of the game, it is the third world of institutional facts rather than the first of observational facts which provides the appropriate framework. Thus, much of the "polarities" of the seventeenth- and early eighteenth-century system depended not on the distribution of capabilities but on dynastic marriages. Despite the fact that certain insights can be gained from treating the international system as a world of natural facts – the statistical knowledge in Searle's example of a football game might not be entirely useless – it should be clear that such knowledge has to be parasitic on the knowledge of the game-structure.

II THE IMPORTANCE OF EVERYDAY LANGUAGE

The previous section was devoted to some of the complexities of various "worlds" and the concomitant epistemological implications.

28

A further implication was that "communication" about facts in the world is influenced by the nature of the world in which we move. Thus, while classical logic assumed that communication among actors is possible on the basis of propositional content, which, in turn, is safeguarded by certain truth functions, the discussion of speech acts showed that such a conception of language is inadequate. Truth and falsity are appropriate criteria only when applied to propositions. Neither the illocutionary nor the perlocutionary effect of speech acts can thereby be analyzed. However, since promising, contracting, asserting, etc., are important parts of our *social* world, we cannot simply exclude these aspects from our theorizing about social reality.

In addition, social reality seems to be even more complicated than speech-act theory suggests. One reason is that speech acts are often not clearly identifiable by performative verbs such as "assert," "request," "demand," etc., but attain this quality solely by *contextual factors*. Consider, for example, the following exchange:

A: (calling) Hi, is Jim there?
B: Yes (just a minute).[24]

While the caller clearly asks to talk to Jim, such a meaning is not conveyed by the terms used. Nevertheless, we all know what is meant and it would indeed be a strange answer if B responded only to the propositional content of this question, said "yes," and hung up. As Stubbs reminds us, the meaning of the request

> could also be conveyed by other sentences, including, I want to speak to Jim; Is that Jim?; Could I speak to Jim?; Give me Jim, please; Jim, please. Such sentences are all different in surface syntax: declarative, interrogative, imperative, and moodless. And they are all semantically different: they differ in the propositions which are asserted, presupposed and entailed. However, in this position in the discourse sequence, these syntactic and semantic differences are neutralized, to make them equivalent as discourse moves.[25]

The upshot of this argument is that in such instances it is the *structure of the discursive interaction* and not semantics or the manifest aspects of the sentences which controls the meaning.

A second point is worth mentioning in this context. While speech-act theory has been quite successful in illuminating the illocutionary force of utterances, the *perlocutionary* effects are not well accounted for. This might be due in part to the easy availability of a test for illocutionary acts. The insertion of a "hereby" brings out this dimension well. It makes sense to say: "I *hereby* appoint you, request from you, promise you," etc. However, the utterance "I hereby persuade you" is close to nonsensical precisely because the success of the action does *not*

29

depend on me, the actor, but on the effect of my act upon the audience. Similarly, "I hereby threaten you" is straining our common-sense understanding. Thus, while these actions are rule governed – and much of the next chapter is devoted to showing how norms are involved in threatening – the rule-guidance is here obviously different from that of the illocutionary dimension. Rather than deriving the meaning from the metaphor of a well-structured game – the conventional aspect of speech acts – perlocutionary effects depend more clearly on *discursive* gambits, by which the hearer is "brought around."

Two Corollaries ①

These observations have two important corollaries. The first corollary is that in examining the bases for our understanding of utterances we cannot be satisfied with highly idealized sets of sentences which are then analyzed in their syntactic and semantic dimension. "Indirect" speech acts are very common occurrences that simply cannot be neglected. The utterance "You look pale" in most cases is not a simple factual statement but is part of a larger context, such as "I worry about you," "Can I do anything for you?", etc. Sentence grammars and semantic investigations ignore, however, precisely this pragmatic dimension of language exchanges, as well as *syntagmatic* chaining of sentences and clauses to larger units or sequences.

There is still another reason why the reduction to an idealized (artificial) language is inappropriate for the investigation of communication in a social world. As we have seen, the "truth conditions" for a sentence are a matter not only of the correspondence between a sentence and the state of the world it depicts, but also of a certain appropriateness depending on the situation.[26] Such "data," however, become available to us only when we take everyday language as our model, instead of beginning with some restricted language captured by an abstract model, and explain actual communication as "deviations" from the ideal of propositional sentences.

The second corollary concerns the way in which persuasion or certain perlocutionary effects can be studied. In the following section I want, therefore, to clarify the issue of perlocutionary force in the case of persuasion. The problem of why and how we give assent to a statement is placed within the wider context of communication. In accordance with the above points, I begin with the analysis of everyday language and examine the reasons by which rational speakers are compelled or inclined to give assent to an utterance.

III COMMUNICATION AND ASSENT

Why can "rational" actors give assent to statements made by someone else? Such statements may concern scientific or logical propositions, or they may entail practical judgments, as mentioned above. The problem of inducing consent can be attacked through a variety of strategies: through restrictions in meanings; through the acceptance of "evidence" for what is the case; or through the stabilization of normatively secured expectations. Although I am not certain that this is an exhaustive set of all strategies available to us, it appears to be a rather comprehensive enumeration. After all, the strategies listed correspond to the syntactic, semantic, and pragmatic dimensions of language respectively. However, since *ordinary language* possesses all three dimensions, it might be useful to investigate further the impact which the selection of one strategy has on the *other dimensions of language*.

Through the restriction on the use of terms and through the developments of rules for cogency in moving from one term to the other, unequivocality can be guaranteed. The consistency of the conceptual framework is thus not only safeguarded, but assent becomes compelling. Consistency is usually considered the domain of logic, as modern logic became increasingly concerned with the *syntactic* dimension of language only. As a matter of fact, the great success in the formalization of language depended crucially upon the restriction of logic to questions of cogency and upon the development of "uninterpreted" calculi. Obviously the communication pattern among persons engaged in logical arguments is monologic, since the success of communication, indicated by a rational assent, is solely dependent upon the correct tracing of logical derivations. In cases in which investigations are concerned with the "semantic" dimensions of language,[27] i.e., the *correspondence* between the calculus and "reality," common understandings are arrived at through the mediation of common objects of experience, and through the acceptance of an unproblematic background knowledge (measurement, theoretical primitives, etc.). The structure of communication among the practitioners (i.e., scientists) remains, nevertheless, monologic. Communication is not dependent in its validity upon pragmatic considerations such as who is entitled to speak, whose objections must be entertained, or upon the preferences of the participants.

However, issues such as personal preferences, authority, etc., become important when we focus our attention on the *pragmatic dimension* of language, a dimension which becomes most noticeable in deliberations about practical matters. Common understandings can be arrived at through the stabilization and evocation of certain generally shared expectations among actors in a specific situation. The medium of understanding is then neither logical cogency nor semantic truth, but rather *claims to the validity of norms* on the basis of which actors can

31

communicate, coordinate their actions, and adjust their preferences. The general problem of assent, therefore, can be formulated in the following way: on the basis of *what reasons* do we ascribe "neustic" force to utterances in various sets of activities, be they logic, science, politics, or law? The neologism "neustic," introduced by Hare,[28] refers in this context to the act of nodding, or better, to the giving of assent to a statement.

Taking "logic" first, it is quite obvious why purely logical arguments are compelling in the strongest possible way. The validity of the derivations is entirely *internal* to a contradiction-free axiomatized system. Persuasiveness in the case of scientific arguments, on the other hand, obviously depends not only on the formal characteristics of a theory but also on experimental evidence. However, criteria such as parsimony, formal elegance, etc., still possess an important residual force in strengthening (or rejecting) data and experiments in support of a theory.

These two points have important repercussions for the treatment of the reasons why we ascribe "neustic" force to norms. While a "scientific" approach to the impact of norms on action often infers this force from the observance of overt behavior (compliance), jurisprudence and legal theory provide more systemic explanations. Efforts such as Kelsen's to represent norms in terms of systematic hierarchies, or in terms of logical structures, can be understood as attempts at reducing problems of validity to a logical issue. This can be done either by treating the neustic-force problem as an issue of validation *within* the recursive functioning of "self-referential systems" (Luhmann) or by leaving the question of why a whole system of rules and norms is valid to some other discipline (Kelsen).[29]

However, such a reduction of the neustic element to a problem of systemic validity buys its persuasiveness at a heavy price. One counterargument might suffice. Even if it were possible to represent the validation of norms as a largely systemic task, such a system of norms would still have to be applied to concrete cases. Since by definition such a system cannot also prescribe exhaustively all possible applications, norm-appliers would still have to argue why a certain case should fall under norm X instead of Y. When a third party is entrusted with the application of norms, this party will be under additional pressure to render a fair decision in the light of past cases, as well as in the light of the particular circumstances which might justify a deviation from the old precedent. The criteria for neustic persuasiveness possibly point, then, in opposite directions. While the systemic criterion favors consistency, the criterion of "justice" could favor a deviation. In the latter case, quite clearly, the neustic force of the argument cannot be based on systemic or logical factors.

Similarly, what counts as a case of self-defense as opposed to aggression, or what is an instance of self-determination as opposed to interference in the internal affairs of a state, cannot be deduced from some system-properties but depends on the evaluation of certain relevant facts. Norm-appliers, therefore, *routinely* face the same problem scientists face only during crisis periods when they are confronted with the problem of validation. In neither case can the persuasiveness of arguments for treating a controversy in terms of calculus A rather than B, or in terms of one set of norms rather than another, be rooted in the validation procedures *internal* to the calculi or in the unproblematic correspondence rules.

[margin note: problems with logical rules of assert]

Given these objections, it should be clear not only that the idea of normative systems (hierarchy of norms) developed by stringent logical calculi might be unrealistic in the sense that such efforts create great practical difficulties, but that such an enterprise might be downright misleading. In other words, we might be well advised to follow up on Hare's suggestion and treat assertions in *all areas* such as logic, science, or law as "speech acts." Instead of making "consistency" and "truth" the paradigmatic cases for deciding validity-claims, as logic and positivism demand, we had better use the model of deciding such questions *discursively* as our "normal case." The worlds of logic and science represent, then, rather exceptional instances in which – through special circumstances – the "pragmatic dimension" of communication often *can* be neglected by the participants in a discourse.

[margin note: four further corollaries]

Four further corollaries follow from these considerations. The first is: since the basis of validity-claims remains problematic in cases of normative statements, as neither an external check nor internal logical criteria are available to settle "practical" matters unequivocally, the issue of why and how certain "opinions" (*doxai:* δόξαι) become authoritative has to be investigated. In particular, one has to inquire into the ways in which traditions, historical experiences, past cases, practices, ideologies, etc., provide support for "reasons" that become socially dominant. Consensus, after all, does not simply emerge out of various debates but is dependent on the availability of cultural, historical, and philosophical experiences by which members of a society share meanings and find solutions to their problems. The second corollary concerns the following: although directives share with assertions a certain neustic feature, significant differences between descriptive and normative utterances exist. Communication in the first case becomes possible through the reference to *external*

[margin marks: ①, ✱, ②]

33

phenomena, while in the second case, the reasons for acceptance are embodied in rules and norms which stabilize mutual expectations. Norms, therefore, more than assertions, are dependent upon the *success of communicative action*, i.e., their perlocutionary effect. However, this perlocutionary effect is not independent of the norms' ability to provide easily recognized templates for solving the problems of social interaction. I shall argue that it is therefore no accident that law largely utilizes types and exemplars of permitted or forbidden actions, rather than exhaustive definitions, or formal syllogistic derivations, in addressing its "subjects."

Corollary three: since "practical" questions can seldom be decided by external referents or by internal coherence arguments, most questions need to be settled by *authoritative decision*. In this context, choice procedures, such as majority rule, cloture of debate, quorums, etc., are important means of arriving at a decision. It is also clear that norms that institutionalize such procedures rely basically upon the effectiveness of communication, i.e., upon the semiotic system by which users indicate to each other in what speech acts they are involved.

The fourth corollary is: within the process of deliberation antecedent to the choice, we can distinguish several modes or styles of reasoning, depending upon the stringency with which norms guide this process. Thus, political deliberations are bounded by norms, insofar as norms determine the persons who can participate in such discussion (citizens, deputies, etc.), and by the procedures that determine when and under what circumstances a particular "speech act," such as, for example, saying "aye" in a parliamentary vote, shall count as an authoritative decision.

IV CONTEXT AND PRACTICAL REASONING

The argument developed in the last section has led to the point where the division between first-, second-, and third-party contexts adopted in the previous chapter can be given greater precision since it can be shown to flow directly from our emphasis on language as a norm-governed activity. Let us remember that according to Franck, the first-party context ("first-party law") is characterized by the issuance of commands which may or may not have generalized character. Depending upon whether the situation-specific elements dominate or whether the *general scope* of the directive is emphasized, we can distinguish between imperatives (commands) and rules. Thus, threats might be situation-specific, for instance, "your wallet or your life," and would therefore not exhibit rule-like characteristics, or they might be

34

issued in a more general version applicable to future contingencies, and addressed to a wider audience. Such rule-like threats can then be cast in an elliptic form as, for example, the motto of the Thirteen Colonies, "Don't tread on me." Threats might also be stated explicitly, as the example of the Monroe Doctrine shows, which specified its range of application by envisioning a clearly defined contingency and by claiming applicability to all outsiders. While there are many more important conceptual distinctions which are as decisive as these commonalities among "first-party" directives, what is crucial for the first-party context is the *imposed* character of the norm,[30] i.e., that the interests, objections, or claims of the addressee(s) are at a minimum, as they are not admitted to an argumentative exchange on an equal basis. Thucydides' Melian "dialogue," which is no longer any genuine dialogue at all, shows most clearly the degeneration of the dialogical format of a discussion and the nature of such an imposition.

The second-party context is characterized by "strategic" behavior among the parties, i.e., by the recognition of interdependence of decision-making, and – in many circumstances – the existence of "mixed motives," or even the perception of common interest. Rules and norms *can, but need not, figure prominently in the actors' choices* since the bargaining between them might include coercive moves. Thus, the resort to norms can be – and frequently is – subsidiary to the process of "breaking the other's will" in order to arrive at a decision. Nevertheless, even in this process of coercion, certain norms might attain great importance because they serve as signals to the opponent when explicit communication has broken down. To that extent, former solutions to a bargain, which the actors view as similar to their present problem, can attain nearly the status of a precedent. Norms can also suggest a particular point on the possibility-boundary of the bargaining space because of their "salience." Splitting the difference, or returning to the status quo, similarly infuses the bargaining process with a normative dimension that often comes very close to the building-up of conventions and customary practices. Zartman's and Berman's argument about the importance of a "formula" and the five competing conceptions of justice in the bargaining process has advanced our understanding of the normative components of negotiations.[31]

Third-party law is the conventional conception of law, i.e., it covers the cases in which a third party applies *preexisting rules* to a given controversy in order either to mediate or settle the submitted issues authoritatively. Although I am indebted to Franck's analysis, I want to add two interrelated points of clarification. The first is that the nomenclature of first-party, second-party, and third-party *law* is somewhat misleading in that it seems to suggest that whenever we can observe the influence of norms we are entitled to call it "law." It is precisely the task for any serious analysis to make distinctions and develop a conceptual apparatus in which differences as well as commonalities of norms and their varying impact on decision-making can be assessed. Since actors normally *do* make distinctions between the prescriptive force of legal norms and imperatives of "comity" or "morality," the distinction between legal and non-legal norms is important for practical as well as theoretical reasons.

The second point of clarification concerns the issue of the "parties" involved. The distinction between first-, second-, and third-party law seems to imply that the conceptual differentiation parallels that of the number of concrete actors involved in a dispute. However, such an easy analogy may be an instance of "misplaced concreteness." I shall argue below in chapter 7 that it is more appropriate to distinguish first-party, second-party, and third-party norms according to the type of guidance these rules and norms provide in the reasoning process. For example, parties which have agreed to let their decisions be directed by recognized norms can even in a bilateral bargaining situation achieve something like a "third-party" law. Thus, the analytical distinctions are more appropriately made in terms of *the style of reasoning with rules and norms* than in terms of the number of distinct actors.

Here Michael Barkun's observation is helpful, suggesting that the transition between dyadic and triadic conflict situations may often be fluid precisely because rules and norms function frequently as "implicit" third parties.[32] Barkun's argument thereby emphasizes (again) the need to make analytical distinctions rather than assume that these conceptually important differentiations coincide with the emergence (or absence) of certain concrete individuals, be they mediators, arbitrators, or judges. Chapter 6 will elaborate on the normative criteria such a discourse will have to satisfy. Parties must grant to each other equal standing and forgo attacks – either verbal or physical – aimed at breaking each other's will. They will therefore have to argue "the merits" of their case and, in doing so, their argument must be cast in terms of universalizable rules.

In this context, the question arises of how a decision based on rules and norms, though *not logically compelling*, can marshal support. My argument below is that rules and norms which are used for arriving at a decision do not function in this choice-process like logical terms or causes but rather as persuasive reasons. This leads me to a brief discussion of the distinctive features of practical reasoning. Practical

practical reasoning

reasoning (having human action as its objective) seems to differ in several important respects from our normal scientific discourse. There is, first, the difference in the underlying principle of organizing phenomena which Kant has pointed out. While we organize phenomena under the aspect of necessity (nature), the concept of freedom provides us with the constitutive principle of understanding human action as resulting from "free will." This creates a special dialectic, as Kant emphasized, in which an actor

① *organizing phenomena.*

> puts himself into another order of things, and into relation with determining causes of quite another sort, when he conceives himself as intelligence endowed with a will and consequently with causality, than he does when he perceives himself as a phenomenon in the sensible world (which he actually is as well) and subjects his causality to external determination in accordance with laws of nature. He then becomes aware at once that both of these can, and indeed must, take place at the same time; for there is not the slightest contradiction in holding that a *thing as an appearance* (as belonging to the sensible world) is subject to certain laws of which it is independent *as a thing* or being *in itself*. That he must represent and conceive himself in this double way rests, as regards the first side, on consciousness of himself as an object affected through the senses; as concerns the second side, on consciousness of himself as intelligence – that is, as independent of sensuous impressions in his use of reason (and so as belonging to the intelligible world).[33]

These considerations lead to a second interrelated difference in practical reasoning. In arriving at a decision, the initial finding of the *relevant premises* from which one deliberates is of decisive importance. Consider in this context the request of a judge addressed to a defendant who has been swimming in a lake in spite of the explicit and widely posted prohibition. The request to "explain" his actions concerns less the subsumption of the factual conditions (i.e., the man swimming) under the general law (i.e., the prohibitions), than the making sure that no *defeating* circumstances can be discovered, or that no other interests and values have to be taken into consideration for an appropriate decision. For example, if the accused can demonstrate that he "jumped in after a child," he would obviously have a good excuse and the mechanical subsumption under the prohibition would be absurd. Would it make any difference if the child could actually swim, and if the defendant knew this? If it was not a child but a dog which the defendant tried to rescue? If the water protected by the prohibition was a drinking-water reservoir, or if it was a private spawning-ground for fish? Therefore, the finding of the relevant "starting-points," rather

37

than the stringency of the final logical deduction, is the important part in this type of reasoning.

The third point of difference from "theoretical" explanations follows from the argument above. In arriving at a particular decision a judge, as well as, in most cases, an actor who follows (or decides to break), a rule, will seek assent to a variety of *practical judgments* which are logically independent of the relevant rule or norm. Thus, whether the swimming was a rescue attempt or simply an act of carelessness cannot be derived from either the norm or the *overtly ascertainable "facts" of the case*. A good (i.e., persuasive) decision will be one in which, however, a rational assent can be gained through the giving of persuasive reasons why these rather than other practical judgments – which would have been possible – were held to be decisive and deserve support.

In this context, the classical teachings about the importance of topoi (τόποι), i.e., "commonplaces" for practical reasoning, become obvious.[34] Commonplaces are not only helpful in the discovery of the *starting-points* for practical arguments, an issue with which the classical teachings about "invention" deal. Topoi, as "seats of arguments," are also decisive for attaining *assent to choices* based on a series of practical judgments. For example, the topos that "more is better than less" is very persuasive as soon as the desirability of a practical matter has been established. The argument utilizing this commonplace becomes controlling by displacing other considerations which could provide grounds for competing evaluations, for example, qualitative distinctions such as in the topos "quality first." Consider in this context the force of Pareto optimality as a decision criterion. It relies precisely on the power of the topos "more is better than less"; it thereby defeats an evaluation of the decision at issue in terms of a *competing consideration*, for instance, one focusing on the *relative*, rather than absolute, gains to the parties involved.

A fourth characteristic of practical reasoning deserves attention. Since choices in a community are mostly made on the basis of equality, the eventual outcomes will be fundamentally influenced by the procedures which guide the choice-process. Choosing and debating *among* actors is, therefore, quite different from solving the choice-problem in the case of an individual. While certain aspects of this choice, or, better, of the deliberation antecedent to the decision, are the same in the individual case and that of a group, there exists a significant difference in collective decisions because procedural rules of debate, fairness requirements, and voting procedures have a significant impact on group decisions. This can easily be gleaned from the following considerations. An individual might freely adjust his "preferences" and change his estimates without violating the requirements of fair play. As a matter of fact, fairness is of no concern in the individual case because, whatever happens, competing ideas, preferences, and priorities are always *those of the individual* and he/she is entitled to give weight to and prefer alternatives freely according to his/her own valuations. In the case of groups, however, the adoption of certain debating procedures, or of putting alternatives to a vote, can mean "stacking the deck" and violating elemental normative requirements of a "discourse on grievances." Here, the "hidden face" of power in setting the agenda is as important a consideration as, for example, the actual vote.[35] The requirement of quorums for collective decisions is crucially related to this aspect. Only with a "critical mass" of persons present can we be sure to have a sufficiently diverse and representative sample of opinions from which we can draw actual proposals in our debates and hope for the emergence of a consensus. The requirements for jury selections make the same point even more emphatically. There, the unanimity rule combined with the diversity requirement is intended to meet particularly exacting standards of fairness.

A fifth decisive difference has to be mentioned also: while "practical arguments" within a discourse of grievances are potentially interminable, since each party can challenge the arguments of the opponent, more specialized techniques are necessary in order to lend persuasiveness to the finality of an authoritative decision. In law, these specialized techniques are based on certain topoi that are *specific to legal orders*. Their function is largely to justify *exclusions* and thus to limit the range of relevant facts and proofs. In this context, the laws of pleadings and evidence deserve particular attention, as do legally imposed deadlines and limits on reasons for appeals. Again, we have returned to the issue of commonplaces and their role in facilitating deliberations and choices in practical matters.

The *formal* characteristics of both types of topoi – i.e., the "commonplaces" in everyday communication, as well as the specific *juridical* topoi – have been investigated by the classical tradition in conjunction with the problem of "rhetorical proofs." I consider this close connection between practical reasoning and legal reasoning to be important and non-accidental. I also maintain that the legal mode of reasoning with rules and norms can be best understood as a specialized case of practical reasoning often expounded in treatises on "rhetoric." I shall discuss this problem more extensively in chapter 8, but for the moment the few remarks in the next section might suffice.

39

V   RHETORIC, PRACTICAL REASONING AND THE CONCEPT OF LAW

For those of us who have become accustomed to identifying rhetoric with technique (or delivery), the connection between reasoning and rhetoric seems rather odd. We have not only forgotten the original links between practical reason and rhetoric, but we have truly become Cartesians, heirs of the Ramist reforms and the logic of Port-Royal, that dismissed all methods of reasoning if they did not agree with the Cartesian ideal of certainty.[36] With the emergence of what the students of eighteenth-century rhetoric call the "elocutionary movement,"[37] rhetoric as a formal discipline "not only renounced her [sic] previous interests in the classical doctrines of invention, arrangement, and style, but undertook also to confine herself to the study or oratorical delivery and its twin aspects of voice and gesture."[38] "Oratory," therefore, attempted to persuade largely by dazzling technique and by the evocation of emotions rather than by the selection and presentation of relevant facts and reasons in the process of deliberation. But it was precisely these latter contributions that classical rhetoric was concerned with in its teachings on "invention" and "style."

In this context, it is important to note that the term "style" entered into everyday discourse via the specialized language of French lawyers in the seventeenth century, who used it to designate the deliberate and appropriate mode of proceeding with a legal argument.[39] Although such a historical note on the etymology of the concept of *style* does not prove my point concerning law as a specialized rhetoric, it nevertheless suggests an important avenue for further inquiry, taken up in chapter 8. While tracing the historical roots of law to the rhetorical tradition is interesting, it was only the work of the "New Rhetoric," in particular the investigations of Chaim Perelman and his circle, that established the *systematic* importance of the quasi-logical foundations of legal reasoning.[40] Perelman and his collaborators demonstrated that in prudential reasoning – and thereby, through implication, also in legal reasoning – the process of inference follows neither the pattern of classical deductions nor that of inductions (notwithstanding the attempts of French courts to present their decisions in short deductions). Measured against the standards of formal logic, the quality of legal arguments is somewhat deficient as it is largely based on paralogical types of inferences, such as the *argumentum e contrario, ad hominem, a simili,* the *reductio ad absurdum,* etc., for which Aristotle's *Rhetoric* provided the theoretical treatment.[41]

40

There is still another, though interconnected, aspect of practical reasoning that makes the classical rhetorical tradition relevant to law. If it is true that one of the major issues in legal arguments is the discovery of appropriate starting-points for arguments and the assignment of "weight" to competing value-considerations, then the process of finding premises has to be subjected to close scrutiny. As mentioned, the classical rhetorical tradition spoke of the problem of *inventio*, i.e., finding the right premises as opposed to drawing appropriate conclusions. Here the topoi (commonplaces) or, as Cicero calls them, the "seats of arguments,"[42] provide appropriate starting points for the discussion of a problem with which the actors or judges are confronted.

The role of commonplaces was dealt with extensively by Aristotle in his *Topica*. Interested in how the arrangement of argumentative steps might influence the conclusions we arrive at, as well as their persuasive character, Aristotle provided an inventory of loosely ordered considerations that are likely to stimulate discussion of relevant aspects of a problem. The topoi, or commonplaces, and the various "catalogues" of topoi provide pointers for discoursive strategies by which crucial facets of a practical problem can be examined and subjected to various challenges in the process of deliberation. The direct relevance of the rhetorical tradition in its attempt to order "subjects" in a topical rather than abstract systematic fashion has been well established for legal arguments. For example, Giuliani has shown that the development of the law of evidence in common-law countries was less a function of the jury system than of the *pleading procedures* which were rooted in the rhetorical tradition.[43] Viehweg has demonstrated the importance of topoi for the codification in Roman law, and through its reception, for civil law systems.[44] These influences are not accidental, as I shall argue, since they are indications for the problem-solving rather than the analytical style of thinking, which underpins jurisprudential activities.

The fact that legal orders with widely different structures and procedures show *topical* orderings not only strengthens the confidence that the observed "rhetorical elements" in law are more than a historical accident, but also call into question one of our most dearly held convictions: that legal orders represent closed systems which are susceptible to complete mapping *and* logical formalization. Rather than sharing this belief in the "systemic" character of law, I shall argue that even mature legal orders are characterized by a much weaker ordering. Such an ordering does not preclude legal thought from following logical canons, but it *does* suggest that the idea of a deductive system as

41

elaborated by the *Begriffsjurisprudenz* (conceptualism) is mistaken. The main characteristics of legal arguments deal with the finding and interpretation of the applicable norms and procedures, and with the presentation of the relevant facts and their evaluations. Both questions turn on the issue of whether a particular interpretation of a fact-pattern is acceptable rather than "true"; consequently, strict logic plays a minor role in this process of "finding the law."[45]

The implications of these arguments for resolving perplexing conceptual issues of the status of international law are apparent. Thus, international law has often not been treated as proper law because it lacked the firm rooting in a sovereign will or because it was not "systemic" enough. My approach offers an alternative to these well-worn theories: an alternative that appears also to be more fruitful heuristically. If social institutions (such as the sovereign) or certain intrinsic characteristics (such as sanctions or a system) are not made the defining characteristics of law, the status of "international law" can no longer be disposed of by purely definitional exercises. On the contrary, my approach opens the door for a more detailed inquiry into the role of norms in the decision-making process of international actors.

As a consequence, this inquiry revolves around two further inter-related problems: the first is the issue of a demarcation-criterion between legal and other types of norms; the second concerns the justification for speaking of the existence of a distinct legal order in international relations. While the first question addresses issues of conceptualization, the other focuses on the impact of law upon actual decision-making. Because I adopt a pragmatic, not semantic, view of law, as stated above, I shall argue that the legal character of rules and norms can be established when we are able to show that these norms are *used* in a distinct fashion in making decisions and in communicating the basis for those choices to a wider audience. Note that such a characterization of law is independent of formal institutions, levels of analysis, or the existence of logically closed systems. With regard to the second question, ascertaining the *impact* different rules and norms have on any particular move in international relations or in the domestic arena can only be decided through an empirical investigation. Here the "standard operating procedures" by which governments dispose of routine decisions are particularly relevant. Furthermore, the investigation of crises – in which these procedures break down and a redefinition of the game is sought – provides us with evidence on the role of norms under non-routine conditions. Such investigations could demonstrate the irrelevance of established norms

42

when high political interests are at stake, although the picture, as it emerges from the concrete studies of crisis-bargaining, is quite different from the widely held belief of the irrelevance of norms in these situations.[46] Even if we agree on the marginal, rather than central, importance of norms in molding the *outcome* of international crises, such an assessment is quite different from the facile dichotomy between the "domestic" and "international arena" where norms count or do not count respectively.

VI CONCLUSION

This chapter has been devoted to an exposition of the methodological position upon which the book is based. Crucial for my argument was the clarification of the assertion that human action is rule governed. While such an assumption does not exclude other types of explanations, it *does* entail certain other methodological commitments which go beyond the epistemology of observational facts recorded in an object-language. It also transcends the teleological explanation schemes of intentions and "rational action." The discussion of the "three worlds" and their concomitant epistemological positions was intended to sharpen the issues and to point to the importance of everyday language in understanding human action. Precisely because syntactic and semantic studies have neglected important aspects of language, and thus of social interaction, a more pragmatically oriented approach based on discourse and communicative action seemed to be required.

Within this framework, the question of how rules and norms guide choices, particularly in cases in which several independent actors have to come to a joint decision, can be posed in a new way. Rules and norms mold decisions via the reasoning process (deliberation). This process departs – especially in the cases of groups – in significant ways from the model of instrumentally rational action. Not only must the discursive treatment of competing claims satisfy certain basic norms, such as equality of standing, non-violence, etc., but arguments within this discourse must also be on the *merits*, i.e., cast in terms of universalizable rules. In addition, the process by which the characterization of actions and the valuation underlying our respective preferences attain assent needs to be investigated further. The section on practical reasoning intended to show how practical judgments become susceptible to a discursive treatment, how the "perlocutionary" power of arguments can be conceptualized, and how persuasion becomes possible.

43

These arguments in turn set the stage for the discussion of authoritative decisions (third-party law). When legal reasoning was placed within the confines of practical reasoning, similarities and differences between these two styles in reasoning could be analyzed in a preliminary fashion, until a more precise determination can be made in chapter 8. Now that the conceptual foundations for the approach used in the book have been laid, the next chapter begins the substantive argument with the examination of the main issues in the present regime debate.

2 ANARCHY AND THE STATE OF NATURE: THE ISSUE OF REGIMES IN INTERNATIONAL RELATIONS

I THE DOMESTIC ANALOGY, REGIMES, AND SOCIAL ORDER

The place of norms in political life has always been controversial, particularly in international relations analysis. The common-sense assumption that "law" begets order and that consequently disorder has to result from either the absence of a normative structure or the ineffectiveness of enforcement seems to have exercised such a powerful hold that people conceived of international politics largely in terms of a negative analogy to domestic politics. The conceptual blinders are so well established that traditionally persons interested in the study of international relations had to group themselves into two virtually exclusive "fraternities." Those who denied that norms are important for international interactions called themselves – with typical modesty – "realists," and those who were interested in norms were labeled "idealists."[1] The advocacy of law among the latter group could then be based on either hopes for a world government, the establishment of peace through law,[2] or on the often somewhat embarrassed admission that international law, although useful for certain purposes, was not really "law."[3] In any case, the underlying dichotomy between domestic (law-governed) and international affairs (anarchy) appeared to be reinforced. World government advocates therefore shared with the realists a common Hobbesian framework.[4] The latter, however, did not account for two major issues: first, the problem of how norms and institutions in general influence decisions and thus create social order, and second, whether and how order is possible in the anarchical realm of international relations.

If we are interested in answering these questions it is clear that we have to overcome the conventional conceptual limitations which impeded more than helped traditional analysis. For this reason I want to utilize the present debate on "regimes" in international relations as my point of departure. Such a strategy appears to be useful because the focus on regimes provides an approach to the function of norms in international relations without involving itself in the quagmire of realist assumptions, or in the often arcane squabbles of legal analyses. Now that the advantages of an inquiry via "regimes" has been stated, two caveats seem in order. The first concerns the current premature emphasis on the question of regime *change*, originally identified with regime decay. This focus not only tends to make regimes little more than reflections of power, but also obscures the way in which norms function in molding decisions. What remains unclear is why actors follow rules in the first place[5] and why even hegemons find it often necessary to resort to norms rather than to direct imperative control based on their "power." The second caveat is directed to the apparent limitation of the regime approach to questions of change in the international *political economy*. If norms and rules are important in molding decisions, then it is not intelligible why such a condition should not also obtain in the "security" area. True, Jervis's and Lipson's arguments seem rather persuasive in pinpointing the reasons why "regimes" are likely to be "weak" in these circumstances.[6] Nevertheless, it would seem necessary to separate the question of the strength, or effectiveness, of rules and norms from the question of their existence and function; otherwise we are likely to end up with a circular argument or some type of *ad hocery*.

In assessing the utility of the regime approach for the study of norms I shall use three criteria: (1) *usefulness*, i.e., the ability of this approach to pose interesting puzzles; (2) *conceptual elaboration*, i.e., the appropriateness (or lack) of the concepts to capture the phenomena under study, and (3) *explanatory power*, most clearly exemplified by the impact of norms on decisions as well as by patterns of deviance or of regime adaptation. The last criterion also includes an appraisal of the importance of "values" for social order and their connection with the more specific norms and rules of a regime. My discussion rejects the conventional dichotomy explaining social interactions either in terms of communitarian attitudes or in terms of individual "rights." An analysis of the two societal models allows then for a characterization of international relations as a "practical association," in Nardin's terms, based on the mutual recognition of rights and shared practices but not on a vision of the good life.[7] It was precisely this concept of a special type of community that gave rise to the conception of *ius inter gentes*, which made the emergence of a state system possible. International law thereby not only emancipated itself from the concept of a natural, or even cosmic, order;[8] it also called into question the conventional

46

way of thinking about law, i.e., that rules and norms can function only in hierarchically and/or teleologically structured social systems.

II THE USEFULNESS OF THE REGIME APPROACH

If patterns of international interactions can be satisfactorily analyzed in terms of power, then utilizing regimes in explanations becomes superfluous.[9] However, in spite of Waltz's assertion that in international relations only the distribution of capabilities matters, his constant utilization of the "market" as an example of systemic constraints belies the possibility of such reductionism.[10] After all, markets are probably *the* social institution which are most dependent upon normative underpinnings. While markets are anarchical in the sense of lacking central decision-making institutions, it is unimaginable that they could function without the common acceptance of the convention of money, without the protection of property rights, and without the institutions of promising and contracting, governed by practice-type rules.[11] In addition, it is one of the most egregious errors of this type of analysis to equate capabilities with power. The incongruency of such an equation was pointed out by Baldwin and needs no further elaboration.[12]

The above considerations clearly indicate that at least some of the objections of structural or neo-realist criticisms to the regime approach are mistaken. Nevertheless, there has been widespread agreement among mainstream political scientists that certain issue areas, such as security, might not be susceptible to regime analysis. For example, Robert Jervis maintains that the incentives in the field of security are likely to defeat the establishment of security regimes, and that the obstacles to maintaining them are also particularly severe. Consequently, "security regimes" can only come into existence under very unusual circumstances, i.e., when all major actors are satisfied with the status quo, and when defensive postures are both distinct and effective.[13] Jervis also argues that a security regime exists only when the established norms facilitate not only cooperation but a cooperative stance of a *particular* kind. He attempts to make the crucial distinction along the short-term/long-term continuum of interest. In order for a regime to exist, there has to be evidence of cooperation "that is more than the pursuit of short-run self-interest. To comply with a robber's demand to surrender is not to participate in a regime, even if the interaction occurs repeatedly and all participants share the same expectations."[14]

Several points are worth pondering in this context. There is, first, the assertion that in testing the existence or the functioning of regimes we are to look at long-term rather than short-term interests. But such an argument appears to be problematic. If it is "interests" we are to consult, then "interests" alone should explain the emergence of cooperation. Norms and regimes are in that case, at best, epiphenomena. It seems, however, that we need norms precisely for the reasons that many actors face each other in single-shot rounds and/or in the absence of sufficient information concerning each other's pay-off structure. In other words, the interacting parties can often neither rely on a common history nor expect future gains through the use of tit-for-tat strategies. Precisely for that reason, it is the function of norms to fortify socially optimal solutions against the temptations of individually rational defections. And it is precisely the internalization of the norms' *generalized* validity claim which bridges the gap among actors who know very little, or virtually nothing, about each other. It is therefore more this generalized attitude – obviously often counteracted by the incentives of defection – than specific utility calculations which explain why socialized actors follow rules.

Utilizing the divergence of individual and collective rationality as a "first cut" in approaching the role of norms in decision-making nevertheless serves a useful purpose, even if we realize that most actors do not face a clearly defined matrix with given utilities, and that the outcome of their choices is very seldom the result of simultaneous choices. Thus, it is often only through the choosing itself – and through the perceived response – that actors become aware of their own utility function as well as that of their opponents. It is here that norms can become particularly useful in defining situations and thus in indicating to the other that one understands the nature of the "game" in which one is involved.

The national security field, rather than the market, provides us, in the case of deterrence, with an appropriate illustration. Precisely because deterrence is a psychological relationship between the contestants, a common universe of meaning is crucial for its proper functioning. When deterrence fails – because one actor did not believe the other would retaliate, because he hoped his defection could remain ambiguous or undetected, or because the reversal of a quick *fait accompli* is considered too costly[15] – the reestablishment of common understandings on the basis of shared meanings becomes important. Note in this context that "irrational" actors such as terrorists cannot be deterred and that therefore a strategy of deterrence crucially depends upon normative understandings. Consider, for example, crisis bargaining, particularly "going to the brink" under conditions of mutual vulnerability. As Schelling has pointed out, the utility of threats in these cases depends more on the intensity and the balance of the interests involved, as well as upon the ability to shift the blame for missing the "last clear chance" before a dangerous escalation,[16] than upon military capabilities. Thus, disparities in force posture matter little in the face of a guaranteed level of destruction. Jervis has shown that under these circumstances the defender of the status quo is likely to have a double advantage. First, attempts to change the status quo will usually shift the burden of "the last clear chance" to the challenger. Second, the intensity of interests establishing the balance of motivations will favor the defender, because actors facing certain annihilation will value their present possession more than the prospects of future gains.[17]

Although this argument is compelling only under conditions of a high degree of informational certainty, some actual examples seem to bear out these hypotheses and thereby show its persuasive force. According to an apocryphal story, Nikita Khrushchev is said to have remarked to a Western correspondent once

> that Berlin is not worth a war, but he is reminded that this shared risk is a two-edged sword. Khrushchev, as if coached by Schelling, replies that "you are the ones who have to cross the frontier," showing in a single vignette that (he) did think in terms of the manipulation of shared risk as well as the manipulation of the status quo as a means to pass the onus of "the last clear chance" to the opponent.[18]

This example is significant since it establishes that even in crisis bargaining situations, much more goes on than the usual haggling about distributional outcomes upon which classical bargaining theory focuses. As Fisher and Ury rightly remark:

> Each move you make within a negotiation is not only a move that deals with rent, salary or other substantive questions; it also helps to structure the rules of the game you are playing. Your move may serve to keep negotiations within an ongoing mode, or it may constitute a game-changing move. This second negotiation, by and large, escapes notice because it seems to occur without conscious decision. Only when dealing with someone with a markedly different cultural background, are you likely to see the necessity of establishing some accepted process for the substantive negotiations. But whether consciously or not, you are negotiating procedural rules with every move you make, even if those moves appear exclusively concerned with substance.[19]

It was the Cuban missile crisis that showed that the acceptance (or reestablishment) of such a common framework of meaning is essential before a solution, i.e., the striking of a deal, becomes possible. Khrushchev's letter to Kennedy, which represented the turning-point in the crisis, eloquently made this point. Knowing that he had over-played his hand, the Kremlin leader signaled that he accepted the definition of the situation as a major superpower confrontation and disclosed his willingness to de-escalate. The crucial passage reads:

> You can regard us with distrust, but in any case you can be calm in this regard, that we are of sound mind and understand perfectly well that if we attack you will respond the same way . . . This dictates that we are normal people, and that we correctly understand and correctly evaluate the situation . . . We however want to live in peace and do not at all want to destroy our country . . . We quarrel with you, we have differences on ideological questions. But our view of the world consists in this: that ideological questions as well as economic prob-lems should not be resolved by military means but on the basis of peaceful competition.[20]

Having established such a framework of rationality, norms can, in addition, provide the templates for solutions. Here the power of precedents, of dividing the difference, or of returning to the status quo ante (because of saliency) has been noted in the bargaining literature.

The Cuban missile crisis shows in still another respect that real-life situations are much richer in their normative texture than the conven-tional games of bargaining theory make it appear. Consider, in this context, Kennedy's insistence on not simply breaking the other's will irrespective of the costs to the other and irrespective of its implications for the future. Rather, a redefinition of the game on the basis of mutual role-taking was sought, which infused the situation with normative considerations that went beyond the immediate question of winning by taking a wider variety of factors into account. Putting oneself into the shoes of the other leads to a sharing of aspirations, fears, and weaknesses that not only reassures the opponent but makes a redis-covery of a common sociality possible. This in turn limits the demands since the perceptions of the opponent, as well as of the stakes, change. In opposing an ultimatum to Khrushchev, Kennedy is said to have remarked:

> There is one thing I have learned in this business and that is not to issue ultimatums. You just can't put the other fellow in a position where he has no alternative except humiliation. This country cannot afford to be humiliated and neither can the Soviet Union. Like us, the Soviet Union has many countries which look to her for leadership and Khrushchev would be likely to do something desperate before he let himself be disgraced in their eyes.[21]

Although the last sentence seems to indicate that such considerations are based on rational calculation, it is nevertheless a type of calculation which is not fixated upon the utilities as measured by the superiority in capabilities to inflict greater pain on the opponent. It is rather a calculation in which a conception of "reciprocity" as an evoked set of commonly accepted values serves as the background for calculation.

The obvious objection to such an interpretation of the crisis could be that Cuba was an atypical situation which is helpful neither for the understanding of international politics in general nor for the resolution of crises in particular. Thus, it could be argued that even admitting the important part norms played in resolving this conflict, it was after all the conventional and nuclear superiority that decided the outcome. While I do not want to deny the importance of military capabilities, it is obvious that these resources mattered largely because they shaped the perceptions of the respective decision-makers. But to the extent that norms are also part of the decision environment, their influence has to be carefully studied as well. Resorting to some reductionist explanations which derive *a priori* the outcomes from the force posture is hardly advancing our understanding.

The limitations of capability analysis become even more obvious in the debate concerning the usefulness of a "countervailing strategy." The underlying idea of this doctrine is that since the threat of nuclear annihilation is incredible, the U.S. needs a variety of options with which to meet Soviet challenges on lesser levels. Such a strategy, then, entails a capability for "limited" nuclear strikes. The particular reconciliation between the requirements of enhancing deterrence and those of providing greater flexibility in fighting a war is, however, hardly convincing. After all, the U.S. capacity to attack Soviet targets selectively with nuclear weapons is less a function of the options created by the American military posture than the (well-founded) fear of Soviet retaliation against our vulnerable population centers. In addition, there is an important flaw in the escalation dominance argument which can be resolved only if we assume that important normative constraints will prevail in a "limited nuclear exchange." As Jervis points out:

> While the countervailing strategy pays at least some attention to the credibility of threats, it completely ignores the need to make credible promises. Unless a war ends with one side running out of ammunition – a most unlikely contingency – some sort of negotiations will be required. Each side will have to believe not only that continued fighting is costly, but that peace is possible. This situation involves

51

making and accepting promises for an immediate ceasefire and the belief that the other is not merely waiting for a favourable opportunity to renew the fighting. The ability to provide the necessary assurances is an indispensable part of war termination, a part no U.S. policy can overlook.[22]

Thus, one of the implications of the nuclear revolution in strategic thought is precisely that threats and force function differently now than they did in the past and that therefore considerably more cooperation among the adversaries is required to make deterrence work. To that extent, deterrence entails the credibility not only of threats but also of promises and commitments (by the power which is threatening) that destruction will be kept in abeyance. This type of normative guidance in crisis situations might not satisfy the requirements of a well-formed regime. Nevertheless, as we have seen, it is of decisive importance for an adequate understanding of international politics.

When we move from crisis to "normal" politics, even the most hardened realists have to confess that the application of force is a very costly way to achieve one's objectives, and that sensible powers have therefore followed a policy of prestige.[23] Prestige itself, however, is an ambiguous concept. It might simply mean establishing a "bad reputation," as gangsters attempt to keep challenges to their position to a minimum, or it may be tied to shared aspirations. Nevertheless, in either case prestige depends on the other person's expectations about the likelihood, scope, and domain of (retaliatory) action. The more explicit this framework becomes, the more prestige becomes mediated by a normative order.[24]

While this observation does not establish the "moral" character of such expectations, it nevertheless demonstrates that power and influence are often derived from the role of a protector of certain rules and core values. The notion of a Great Power (in the European state-system) and of hegemonic leadership (in ancient Greece) are cases in point.[25] Whether it is useful to endow the "rules of the game" with the dignity of some type of legal force, as some scholars suggest, is a difficult question.[26] Nevertheless, the embeddedness of the power-game in a shared normative structure shows that the alleged antinomy between power politics and following the rules of the international game is largely mistaken.

The discussion of "reputation" and "rules of the game" leads us back to Jervis's second point: the argument concerning the commands of a robber in forcing a particular action and the role of expectations. While Jervis is in a way correct in denying regime status to the expectation of being robbed (even if repeatedly), the reasons for doing so remain obscure. It seems that three further problems need clarification: (a) the implied identification of norms and rules with "commands"; (b) the denial of rule-status to "illegitimate" demands as judged from a certain base-line of expectations; and (c) the lack of a distinction between explicit and implicit rules (the latter giving rise to "expectations" but not to a full-fledged regime). A brief discussion of these issues is appropriate.

Mistaking norms and rules for commands has a long and distinguished ancestry, shared by such unlikely companions as positivists, voluntarist philosophers, and theologians.[27] But even in the last case, when the obligatory character of prescriptions is derived from an absolute sovereign – God – language clearly distinguishes between a *command* and a *commandment*. While commands are situation-specific, commandments (which show rule-like features) are always thought to be applicable to broad classes of events.[28] Rules, as Hart points out, are "standing orders."[29] This characteristic is best elucidated when rules are stated in the "if–then" form, indicating the circumstances and range of the rule's application.[30] Rules are also valid *erga omnes* (applicable to all) and are thereby quite different from commands. After all, the famous gunman asking for your wallet is not claiming to have established a rule or norm also applicable to *himself*.[31] The latter corollary is surely not part of the language-game of asking for "your money or your life." Even when rules empower someone to issue commands, the command and the rule are clearly distinguishable. As Kaplan and Katzenbach state, rules that empower in this sense are always part of a larger normative context.[32] It is the lack of legitimacy of such demands that makes the acceptance of "being robbed" as part of the normative discourse implausible, even if it is based on stable expectations.

This leads me to the second silent premise in Jervis's (and Hart's) account: the identification of a "rule" with legitimacy. Such an identification is surely in order when we use rules and norms within a discourse on grievances, i.e., when we try to come to a fair decision as to the violation and/or weight of the contenders' respective claims. However, there are some circumstances in which we can appropriately use the term "rule" nearly interchangeably with that of "generalization," and can do so without much concern for the rule's legitimacy. Consider once more the example of the gunman, but this time from the perspective of the average New Yorker, who will not fail to tell you that "you will get robbed if you go through Central Park at dawn, dusk, or night." Even the police are most likely to shrug their shoulders if someone complains about this intolerable situation. In other words, there seems to be a pretty well-established "regime" in place, in spite of its illegitimacy. Given the difficulty in enforcing the law in the face of large-scale non-compliance, everybody is supposed to take this generalization as a "rule" *for* his/her behavior, and is not to venture into the park at certain times.

Thus, the notions of "rule" and "legitimacy" appear to be more contingently related to each other than both Jervis and Hart claim. It is precisely this reason which justifies the distinction among different *contexts* in which rules are used, as made by Franck. Thus, what is acceptable in one context, for instance, giving advice to someone and thereby treating robberies as a "given," is not necessarily so in another context. For example, it would be adding insult to injury to tell an aggrieved person in a court of law that he/she did not suffer unjustly because being robbed was, after all, what he/she had to "expect."

There remains the third problem, mentioned above, i.e., the nature of norms themselves. It leads to the argument that certain rules of the game, although giving rise to expectations, are not full-fledged rules, but – at best – implicit or tacit norms. Again, a short reflection shows that the term "tacit" is used in a variety of senses. Thus the observance of SALT II by the U.S. until May 1986 was due to a "tacit" agreement because the treaty was never ratified and had expired long before the U.S. deviated from the stipulated numbers of warheads. However, since the administration repeatedly announced its intention to abide by the treaty one has to wonder to what the term "tacit" refers in this context. Similarly, unilateral announcements, such as claims to the exclusive use of ocean space for purposes of testing missiles or atomic weapons, have been heeded by both the U.S. and the U.S.S.R., and the compliance with these requests has been explained in terms of a tacit understanding. Furthermore, there are the famous rules of the game which developed in the Korean War and which Schelling mentions,[33] such as not bombing beyond a certain meridian, or river, in return for a similar restraint on the part of the opponent. In these instances the "bargaining" was truly tacit as no formal written or spoken communication took place and the opponents had to communicate "by doing." Finally, there are certain instruments, such as the Helsinki Accords, or certain gentlemen's agreements within the I.M.F.,[34] which are the result of very explicit bargaining and even drafting, whose binding force is, however, again held to be "implicit," or "tacit."

If we want to understand how norms work we obviously need a clearer conceptualization. The two-by-two table below (figure 1) is an attempt to deal with the, at first, bewildering complexity of the

54

	COMMITMENT	
	tacit	explicit
tacit	"unspoken rules" Schelling's rules	custom/convention "implied" contracts
EXPRESSION explicit	gentlemen's agreements unilateral declarations	contracts/treaties

Figure 1

examples above. The first variable concerns the issue on the basis of what reasons a validity-claim is implied (commitment); the second variable deals with the tacit (implicit) or explicit nature of the (verbal) formulation of the norm.

The least problematic cases fall into the cell on the bottom right. The validity of the explicit commitment is governed by practice-type rules which are well codified (Vienna Convention on Treaties, "restatements" of contract law, codes, etc.). The top right and bottom left cells are to a certain extent "mirror images," as they vary either the explicitness of the rules, i.e., their expression, or the explicitness of the commitment itself. Thus, while custom is as binding as the obligations incurred through formal contracting, the implicit, or tacit underlying rule (*opinio iuris sive necessitatis*) often makes it difficult to ascertain precisely what counts as custom. The reasoning of the I.C.J. in the *North Sea Continental Shelf* and in the *Asylum* case show this clearly.[35] On the other hand, within well-defined practices, a mere "sign" (such as hailing a cab) is sufficient to construe an obligation. Although the boundaries between these cases and gentlemen's agreements are often fuzzy, there seems to exist an important distinction in that the expression of the commitments in the latter case is, as the I.M.F. example showed, very specific, while the nature of the obligation remains ambiguous.

Implicit rules in the top left cell, or as Paul Keal has called them, "unspoken" rules,[36] are the least understood rules. They emerge largely through *unilateral* calculations which may take verbal as well as non-verbal clues into account. Although the inclusion of verbal messages seems to violate the "implicit" character of the rule in question, it is important to realize that "implicitness" and "explicitness" do not necessarily refer here to the existence or absence of verbal utterances, but rather to the rule's function within communicative action. The

55

decisive criterion is whether direct communication takes place among the parties in regard to the norm, or whether its operation is unilaterally inferred or imputed from the other's action. These calculations occur on the basis of expectations about alter's reaction to ego's action. For international politics, this results in the following dynamics:

> A's expectations of B will include an estimation of B's expectations of A. This process of replication, it must be noted, is not an interaction between two states, but rather a process in which decision makers in one state work out the consequences of their beliefs about the world; a world they believe to include decision makers in other states, also working out the consequences of their beliefs. The expectations which are so formed, are the expectations of one state, but they refer to other states.[37]

Although expectations which prove to be correct in a number of instances thereby attain a certain stability and provide some guidance for decision-making in analogous situations, compliance with these unspoken rules will be unproblematic only when the perception of a common interest is sufficiently strong. Obviously, this will be the case in instances in which the situation resembles a "game of coordination," i.e., when the interests of the interacting parties are neither opposed nor mixed. To that extent Hume's example of two men coming to a tacit agreement about how to row a boat is insructive.[38] However, if states perceive the situation as one of resembling a prisoners' dilemma (i.e., when mixed motives prevail and the incentives to defect are larger than those to cooperate), rules and norms, which attempt to shore up the cooperative solution, will be under pressure. In addition, rule-guidance will be weak since no explicit discourse *about* the tacit rule is possible without either opponent wanting to enter into such a discussion. Not only, therefore, are violations difficult to detect and communicate, but there is the additional problem that no explicit discussion about either scope or applicability of such a rule to a controversy is possible.[39] Casting rules in explicit verbal form is not only the most basic form of institutionalization; it also makes the violation of rules *separable* from the overall pattern of social interaction. It thereby enables disputing parties to discuss their "grievances" in the face of disappointments about each other's conduct.

The above considerations could be useful for advancing the discussion of security regimes, which are often made up by such tacit understandings. Furthermore, it is also clear that even explicit rules are in themselves insufficient to make a regime "robust," i.e., able to survive intended or unintended acts of defection. Since no rule in itself can specify all possible ranges of application, disputes are bound to arise concerning "the meaning" of crucial terms or the relevant characterization of a particular action. To that extent a dispute-settling mechanism becomes necessary even if explicit rules and norms have been agreed upon, and the parties can be assumed to be willing to abide by the agreement.[40] The importance of the Consultative Committee for the functioning of SALT I should be emphasized in this respect.[41]

III CONCEPTUAL ELABORATION

The above discussion dealt largely with the usefulness of regimes for analyzing international relations in general or certain issue areas within it. The last few remarks have already also raised some further questions about the appropriateness of the conceptual apparatus of the regime approach. Not only have regimes been called "woolly concepts," but, it has been argued, the impetus for developing regime analysis derived more from the faddism of the "profession" than from the requirements of the field or subject matter.[42] Although I think these conclusions are exaggerated, serious conceptual problems remain.

According to the "consensus-definition" in the special issue of *International Organization*, regimes are "sets of implicit or explicit principles, norms, rules, and decision-making procedures around which actors' expectations converge in a given area of international relations."[43] With the conflating of informal understanding (tacit or implicit rules) with explicit norms, and the lumping together of rules and formal institutions, important information concerning the functioning of rules as well as the distinctive contribution of formal organizations is lost. Similarly, although rules, norms, and principles are distinguished from each other, it is not clear what the basis for their prescriptive force is, a dimension which obviously unites all these concepts. Besides, there is no criterion for the differentiation among norms other than the logical category of specificity–generality, pointing to a certain conceptual impoverishment. As my previous discussion concerning instruction-type rules, practices, precepts, and principles shows, conceptual distinctions among norms are *as* important as their common status as directives.

Finally, the definition of regimes in terms of convergence of expectations is also misleading. While the convergence of expectations might be a sufficient reason for following norms that are virtually self-

57

enforcing (coordination-norms), it is precisely this convergence which has to be explained in the case of PD situations when the demonstration of long-term joint gains is often not sufficient to motivate actors to cooperate. As the debate between mercantilists and free traders shows, the "relative gains" problems might be decisive in the minds of the actors and thwart cooperative ventures even in the face of mutual gains.[44] Consequently, much will depend upon the ability of the participants to overcome the impediments to cooperation by persuasion and/or the establishment of formal institutions. The present emphasis on the collaborative potential of rational pure egotists and on the emergence of collaboration through reciprocity seems, therefore, somewhat exaggerated.[45] Given the fact that unlike laboratory experiments, "moves" in the real world are fairly complex, ambiguous, and in need of interpretation, the issue in international relations is precisely to figure out what represents a concession, that, in turn, deserves reciprocation. For example, Soviet signals after Stalin's death were not taken seriously by the U.S. since Washington believed that Russian accommodation was a sign of the internal weakness of the Soviet system, which required the crowding of the opponent rather than a tit-for-tat strategy.[46] Similarly, unilateral troop reductions or the cancellation of weapons programs might be dismissed by the opponent as caused by domestic or economic difficulties rather than by the willingness to commence a self-reinforcing spiral of cooperative ventures.[47]

In addition, cultural factors decisively influence our interpretations of what is a concession and what deserves to be reciprocated. Besides, we usually do not reward "good" behavior, except in cases of imbeciles or during periods of "moral training" of children.[48] Nobody in his right mind would consider rewarding someone who claims not to have lied, or to have desisted from robbing or stealing. It is against this "normal," i.e., *normatively expected*, behavior that we judge uncommon efforts, which justify special responses. Even if something is clearly recognized as a gift, we usually tend to reciprocate only when we consider the donation a costly matter for the donor as well as an indication of some special attention he/she thereby displays. The "gold watch" at the retirement party hardly evokes gratitude, and a meager gift such as a ballpoint pen "in recognition for special services" counts more as an insult than as a gift, the assertions of utilitarians notwithstanding.[49]

Although it is always difficult to make analogies between international relations and interpersonal relations, nevertheless it seems that the same reasons inhibit reciprocation in foreign policy. Treating

58

prisoners of war, for example, according to the Geneva Convention (when there was no cause for retaliatory measures), or allowing the normal functioning of embassies, etc., are gestures which, although not unimportant in themselves, are unlikely to arouse much enthusiasm for reciprocity.

Further complications arise for regime-analysis from the fact that often *various* norms regulate action in *conjunction* and that they stand to each other frequently in a relationship of sub- or superordination. The regime literature distinguishes in this context between *principles* (which are "beliefs of fact, causation, and rectitude"), *norms* (which are standards of behavior defined in terms of rights and obligations), and *rules* (which are prescriptions or proscriptions for action). In addition, *decision-making procedures* refer to "prevailing practices for making and implementing collective action."[50] I do not want to enter into an extensive discussion of these distinctions; however, the implied hierarchy among them, derived from the free-trade regime of the post-war era, is too instrumental and simplistic.[51] In most cases, especially in international relations, such simple, instrumental relationships between overarching principles, norms, and rules do not exist. Two reasons suffice to show why this is so.

First, regimes are usually the result of accretion and incremental choices. Consequently, there is neither a deliberate design nor consensual knowledge, as in economic theory, which clearly links principles and norms. One suspects therefore that the special case of economics is highly misleading, when taken as the paradigm for the normative components of regimes in general. Second, even when regimes are explicitly negotiated and thus some purpose or underlying (legislative) will can be construed,[52] most explicitly negotiated regimes serve not only one, but several purposes. Some more specific rules or norms might be compatible with one legitimate purpose, but not with the other, leaving us often at a loss in determining what type of trade-offs were intended by the negotiators. Here the jurisprudential literature is helpful. The discussion about naive instrumentalism in law has shown that many legal purposes are not susceptible to the neat distinction between goals and means.[53] Precisely because goals such as fairness, predictability, and reliability are inherent in the *legal process* itself and are safeguarded as such, they fit neither the conception of a goal that a particular law or statute proclaims to serve – like the "enhancement of highway safety" or the "prevention of restraint of trade" – nor the concept of a means.

These last remarks have important implications for the determination of the identity and change in regimes, as the following example of

the I.M.F. rules shows. While the original arrangement forbade floating and made parity adjustments dependent upon *ex ante* approval of
the Fund, the present Article IV is considerably softer.[54] Violations can
now only be established *ex post* by a decision of the Fund concerning
policies for which the member state did not have to seek approval from
the organization. Furthermore, a variety of policies concerning interventions in currency markets are now possible, and the policy rever-
sals of the Reagan administration demonstrate this. Has the regime
changed? The answer is "yes" and "no," depending on the purposes
for which the explanation is tendered. Conventional regime-theory
suggests that a regime changes when norms and principles change but
that it remains the same when only rules change.[55] Although such
distinctions are helpful as a first cut, they are far from uncontroversial.
Since monetary stability and an increase of trade are now as before the
declared purposes of the regime, the principles have *not* changed,
though the Second Amendment allows floating. Whether we perceive
a change *of* a regime or *within* a regime much depends upon our
perspective and purposes. If we are interested in policy questions such
as the distribution of burdens, i.e., who is obliged to intervene, we are
likely to diagnose a *regime change*. If we are interested in the "system"
as such, it is of lesser importance who plays an interventionist role (as
long as someone does), and we are consequently prone to see the
change only *within* a regime.[56]

This phenomenon of shifting conceptual boundaries is common
enough from organization theory and law. Whether, for example, a
Ford auto worker belongs to the organization (as a worker) or to the
environment (as a customer) depends upon the purposes of analysis
and cannot be decided *a priori*. Similarly, law specifies different
boundaries for corporations, depending upon questions of liability, tax
purposes, nationality, etc. The reason for this, at first, confusing
multiplicity of definitions and boundaries is that "regimes," "corporations," and most "historical individuals"[57] such as "revolutions," etc.,
are largely analytical constructs and not concrete entities of the outer
world. As conceptual creations, such concepts and systems are embedded in our common-sense understandings, but their use is at the same
time influenced by the particular purposes for which we undertake an
analysis. While for many purposes the common-sense understandings
are sufficient to indicate intersubjectively shared demarcations – the
dependence of the original conceptualization of regimes on the consensual knowledge of liberal economics was noted above – for other
purposes no such unequivocal understanding exists. Regimes like
revolutions, states, or power become "contestable concepts."[58]

60

IV EVIDENCE AND THE IMPACT OF NORMS

The strength of a regime has conventionally been explained either by the availability and power of a hegemon, or by the coherence of the principles, norms, and rules of the regime. Either explanation, though insufficient in itself, attains some plausibility because it appears to be related to two familiar paradigms that structure our perception of international relations. At the root lies either the Hobbesian image of international relations (i.e., the conventional realist interpretation of Hobbes), or the more benign Lockian (Humean) version, in which actors through "reason" accept certain limitations in the pursuit of their objectives.

The hegemonic stability thesis, close to the neorealist paradigm, reduces the impact of normative structures on actions to some reflection of power. It is, however, somewhat embarrassed by the "lag" between the decline of the hegemon's capabilities and regime decay.[59] In this view, regimes act largely as constraints upon action and, as proximate causes, determine the outcomes. However, as the jurisprudential discussion has shown, only very few rules and norms are simply constraining;[60] many legal prescriptions are rather *enabling* rules that set actors free to pursue their own goals. Rule-following is therefore not a passive process in which the impact of rules can be ascertained analogously to Newtonian laws governing the collision of two bodies: it is, rather, intensely dynamic. Actors are not only programmed by rules and norms,[61] but they reproduce and change by their practice the normative structures by which they are able to act, share meanings, communicate intentions, criticize claims, and justify choices. Thus, one of the most important sources of change, neglected in the present regime literature, is the *practice of the actors* themselves and its concomitant process of interstitial law-making in the international arena.

The Lockian or Humean perspective, on the other hand, emphasizes *coherence* of the regime components as an indicator of regime strength. The unexamined, additional premise seems to be that actors guided by "reason" usually follow rules and norms, unless internal contradictions within the normative structure create opportunities for defections, either by making confusing demands, or by providing loopholes for noncompliance.

However, compliance and consistency might be more contingently related in regimes, as Haas observes. His investigation of the U.N. security regime[62] concluded that the improvement of regime coherence during the first period (i.e., the concert, 1945–1947) did not lead to a stabilization in the second period (permissive enforcement with balancing, 1948–1955). Similarly, the innovation of "preventive diplomacy," which provided a coherent alternative pattern of conflict management, decayed rather than prospered after the 1960s. Haas suggests that the new consumers of the regime, who increasingly entered the U.N. during this time, refused to go along with the elaborated procedure and made it impossible for the Secretary General to routinize and stabilize the procedures.[63] Although this explanation plays down the unwillingness of the Great Powers to accept an activist U.N., it shows that "effectiveness" raises a whole host of issues that cannot be reduced to problems of the coherence of the regime structure.

Thus, there does not seem to exist a clear logical relationship between higher-order norms and more specific rules on the one hand and regime strength on the other. Consequently, it is less than justifiable to infer regime strength from the logical properties of a normative structure. After all, it is the inconsistency and the value opportunism of the legal order that prevent us often from knowing what "the law" is until a court has authoritatively established a link between rules and principles, or between conflicting rules themselves. But this lack of clarity does not necessarily imply regime weakness. From experience we know that effective regimes, such as constitutions, frequently show important discontinuities between specific norms and higher principles, quite aside from the fact that many of the higher principles are expressions of *competing* values. Liberty and equality can give rise to mutually contradictory prescriptions, and a variety of more specific regulations might be compatible with the same higher norm or principle. For example, segregation, as well as desegregation, was held to be compatible with the equal protection clause of the Constitution. While we all interpret the change from the "separate-but-equal doctrine" to the present holding as progress, and as an increase in the enlightenment of the courts and the public alike, there are several issue areas in which such an argument is not as easily made. What is "due process," and whether it necessitates a wider or narrower scope for the exclusionary rule of evidence, is much less readily ascertainable. Such an assessment depends upon a variety of policy considerations and interacting standards that cannot be easily accommodated within one single deductive conceptual scheme or even within one evolutionary theory.

The strength of a regime, therefore, does not seem to result from the logical neatness of relating rules and higher principles to each other, but rather from the deference to *authoritative decisions* that establishes

62

what "the law" is, or from the acceptance of norm-regulated practices. In other words, the crucial variable here is *institutionalization*, i.e., the acceptance of decisions as authoritative which are either rendered by dispute-settling organs or which have been made collectively. Although a look at *behavior* is certainly necessary when we want to decide on the effectiveness of the rule-guidance provided by a regime, the converse inference that a regime must be weak when we observe inconsistent behavior does not necessarily follow. Ruggie's example of the violation of GATT rules[64] shows clearly that regimes can survive even if certain practices are inconsistent with the prescription. Again, the jurisprudential writings about the effects of noncompliance are useful in this respect. Some brief remarks suffice in this context.

First, as everyone familiar with international law knows, not every violation of, for instance, a bilateral or multilateral treaty *ipso facto* annuls the treaty. In order even to suspend a particular agreement, the breach has to be material, i.e., of sufficient gravity and centrality to its purpose.[65] Thus, parties, especially in cases of multilateral agreements, can probably live with a great deal of inconsistency as long as they can reestablish some form of consensus, and/or no other viable alternative exists. Second, in deciding whether a particular violation demonstrates the end of a regime, it is important to look to the justification proffered by the violating party(ies). Admission of guilt, apologies, pleas for "understanding the extreme circumstances that forced such an action," etc., are very important indicators for the acceptance and validity of the prescriptions and, therefore, for the force of the regime. Although pleas and excuses can naturally be cynically manipulated, disregarding them and looking simply at overt behavior cannot claim by itself to disclose more accurately what is the case. Because human actions need interpretation, the justifications and excuses are important yardsticks for appraising particular choices. Actually, violations of a rule when *admitted* might strengthen the future adherence to the rule by the trespasser and others alike.

These considerations show that, except in extreme cases – such as when noncompliance is widespread, persistent, and unexcused – no facile inferences can be drawn from observing overt behavior. Precisely because rule-following is part of moral assessments, the question of whether a norm predicted the actual outcome accurately telescopes several important concerns that ought to be distinguished into one factual observation. In this context it is important to realize that actors often follow specific rules not only because this or that regulation happens to further their particular interest. Our attitudes towards the norms in a society are largely formed by the respect towards "the law" which was inculcated during socialization. Thus, while we may object to *this* or *that* law, compliance with norms is significantly shaped by our values, among which deference to "the law" is one of the most important.

V NORMS AND VALUES

As stated, values influence our choices largely via the evocation of emotional attachments rather than through readily available cognitive patterns characteristic of rules. Again the domestic analogy seems to explain the phenomena in question. While the domestic arena is characterized by a value consensus, in the international arena such considerations are, if not entirely absent, at best of minimal importance. Although I do not want to take issue with the last observation, the argument might indeed prove too much. From the observation of the often murderous infighting among people who profess the same values, such as "true believers," we can see that common values by themselves are insufficient to ensure cooperation and avoid conflict escalation. On the other hand cooperation can take place in the absence of a value consensus. A more detailed examination appears appropriate.

As a first step I want to exemplify the difference in the impact of norms and values by means of two ideal-typical theories of society that root social order in either values (attitudes) or in rights (norms). Let us begin with "values."

In the language of instrumental rationality we are accustomed to deal with values as "preferred events" or simply as "goals." However, I want to argue that values guide actions in a way different from instrumental rationality.[66] Values are not only more general than rules, or norms, but they influence decisions on the basis of largely cathectic considerations. As opposed to rules which prescribe specific *actions*, values inform the *attitudes* of actors. Rather than addressing the rational calculating abilities of decision-makers, values serve to strengthen the will and the emotional attachments to social objects, or states of affairs. Decency, justice, goodness, etc., are values in this sense.

The importance of values that go beyond the particular instructions transmitted by rules (or the less specific but still action-oriented *principles*) becomes obvious when actors know (or imagine) that a "way of life" might be at stake in a particular situation, and when they also realize that immediate individual gains defeat long-term individual or social purposes. Values are therefore important in overcoming the

64

"weakness of will" problem by stressing the importance of character and reputation in a society and by insisting on the importance of social solidarity and the spirit of sacrifice and self-abnegation.

Perhaps disenchanted with the abilities of clever actors to interpret the law to their benefit, some political theorists and charismatic leaders have argued against a "juridification" of social life and have therefore emphasized communal values and attitudes rather than rules and norms. It was Rousseau who, starting from the importance of sentiments to be inculcated through socialization in the family,[67] attempted to reconstruct political life along the lines of sentiment and values rather than along those of interest and normative guidance. He emphasized shared values and the emotional reaffirmation of unity through symbols, ceremonies, and games, rather than through arguments, debates, and third-party decisions. The latter measures are typical for the normative guidance which rules provide.[68] The idea that a perfectly socialized man is united with his fellow man through an attachment to basic values and shared emotional experiences has then been a train of thought in political theory from the utopian advocacy of small face-to-face communities to the "new man" in Marx and Mao. This new "species being" is supposed to act out of feelings of solidarity rather than self-interest,[69] and the political order which unites these beings is either idyllic and abundant, or Spartan in its simplicity. However, both versions share the taboo on conflict and on institutionalized means of resolving disagreements. Thinkers in this tradition either assume that conflicts will end in the future, or that they are the result of particular "troublemakers." These persons are then simply exiled, "lost to the world," as in More's Utopia and in many American utopian communities,[70] or they are – given the less benign circumstances of Stalinism or Maoism – physically eliminated.

Speculations based on emotional attachments and solidarity have been opposed by those theorists who emphasize the stresses and strains which appear in societies characterized by an increasing division of labor and the break-up of the face-to-face contacts of primitive society.[71] This type of literature stresses the emergence of calculating rationality, the victory of bureaucratic organization, organic solidarity, and the rationalization of law over the communal values of traditional orders.[72]

Although actual societies do indeed differ in the extent to which they stress accommodation and communal values or emphasize controversies, adversarial settings, and "rights," it is questionable whether either ideal type alone provides much insight into the sources of social order. After all, even modern societies with highly technical regulations must make the "nation" a love-object that arouses deep feelings of attachment. Personal identities and the possibility of rational action depend on the creation and stabilization of such "love-objects,"[73] as does the ability of collectivities to transcend "generations" and particular interests[74] (Rousseau's *volonté de tous*). On the other hand, even the most charismatic leader soon feels the need to institutionalize the "right way of life." This amounts, however, to the creation of more specific norms and, connected with them, formal procedures to settle disputes, arising out of the application and interpretation of norms.

Viewed from this perspective, even the international system of today illustrates some of the traits represented in these two models. On the one hand, our discussion of rules and norms showed that the international anarchy does not necessarily entail the absence of norms. On the other hand, it also is quite clear that neither the preservation of a way of life nor the maintenance of any particular configuration of the system – short of the total destruction of civilization through nuclear war – is one of the "transcendent preferences" of the actors and their respective publics. Thus, while the international arena is hardly one which is characterized by the absence of norms, the lack of "love-objects" located at the supra-national or even transnational level[75] is hardly debatable.

Nevertheless, I do not mean to suggest that *all* value considerations are absent from international politics. For example, Hoffman's recent discussion of "duties beyond borders"[76] goes well beyond examining goals in the conventional repertoire of statecraft. Furthermore, human rights abroad,[77] as well as questions of intergenerational justice, *do* increasingly appear as issues in the policy debates within many domestic societies.[78] The greater awareness of the potentials of world-wide pollution – particularly well driven home by the tragic mishap in Chernobyl – is another indicator for the slow, but nevertheless perceptible, articulation of wider policy concerns on the basis of more inclusive values.

The resort to values as the foundation of a way of life also forms a residual but important technique for judges in "finding" the law. Judges who have to close gaps or assign weights to competing normative principles often have to resort to values in order to lend persuasiveness to their arguments. Given that this is a technique into which all professional "rule-handlers" have been socialized, it is not surprising that even the judges of the I.C.J., in spite of their awareness of the tenuous social backing of international legal norms, have repeatedly invoked the "aims and purposes of the Charter," "the interests of the international community," and even "natural law."[79] They went

66

thereby well beyond the explicit "sources" of international law as enumerated in Article 38 of the I.C.J. statute. Such conceptualizations provide important new crystallizations for assessing the changing nature of international affairs and for the formulating of alternative forms of consensus across state boundaries.[80] Nevertheless, it is quite clear that the values invoked by various global activists or I.C.J. judges have more symbolic than direct emotional pull in galvanizing the relevant publics. The time when the international arena might move from a "negative community" to a conception of a "global community" still seems far off.

VI CONCLUSION

In a way, our inquiry has come full circle. In trying to refute the argument of the international arena as a norm-less anarchy, we focused our attention on the present regime debate in the hope that this approach might provide some answers. Although certain important insights could be gained from this debate, there remained several conceptual problems that inhibited an accurate assessment of the role of norms in international life. The review of the regime approach focused therefore on three crucial areas: the usefulness of the approach, its conceptual elaboration, and the impact of regimes upon action.

The discussion of "tacit" rules and the problem of the normative underpinnings of deterrence was designed to show that norms have some important functions even to the realm of national security. The discussion of the conceptual elaboration of regimes established that the distinction among different types of norms and their links suffer from too instrumental a view of the function of norms. This flaw made it imperative to develop an alternative for representing the super- and subordination of rules, norms, and principles and their influence on choices through guiding the reasoning process of an actor. Only in this way could a more appropriate measure for the existence and the "strength" of a regime be found. While these avenues for further research seemed promising in resolving some of the conceptual puzzles of present regime analysis, the argument that regimes are probably most of the time "contestable" concepts showed the limits of regime analysis.

The question of the "impact" of norms upon choices led also to a discussion of the role of "values" and their contribution to the establishment and maintenance of social order. Two polar models of society were discussed, i.e., one which is largely attitudinal and value based (communitarian model), and one which emphasizes rights and rules (liberal model). These polar types are obviously only heuristic, since most societies exhibit features of both ideal types. Nevertheless, societies can be distinguished according to predominant modes of resolving conflict specific to either type. These considerations led me back to the theme of the "sources" of social order with which this chapter began. It also provided a preliminary answer as to the appropriate characterization of the present international arena. While the international domain is a far cry from an unregulated or anarchical state, value considerations providing the foundations for the generalized attitude towards socially recognized "others" are rather weakly articulated. Although global issues are gradually leading world public opinion to adopt more inclusive values, the international arena is still but a "negative community."

3 THE EMERGENCE AND TYPES OF NORMS

I INTRODUCTION

The investigation of the previous chapter has led us to the point of having to revise most of the conventional beliefs about "law and order." Three further questions have emerged that will guide the inquiry in the next few chapters. The first question deals with the problem of how norms in general function and which different norm-types exist. The second question concerns the prescriptive force of norms, i.e., why and in what circumstances certain norms provide "reasons" which decision-makers will find persuasive, and to which they will therefore defer. Finally, there is the question of an appropriate demarcation-criterion allowing us to distinguish between "legal" and other types of norms.

In this chapter I intend to take up the first problem and also tackle the question of the "emergence" of norms through either spontaneous generation or through explicit procedures. While the issue of "tacit rules" has already been dealt with, the generation of *explicit* conventions, i.e., rules and norms in intersubjectively communicable form, needs elaboration. Furthermore, the various distinguishing characteristics of several norm-types makes it necessary to deal first with the "generic" features of all norms and rules. I maintain that all rules and norms are problem-solving devices for dealing with the recurrent issues of social life: conflict and cooperation. Here, the public-choice perspective provides a useful starting-point. To the extent that scarcity of time, of space, or of available "goods" exists, individual actors cannot achieve their goals without interfering with each other's pursuits and/or experiencing actual conflict.

An example of interference resulting from scarcity could be the crowding on a beach in which one set of actors wants to sunbathe in peace while the other prefers to play ball.[1] Given a longer beach, interference could easily be avoided by moving. However, given the

69

facts of social life, i.e., scarcity and non-identical preferences, norms provide guidance and solutions to problems by directing actors to act in specified ways. Thus, rules and norms link individual autonomy to sociality. On the one hand they leave each actor free to decide for himself/herself which goals to pursue – even to break the rules – while on the other hand they safeguard the conditions of social coexistence. Three distinct ordering functions can be discerned within the universe of norms. First, by "ruling out" certain methods of individual goal-seeking through the stipulation of forbearances, norms define the area within which conflict can be bounded. Second, within the restricted set of permissible goals and strategies, rules which take the actors' goals as a given can create schemes or schedules for individual or joint enjoyment of the scarce objects. Third, norms enable the parties whose goals and/or strategies conflict to sustain a "discourse" on their grievances, to negotiate a solution, or to ask a third party for a decision on the basis of commonly accepted rules, norms, and principles.

Although I will show that different rule- and norm-types are correlated with these three ordering functions there is, nevertheless, a great deal of interdependence among the functions of norms. Let us recall once more the example of the crowded beach. The main role of norms here is simply to create specific "separation-schemes" which minimize interference and channel conflict. Such an effective separation-scheme can be worked out by providing a schedule for alternative uses of the beach at given times (providing naturally that the number of separated activities does not in turn crowd the schedule). Other separation agreements might establish a sequence or a priority-rating among the competing claims, e.g., through the simple rule "first come, first served," or through the establishment of exclusive rights.

Nevertheless, norms regulating forbearances, such as not to use violence, play an important though residual role, even if the "beach rules" posted are likely to mention only the schedule. As Hobbes already saw, competition over the acquisition of scarce goods is sooner or later bound to result in competition for power, i.e., the ability to "get" scarce goods. This can be done by influencing the actors either through the threat of deprivations or through the promise of inducements. Both influence attempts have often been lumped together as manifestations of "power." However, significant asymmetries exist in the case of "positive" sanctions (inducements) and negative sanctions (threats).[2] While threats are cheap when they work and expensive when they fail (because one has to make good one's threat), inducements are expensive when they work and cheap when they fail. The reasons why the most fundamental rules in any society concern

70

"forbearances," i.e., rules threatening sanctions, rather than offering positive inducements, is obviously related to this point.

Another asymmetry also has to be mentioned. Since inducements are usually an expensive way to prevail, they create an incentive for false promises and lies. This is the reason why norms against lying (protecting the veracity of factual information), norms against the resort to violence (bounding of conflict), and norms against the breaking of promises (*pacta sunt servanda*), as well as norms settling the orderly acquisition and transfer of "property," have been called "laws of nature" by Pufendorf,[3] or the "minimum conditions of social coexistence" by Hume[4] and his successors, such as Bull.[5] Precisely because these norms are "constitutive" of society they are held to be natural, in the sense of being "fundamental."

These initial thoughts can now serve for establishing the steps in the argument of this chapter. I want to begin by showing how norms function in cases of independent and interdependent choices. Furthermore, I intend to investigate the differences that arise when norms emerge through iterative bargains and remain silent, i.e., are based solely on expectations, or when they attain firmer status by explicit, intersubjectively communicable formulation. In a third step I attempt to distinguish various rule- or norm-*types* by showing that these various types function in substantially different manners in a variety of recurrent social situations. These situations, in turn, can be described and analyzed in terms of several "games," familiar from elementary game-theory. Here I shall use both Duncan Snidal's analysis,[6] which is based on two prototypical models, i.e., PD games and coordination games, and Edna Ullman-Margalit's suggestions of a third set of norms, i.e., norms of partiality.[7] However, unlike either, I am concerned neither with building formal models nor even with the expansion of the heuristic power of game-theory through the modification of certain assumptions, as, for instance, in Snyder and Diesing's fundamental study on crisis bargaining.[8] The use of game matrices in my case is merely *illustrative*. The persuasiveness of the argument therefore does not lie in the formal derivation of my conclusions from a set of axiomatic assumptions, but is indebted to practical philosophy and linguistic analysis.

In section II I am concerned with the "emergency" of rules and norms under circumstances where no explicit communication is allowed. To that extent, the analysis commences here where the preliminary discussion of tacit rules in the last chapter left off. Having shown the problem-solving characteristics of all rules and norms, I explain the emergence of tacit rules by using Kelley's and Thibaut's laboratory experiments[9] concerning the "minimum social situation." The discussion of coordination norms then shows the transition to situations in which *explicitly* formulated and intersubjectively communicable rules become necessary.

Section III applies these theoretical considerations more explicitly to some of the puzzling problems of international relations. Precisely because even widely accepted customary practices are far from uniform, actors need some type of *Gestalt* to recognize both behavior that is deviant – but which still resembles the customary practice – and criteria for judging conduct which would indicate the absence, or desuetude, of custom. I shall argue that it is largely the underlying *rule* or norm and not the observable overt behavior which gives a customary practice its recognizability and coherence. Furthermore, as a short interpretation of Pufendorf's discussion of the conventions of war shows, not all rules have sufficient "normative pull" to establish a customary practice. These considerations, in turn, occasion once more a discussion of the "rules of the game" and their function (and limitations) as a means of conflict management in the international system.

Section IV investigates the problem of norm-generation in situations in which the actors' motives are "mixed," i.e., when common as well as opposed interests can be assumed. I maintain that the rule-types which are designed to overcome the disjunction between the individually and collectively desirable state of affairs are practice-type (or institutional) rules and precepts. It is relatively easy to show how these norms influence actors by either strengthening their "trust," or by attaching negative sanctions to otherwise individually profitable defections. However, explaining the prescriptive (deontic) status of these norms is more involved and can no longer be explained in terms of instrumental reasoning, attempts of rule-utilitarianism notwithstanding. A short conclusion (section V) summarizes the main arguments .

II THE "EMERGENCE" OF RULES

The generic features of rules

Rules, as we have seen, are a type of directive that simplify choice-situations by drawing attention to factors which an actor has to take into account. Rules are therefore not situation-specific, like imperatives, but delineate *classes* of events by specifying the set of circumstances in which they are applicable. Thus, rules might simply

72

embody experiential knowledge concerning the causal nexus among natural phenomena and the likelihood of attaining one's goals in given circumstances. The obvious examples for this category are "instruction-type" rules such as "do not plant tomatoes before 15 April." This rule indicates the day when the frost season (for a given region) has ended and it further identifies frost as the most important factor "causing" the plants to perish.

The above example provides two important correctives to some of the most egregious errors in accounting for the action-guiding function of rules and norms. The mistake of identifying rules with "commands" has been pointed out on the basis of the specificity/generality criterion. Also, in the case of instruction-type rules, we can clearly see that the force of such rules does not derive from the issuance of an authority but rather from the "hypothetical imperative" that results from the empirical regularities we encounter in pursuing a self-chosen goal. Thus, an actor can quickly exempt himself from the demands for compliance by disclaiming interest in the purpose for whose achievement the rules provide instructions. Commands obviously function differently.

Another, equally important, corrective is the realization that the action-guiding function of rules does not derive from their imperative mood or linguistic form. A variety of linguistic formulations provide equivalent meanings and the prescriptive force of a norm, consequently, cannot be identified with particular modes of expression. Many directives in rule-form, such as the indicative statement printed on notes of German legal tender that "anyone counterfeiting notes will be imprisoned for not less than two years," have to be taken as directives in spite of the descriptive phrasing.

The last remarks lead me to another important issue, i.e., why it is often necessary to cast rules in explicit verbal form and thereby make the transition from a habit, or a tacit rule, to (at least) a customary norm. After all, a rule can exist and guide practices, even if it is not explicitly formulated or communicated. For example, most native speakers of a language follow complex speech-patterns but would have difficulties in formulating the underlying rules. Obviously, through the explicit formulation not only does rule-guidance become firmer – even in the absence of formal enforcement agencies – but the articulation of rules in explicit form is crucially related to our ability to bound conflict and decide grievances without disrupting the overall pattern of social interactions. In attempting to prove this point, I shall start out with an experiment which models a minimal social situation and investigates the role of reciprocity in structuring social interactions. The weakness of tacit rules to which reciprocity may give rise is then discussed in terms of two examples: one, the "rules of the game" in international relations, and two, Pufendorf's observations on the rules of warfare. A short contrast between Pufendorf's treatment and the modern teachings on custom shows the important differences between mutual expectations based solely on reciprocity and the emergence of more explicit (customary) norms.

Tacit rules

Imagine two persons placed in separate rooms without either the knowledge of the other or the means to communicate with each other. Each of the participants in this experiment can press two buttons that control an "outcome" for the other person: the left button delivering a reward, the right one a punishment.[10] Ignorance of the functions of the buttons and lack of communication now make it necessary that these participants "make sense" out of their situation and achieve some type of control over it. This is done first by realizing the interdependence of their choices, and then by the formulation of a maxim for choice by each participant as to the appropriate decision in the next round. It can now be shown that by following a simple instruction-type rule, a stable, mutually beneficial situation arises if both parties manage to realize the interdependence of their responses.

In order to understand the importance first of the instruction-type rule of win/stay, lose/change, and then of timing, consider the following sequence of decisions. Person A pushes the left button and B follows suit. Given this rather accidental coincidence of responses both players are able to build a stable reward-structure, as no one will have an incentive to "defect" in subsequent trials. Now assume that A pushes "reward," while B punishes A by pressing the right button. A will now have to change in accordance with the rule and thus deliver a punishment to B. This will cause B to change also, and B will next time push the button rewarding A. A, in turn, having been rewarded, will persist in punishing B. This will cause B to change and punish A, who in turn has to change and thus reward B. But B will now persist in the previous strategy that brought him a reward, and he will thereby punish A again. It is rather questionable whether the two parties will ever be able to break these destructive cycles. One way to escape this predicament is, however, provided by the synchronization of choices. Thereby people become aware of the interdependence of their actions, and this can "solve" the simple coordination problem.

Assume now for a moment that both perceive a clock (or even the stronger case that they have been instructed to press a button every minute on the minute). The sequence of events is then the following (if we do not start right away with the accidental pushing of the reward button): A presses (reward) and B pushes (punishment). This means that in the next round B will "stay" while A has to change. But since A has, through his change, punished B in the second round, both have lost and must change. A, as well as B, will therefore press in the third round their respective "reward" buttons. Assuming that no one changes his strategy out of purely idiosyncratic reasons, a stable structure of "rewards" will result.

This example seems to suggest several things. First, it clearly shows that norms, *in addition to interests*, are necessary in order to arrive at cooperation. To that extent, the dictate of self-interest (win/stay, lose/change) is by itself insufficient – in the absence of certain conditions – to lead to stable cooperative outcomes. The niceness-rule in Axelrod's tournament approach[11] obviously telescopes two distinct problems into one choice, i.e., the decision to adopt a contingent self-interested strategy (tit for tat) and the impact of a norm on the basis of which stable coordination becomes possible. The latter problem is neglected (or implicitly solved) by requiring a cooperative play in the first round, by the requirement of simultaneous choice in game-theory, and by the clear understanding of what outcomes will result from the contingent choices since the players face a well-defined game-matrix.

Second, it might be tempting to see in the above example the emergence of the norm of reciprocity. But such an interpretation is misleading since, again, too many distinct problems are thereby aggregated. Reciprocity seems to cover a much wider range of situations. Besides, it is not clear whether we need "reciprocity" in order to explain the choice of strategies among "rational" actors, instead of deriving it, as is usually done, from the rational choice *of* self-interested actors. It is precisely this confusion which derails the rule-utilitarian attempts at explaining and justifying the adoption of norms, which will be dealt with below.

Third, in the example of the "minimal social situation," the issue of simple coordination of two contingent choices arose, but the situation was one in which the interests of both players are *not* mixed given conventional standards of rationality. Thus, while all norms in *social life* help coordinate interdependent choices – as this is just another way of saying that norms are generically problem-solving devices – not all of them satisfy the conditions of "norms of coordination." In order to see the properties of coordination norms more clearly, consider the games of coordination shown in figures 2–8.

Coordination games are naturally formalizations of frequent social

	C_1	C_2	C_3
R_1	1.5 meet 1.5	0.2 0.5	0 0.5
R_2	0.5 0.2	1.2 meet 1.2	0 0.2
R_3	0.5 0	0.2 0	1 meet 1

Figure 2

	C_1	C_2	C_3
R_1	1 meet 1	0 0	0 0
R_2	0 0	1 meet 1	0 0
R_3	0 0	0 0	1 meet 1

Figure 3

	C_1	C_2	C_3
R_1	10 10	0 0	0 0
R_2	0 0	9 9	0 0
R_3	0 0	0 0	10 10

Figure 4

76

	C_1		C_2		C_3	
R_1		4		0		0
	6		0		0	
R_2		0		5		0
	0		4		0	
R_3		0		0		6
	0		0		4	

Figure 5

situations which confront actors with the need to choose an action (X) on the condition that others do the same (although other alternatives might have been equally acceptable in case there was the assurance that the relevant other(s) would select them). The best example is perhaps Schelling's problem of the two friends who agreed to meet but forgot to make the place explicit.[12] Their meeting then will depend on whether each of them chooses a place which he/she thinks the other will select. Let there be three places with R_1 through R_3 being the actions of actor A, while C_1 through C_3 are those of actor B. In such a case we have the problem of "pure coordination" represented in Figure 2, although this case might seem "trivial" (since R^1C^1 is not only an equilibrium but also best for both). In Figure 3 this requirement is relaxed, i.e., a non-trivial case of pure coordination is given. Figure 4 again shows a coordination game that is trivial insofar as the least preferred outcome for both parties is the one which provides the solution to the coordination problem because of its "salience."[13] Finally, Figure 5 illustrates that coordination problems proper can occur in situations in which less than full symmetry of interests prevails.

In order to understand how norms can provide a solution to these problems of coordinated choices, let us focus on the characteristics that are to be found in all of these games of coordination. First of all, all coordination games involve situations of interdependent decisions in which the interests of the participants are neither mixed nor mutually exclusive. This coincidence of interests need not be perfect (as demonstrated by Figure 5, which represents nonsymmetrical pay-offs). Thus, although the parties are probably not indifferent as to which of the

77

equilibrium points is chosen, the coincidence of interests still prevails and, thus, *any* coordination equilibrium is preferred over any other set of possible choices.

Second, in coordination games no strategy is dominant, i.e., preferred irrespective of the other participant's choice, and "no choice of action is safe either in the sense that it guarantees at least some fixed return or in the sense that it prevents the worst outcome from being brought about" (by a failure of coordination).[14] Third, in any coordination game there exist at least two equilibrium points that are "proper coordination" equilibria. A proper coordination equilibrium, in turn, is defined as a coordination equilibrium in the strong sense, i.e., "at least one actor would have been worse off had anyone alone acted differently."[15]

How can coordination problems be solved, and what roles do norms play in guiding the choices of the participants? A closer look at matrices 1 and 3 reveals that solutions are already prefigured by the pay-off structure. To that extent, the pay-off matrices themselves have a function similar to that of a norm. They provide so to speak the equivalent of the "clock," or of the instruction to press the button every minute on the minute, in Kelley's minimal social situation experiment.

Games 4 and 2 have no obvious solution since 2 is indeterminate and in 4, cell R_1C_1 favors Row, while the other coordination equilibria benefit Column. It is here that norms different from the dictates of individual rationality have to aid in the solution of the dilemma. A proper point of convergence, if it is found at all, is due to specific circumstances in which the game is played, or to the common knowledge of some idiosyncratic features. It has been the merit of the investigations of Schelling and Lewis[16] to clarify further the solutions of coordination games and the role of rules or, as Lewis calls them, "conventions." Aside from salience, or precedents, other cultural norms might be sufficient to resolve the embarrassing problem of coordination through convergence. Furthermore, as long as the interacting parties share a common background, the rules serving as solutions need not be explicitly formulated, as they are implicitly understood.

Explicit rules

The upshot of the last remark is, however, that an explicit formulation will be necessary in cases in which the interacting parties do not share in a common history or culture. A second condition which seems to make an explicit formulation necessary deals with the issue of the imprecision of tacit rules, especially when a great number of participants play the game in a variety of forms. As Ullman-Margalit points out,

> while a regularity extracted from past events might somtimes be continued in more than one way, a norm will provide the principle of continuation which will resolve potential ambiguities in most future events. To wit: a chain of past solutions to a recurrent coordination problem might fall under several regularity descriptions that fit, but which might guide to different actions in a given new instance. A norm, by fixing on a unique, fitting description of the regularity, provides a unique guidance for action in normal future cases.[17]

Third, the formulation of an explicit coordination norm or rule is required in cases where a deadlock among various equilibrium points cannot await the emergence of a settled practice because of the compelling character of the coordination dilemma. Such situations usually call for the issuance of a *decree* by the public authority or for an explicitly negotiated norm. For example, nobody would think of leaving the establishment of rules of traffic on a river or lake or in a skiing area to the emergence of a practice.

Another example of the need for an explicitly negotiated norm is the allocation of frequency bands of the radio spectrum to a variety of users even in the absence of shortages. Although no nation is likely to care much about which frequency it is to use, as long as others do not interfere, an incredible scramble for frequencies would ensue, with enormous bargaining costs for all participants, in the absence of an agreed decree of allocation.

Finally, an explicit formulation of an underlying rule solving a coordination problem seems necessary when the solution is likely to engender further debate. This is likely to be the case when coordination games become increasingly *impure*, i.e., the symmetry condition of pay-offs is weakened. Consider, for example, Figure 6, where the "salience" of R_2C_2 is counteracted by the higher pay-offs to both actors in R_1C_1 and in R_3C_3. The impure characteristics of a game of coordination are heightened in Figure 7. Technically speaking, we still have here a coordination game, since R_1C_1 and R_3C_3 are equilibrium points and neither party can deviate unilaterally and hope for a better pay-off. The great difference in the relative pay-offs to each party and the exact opposition of the equilibrium points in providing Row or Column respectively with the larger pay-off will create problems in settling on one equilibrium point. Naturally, there would be the possibility of agreeing on the alternation between R_1C_1 and R_3C_3 if considerations of

79

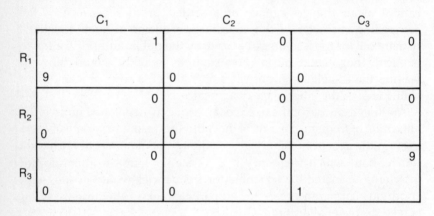

	C_1		C_2		C_3	
R_1		5		0		0
	6		0		0	
R_2		0		4		0
	0		4		0	
R_3		0		0		6
	0		0		5	

Figure 6

	C_1		C_2		C_3	
R_1		1		0		0
	9		0		0	
R_2		0		0		0
	0		0		0	
R_3		0		0		9
	0		0		1	

Figure 7

"justice" were a motivating factor in the recurrence of choices. It is, however, also possible that considerable bargaining through threats and strategic moves ensues in order to decide once and for all which equilibrium is decisive for future rounds. If this situation is not supposed to degenerate into a constant chicken game, a rule will have to be found which the participants accept. Thus, an arrangement that provides for the alternate selection of R_1C_1 and R_3C_3 solves the coordination problem, but it is also "fair" by being impartial between the interests of the two contenders. Consequently, it is likely to be more stable than a rule which settles arbitrarily upon one coordination equilibrium point for all future rounds.

As an illustration of such an iterative, impure coordination game, divestment clauses could be mentioned which guarantee foreign investment. In allocating the different and unequal pay-offs at different times, a "fair" solution to the impure coordination game is reached. The investor is guaranteed unimpeded business and/or tax advantages for twenty years, while the host state is entitled eventually to take over the enterprise.

Figure 8 shows an interesting variation on the coordination problem which has a certain "twist" to it. First, it is a very "impure" game;

	C_1	C_2	C_3
R_1	3 10	0 0	0 0
R_2	0 0	5 5	0 0
R_3	0 0	1 6	0 0

Figure 8

second, it seems quite stable, although the solution R_1C_1 is no longer an equilibrium point (Column-chooser would have been better off by selecting C_2). If he tries, however, to convince A through a strategic move that he will choose C_2, his threat is empty, as Row can threaten to pick R_3, which will in that case quickly lead Column back to select C_1.[18] Why does one need rules in such a situation, which, although no longer a game-theoretical equilibrium, appears to be stable? Are rules in such situations mere epiphenomena hardly needed for a solution to the recurrent choice-problem? I do not think that such an interpretation is correct. It should be obvious that rules are not simply redundant, even in such situations. They simplify choices insofar as they prescribe certain moves, and thus significantly reduce the high costs of bargaining via strategic moves.

III TACIT RULES, RULES OF THE GAME, AND THE PROBLEM OF "CUSTOM"

Our discussion of "tacit" or unspoken rules[19] derived their emergence from the mutual expectations of two actors. To the extent that these tacit rules are based on the inferences in which each actor works out for himself beliefs about the world, they provide an actor with the incentive of denying the existence of such an understanding without incurring the opprobrium of violating a rule. Tacit rules appear, therefore, to be dependent for their proper functioning on the back-up of social pressures generated by face-to-face relationships. Otherwise, they have to be transformed into explicit coordination norms, if the parties are to tolerate deviations oscillating within a certain range of common understandings. Since these points are of considerable importance for tacit understandings in international politics, some further discussion seems warranted.

Consider, first, the case of a face-to-face relationship. A husband who usually comes home at the same time from the office may give rise to certain expectations on the part of his wife. A sudden break in this pattern will therefore cause upset, since his wife is likely to complain that she was disappointed in her reliance on this pattern. As in any good relationship, such a complaint calls for a discussion in which both parties have to put forward explicitly their reasons for creating and then disappointing the expectations. Because the usual assumption is that the partners value their relationship, a resolution to the conflict can easily be achieved. Nevertheless, what is necessary is an explicit communication *about* the tacit rules.

Nothing will escalate conflict more quickly than when the husband denies the experience of the wife by arguing that no such tacit understanding existed. This strategy, popularly called "gaslighting," is very destructive of any interaction: it not only denies certain obligations that may arise for "alter" out of the reliance by "ego," but, in addition, it calls into question the normality of the person having relied on the predictability of the other. By "denying the experience" of the other, one also implies that the other person's understanding of the relationship, as well as of the common social world, is faulty or mistaken. Such an attitude is quite different from acknowledging the partner's reliance on the pattern while at the same time arguing that this behavior should not have been taken as an indicator of future performance. Pleading special circumstances which necessitated "exceptions" to this tacit rule, or proposing a new "codification," modifying or even abrogating the previous understanding, is also quite different.

These theoretical considerations are also important in international relations. As Schelling has shown, tacit understandings are important devices for keeping the international game within certain bounds of mutual expectations and thus half-way predictable and "rational."[20] Indeed, a variety of such understandings, usually called "rules of the game," have characterized the European state system as well as post-war international relations. These rules of the game[21] mediated between the universalist, explicit legal prescriptions on which the state system was based (sovereign equality), and the realities of differentials in power which influenced the way the actors played the game and managed conflicts. Basically, three types of devices have evolved: *spheres of responsibility (spheres of influence), spheres of abstention*, and *functional regimes.*[22]

Functional regimes depend upon the explicit agreement of actors to "depoliticize" an issue area and to "unbundle" the package of territorial rights in order to allow for the competing uses of a transborder resource. Therefore, technically they do not fall within the domain of tacit rules, despite their membership in the set of "rules of the game." Their effectiveness depends not only upon the stability of the parameter conditions but also on their continual updating and upgrading in order to manage interaction effects. The Antarctica regime[23] is instructive in this respect.

"Spheres of responsibility" lead a somewhat shadowy existence because they sometimes mix explicit rules with the unilateral arrogation of competence. Frequently, attempts are made to fortify such unilateral claims through the announcement of a *doctine* (Monroe Doctrine, Brezhnev Doctrine). As a special version of spheres of responsibility, we encounter territorially defined "spheres of influence" which need explicit, though not necessarily official, formulation and recognition. Finally, "spheres of abstention" are the least formal arrangements, consisting largely in tacit rules. Consequently, as we would expect, they are very prone to breakdowns, as the short-lived détente between the U.S. and U.S.S.R. in the seventies demonstrated.

Spheres of responsibility

Spheres of responsibility can be defined either functionally or territorially. The former version appears to have been important in defining the role of a "great power" – a notion which came into existence after the Congress of Vienna. It designated a power with system-wide interests as well as a say in matters pertaining to the management of the system. Managing the security issues in the classic conception of politics involved largely the issues of a balance of power. Metternich attempted, however, to stretch the meaning of "security" to include also the internal constitution of the states (Congress of Verona). England's reluctance to accede to such an understanding within the Concert[24] clearly showed that purely functional, system-wide specifications of responsibilities of a Great Power led easily to conflicts for two reasons: one, varying conceptions of legitimate sovereignty existed among the conservative and liberal participants; and two, the respective interests of various Great Powers showed significant geographic discontinuities.

Gradually, *territorial* "spheres of interest" emerged most clearly on the European frontier (the Balkans) or on that of the colonial world (Persia!). As the clashes between Russia and Austria over the Balkans demonstrated, conflict increasingly involved the use of internal political groups (Pan-Slavism) and/or strict territorial division and incorporation (Bosnian crisis of 1908). The latter solution, however, became increasingly unviable when the system's flexibility decreased. Nationalism, as well as the interpretation of politics in Darwinian terms, i.e., as the survival of the "fittest," made calculated territorial compensations difficult, if not downright illegitimate. A rational balancing through territorial adjustments increasingly created "scores." Consequently, territorial adjustments could no longer provide acceptable solutions.[25]

The notion of a special "sphere of responsibility" surfaced again at the end of the Second World War when the Allies discussed the structure of the post-war international order. Roosevelt's idea of the "Four Policemen," and Churchill's conception of a world organization as a framework for *regional arrangements* have to be mentioned in this context.[26] The inability of the Great Powers to come to some substantive understandings concerning either their collective responsibilities or their mutually accepted preponderance in certain regions indicates, however, not only that these notions were imprecise, but that they contained conflicting elements.

The Western conceptions of the future international order never resolved the tension between the principles of universalism and the regionalist bias which Churchill, and even sometimes Roosevelt, exhibited. The U.N. was, therefore, right from the beginning, based on an uneasy compromise between the claim of universal competence to deal with all matters of peace and security (even against non-members, since the Security Council was entrusted with the "enforcement" of peace), and the concept of permissible "collective self-defense" and regional alliances.[27] In addition, the two main protagonists, the U.S.S.R. and the U.S., did not share a common understanding concerning the legitimacy and limits of Great Power influence in their respective spheres. For this reason, the informal agreements, such as Churchill's proposal of apportioning influence in the Balkans on the basis of either exclusive or shared zones of preponderance, were doomed to failure.[28] For one thing, the U.S. refused to recognize such deals; but even if they had been accepted, the Soviet conception of interest was so extensive that it increasingly meant the virtual exclusion of all foreign influence, or even of constitutional limitations.[29]

In this way, similarities and differences between the management devices in the nineteenth century and modern times can be established. First, there appears to be a striking similarity in the change from the more *universal* conception of a functional, general responsibility for peace and security to a more solidly defined, *particularistic* sphere of influence. What is surprising is the rapidity with which this change occurred in the post-war era. While various forms of the European Concert functioned (admittedly with different degrees of success) for some ninety years,[30] emphasizing universal competence but slowly changing to regionally specific spheres, this drastic shift took only a few years in the post-war era. The result, however, was not mutual accommodation but rather the exacerbation of tensions in the Cold War.

A second similarity between the nineteenth- and twentieth-century developments appears: it is the salience of the internal regimes for the maintenance of international order. The patterns show, however, an inverse historical sequence. Metternich failed to win acceptance for the extensive interpretation of Austria's security interests, which led then to a more moderate interpretation of domestic challenges to the international order. Soviet insistence on implausibly extensive security interests, on the other hand, resulted in hostility and the breakdown of interactions. Finally, in the post-Second World War era, a *de facto* accommodation occurred which limited these extensive security interests to a particularistic sphere by adding some notion of ideological preponderance to the classical notion of a sphere of influence. Regimes which are based on ideologies contradicting that of the respective Great Power in the region can be changed or suppressed. The similarities between the U.S. assertion of primacy in the Western Hemisphere and Soviet behavior in the Eastern bloc has been noted. Still more important is that both powers have found it necessary to develop extensive explicit rationales, communicated in the form of doctrines.[31]

Certain dissimilarities also exist: the accommodation of the post-war era was not backed by mutual explicit agreements, as used to be the case in previous times. Even the Helsinki Accords, desired by the S.U. as a ratification of the status quo – and by the West for precisely the opposite purposes (*vide* the Western emphasis on the human rights provisions in "Basket Three") – do not have the obligatory character attendant on treaties. Technically speaking they are not treaties, and thus the "rules of the game" which have emerged resemble still "tacit rules." In accordance with the argument in chapter 2 it is clear that these rules are tacit only insofar as their *obligatory character* is concerned; their *expression* has become rather explicit.

The last point establishes another significant dissimilarity between the European states system and the modern international system. Endowing spheres with legal character had two consequences: one, it created enforceable "rights" among the contracting parties; two, it imposed a regime upon the "locals." Since in international law agreements cannot bind non-participating third parties (*pacta tertiis nec prosunt nec nocent*), the nonrecognition of the local powers as full subjects of international law was therefore a precondition for such a regime. With the acceptance of territorial sovereignty as the universal organizing principle in the present international arena, a legal expression of such agreements is prohibited. Consequently, such understandings can have only the status of tacit or *unspoken rules*, since formal agreements are illicit, and violate a peremptory norm of international law.

Great powers nevertheless have to communicate to each other how they wish to play the game by marking off certain spheres as their bailiwick. They often resort to "doctrinal" policy pronouncements in order to give respectability to their claims couched in rule-form. But as our discussion shows, tacit rules, when cast in explicit form as doctrines, resemble *general threats* more than conventions or rules, in the "third-party" mode of rule-use.

Spheres of abstention

The most appropriate example for tacit rules in the motley array of the "rules of the game" seems to be "spheres of abstention." These devices were either tacitly agreed to by the superpowers themselves or were explicitly created, first by the U.N. through "preventive diplomacy,"[32] and then tacitly consented to by the superpowers. However, in the latter case, as soon as the question arose for what *purposes* the U.N. troops were used – aside from reestablishing minimal control of the situation – preventive diplomacy failed, as the ill-fated Congo operation shows. The vocal opposition of the U.S.S.R., and her refusal (together with that of France) to pay for the operation, led to a financial crisis which clearly and narrowly circumscribed future U.N. activities in this field.

Similarly, the subsequent tacit understandings among the superpowers to leave most of the developing world to its own devices came to naught during the Ford administration, and it contributed significantly to the demise of détente. The tacit understanding of abstention was susceptible to subversion because relatively large gains could be reaped from very limited involvements, particularly in the weak states of Africa. The realization of these possibilities by both sides dramatically changed the definition of the game. The competition was increasingly interpreted as a PD situation rather than an impure game of coordination. In addition, the intervention via proxies (Cuba) appeared to enable the intervening party to disclaim responsibility[33] and thereby make deviation virtually costless. Later historical evidence showed that such an interpretation of Soviet moves in Angola and Somalia was rather exaggerated. Nevertheless, there is no question that these were the fears among the U.S. policy-making community at that time.

Finally, the value of détente itself became questionable since détente was based on the recognition of the Soviet Union as an equal world power. However, U.S. policy increasingly tried to delink the Soviet–American understandings concerning nuclear parity and arms control from the conflicting interests in certain regions. For example, attempts by the Soviet Union to propose a joint undertaking in the Middle East, and to transform détente thereby into an entente, were rebuffed by the United States through the drastic measure of a nuclear alert.[34] While "linkage" was intended by the U.S. (and opposed by the U.S.S.R.) in certain areas (détente and economic help), it was invoked by the Kremlin (and negated by the White House) in others (condominia).

Negative understandings are – aside from the extreme case of mutual assured destruction, or "fear of violent death," as Hobbes would have called it – very weak and subject to defeating considerations precisely because an agreement of abstention about the limits of allowable influence is often too ambiguous. Furthermore the perception of *mutual interest* is not shored up by rights which could demonstrate to the participants the tangible *quid pro quo* and which also could insulate a "violation" from the overall patterns of social interaction.[35] Only explicitly formulated rules make it possible to discuss diverging expectations, and to justify deviations and exceptions without calling into question the nature of the social relationship as such. Having a right means, after all, that I can insist on something without being dependent on the intimate back-up of face-to-face relations or upon the good will of others. On the contrary, as rightholders we can have the legitimate expectation that others will understand and respect our insistence without necessarily taking it "personally," i.e., calling the present relationships into question. A society without rights seems to be one in which the low level of tolerating conflicts leads either to the enforcement of unbearable conformity or to disintegration.

Since these considerations of tacit rules have important implications for "custom" in international law, a brief discussion seems appropriate.

CUSTOM

"Custom" seems to satisfy more clearly the requirements of coordination norms, or conventions, than the various "rules of the game" discussed above. Nevertheless, some of the same problems of tacit rules arise in connection with the question of why and when a particular widely observed practice among nations attains "customary" force. What is at issue in this case is the change of character in the rule, i.e., from an imputed or generally observed rule *of* behavior to a rule *for* behavior. Only through this reflexive understanding can a rule guide choices by providing the template for resolving a (coordination) dilemma. In this context, Pufendorf's discussion of the tacit rules of chivalry can serve as a starting-point for our examination of the problem of custom:

> Among many writers there is also gathered under the term law of nations certain customs which amongst most nations, at least those that lay claim for themselves to some repute in more refined and human deeds, are observed by a certain tacit agreement, especially in warfare . . . Now although such customs seem to have an obligation arising from some sort of tacit agreement, still, if a man who is waging a legitimate war neglects them, and declares that he will not be bound by them, providing a course opposed to them is possible by the law of nature, he may be accused of no fault other than a kind of ungentle-manliness, in that he has not adapted himself to the number of those by whom war is considered one of the liberal arts . . . Since, however, these reasons [underlying the customs] are not general, they cannot constitute any universal law such as binds all people.[36]

There are several points in this passage that warrant some further interpretation. There is, first, the argument that customs are not binding since they arise from a tacit rule. Nevertheless, a unilateral declaration of their nonobservance seems required, precisely because even such rules induce some type of reliance. Second, these practices are neglected as a "source" of law for the regulation of the conduct of war (*ius in bello*). Their utilization seems, rather, subordinated to the just war doctrine (*jus ad bellum*), although obligatory injunctions are thereby not ruled out if they are based on the compelling character of the "law of nature" (*ius naturale*). The latter obliges, however, by means of general precepts rather than by the existence of certain practices (*consuetudines*) or even agreement (*per conventionem*).

The last point, which seems to argue against agreements as instruments for the creation of obligations, is misleading if not qualified further. Pufendorf clearly implies in several places that it is through the institution of promising and contracting that obligations *can* be created. Thus, he seems to suggest two things here. In taking "convention" in the technical sense, rather than as a synonym for contract or treaty, he argues that the observation of certain uniform regularities based on tacit rules does not create obligations. In addition, he holds that the force of a prescription in the realm of international relations (*ius inter gentes*) cannot simply be derived from the uniformity of regulations in various domestic legal systems. The latter laws "are common to nations, not because of any mutual agreement or obligation, but they agree accidentally due to the individual pleasures of legislators in different states."[37] The former, i.e., tacit rules, lack, aside from the "necessity" acquired through the use of a "hypothetical" precept of natural law, the *articulation in rule-form* underlying the behavioral regularity. Only through the explicit articulation of the tacit understanding is the necessary reflexivity attained.[38]

Anybody familiar with some of the discussion surrounding the problem of custom and the sources of international law will notice some interesting similarities and differences. On the one hand, it seems that the drafters of Art. 38 of the Statute of the International Court of Justice have taken a more naturalist position than Pufendorf. The article lists the "general principles recognized by civilized nations" as one of the "sources" of international law. These are precisely those principles which, according to Pufendorf, are only "accidentally common" to the various national legal orders and which, he surmises, lack the binding quality of law.

On the other hand, the implicit argument in the I.C.J. definition of custom "as evidence of a general practice accepted as law"[39] appears to agree with Pufendorf's point that a behavioral regularity based on a unilateral imputation is insufficient to establish the obligatory force of a practice. For custom to exist as a legally binding practice it must possess an ascertainable rule underlying the behavioral regularity. This rule must not only be articulated in order to move from the rule *of* behavior to a "standard" or guide *for* behavior; in addition, the I.C.J. stated in its North Sea Continental Shelf decision:

Not only must the acts concerned amount to a settled practice but they must be such, or be carried out in such a way, as to be evidence of a belief that this practice is rendered obligatory by the existence of a rule of law requiring it. The need for such a belief, i.e. the existence of a subjective element, is implicit in the very notion of the *opinio juris sive necessitatis*.[40]

A further discussion of the specifically *legal* character of a rule, i.e., the illumination of the *opinio juris sive necessitatis* part of the argument, will have to wait until later. For the moment it is important to notice that the modern use of multinational conventions as evidence for the existence of custom decisively reverses the classical priority of treaties over that of mere custom. If a multilateral convention is, for instance, seen as declaratory of international custom, even non-members are obliged. To that extent the characterization of legal developments in the international arena as a simple progression from custom to treaty needs an important correction.

IV

Our discussion until now has emphasized the generic function of rules and norms in simplifying the choices of independent actors. It has also focused largely upon situations in which the agents' interests were either identical or complementary. The coordination and interference problems that arise in these contexts can usually be resolved by coordination norms, i.e., directives, customary norms, and – in certain cases of impure coordination games – rights.[41]

However, there exist other types of norms that are particularly important for the resolution of more deep-seated conflict. In cases in which the interests of the interacting parties are "mixed" they find themselves often in a situation resembling a prisoners' dilemma. As is clear from the original story, no such dilemma *need* arise if both parties trust each other. Remember that the two vagrants who have been locked up in separate cells and who are each promised a release by the district attorney in return for turning state's evidence could decide not to fink on each other. But such a reliance on the other presupposes trust, which is difficult to marshal if both prisoners face the situation unprepared. Trust between the two prisoners could have been strengthened, however, by an advance discussion of what to do in case of their capture and by their mutual promise to each other not to cooperate with "the law." The individual incentive of defection could have been weakened by "promising," i.e., by utilizing a social institution governed by rules, and by trusting each other in accordance with the precept that one ought to keep one's promises.

Thus, it has often been maintained, there are basically only two ways of solving the prisoners' dilemma: either one can attempt to influence the parties' probability-calculations concerning the likelihood of the other's defection[42] or one can try to affect the actors' utilities directly, for example, by threatening sanctions. In both cases, however, the solution consists largely in a redefinition of the game through the modification of the pay-off structure. Norms are important in both cases. On the one hand, legal sanctions are designed to prevent defections from the socially optimal solution by making the strategy of individual utility-maximization costly. On the other hand, certain norms strengthen trust, such as those underlying promises or agreements. They are intended to shore up the collectively beneficial solution by reassuring the individual who is choosing in the face of an apparently profitable defection by the other party. Since the problems of legal sanctions will be taken up later, I want to focus in this chapter on the institutions of promising and contracting, both of which are governed by practice-type rules.

PRACTICE- (INSTITUTION-) TYPE RULES AND PRECEPTS

In analyzing this rule-type, it is perhaps best to consider Austin's illuminating discussion of "performatives" that gave rise to the theory of speech acts. In noting the asymmetry between the use of the first-person indicative present and other persons and tenses of performatives, Austin writes:

> If I utter the words "I bet . . .," I do not state that I utter the words "I bet," or any other words, but I perform the act of betting . . . Similarly, an anxious parent, when his child has been asked to do something may say "he promises, don't you, Willy?" but little Willy must still himself say, "I promise" if he is really to have promised. Now, this sort of asymmetry does not arise at all in general with verbs that are not used as explicit performatives. For example, there is no such asymmetry between "I run" and "He runs."[43]

The institution of promising is relatively simple in its rule-structure; it seems that one has only to use the words "I promise" in order to make clear that one is performing the act of promising. More elaborate rules are required for making a contract. Furthermore, there seems to exist a similarity between practice-type rules and instructions or

91

decrees. Both kinds of rules appear to provide instrumental guidance for the achievement of a goal. However, the cases differ significantly in that in the case of an instruction the relationship between following the rule and achieving the objective is *empirical*, while in cases of practice-type rules the connection is simply *logical*: moving the rook and king at the same time means simply, within the game of chess, "castling." Practice-type rules usually concern performances and thus specify the conditions under which a given action – often characterized by such terms as "hereby," "therefore," etc. – shall be held valid. They try to limit the circumstances which might serve as defeating reasons for the validity of such an act. Austin's discussion of "infelicities" which can void the effects of the speech act is illuminating in this respect.[44] The rules governing contracts or, in the international arena, treaties, attempt, therefore, to avoid these "infelicities" by specifying as precisely as possible the circumstances when a contract or treaty is void (for example, because of the lack of capacity of the agent to contract) or becomes voidable (for example, through changed circumstances, i.e., the famous *clausula rebus sic stantibus*).[45]

Furthermore, while all speech acts executed in accordance with practice-type rules require the agent's free volition, a usually well-stipulated set of prescriptions tries to objectify the subjective aspects of the situation. Thus, by acting in a specified fashion (whose ritualistic aspects are still visible in many legal orders), "society" wants to insure that the individual is not only utilizing a particular practice *but that he/she knows* that he/she is utilizing it. Again, the "thereby," the lifting of the hand to swear, the solemnity of expressions, etc., are of relevance here as they exclude the erroneous or unconscious performance of an act. The reason for such formulas is that questions of intentions can be settled more easily. Instead of attempting to second guess the state of mind of the persons, courts can ascertain or impute intentions from *empirical facts*, such as: Did he utter certain words? Has she signed a paper which has "standard contract" on its first page? etc. Further challenges have then to argue for exemption from the obligation because of circumstances, or attack the institution as such (for instance, of will-making, contracting, etc.). The latter argument is counteracted, however, by the general, and widely accepted, precept that one has to obey "the law."

This leads us to a discussion of the last rule-type: *precepts*. While practice-type rules are characterized by their specificity and the constitutive nature of a given "performance," precepts are prescriptions of the highest generality which try to overcome the dilemmas between self-interested and socially desirable actions. Precepts such as "do not lie," "love your neighbor," or, perhaps most obviously, the Golden Rule (do unto others as you would have others do unto you) are good examples of this genre. Characteristic of this type of rule is that it does not contain a specific range of application. In addition, precisely because the claim to validity of precepts is based on a categorical, rather than a merely hypothetical, imperative (characteristic of instruction-type rules) these rules do not seem susceptible to recission. Only certain exceptions and excuses, depending on circumstances, can restrict their scope. This lack of specificity, as well as the admission of exceptions upholding at the same time their *universal* claim to validity, creates particular difficulties in applying these rules to concrete cases.

Obviously precepts figure prominently in the moral discourse, and much of the often interminable nature of a moral discussion results from this lack of specificity. However, matters are still more complicated since precepts are frequently linked to certain practices, as the example of "promises (or treaties) shall be kept" shows. Nevertheless, the distinction between these two types of rules is not thereby obliterated. While precepts largely provide the sufficient *backing* for validity-claims of certain practices, practice-type rules define the *practice itself*, i.e., what shall count as a treaty, promise, contract, etc. Therefore, when precepts have legal standing they do so by being standards or *principles* (in Dworkin's sense) rather than strict rules, an important distinction that will be elaborated further in chapter 7.[46]

The connection between various rule-types in the above example shows one further important point for a theory of law. The hope to find "legal rules" as coinciding with specific rule-types appears to be frustrated. The conceptual distinctions between, for example, law and morals obviously have to be based on a different demarcation-criterion since all rule-types enumerated here may play a role in a legal system. But if this is true, then the functioning of law in a society also seems to depend upon its embeddedness in the socially shared assessments of the obligatory nature of certain moral standards and principles that "lend force" to the practices and institutions regulated by law. To that extent, the demand that one ought to obey "the law" is a moral precept of overarching importance.

V CONCLUSION

This chapter was concerned with the "general features" of all rules and norms. In a first step I treated them as problem-solving devices in situations in which actors with non-identical preferences meet and cannot pursue their goals without interference. I tried to

93

show not only that rules emerge even in the absence of explicit communications, but that rules in explicit form are necessary in order to overcome the conflicts that are bound to arise.

Aside from instruction-type rules, various coordination norms such as conventions, decrees, and – in a preliminary fashion – rights were discussed. The conceptual analysis of tacit and explicit norms of coordination occasioned an examination of the "rules of the game" in international relations as well as custom. Both phenomena are often treated as silent or tacit agreements and are then analyzed in terms of coordination norms. However, it became clear that the "rules of the game" do not constitute a well-defined subset of norms. They represent rather a wide variety of rule-types, with differing degrees of explicitness, and are based on a variety of validity claims. The discussion of functional regimes, spheres of responsibility, spheres of interests, and spheres of abstention proved illuminating in this context. It showed that certain of these "rules of the game" resulted from contractual relationships, while others are basically only generalized threats that strain the concept of rules. The problem of custom, examined by means of a comparison of Pufendorf's writings with modern doctrines, attacked the problem of the transition from a unilateral (imputed, or "tacit") rule *of* behavior to that of an intersubjectively shared rule *for* behavior from still another angle.

Section IV, finally, attempted to show a certain correlation between certain rule-types (institutional rules, practices, and precepts) and recurrent social situations that embody conflicting as well as common interests of the interacting actors. After it had been shown how rules and norms either shore up trust or attach penalties, their contribution to the resolution of conflict among actors with mixed motives could be assessed.

4 THE FORCE OF PRESCRIPTIONS: HUME, HOBBES, DURKHEIM, AND FREUD ON COMPLIANCE WITH NORMS

I RULE-TYPES AND EXPLAINING RULE-FOLLOWING

Why do actors follow rules? The argument developed in the previous chapter appears to provide an easy answer to this problem. Having stressed the problem-solving character of rules as their generic feature, we seem justified in arguing that all norms are simple instruments for arriving at a decision. By typifying and simplifying situations, rules serve as guides for action. The obvious example in this context was the instruction-type rule. Taking instruction-type rules as the prototype or model of all rules, however, would be seriously misleading because the grammar of "following a rule" is considerably wider than that of attaining one's goals through instrumental guidance. Different types of rules exist and function often "heteronomously," i.e., instruct us what interest of *others* we have to take into account while making our choices. Under these circumstances instrumental explanations fail. Consider the precept of "do not lie," which is supposed to counteract the powerful incentive "to have one's cake and eat it too." While everybody agrees that everybody is better off in a world that works on the presumption of mutual veracity, it is obviously often to the advantage of the individual to lie. Attempts at explaining the adoption of such precepts in terms of the long-term "rational self-interest" of the actor run into serious difficulties, which already puzzled Hume.[1]

Furthermore, unless one makes a whole host of additional (and often quite implausible) assumptions the adoption of a "regime" cannot be satisfactorily explained by utilitarian arguments.[2] Thus, although in a way practices and precepts embody guidelines about how to act, very much like instruction-type rules, they are quite different in other respects. As we saw, the difference between "precepts" and instructions consists simply in this: the force of the instruction-type rule is purely *hypothetical*. The injunction against lying, on the other hand, is *categorical*, and that means the actor cannot exempt himself/herself by a simple disclaimer.

Principles provide an additional puzzle for an instrumentalist account of the functioning of rules and norms. Take the principle of doing no harm to anyone (*neminem laedere*), for example. While instrumental rationality presupposes as a minimum condition *intentional* action, the norm against harm to others also covers outcomes that result from negligent or non-deliberate conduct. Since negligent or careless actions are by definition *unintended*, the expansion of the norm "do not carelessly or negligently injure someone else" provides precious little guidance. In certain simple situations such as playing with explosives or driving at unreasonable speed, the meaning of the principle seems both clear and sufficient. In other less patently dangerous and reckless situations, rule-guidance becomes indefinite "because there is no specific action the rule enjoins us to do or to forbear from; one cannot even begin to be careful unless one also knows what to be careful about."[3]

Since in cases of assessing liability, institutions are essential for the admissibility and the enforcement of claims, and since various social orders have widely diverging regulations concerning the conduct of tortfeasors, there is a general tendency to derive the obligatory character of heteronomous rules from the existence of an *effective sovereign* whose will has to be obeyed. But to a certain extent this is putting the cart before the horse, since the sovereign – even in the Hobbesian construction – depends for its existence upon a contract, i.e., precisely the common acceptance of a practice, regulated by rules which it is supposed to explain.

Finally, one could be inclined to conceptualize the "constraining force" of all rules in terms of internal restraints experienced by the actor. To that extent Durkheim's argument of rules as "social facts"[4] seems to fit precepts and principles well. The *moral* character of many rules, such as the precepts of keeping one's promises, or the injunction against lying, has induced some theorists to argue that all rules are means of *constraining* individual actors. Such constraints secure a functioning society by giving precedence to social, rather than merely individual, interests. However, many rules are, as we have seen, of an enabling rather than a restraining character. In addition, many prescriptions seem rather morally neutral in their demands and might concern rather technical limitations, such as the specifications for deadlines.

These initial remarks raise several points worth pondering. There is first the realization that different rule-types correspond to different recurring social situations, as discussed in the previous chapter. Second, these various rule-types also appear to function quite differently from each other. Third, our common-sense notions, as well as our conventional theories of why we as actors comply with norms, appear to raise more puzzles than they seem able to solve. To each theoretical position a counterexample can be quickly constructed.

I suspect that these failures result from mistakenly identifying compliance with one type of rules or norms with rule-following in general. For example, coordination norms and instrumental rules fit well the argument of rule-utilitarians, such as Hume's. The Hobbesian perspective, on the other hand, emphasizes the importance of institutional sanctions in the case of practice-type rules and precepts. Durkheim's idealist position, finally, stresses the importance of emotional attachments to social objects that are experienced as "sacred" and that serve as an internal constraint upon an actor's choice. In particular, Durkheim's later work advances our understanding of the role of norms further. At that stage, Durkheim is interested in societies in which the normative force of prescriptions is no longer based on either the shared emotions or on a purely instrumentalist point of view. The prescriptive force of norms appears then as a claim to validity which is mediated by language and which can be validated discursively.

This last point has important implications for understanding the role of norms in social life. Since rule-following does not involve blind habit (except in limiting cases) but argumentation, it is through *analyzing the reasons which are specific to different rule-types that the intersubjective validity of norms and thus their "deontic status" can be established.* To that extent the three perspectives of Hobbes, Hume, and Durkheim can be shown to be special cases of a more encompassing theory of communicative action in which validity claims can be raised and decided.[5] The question of compliance with norms is part of a wider argument through which individuals act in a social context, enabling society as well as the "self" of an actor to reproduce themselves. *The important issue for investigation then becomes under what circumstances which type of reasons serve as a sufficient justification for following a rule.* Noncompliance is also more complicated, especially in rule-systems that do not possess effective norm-setting (legislative) institutions. Particularly in the case of international relations, noncompliance cannot be understood simply as "regime decay" or as a pathology, at least not until further qualifying conditions have been specified.

The approach outlined above, indebted to linguistic analysis and to practical philosophy,[6] violates several of the most dearly held convictions in the social sciences. The assertion that a discussion of normative issues is possible must appear strange to all those who adhere not only to the strict fact–value distinction, but who treat values and norms as being all of the same cloth. Furthermore, the guiding function of norms has to be conceptualized in positivism as a stimulus that determines – but, on account of a variety of interfering factors, only probabilistically so – the decisions of actors.[7] I think both of these tenets identified with contemporary social science are mistaken. It might therefore be useful to begin the next section with a refutation of this epistemological position in order to clear the ground once and for all before turning into a systematic exposition of the various theories mentioned above. I begin in the next section with the demonstration that norms and rules do not function like causes. Consequently, even the weaker version of the argument of the probabilistic impact of norms on action is erroneous. "Explaining" an action is more complex, since the place we accord to norms in guiding decisions is apparently not independent of a whole variety of other concerns, such as the agency of an actor or the actor's responsibility. Indeed, often the concept of "cause" itself is problematic, as we have seen. Take, for example, causal explanations in a murder trial: the district attorney calls the jealousy of the accused the cause of death, while the coroner lists the entering of a knife below the fourth rib and the concomitant lacerations and blood clots as the "cause." What we accept as adequate explanation obviously depends on our interests and upon the context and roles that we consider to be germane to our assessment.

Section III is devoted to the treatment of Hume's and Hobbes's perspectives on norms and their reasons for inducing compliance. I will try to show not only the defects of these theories but that the prudential reasons advanced by Hume and Hobbes fail to account adequately for the prescriptive force of certain rule-types, such as institutional or practice-type rules and precepts. Section IV is therefore devoted to the complexities of institutional rules, which are exemplified by fifteen cases taken from contract law. In discussing these cases it will become obvious why Hume's prudential argument about reputation, as well as Hobbes's "solution" to the vagaries of sequential contractual performance, is unable to explain the obligatory character of promissory commitments and their concomitant phenomena: excuses and exemptions.

Durkheim's and Freud's approaches to norms are taken up in section V. This discussion advances our understanding of normative regulation for those cases where the directive force no longer aids the individual actor in choosing his preferred goal (or the most adequate means for attaining it), but where the *goals themselves*, pursued by several actors, collide. In this case, norms have the task of mediating among the competing goals. While it is conventional wisdom that such a conflict is not susceptible to reasoned argument, I shall argue that such collisions *do* have some type of rational solution when something like a moral point of view emerges. This argument then prepares the way for chapter 5, where the criteria for such a "discourse on grievances" is examined by means of an interpretation of Pufendorf's absolute and hypothetical laws of nature. A short summary in section VI attempts to tie together the main strands of the argument in this chapter.

II EXPLAINING BY NORMS

An attempt to explain human action in terms of underlying factors is conventionally required to satisfy the standard criteria of science. As Hempel and Popper have shown, a scientific explanation is not solely a matter of using measurement procedures – they are often relegated to an unproblematic, background knowledge – but consists in an explanation-scheme that employs general laws and initial conditions and which results in a testable, conditional prediction (explanation) by logical implication.[8] In this context the criterion of refutability or corroboration is of particular importance. It not only ensures the truth value of a theoretical construct but also leads to self-correction, and thus to the growth of knowledge, when empirical evidence shows the inappropriateness of a proffered conditional prediction.[9] While the "fit" between a theoretical structure and reality always remains problematic, the corroboration of logically derived hypotheses in empirical tests is evidence of both the appropriateness and the heuristic power of the approach or theory.

Even this standard account of scientific explanation, however, needed correction. Progress through self-correcting experiments was not as automatic as initially assumed. Indeed, crucial experiments usually attained their decisive status not in the course of normal testing – where the scientist could always explain the divergence between expected and obtained results as caused by errors or interferences – but rather *ex post facto*, after a new theory had labeled the observed failures as decisive.[10] If the experimental refutation of singular hypotheses no longer decided the appropriateness of the theoretical structure, on what basis could science produce warranted and cumulative knowledge? Unless one was willing to entrust the progress of knowledge to the idiosyncrasies of individual researchers,[11] a new "objective" yardstick had to be found. It is in this context that Imre Lakatos's proposal has to be understood. It introduced the "fruitfulness" of a whole research program as a criterion. Single instances of failed predictions (explanations) no longer need refute a whole theory. Rather, the failure of the entire theoretical framework (research program) to provide novel insights and to integrate discordant discoveries without resorting to obscurantist, *ad hoc* auxiliary hypotheses becomes decisive. Heuristic fruitfulness as a criterion prevents the premature rejection of a theory that has led to several new insights, but failed in a single test case.[12]

The last point is of particular importance for an approach that tries to explain human action in terms of underlying norms or rules. Since rules and norms are valid even if they fail to guide action in one or several cases, the question of whether and how rules and norms influence decisions cannot be "tested" if one uses strict refutability as a condition *sine qua non* of an appropriate explanation. On the other hand, "fruitfulness" seems to allow for a probabilistic interpretation of the influence of norms and rules upon behavior. In this version rules and norms can then become "causes" in that they determine, but only *probabilistically* so, outcomes (decisions).

However, such an interpretation of explaining by means of norms is questionable. Although norms and rules might function in certain contexts like causes, their influence on human action is not adequately captured in probabilistic statements about future conduct. As already pointed out, even causal explanations answer to a variety of concerns. Since norms and rules are not only used in listing the antecedent conditions of an action, but also in assessing responsibility and in ascribing praise or blame, "explaining" an action is significantly shaped by the moral discourse and by our pragmatic interest. Probabilistic statements about *empirical* regularities, on the other hand, are solely constituted by their reference-class, by the ranges of numerical values within which the measurements of the crucial variables have to fall, and by the "methodological rule" which decides that *reproducible* deviations from those ranges refute the theory.[13]

One further issue remains to be clarified: whether explaining by means of rules and norms is the same as indicating the intentions of a given actor or referring in the explanatory account to his "mental states." The first part of the statement is exemplified by Hart's discussion of the "internal" aspects of rules; the second part needs an elaboration of the "objectivity" (or at least the intersubjectivity) of rules that will distinguish rule-following from indicating idiosyncratic preferences. Hart's starting-point is the conceptual distinction between habit, resulting in a uniformity of behavior, and rule-guided regularities of behavior:

> A social rule has an "internal" aspect . . . What is necessary is that there should be a critical reflective attitude to certain patterns of behavior as a common standard and that this should display itself in criticism (including self-criticism), demands for conformity and in the acknowledgments that such criticism and demands are justified.[14]

But by emphasizing the internal aspect as it enters our discourse through the normative terms "ought" and "must," "right" and "wrong," Hart is careful to distinguish the standard function of a rule from the private mental states of those following it. Similarly, understanding rule-following differs from an exercise of empathy,[15] as practice-type rules nicely illustrate. For example, when I ask for an explanation of a certain move in chess, such as castling, answers referring to the state of mind of the actor are usually considered inappropriate or at best subsidiary to explanation in terms of the underlying rules. Thus, to explain that one felt a certain pressure, or liked castling, is sensible only when it is related back to the rule-structure of the game. Even in the case of promising and contracting, which require consideration of the intentions of the parties, intentions defined as validating conditions of the performances are *not* the same as mental states accompanying the performance. Consider the "I do" uttered by a person during a marriage ceremony.[16] Although it would be strange if a person had no doubts on that occasion, possible anguish or even mental reservations usually do not invalidate the act. True, lack of intent *might* be an invalidating reason, but to establish such a lack requires an operation other than a simple reference to mental states on the occasion of the performance (for instance, proof that it was a "shotgun marriage"). Given these considerations, social scientists have tended to explain all of social action in terms of rules or, more particularly, in terms of practice-type rules.[17] In this sense, explanation involves the identification of the rules that constitute a "form of life," and forms of life are given and have to be accepted.

But there are good reasons to be cautious in this respect. After all, many social situations are not so clearly structured as games, but they have to be enacted; that is, which set of rules applies in a concrete case is part of the transaction of mutual sense-making among actors. In chess, the binary choice of "allowed" and "not allowed" moves is exhaustive, and the umpire reduces the ambiguity of actions in, for example, a baseball game to the same simplicity. But in the moral realm umpires cannot usually solve by a simple fiat the problems that arise. Besides, in international relations, where authoritative determinations analogous to umpires' rulings are the exception, the parties themselves must interpret each other's moves and constantly renegotiate the reality in which they operate. Similarly, while the question "Why should I follow this rule of chess?" is nonsensical within the game, the question "Why should I follow this legal prescription?" is not equally meaningless (nor is a possible answer necessarily a purely extralegal matter, as some jurists would have us believe). Courts have traditionally taken a variety of positions, depending on circumstances, in enforcing promises and contracts and have developed a whole host of exceptions and excuses that defeat the obligations resulting from the utilization of well-established and recognized practices.

"Theories" which deal with rule-following must therefore not only attempt to explain why actors follow rules in general, but also give a rational account of admissible exceptions and excuses. In this context, utilitarianism and decisionism are particularly important, since they explain inconsistent rule-following either in terms of one underlying principle – that of utility – or in terms of the "will" theory of the sovereign who "makes" the law, enforces compliance, or allows for exceptions through the decisions of certain institutions. The next section examined both of these approaches.

III HUME AND HOBBES ON THE PRESCRIPTIVE FORCE OF NORMS

Hume on conventions

In section II of the book "On Morals" of the *Treatise*, Hume deals with the question of the emergence of norms and their prescriptive force. Forgoing a metaphysical principle or common goal, Hume explains society in terms of selfishness and limited generosity of actors who have to cooperate in order to achieve their ends. This explanation requires "artificial virtues" – that is, "conduct in accordance with, or a disposition to observe, general moral rules or conventions."[18] Hume then discusses three sets of rules. They basically deal with institutions of promise-keeping, with the stability of possession, and with the transfer of property. Quite aside from his conservative preferences, he seems to presume "that different degrees of utility achieved by alternative rules are negligible compared with the overriding good of social order served by any of them."[19] The reason for this position is the implicit argument that for such specific rules to have arisen and to have obtained social prominence they must correspond to other human "inclinations," i.e., factors that buttress their acceptance beyond the obvious criterion of social utility. Thus, the utilitarian argument is paralleled – and to a certain extent even superseded – by a cognitive interest that endows certain rules with a prescriptive status.

The argument that it is *salience* which lends prescriptive force to norms is further exemplified for Hume by the rule of international law that bays and firths belong to the surrounding state. "These [bays] have properly no more bond or union with the land than the Pacific ocean would have; but having an union in the fancy . . . they are of course regarded as an accession."[20] Thus accession, based primarily upon the "imagination's fancy," might be sufficient justification for a claim that gives rise to the obligatory character of a rule.

Even within a rationalistic perspective, however, many occasions arise where no single obvious principle recommends itself as a convention. In such cases, Hume's claim that the prominence or salience serves as a sufficient basis for the prescriptive status of a norm can be defeated by other considerations. This is particularly true in cases in which norms cement a status of (extreme) inequality and thus become susceptible to a variety of criticisms. Do rules matter, given these circumstances? Our discussion in the previous chapter has already suggested an answer. Rules as standing orders can significantly reduce bargaining costs by raising the costs of noncompliance. Otherwise, a considerable amount of bluffing is to be expected in the absence of a "legitimate" (i.e., accepted) rule fortifying the particular outcome.

Nevertheless, what are the reasons why participants might accept as legitimate such a regime of inequality? Although rules are obviously not neutral as to the distribution of benefits, their impersonal character distinguishes them from immediate (and more blatant) exercises of power. This difference has two consequences. It shifts concern away from this or that concrete dispute and toward the problem that a particular solution in accordance with rules is "just the way the ball bounces." Furthermore, to the extent that all are subject to the same prescriptions, and that advantages are inherent in *positions*, competition is diverted from actual pay-offs in any concrete bargaining situation to access to privileged positions. As long as people perceive access to be reasonably free, they are likely to tolerate a great deal of inequality in the hope to "make it" to the top – mythical as such expectations might be. Moreover, inegalitarian norms are not in themselves unjust. Possible justifications are that total pay-offs to

103

society are larger than in a more egalitarian distribution.[21] Similarly, although on a much more restricted scale, John Rawls's "difference-principle" allows inequalities as long as the least advantaged person benefits.[22]

These last remarks involve reasons for rule-following in "hard cases" and thus the effort to supply validating principles upon which the prescriptive character of rules is based. They also show that these reasons are defeasible and that rules need not contribute solely to social integration.[23] Rather, rules may also provide the fissures of society when the regime itself comes under pressure and the defenders of "law and order" face those advocating new rules, usually in the name of inherent or natural rights.

The rule-utilitarian solution to the problems of cooperation is further open to a variety of other criticisms. We have already mentioned one such objection: Hume assumes that the choice of rules concerning the concrete regulation of property is relatively unimportant when contrasted with the utility of the property regime as a whole. He thereby not only commits a kind of liberal fallacy (as do Rawls and McDougal after him),[24] but he is also strangely insensitive to the problem of differences in outcomes connected with different regimes. Even assuming the Pareto optimality of various regimes, no convergence upon any particular set of rules need result as long as these regimes benefit various actors in a differential fashion. Indeed, it is more likely that considerable bargaining will occur in such a multiparty context, and hence the acceptance of a particular rule-set requires further explanation. Even if we deal only with various coordination norms, several other factors seem to be important: to wit, whether the common good of a regime can be provided only conjunctively, i.e., through universal cooperation, or whether it is available even in cases of less than general participation (disjunctive procurement). Furthermore, it seems rather important whether the participants can exclude noncooperative actors from the benefits of the common good[25] or whether such a possibility does not exist. Four examples below are designed to illustrate the effects of these variables.

Assume seven adjacent property-owners who either decide (or are forced) to build a sewerage system. The configuration of the properties is the following: A sits at nearly the lowest point. C and B are located on a hill.

The obvious routing of the sewage canals including all the participants is option I: an X which crosses at A's property, where a small sewage plant is also located (x1). The price for this option is $280,000 and each member's share is therefore $40,000. A, however, being in a

104

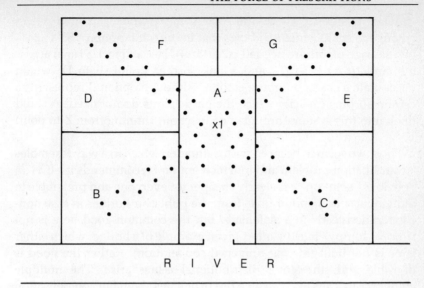

Figure 9

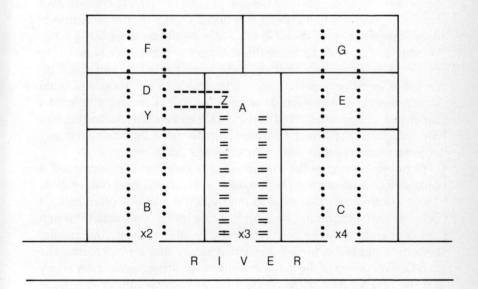

Y–Z = extension to A

Figure 10

105

strategic position vis-à-vis the others, might refuse, or hold out in paying his share, since he knows that in the other option – $300,000 – two sewage plants are needed (x2 and x4). He can block a canal across his land (from B to C), and a link further uphill (E to D) would necessitate a costly pumping-station. Although option II represents a certain surplus capacity which the participants do not need, A could hook into this system through a connection, running from Z to point Y.

Thus, we seem to be faced with a situation which in a way resembles a coordination problem and in which option I recommends itself as an "obvious" solution. It is clearly cheaper for everyone and preferable to individual action and/or fines from the public authorities in case non-cooperation leads to a stalemate. But the common good here is not simply "lumpy" like the often-given example of a bridge, which either is or is not built (forcing universal cooperation). Rather the good is divisible and, therefore, distributional issues arise. The multiple equilibria are thus likely to give rise to debates about fair compensation principles and/or to bargaining in which certain similarities to playing "chicken" appear. Appeals couched solely in terms of cost might not be persuasive to A, since he has the prospect of paying considerably less if he "hangs tough." Even if option II is chosen, the price to A is only somewhat more than his fair share would be in option I. Conversely, cost-appeals alone might no longer be persuasive to the other participants after their feathers have been ruffled. Given the non-cooperative attitude of A, they might decide to go ahead and build option II and exclude A from the hook-up. A is then forced to build a canal and set up a small filtration plant (x3) for his own use, costing him $46,000. Thus, the other participants can punish A by making him pay at least a sum close to their own expenses under option II.

Example 2 concerns the case in which a common exclusive good is provided in a disjunctive fashion, i.e., without universal cooperation. Thus, asymmetries that exist in international relations often make it possible that a common good, such as free trade, is provided through the cooperation of the major powers. Sooner or later, the smaller countries might be forced to participate in this arrangement. The E.E.C., composed of the major European countries, made it necessary for the smaller nations to create a counterassociation for free trade (E.F.T.A.). Over time, the United Kingdom had to abandon its role in the latter organization and apply for full membership in the E.E.C. while the other countries requested associate status. Similarly, in spite of the Soviet Union's original refusal to participate in the I.A.E.A., the success of this organization resulted in a Soviet reassessment and her joining of the agency.[26]

Example 3 represents the situation in which the common good has to be provided under conditions of conjunctive supply and nonexclusivity. Thus we have the classical multi-person prisoners' dilemma that Schelling mentions, such as overcrowding of parks and freeways, fishing agreements, public vaccination, etc.[27] Although there might be "rivalry" in consumption, and therefore the condition of "joint supply," necessary for a genuine public good, is not present, the characteristic of nonexcludability results from the inability or the great costs of instituting effective measures of exclusion. The main factor inhibiting cooperation is the need for universal participation; precisely because of this exacting requirement, there is the fear that no such arrangement is likely to succeed. In the often-discussed "tragedy of the commons,"[28] the individual villager is said to continue with the overgrazing because of his greed. But such a choice is as likely to be induced by the feeling of uselessness of cooperation in the face of the odds. Therefore, overgrazing could be rather a "defensive" action of avoiding losses rather than a dictate of greed. The results of certain experiments seem to bear out this conclusion.[29]

Example 4, finally, concerns the case in which the common good can be provided disjunctively, i.e., less than universal cooperation is necessary. The common good can be provided by "hegemons" or a smaller group (which in turn might profit disproportionately) because cooperative members know that their contribution will not be useless. On the other hand, free-rider tendencies will appear precisely because *others* know that despite the low level of cooperation the common good will be procured. The representation of these instances in cases of a multiplicity of participants results in the two-by-two matrix shown in figure 11.

As figure 11 suggests, the conventional "solutions" to these problems are impeded by two distinct motives: fear and greed, which classical game-theory lumps together in the "utility maximization" criterion of rationality. *The point is not that these two motives can be aggregated, but rather that in understanding the problems of cooperation it makes sense to find out under what conditions which motive is likely to become dominant.*[30] To that extent *a priori* conceptions of rationality are not helpful, as they are likely to misdiagnose the problem of how to eliminate the obstacles to cooperation. Consider Example 1 above: if "ought" considerations enter into A's calculation, they are certainly not those of norms or rules. Since he is within his "rights" to refuse to

	EXCLUSIVE	NON-EXCLUSIVE	
CONJUNCTIVE Greed	I Generalized coordination game Convention Appeal to values and/or establishment of exclusivity (sewer example)	II n-person PD Contract, public authority Enforcement (Tragedy of the commons)	Fear
Fear DISJUNCTIVE	III Coordination among "powerful" Convention Bargaining concerning expansion of participation and benefits (Britain joins EEC)	IV Hegemonic leadership K-groups Burden sharing arrangements Free-riding: Arm-twisting (Alliances)	Greed

Figure 11

participate and bring about a socially desirable state of affairs, appeals to him will have to be couched in terms of general values such as good neighborliness, fairness, equality, etc. Similarly, such appeals will be part of persuasive strategies in the case of cell IV, where a hegemon will attempt to twist arms and get others to shoulder their "fair burden." Fear, on the other hand, prevalent in cases II and III, has to be counteracted in a different fashion. It will impel outsiders to join as soon as there are assurances that the common good will be provided. A certain bandwagoning effect is likely to occur, even if the future benefits as compared with the costs are highly uncertain and perhaps not even susceptible to a clear assessment.

Since classical utilitarianism attempted to explain cooperation (as well as defection) without a disaggregation of the motives of fear and greed, several adjustments of its original position became necessary when cooperation had to be explained under conditions of an apparent disjunction of individual and collective rationality. These modifications were, for instance, based on the iterative aspects of many social situations in which the same players interact without full knowledge of the number of rounds. Thus, "shadow of the future" attained its importance. The need for (or the possession of) "reputation" represents another elaboration of the same original paradigm, as does the shift from act-utilitarianism to that of rule-utilitarianism. Finally, through the institution of a "sovereign" the actors' utility calculations were altered by the threat of sanctions so that it became rational to follow the dictates of reason, or as Hobbes has it, the "laws of nature."

Although all of these attempts clarify certain aspects of social action, serious conceptual problems remain which show the limitations of purely prudential arguments in understanding cooperation as well as (non-violent) conflict over goals. A more detailed discussion seems justified. Let us begin with the "long-term" utility considerations which allegedly induce rational egotists to cooperate. Given recurrent and unknown numbers of PD rounds such a stance can be elicited, as Axelrod argued, through the choice of a tit-for-tat strategy and the application of the niceness rule.[31] However, in addition, the actors must face in iterative bargains a pay-off matrix in which their utilities are *cardinal* rather than merely ordinal. The last, rather strong, requirement becomes clear when we realize that otherwise none of the participants is able to make a "rational" long-term or overall utility assessment.

Hume's argument concerning reputation introduces another variation in the utilitarian explanation scheme. In many social situations resembling a PD game an individual who has acquired a reputation not only chooses but also induces the others to follow a cooperative strategy. In addition, reputation has, in a way, a life of its own. It can be transferred from one game with one set of people to another. People who know that X was a reliable cooperator with Y and Z will trust him/her, assuming a certain consistency in his/her attitude or "character." Reputation therefore often resolves the information problem that otherwise inhibits coordination among nonparticipants or makes cooperation possible only if the same players consistently interact with each other and have an immediate chance of retaliation. Still, as Philip Heymann writes, reputation is not enough in a world of rational egotists, unless they have learned to value honesty and trustworthiness as such:

> the unhappy fact of the matter is that there is only a rough congruence between the self-interested dictates of reputation and the requirements of mutually beneficial patterns of coordination. The benefits of coordination frequently depend upon trust that agreed freedom of action will be honored in spite of conflicting temptations. But the effects of reputation provide some basis for such trust only when a limiting set of conditions is met; any violation must be known; it must be known by a party whose reactions to the violation are important to the violator; and the expected cost to the violator must exceed the benefits of giving in to the conflicting temptation. Plainly, if we had to rely on reputation alone, the benefits of coordination would escape us in a myriad of situations.[32]

It seems that except in the special circumstances Heymann mentions, prudential or (act-)utilitarian considerations cannot provide sufficient reasons for rule-following. The conventional strategem has therefore been to argue that only *act*-utilitarianism is unable to overcome the disjunction between individual and collective rationality. *Rule*-utilitarianism, on the other hand, was supposed to correct these shortcomings. However, as we will see, rule-utilitarianism does not do much better on this score. True, while the act-utilitarian could never be bound by a promise in case the general utility of breaking a promise was greater than that of keeping it, the rule-utilitarian has to evaluate alternative *regimes* and calculate their overall utility. The argument, as Harsanyi shows, can then take two avenues.[33]

One is that the choice of a regime is made by an all-wise, ideal universal legislator, who knows all the benefits and effects each rule of a code or regime would have upon people's incentives and expectations, and who can thus assess which combinations will produce the highest overall benefit. This fiction obviously takes care of the practical informational impossibilities of accounting accurately for all advantages and drawbacks of a regime by eliminating them through assumption. Nevertheless, it will not do logically, *even if we were somehow able to find such an incredibly wise legislator*. First, as should be clear, the problem reduces itself to an *act-utilitarian* choice by the legislator, a choice which is then governed by the rationality of the simple goal–means concept of rationality. Thus, the problems are solved only by having them assumed away. Second, and even worse, the utilitarian account of compliance with a regime becomes *incoherent*. It is simply incompatible with the utilitarian premises that an actor can "take someone else's word for it," instead of making his/her *own* utility calculations. Therefore, to "trust" the choice of an all-wise legislator is as impossible for utilitarian actors as feeling someone else's pleasure.[34] Bentham's remarks about "nonsense on stilts" seem quite applicable here.

There exists still another avenue, however. In case we do not want to make the heroic assumption of an all-wise legislator, we can become Humean rule-utilitarians who either stress the development of custom through usage, or the contractarian character of regimes. But these versions, too, result in puzzles. For a clearer understanding of these problems, consider the problem of lying. Typically, the individual who is considering the telling of a lie will do so because of the higher return of the defection strategy (lying) in contrast to telling the truth (cooperation). According to the rule-utilitarian account, a liar can be confronted with the argument, "But what would happen if everybody acted in such a fashion?" Thus, in cases when the veracity of the interacting parties is at stake, this naive version of the "generalization-argument"[35] is supposed to induce cooperative choices among the actors. Similarly, when the burden-sharing of a public good is at issue, the argument is credited with counteracting the free-rider tendencies among utility-maximizing rational egotists. The argument usually takes the following (more explicit) form: "The consequences of everyone's doing X are undesirable (harmful, destructive). Therefore it is wrong for anybody (you, the wavering actor) to do X. Conversely, the consequences of doing Y are good, so you ought to do Y."

Clearly, this argument cannot be logically valid, since a little reflection produces many examples illustrating the absurdity of the inference. Thus, even though it is desirable to produce food, one cannot conclude that it would be desirable for all of us to produce food. In the same vein, we are entitled to hold that being deprived of one's freedom is clearly undesirable. But although nobody is likely to prefer to have his/her freedom curtailed – pathological cases excepted – we cannot conclude that putting people in jail ought not to occur.[36] The possibility of a society in which people can freely pursue their legitimate interests seems to depend – to a certain extent at least – on the willingness of the public officials to do precisely this.

Be this as it may, we are left with the puzzling recognition that we nevertheless *do* find the generalization argument persuasive, and that the logically "correct" (counter-) argument strikes us as rather unsettling. Consider in this context the exchange in *Catch 22* between Airman Yossarian and his Major, whose name is also Major. The officer insists that the airman should sign up for another tour of duty. Yossarian, tired of the war, says:

> "I don't want to fly milk runs. I don't want to be in the war anymore."
> "Would you like to see your country lose?" Major asked.
> "We won't lose . . . Some people are getting killed and a lot more are making money and having fun. Let somebody else get killed."
> "But suppose everybody on our side felt that way."
> "Then I'd certainly be a damned fool to feel any other way, wouldn't I?"[37]

Phrasing the problem in terms of a prisoners' dilemma is helpful since it elucidates the ironies conveyed in Yossarian's response. It becomes clear that the naive version of the generalization argument persuades only if "bunching" has taken place. "Bunching" occurs when the state of the world is dissected into *two* and *only two alternatives*: one of cooperation and one of noncooperation. In addition, it is

111

assumed that *either* state can be brought about through the choice of the addressee. Since the noncooperative choice leads to unfortunate consequences for all, including the chooser, cooperation is imperative upon him/her.

In terms of a PD matrix, only the top left and the bottom right cells are considered as possible outcomes. There are only two possible outcomes precisely because "bunching"[38] eliminates the possibilities of my cooperating while the others do not (or vice versa). But it is not difficult to see that bunching in cases *where other people are involved* imparts some type of magical thinking into the situation. The mythical assumption here is that *my* action can produce either universal cooperation or noncooperation. Yossarian's response addresses both simplifications. First, he argues the insignificance of his defection, i.e., that others would not be influenced. He accepts, however, the bunching proposition in his second comment. But since he assumed that all others choose the non-cooperative solution instead of Major Major's cooperative stance, he is "justified" again in refusing to serve.

Thus, the long-run utility argument based on the generalization principle for complying with practice-type rules and precepts is considerably less persuasive than usually assumed. The reason is not simply that in the long run we are all dead, but rather that a strict rule-utilitarian position entails serious conceptual difficulties. Hume himself appears to have recognized this fact when he critically discussed the argument that "Honesty is the best policy." In a remarkable passage of his *Inquiry*, he appears to concede that without additional strong assumptions concerning the desirability of a moral life, the principle of long-run utility embodied in rule-utilitarianism is insufficient for inducing compliance with rules among self-interested actors. Hume writes:

> That honesty is the best policy may be a good general rule but is liable to many exceptions. And he, it may perhaps be thought, conducts himself with most wisdom who observes the general rule and takes advantage of all the exceptions.
>
> I must confess that if a man thinks that this reasoning much requires an answer, it will be a little difficult to find any which will to him appear satisfactory and convincing. If his heart rebels not against such pernicious maxims, if he feels no reluctance to the thoughts of villainy or baseness, he has indeed lost a considerable motive to virtue; and we might expect that his practice will be answerable to his speculation. But in all ingenuous natures the antipathy to treachery and roguery is too strong to be counterbalanced by any views of profit and pecuniary advantage. Inward peace of mind, consciousness of integrity, a satisfactory review of one's own conduct – these are

112

circumstances very requisite to happiness and will be cherished and cultivated by every honest man who feels the importance of them.[39]

While these objections to rule-utilitarianism result mainly from the difficulties that arise from the long-run argument concerning individual utility calculations, there are, as we have seen, also difficulties in arriving at a solution in multi-party bargaining situations. One way of dealing with these issues is to simplify the complexities of the situation drastically. Two devices recommend themselves: either the number of participants has to be reduced or the set of available alternatives has to be limited. The former can occur through delegation and the acceptance of majority voting. Finally, as a variant of the reduction of participants, there exists the possibility of external imposition by a sovereign who effectively attaches sanctions to his command, the alternative that Hobbes espouses. Thus, in a way, one could argue that Hobbes represents a special case within the wider social-choice perspective rather than an independently articulated theory. However, the Hobbesian solution to overcome recurring PD situations through "contract" *does* introduce several new elements which deserve further attention.

The Hobbesian dilemma and its "solution"

Although Hobbes has been commonly identified with the Austinian command theory, he expounds a much more sophisticated theory of norms and institutions. First of all, Hobbes appears to be aware that commands by the sovereign are an extremely costly way to attain social order. It is precisely this type of costs that rules are designed to overcome. In at least one of the examples he uses, the problem of impersonal and intersubjective rules guiding action becomes visible. Considering the performance of contracts, a practice constituted by rules, he writes:

> If a covenant is made, wherein neither of the parties perform presently, but trust one another in the condition of mere Nature (which is a condition of Warre of every man against every man) upon any reasonable suspicion it is Voyd. But if there be a common Power set over them, both with right and force sufficient to compell performance, it is not Voyd. For he that perform first, has no assurance that the other will performe after; because the bonds of words are too weak to bridle men's ambition, avarice, anger and other Passions, without the fear of some coercive Power . . . but in a civill estate, where there is a power set up to constrain those that would otherwise

113

violate their faith that fear is no more reasonable; and for that cause, he which by the Covenant is to performe first, is *obliged* so to do.[40]

Several points are worth pondering in this context. One might be inclined to argue that Hobbes derives the success of the interaction from the coercive power of the sovereign. However, the relationship that results from the transformation of a bilateral bargaining situation into a trilateral one (through the inclusion of the sovereign) is more complicated. First, the order that results is not primarily a function of the coercive power of the third party. Rather, order stems from the experience of trust, or "assurance," as Hobbes himself calls it. Second, trust in the Hobbesian sense is *no longer* a simple human quality dependent upon personal acquaintance. Instead, it is mediated through a social institution. It is *trust in a general system of expectations*, a system that continues to exist even in the face of occasional, perhaps even deeply felt and resented, disappointments. Trust in the system is guaranteed by the intersubjectivity of the rules defining practices, such as promising and contracting. Third, Hobbes invokes "reasonable-ness" as a standard for obligation. Thus, the presence of the sovereign can for the most part remain residual, an implicit threat, rather than an explicit third party to the transaction.

This interpretation of Hobbes appears to be at odds with conventional structural realism, which stresses power and downplays the importance of norms. Nevertheless, it is Hobbes himself who emphasized the importance of expectations for social order. True, there is a contingent relationship between expectations and the role of force, because Hobbes believes – in accordance with his pessimist view of human nature – that it is mainly fear (rather than the perception of mutual advantage) and the avoidance of a social evil (rather than the idea of a common good) that motivate people. However, since continual enforcement is not viable, every exercise of coercive force has to be transformed into one of "power," that is, linked to expectations which not only force an actor to act in a certain way but also inform him/her why he/she is being forced and how the unenviable consequences can be avoided in the future by complying with norms. Thus, Hobbes is much more interested in the *latent* presence of the sovereign, mediated by the establishment of the common meanings of words, and appropriate beliefs, including an officially propagated religion, than in coercion and its instruments.[41] Such an interpretation also suggests that a variety of rather complex social arrangements has been aggregated under the rubric of "contract" and that disentangling them might be useful for a fuller understanding of the interaction between formal institutions and normative structures.

114

On the most basic level, the establishment of a sovereign relieves the parties even in single-shot transactions from the fear of being played for a "sucker." This fear is naturally aggravated by the sequential performance of the obligation, as pointed out. Although the role of the sovereign remains in most cases residual – as the common knowledge of a third party's existence is usually sufficient in structuring mutual expectations – the institution of contracting raises other important problems.

Contracting is possible only when property rights are well established and protected. It is here that governmental powers become particularly important. Governments are therefore not only residual "enforcers" of transactions, seeing to it that the transfers take place in accordance with the wishes of the contracting parties, but they also play a much more interventionist part as defenders of the original entitlements.[42] Furthermore, if rights have been infringed, the role of the sovereign is often interventionist in still another respect: it becomes the "authority" which is entitled to assess damages according to certain (liability) rules. Thus, the enforcement of contracts, the guarantee of property rights, and the power of authoritatively deciding on restitution or damages raise many more, and quite different, issues from those of simple threats with which Hobbes is often identified.

Let us begin with property rights. Since exclusiveness is one of the characteristics of property rights, we can see how the assignment of such entitlements counteracts the fear generated by some types of a generalized PD situation, depicted by Hardin's "tragedy of the commons." While the exclusivity of rights has often been decried as the foundation of inequality, property rights have important social benefits even on the international level.[43] Under certain circumstances rights not only ensure the best use of a resource, given the preference of the actors, but also prevent the consumption function of the participants from being skewed toward early use, thus contributing to the early exhaustion of the commodity. (This is the familiar "common pool" problem.) Significantly, the new draft treaty of the Law of the Sea Conference (UNCLOS III) has dealt with the problem of managing the living resources of the sea largely by expanding the property rights of coastal states (with minor provisos for the preferential treatment of claims made by noncoastal states).[44] Such a regime obviously sacrifices important communitarian values, which had given rise to the concept of a "common heritage." However, this property-regime is cheap to maintain and probably more effective when compared to more elaborate but complicated communitarian alternatives.

In the case of a transfer of rights, the role of the public authority is restricted to safeguarding the initial entitlement and the terms of the "deal." Only the buyer and seller can set the "price" for the right.[45] However, rights can be infringed upon sometimes through inadvertent action or other special circumstances. The straying of cattle into a neighbor's property, ruining his crops, is the usual textbook example for the latter problem. In that case, the contract solution does not provide for a resolution through the interactions of the affected parties. Rather, the contract involves here the resort to the public authority for remedies. Liability rules therefore leave the various parties free to pursue their ends, provided they are ready to pay damages in cases of interference. Such rules therefore not only presuppose the existence of an effective mechanism for settling disputes, but also assume a clear understanding of the various costs resulting from a particular interference. But since we live in a world of imperfect knowledge and since neither the victim nor the tortfeasor is entitled to set the "price" for the infringement of rights (because of the undeniable incentive of "strategic behavior"), it is clear that such decisions involve a large amount of discretion. Furthermore, the result and the acceptance of any particular decision of the authorities by the litigants and – more importantly – the "audience" depends to a large extent upon the generalized respect for "the law" and the sovereign rather than on the rational assessment of the various gains and losses in a particular case, or even several instances.

The interventionist position of the sovereign can be seen even in the law of contract, when the "sovereign" has increasingly moved away from simply ascertaining the will of the parties, such as in *Norrington* v. *Wright* (1885),[46] to the consideration of a wider variety of factors, such as in *Helgar Corp.* v. *Warners Features* (1918).[47] In weighing the type of damages resulting from a breach of contractual obligations the sovereign expanded the set of relevant considerations from the ascertainment of the "will" of the parties to those of "justice" in general.[48] Precisely for these reasons the discretionary powers vested in the sovereign have to be carefully bounded by normative constraints. Governmental powers are thus a very special type of rights in that they not only grant to office-holders a certain authority, but they impose at the same time specific *duties* as to the scope and domain of their rights. Normal rights, on the other hand, are characterized by the fact that the right-holder can choose whether or not to exercise his/her rights and that those bearing the correlative duties are *different persons*.

From these brief remarks it can be seen that the Hobbesian construction of a sovereign and his powers, leaving him in the "state of nature"

116

vis-à-vis his society, fundamentally misdiagnoses the problem of authority. It takes only a little reflection to realize that, given Hobbesian premises, no "contract" setting up a governmental authority would ever be possible. Furthermore, no government could stay in existence – should it have been established by some miracle – since disinterestedness and impartiality cannot be assumed on the part of the sovereign as long as he remains in the state of nature.

There remain additional issues in the institution of contracts, even among private parties, which need further discussion. It is precisely the issue of what is just or fair under given circumstances which introduces complexities into contracting that make it impossible to derive obligations simply from the binding character of institutional rules.

IV THE COMPLEXITIES OF INSTITUTIONAL RULES: THE CASE OF CONTRACT

From this argument concerning the importance of expectations mediated through institutions several corollaries follow. First, as we have seen, Hobbes's solution is neither exhaustive of the role of third parties nor does it deal adequately with the problem of rule-guidance in a variety of situations. In short, rules and norms serve a much greater variety of functions in two and three-party contexts. These can be represented in a two-by-two matrix, depending on whether we deal with a two-party (bargaining) or a three-party context, and whether we deal with the prevention of mutually destructive solutions to the dilemma, or with the problem of enforcement. (In figure 12 the *ex ante–ex post* dichotomy is designed to reflect the latter condition.)

From this little representation it becomes rather clear that the problem of rules (norms) guiding conduct cannot be reduced to one of sanctions (subsection IIIb), or enforcement (subsection IVb), or that of authoritative norm-application (subsection IVa). But even if we deal with instances of adjudication, the roles norms play in other contexts have to be taken into account as they could void the contract. Most obviously, this is the case when courts have to ascertain whether the parties had satisfied the *conditions* for making a contract (for example, had they "capacity" to contract in that they were, for instance, not minors?) and whether there was a "meeting of the minds" at the time the parties arrived at a substantive understanding or deal.

Furthermore, cases arise in which courts have to go farther in their

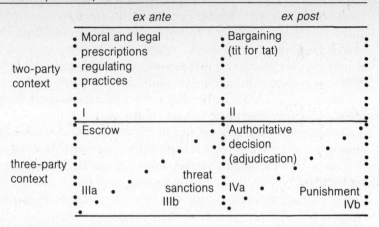

Figure 12

probings than simply ascertaining the intentions of the parties and the conformity of their dealings with the formal requirements of contract law. Consider the following cases:

1. A, a contractor, obliges himself to build a house for B. Shortly before completion the ground shifts and the house is practically destroyed. B now requires the contractor to build him a new dwelling. The contractor obliges, only with the same result.[49]

2. The same as above, only that the house is not destroyed and payment is to be made in only two installments. After eight months all work is substantially completed, but the contractor is behind in landscaping as specified in the contract. B alleges a violation of the contract and refuses payment of the second installment.[50]

3. C purchases a red Camaro from X and pays in full. When the car is delivered, it is blue. C requests his money back because of a breach of contract. X refuses, claiming the breach (wrong color) is not of a "material" nature.[51]

4. F purchases cotton from a seller in India. The cotton is supposed to be delivered on a ship called *Peerless*. When the ship arrives (the cotton prices having drastically declined), F refuses the merchandise, claiming that he intended to take delivery from another ship also called *Peerless* that had landed earlier.[52]

5. A applies for a life insurance policy. The medical examination shows that his health is excellent. After a year, he is killed in a car accident. The life insurance company refuses payment, claiming no contract existed since it never signed and returned the policy

118

to the deceased. Together with this refusal, the insurance company returns the four quarterly payments.[53]

6. Z, who knows that his house is infested by termites, replaces the infested parts of the structure but does not treat the house for infestation. He sells the house to K who, during the bargaining, never asked about termites or the possibility of infestation. Z is silent on this point. When the damages are discovered by K after the sale, K requests his money back. Z refuses, arguing that he never intended to mislead the buyer, would have disclosed the damage when asked, and therefore should not have to bear the burden of K's negligence in inquiring when buying a house which was open to his inspection and was bought "as if."[54]

7. A railroad company sells tickets which have very explicit waivers of liability on their back. X buys a ticket, notices these waivers, argues with the ticket salesman, but mounts the train. Because of negligence (faulty equipment and the engineer's mistake), the train derails and X is injured. The railroad refuses to pay damages.[55]

8. A prospector sells B a stone for one dollar which turns out to be a rough diamond. A demands the return of the stone on the basis of error.[56]

9. A sells B a cow which both assume is barren, but is actually pregnant at the time of sale. When A realizes this he refuses delivery.[57]

10. A promises B, his nephew, $5,000 if he does not smoke and drink before his twenty-first birthday. By the time B is 21, the uncle is dead and the executor of the uncle's will refuses payment, claiming that the promise lacked "consideration"[58] since it benefited only the promisee.[59]

11. G, a master of a ship, promises his crew, while in rough seas, a special bonus if they exert themselves in order to safeguard ship and cargo. Later, when safe in port, he reneges on his promise and the seamen sue for their bonus.[60]

12. A and B make a contract that S is to render a benefit to C. C, not knowing about his good fortune at the time of the agreement, is overjoyed when he hears about it and expects A to perform. Over a period of time, A makes excuses and finally tells C that he and B have agreed to invalidate the original agreement. C, although not part of the original contract, insists on performance.[61]

13. B rents a room from C. The room has not been used for several years and B discovers a big envelope with money. C admits not

being the owner and, in fact, the owner cannot be traced. Has C a right to the find (since it is his house) or is B, who not only found the money, but also found it in his rented room, entitled to the sum, or should it be shared?[62]

14. In a storm a freighter loses part of its cargo, which belongs to several owners who had contracted for the transport. Should the loss be "where it falls," i.e., those owners who lost their property are entitled to nothing, while the lucky others do not share the losses? Should the owner of the vessel bear the burden or should some type of burden-sharing be imposed by the court?[63]

Several points emerge from the analysis of these few cases. First, Hobbes's prototypical example of a contract involving *sequential performance* is quite limited in showing the complexities of contracting, as well as the problem of trust and assurance necessary to facilitate exchanges. These impediments are not alleviated by simply entrusting the institution of the court (as the representative of the sovereign) with a more explicit presence than that contemplated by Hobbes. Even if one takes Holmes's realist position of the bad man (and its corollary that the law is what the courts do), one has to know – especially when one is one of Holmes's (or Hobbes's) "bad men"[64] – what the principles *are* according to which courts are likely to decide. To argue that it is those interests which are safeguarded by the contract or promise is not very helpful, since courts enforce certain promises and contracts while they refuse to do so in other cases. After all, contracts when entered under duress, or when made *contra bonos mores*, are void. Similarly, promises – unless given under a seal[65] – are in common law countries usually enforceable only when they imply "consideration." Thus, the argument of the executor in example 9 is based on this doctrine, while in case 10 the court held that the nephew's compliance with the uncle's demands (even if they benefited him and not the uncle in the sense that it led to a healthier lifestyle of the nephew) established sufficient "consideration."[66]

Similarly, even when express promises are lacking – i.e., when a doctor treats an unconscious man who dies and when the doctor then asks for payment for his services from the deceased's estate[67] – courts are often inclined to "imply promises and fill in the missing terms and, in general, pursue the beneficent end of making contracts for their parties."[68] At times, such discretion leads to, at first sight, quite startling results, as Lord Kenyon in *Harris* v. *Watson* (case 11 above) shows. Referring to the doctrine in maritime law that the crew are to exert themselves in order to save a ship, Kenyon denied the request for the bonus payment on policy grounds:

> If this action was to be supported, it would materially affect the navigation of this kingdom . . . for if sailors were in all events to have their wages, and in times of danger were entitled to insist on an extra change on such a promise as this, they would in many cases suffer a ship to sink, unless the captain would pay any extravagant demand they might think proper to make.[69]

Thus, higher-order principles and/or policy considerations may be invoked to void promissory or contractual obligations. This is quite at odds with the conventional conception that the court's task is simply to enforce the parties' will. In the latter case, relief would be narrowly circumscribed by error or fraud at the time when the parties made the agreement. Example 9 is to that extent a classical case in which the mistake on the part of the seller provides the reason for releasing him from the contractual obligation. Case 8 seems to fall into the same category, although the court went the other way. The justification was that it was not so much a "mistake" as the speculative nature of any dealings among prospectors which governs such transactions.[70] Since both buyer and seller are aware of the potential windfall, such bargains are enforceable since they are not based on the common conception of error.

Case 6 appears to be similarly situated. The question is not so much what the factual situation was, but to what extent courts can be invoked to provide relief if one of the parties fails to have adequate understanding of the situation while making the contract. The issue is therefore whether there is a duty to disclose essential defects in the *precontractual* phase although no fraudulent intention need be present. Civil law countries have developed the doctrine of *culpa in contrahendo*,[71] which imposes a duty of disclosure on the seller. The common law also has increasingly stressed the principle of good faith[72] as a precontractual duty against the "arms' length doctrine" of former times.[73] These principles are operative in case 5, in which the undue delay of signing a policy cannot be pleaded as a defense. The fact that technically no contract was in existence is defeated by considerations of equity. In addition, the receipt of premium payments might be construed as a functionally equivalent action to a formal signature.

Case 4 raises the same issue, whether a contract was or was not in existence. When *Ruffles* v. *Wichelhaus*[74] was decided, the Court held that there was "no meeting of the minds" and therefore no contract.

Consequently, it held for the defendant, who had refused acceptance of the cotton as well as payment. However, even if there might have been a mistake preventing an exact "meeting of the minds" among the contracting parties, the question is still whether this mistake was of such a material nature as to justify the conclusion of the Court. It is exactly this distinction between material and non-material breaches on which the decisions in Cases 2 and 3 turn. While the failure to finish the landscaping work constitutes a breach of contract, it is not "material" enough to justify nonpayment (save keeping a small amount in escrow). On the other hand, the classical "perfect tender rule" applied to sales contracts provides that even minor deviations in the quality, quantity, and number (or color) voids a sales contract.

Cases 1, 7, 12, 13 and 16 raise more difficult issues for contracts as they turn (like Case 9) largely on policy considerations. Here, the limits of the institution of contracting (Case 12) are at issue by either including or excluding benefits to third parties or by allocating risks and liabilities in a principled fashion. The invalidation through the courts of many waivers of liability in standard contracts, as well as the development of the doctrine of "frustration" (for example, releasing the builder in Case 1 from his strict liability), has occasioned the present discussion in jurisprudence about the "death of contract." It led to the suggestion that contracts should be emancipated from the institution of promising and be absorbed into the law of torts.[75] This debate is not merely academic, since it revolves around the problem of what principles and norms are applicable in construing contractual obligations or in filling in the "gaps" when unforeseen circumstances arise.[76] This leads us back to the question of why we should comply with institutional rules, i.e., why are contracts and promises binding?

V THE LIMITS OF PRUDENTIALISM: DURKHEIM AND FREUD ON NORMS

We started out with the rule-utilitarian position of Hume and saw that his argument, elaborated on the basis of "coordination norms" and instrumental, instruction-type rules, could not satisfactorily deal with certain problems of institutional or practice-type rules. In particular, Hume's argument about the need for reputation and the long-term interest in keeping one's promises works – if at all – only under special circumstances. In addition, there is a hint that it is logically faulty (*petitio principii*). Since both the loss and the acquisition of a reputation presupposes the general acceptance of the practice, reputation cannot be invoked as the *reason* for the acceptance of the practice. Hobbes's attempt at explaining rule-following for the cases of practice-type rules fared not much better. His paradigmatic case of sequential performance of contracts is far too simple to cope with the complexities of the institution of promising and contracting. The selection of the fifteen cases above was designed to show a variety of problems which are likely to arise. Three corollaries follow from these considerations.

Three corollaries

One, it became clear why realism quickly has to become *legal* realism. ① After all, the sovereign "command" has to be applied to the controversy and therefore needs interpretation. Two, our discussion demonstrated that compliance with decisions by a court is something different from compliance with simple rules. It becomes what Fisher ② calls "second-order compliance."[77] Although this deference to authoritative decisions is parasitic upon the compliance with standing rules (first-order compliance), it has some distinct features, as we shall see in chapters 7 and 8. Three, the interpretation of Hobbes showed that while compliance with a court decision is explainable in terms of the original "contract" establishing the sovereign, his theory fails to ③ account for the binding character of the social contract itself in the state of nature. Arguing that the original contract is binding because it is a promise pushes the argument only one step further back. It seems that no purely prudential reasons suffice to establish the obligatory character of certain practices such as contracting and promising. If it is not prudence alone, what other considerations become relevant? I shall argue that only the emergence of a "moral point of view" can resolve some of the puzzles.[78]

DURKHEIM AND THE MORAL CHARACTER OF RULES

Why should one keep one's promises? It is here that Durkheim advances our understanding by pointing to the importance of the extended "self" and to emotional attachments created through ritual activity and through communicative action. Rituals not only bond people together, calling attention to their relatedness in a compelling fashion, but also give meaning to social interactions by enlarging the "self" of the actors through the inclusion of societal concerns. Thus, the emotional roots connecting the "self" with significant others remain important even after primitive bonding is largely supplanted by verbal argument. Communicative action, which evolves when ritualistic bonding in primitive society comes under pressure, establishes a conceptual frame within which the force of norms as conduct-guiding devices can be discursively ascertained.

123

Durkheim deals with the problem of norms and conduct-guiding rules in the context of his discussion of "social facts," which individual actors experience as external constraints. Furthermore, Durkheim maintains that certain social phenomena are best investigated by tracing their origins to a collective experience and that there are significant analogies between the sacred and the moral. This last claim allows for a clearer conceptualization of obligation by rooting it in the experience of the sacred. Sanctions are then no longer simply the penalties attached to certain actions by the Hobbesian sovereign, who thereby changes the utility calculations of the individual. As Durkheim emphasizes again and again, the term "moral authority" is "opposed to material authority or physical supremacy."[79] Furthermore, moral facts expressed in rules of conduct are valid not because of threatened deprivations, but because of their duty-imposing character, which is in turn the precondition for the legitimacy of physical sanctions.

The phenomenological analysis proceeds by focusing on the similarities between the force of the sacred and the force of moral authority. In both cases the feeling of obligation is characterized by a particular attitude and an *ambivalence of emotions*. The attitude toward the sacred and toward moral authority consists in transcending purely self-interested concerns. As Jürgen Habermas points out in his interpretation of Durkheim:

> In honoring the sacred during a cultic activity, in complying with ritual prescription, etc., the individual divests himself from his . . . utilitarian attitudes. Without having regard to the imperatives of self-preservation or self-interest he commits himself with all the other believers to a communion; he is integrated with the impersonal force of the sacred which transcends all individuality.[80]

Emotional ambivalence in the presence of the sacred (which is simultaneously "the prohibited and untouchable" as well as the "loved and the desired whose nearness is sought")[81] is paralleled by the ambiguity between denying one's spontaneous inclinations and the enthusiasm for the good in a moral action. On the basis of these similarities Durkheim finds the religious roots for moral obligations, though not without secularizing religion in one important respect:

> Morality would no longer be morality if it had no element of religion. Apart from this, the horror which crime inspires is in all ways comparable to that with which a believer reacts to sacrilege. The respect which we have for the human being is distinguishable only very slightly from that which the faithful of all religions have for the objects they deem sacred. This characteristic, sacredness, can be expressed, I believe – and I feel bound to express it – in secular terms.

124

That is, in fact, the distinctive mark of my attitude. Instead of joining with the utilitarians in misunderstanding and denying the religious element in morality, or hypostatizing with theology a transcendent Being, I feel it necessary to translate it in rational language without thereby destroying any of its peculiar characteristics.[82]

Thus Durkheim transforms religion from a historical event of revelation, or from the inception of a practice (ritual), to one of the transcendence of the individual in the direction of an ideally symbolized society. This society, in turn, guarantees in its rites and myths the cohesion and coherence of the world, as well as the objectivity of the moral order. With its duty-imposing claims upon the individual, it is the absolute, and at the same time only a relative order, for all obligation results from the form of life that characterizes a specific society.

Nevertheless, Durkheim realizes that a fundamental change in the moral character of rules and obligations occurs when language intervenes. Solidarity, the moral basis of the society, which was previously largely guaranteed by shared religious practices (rites), is now transformed into a justificatory argument. The commonality of experience is no longer one merely of sentiment; it depends rather upon the success of *communicative action*.[83] Claims to validity have become the basis for the prescriptive character of rules. Customary norms have lost the naive respect upon which they relied and have to be tested and corroborated by justificatory arguments. Rules themselves are vulnerable to defeating reasons, and exceptions and exemptions restrict the scope of rules, depending upon a whole host of interacting factual and value claims. In other words, the homogeneity of prescriptions, all originally experienced as sacred, is differentiated. Within the normative realm principles and rules can be distinguished, and different rule-types can be identified. Durkheim's analysis helps us clarify three points, although with different degrees of success.

First, it enables us to clear up one of the fundamental misunderstandings common to law and morals alike: that the obligatory force of a rule or norm derives from the issuance of a *command* by God or the sovereign. This command theory seems to be acceptable only as an explication of the experience of the sacred. Justifications in terms of intersubjective reasons, on the other hand, are *claims to validity* that can be decided only discursively. Deliberation, rather than following another's command, is the prototype for deciding moral questions.[84] Deliberation and persuasion are similarly characteristic of legal decision-making, as the metaphor of "finding the law" and the need for reasons offered in a judicial pronouncement indicate. After all, without such reasons a decision is usually considered illegitimate and in violation of "the law." Secondly, Durkheim is helpful in advancing the analysis of the reasons for the obligatory force of practices like promising or contracting by showing their roots in rituals. As we have seen, practice-type rules contain instructions for performances. Performative expressions, such as "hereby," or the affixing of signatures or a seal (the ritualistic character of these gestures is still evident), specify the conditions under which a given action is valid; the enforcement of promises without "consideration" but given under "seal" is a good example.

The third contribution of Durkheim's theory is his emphasis on *emotions* for social life. By making the society the love-object of actors, the individual identifies himself/herself with the collectivity and attains in this process also a "self." Identity is guaranteed by the structure of relations that we have wanted because we loved the others and which

> we cannot fail to want and to love because otherwise we would lose ourselves and our capacity for wanting and loving . . . We are certain of loving and wanting them and of being loved and wanted in return. It is precisely because they are stable love objects and a source of certainty that we are able to live without continually being thrown into total crisis.[85]

But by the creation of love-objects, there are also those who become objects of our aggression. It may be that they are our personal enemies, but "more often than not these objects of aggression are . . . institutionally defined."[86] Durkheim failed to deal with this other side of social solidarity, although his treatment of the "sacred" which is experienced with "awe" and with an intense *ambiguity of feelings* could have led to a more systematic treatment of aggression and social conflict.

It was only Freud who systematically developed these ideas. The initial experience of ambiguity of emotions vis-à-vis love-objects shows the presence of two conflicting emotional principles, Eros and Thanatos. The differentiation process can be studied in individual as well as social development. Criticizing the utilitarian account of social solidarity, Freud remarks:

> The interest of work in common would not hold society together; instinctual passions are stronger than reasonable interests. Civilization has to use its utmost efforts in order to set limits to man's aggressive instincts and hold the manifestations of them in check by physical reaction-formations. Hence, therefore, the use of methods intended to incite people into identifications and aim-inhibited

126

relationships of love, hence the restrictions upon sexual life and hence too the ideal's commandment to love one's neighbor as oneself . . . civilisation is a process in the service of Eros, whose purpose is to combine single human individuals, and after that families, then races, peoples and nations, into one great unity . . . But man's . . . aggressive instinct . . . opposes this programme of civilization . . . What means does civilization employ in order to inhibit the aggressiveness which opposes it, to make harmless, to get rid of it, perhaps? This we can study in the history of the development of the individual. What happens in him to render his desire for aggression innocuous? Something very remarkable . . . His aggressiveness is introjected, internalized; it is, in point of fact, sent back to where it came from, that is, it is directed towards his own ego. There it is taken over by a portion of the ego which sets itself over against the rest of the ego as super-ego, and which now, in the form of "conscience" is ready to put into action against the ego the same harsh aggressiveness that the ego would have liked to satisfy upon other, extraneous individuals.[87]

In short, social solidarity becomes possible through the displacement of aggression to *impersonal norms*, and it is now largely the normative structure which determines which objects are to be loved. "In this system of symbols, the norms therefore constitute the boundary inside of which eros is to be found and outside of which lies aggression."[88] The shift from the undifferentiated feeling of ambiguity to a moral order which links emotions to normative structures in the mature personality had been foreshadowed by Durkheim's studies into the origins of primitive religions and the emergence of morality. However, Durkheim's work did not provide a clear picture of how emotional attachment and normative structures relate to each other at a stage when communicative action and the ascertainment of validity claims have taken over the functions of ritual activity in procuring social solidarity.

In one of the most moving scenes of his *Eumenides*, Aeschylus depicts this change, in which the revengeful impulses, symbolized by the Furies, become the good spirits (Eumenides–Εὐμενίδες). Subservient to the law, to the *dike* (δίχη) of Zeus, they are also now the law's implacable avengers. It is this reconciliation of the destructive impulses with the normative order which creates the community characterized by brotherly love (φιλία–*philia*), in which persuasion and argument rather than revenge and force reign.

> *Athene*: Now for the love that you perform, to this dear land my heart is warm. Holy persuasion too I bless, who softly strove with harsh denial, till Zeus the Pleader came to trial, and crowned Persuasion with success . . .

127

Chorus: Let civil war, insatiate of ill, never in Athens rage. Let burning wrath, that murder must assuage, never take arms to spill, in this my heritage, the blood of man . . . Let all together find joy in each other; and each love and hate with the same mind, as his blood-brother; for this heals many hurts of humankind . . .

Athene: . . . Great gains for Athens shall arise from these grim forms and threatening eyes. Then worship them with friendly heart, for theirs is friendly. Let your state hold justice as her chiefest price and land shall be great and glorious in every part . . .

Chorus: . . . Now great, all seeing Zeus guards the city of Pallas; Thus God and Fate are reconciled.[89]

VI

This chapter attempted to answer the question of why actors "follow" rules. Starting with the "problem-solving" approach developed in the previous chapter, the argument was developed in four steps. First, I tried to correct the largely mistaken notion that explaining an action in terms of norms entails a (probabilistic) prediction about future conduct.

The second step involved the explanation of rule-following in terms of the standard rule-utilitarian account, i.e., showing that the action was in the interest of a given actor. While in narrow act-utilitarian explanations there is no need for the inclusion of rules and norms, rule-utilitarianism, such as espoused by Hume, argues for the long-term utility of the adoption of regimes by individual actors. But as the problems with the generalization argument and those arising out of multi-party bargaining situations showed, the rule-utilitarian account needs substantive revision. I then discussed the Hobbesian version of rule-following, which seemed to be a special case of the prudentialist stance inherent in utilitarianism.

The third step involved the demonstration that Hobbes's solution to the problems raised by practice-type rules (contracting) is rather limited in its relevance and in its dealing with the complexities that actors encounter in making promises to each other and in obligating themselves through contracts. A set of cases taken from contract law demonstrated the inadequacy of explaining rule-following in terms of the paradigm of sequential performance of contracts.

The discussion of Durkheim's "idealist" position, examined in a fourth step, was designed to go beyond the inadequacy of a purely prudential stance in the case of practice-type rules and precepts. Durkheim's analysis of the experience of the "sacred" provided important clues as to the importance of verbal argumentation at a time

128

when the cohesion of a society is no longer experienced on the level of emotions or common rituals. Nevertheless, Durkheim's inability to come to terms with the ambiguity of emotions inspired by the sacred prevented his analysis from proceeding.

The brief discussion of Freud indicated in what direction Durkheim's analysis has to be developed further. It also attempted to demonstrate that rule-following in the case of practices and precepts has to be understood against a considerably wider conception of the "self" than that of (rule-) utilitarianism. Precisely because the individual experiences a conflict with others concerning the goals, the issue arises of how such conflicts can be mediated by norms and rules. The argument of the next chapter therefore deals with the criteria for a discourse on "grievances," through which conflicts over goals can become susceptible to a rational treatment even if no unique and compelling solution emerges. This discursive treatment of conflict in terms of competing validity-claims, in turn, provides the background for the discussion of law as a specialized style of reasoning in chapter 8. Through the adoption of certain additional techniques to cases and controversies, authoritative decisions can resolve conflict among the contending parties by settling on one among several, perhaps even equally possible, alternatives.

5 THE DISCOURSE ON GRIEVANCES: PUFENDORF AND THE "LAWS OF NATURE" AS CONSTITUTIVE PRINCIPLES FOR THE DISCURSIVE SETTLEMENT OF DISPUTES

I

The argument of the last chapter, concerned with the "reasons" in support of rule-following, called into question our conventional way of viewing judgments about practical matters as indications of personal preferences, or as expressions of idiosyncratic feelings. Since in the pursuit of our goals we do interfere with each other's purposes, certain norms and standards, backed by our sentiments of approval and disapproval, make it possible to advance claims without simply resorting to solipsistic statements such as "I like" or "I dislike."

Nevertheless, even after we had left the purely idiosyncratic grounds of personal desires and passions, reasoning with rules as conceived by rule-utilitarians proceeded largely along the lines of instrumental rationality. In other words, providing reasons was seen solely from the perspective of the effective pursuit of the actors' "long-term interests". However, practices and precepts also exhibit certain other features, such as the protection of other persons' interests, which make these norms quite unlike instrumental rules. Attempts to explain the obligation inherent in practices and precepts in terms of individual long-term utility calculations failed, as our discussion of promise-keeping suggested. Thus, to reduce the problem of rule-following to *prudential* considerations[1] appears to be unsuccessful, and the argument above shows why. In the case of prudential considerations our reasoning deals largely with the choice of means for the achievement of self-chosen goals. Since promises and precepts have important other-regarding dimensions, these actions transcend the boundaries of simple prudential choices.

130

Our grievances, on the other hand, arise largely from the collision or conflict of our *ends*. It becomes necessary, therefore, to elucidate what the non-idiosyncratic conditions and presuppositions of our discussions and determinations are about, on the basis of which we can assess the relative merits of our claims. In this context two questions deserve attention. First, there is the issue of "rights," i.e., those claims or entitlements which enjoy a particular form of social recognition and which figure prominently in our discourse on grievances. Second, the conditions, or constitutive elements of precisely this discourse, in which we argue about the priority and weight of our claims, need further clarification.

Thus, although we started our investigation on the basis of a public choice perspective in which compliance with norms – if at all – derives from our desires rather than from "reason," the emerging analysis suggests a much closer connection between reason and the choice than the original Humean perspective implied. Assessing this concept of reason, Samuel Stoljar points out:

> reason is no longer taken in a cognitive sense, as a self-sufficient source of morality, but is given an analytical and self-reflective role; reason simply becomes our logical way of finding or of constructing a framework within which an orderly (and concludable) argument can be carried out. In this way, just as prudential rationality offers external or supra-personal criteria in terms of which the practical reasons we give for an action can be adjudged as being right or wrong, so in the moral field rationality now provides, in a comparable procedure, those external or independent standards, without which we cannot reason about, let alone settle, our interpersonal grievances or complaints.[2]

In this chapter I want to develop these thoughts further; first by a negative step, i.e., the demonstration that the difficulties encountered in the rule-utilitarian account are not peculiar to rule-utilitarianism. They reappear even in a deontological theory, as is brought out by a brief discussion of Kant's categorical imperative. The second step is the positive demonstration that these difficulties can be overcome through the introduction of *substantive* principles which allow for the ordering and discursive treatment of the grievances.

However, one caveat should be added immediately. The ordering of claims does not satisfy the conditions of a (deductive) moral "theory,"[3] and therefore its conclusions are not necessary or compelling. Discourses allow only for a much weaker form of ordering, for which the "topical" discussions in practical reasoning or the expounding of "cases" in law provide examples. Nevertheless, the usefulness of such

131

a framework for arriving at a decision is far from negligible. In elaborating on these conditions I shall use Samuel Pufendorf's teachings on the "laws of nature" as my main guide. The interpretation of these texts will show the close association between legal and moral reasoning in some type of naturalist mode. Since Pufendorf develops his ideas in connection with some of the puzzles of international law, a closer examination of his writings will also demonstrate the relevance of this admittedly rather abstract discussion for international relations.

In order to develop these thoughts more fully, my argument will take the following steps. In section II I discuss the difficulties of the generalization argument and the categorical imperative in generating principles which would allow for a clear and defensible recognition of our duties and/or rights. I first try to show that the "consistency" argument inherent in the generalization argument, as well as the narrower and wider grounds of the categorical imperative, tends to become incoherent. In a second step I intend to demonstrate that the fallback upon utilitarian criteria does not eliminate such problems either. Thus, I conclude that *formal criteria* alone are probably insufficient and do not provide the necessary guidelines for deciding such questions. However, I argue also that problems of conflicting goals *are* susceptible to a discursive (intersubjectively valid) solution. The constitutive conditions for an intersubjective discourse on grievances, as well as its substantive principles, are introduced in sections III and IV by means of an interpretation of Pufendorf's absolute and hypothetical laws of nature. The absolute laws contain the substantive principles of no-harm and equality for the persons claiming grievances, as well as special duties to advance others' interests under certain circumstances. The "hypothetical laws" of nature and, in particular, that of promise-keeping, are able to explain the special obligations incurred in using practice-type rules. This approach opens the way for an analysis of "rights" which are parasitic upon certain practices for which "promising," creating *in personam* rights, is paradigmatic. Section VI, the conclusion, provides a brief summary of the most important points of the argument in this chapter.

II GENERALIZATION AND THE CATEGORICAL IMPERATIVE

The discussion of the naive version of the generalization principle (the Golden Rule) showed the limitations of prudentialism in establishing the obligatory force of certain types of norms such as

132

practices and precepts. Since this approach makes the fulfillment of obligation dependent upon the yardsticks the individual is willing to accept in a logically consistent manner, we have no defenses against either the morally indifferent or the fanatic, since the "obligation" of others depends upon our (im)moral idiosyncrasies. Consider, for example, the "sincere Nazi" who would be perfectly willing to take the consequences of being sent to a death camp if he were Jewish or a gypsy, or had some other "undesirable" ancestry. As long as he is "consistent" he would be morally entitled to have his perversions enforced. But such a position borders on madness. Besides, as the last example suggests, the consistency-criterion will provide incentives to invent spurious classes of people, or circumstances, by which the actor prescribing such a rule can exempt himself from the consequences. Thus, whites may invent special rules which apply only to blacks (or vice versa), and while most of us shrink before admitting such a clearly discriminatory rule (especially when applied to people of the same society), there is an easy way out even for that eventuality: all one needs to claim is that the "others" are not part of the "society" to which the rules apply. Unfortunately, these are not imaginary examples, as "apartheid" and the establishment of "Bantustans" show.

Given these difficulties that arise from the application of the Golden Rule, it becomes understandable that Kant dismissed that argument as insufficient to provide guidance in cases when our ends collide. In one of his crucial conceptual distinctions, he separates precepts of prudence (hypothetical imperatives) from the "categorical imperative" that prescribes what ought to be done not in pursuit of some other purpose, but irrespective of whether a course of action suits us or not. Rules are obligatory if they can be shown to satisfy the criterion of the categorical imperative, which states that one should "act on that maxim that one can at the same time will to become a universal law."[4] Thus, the categorical imperative contains two criteria: that of universalizability, and that which makes such a prescription "willable," for which Kant advances wider and narrower grounds.

To the extent that universalizability is invoked, it simply means that actions cannot be based on purely idiosyncratic preferences. Thus, as Stoljar reminds us, all value-judgments with any claim of validity have to be universalizable. Even a judge at a cat show, who decides that the male tabbies "Slitz" and "Moritz" are first-class specimens of their breed, implies thereby that he will have to judge any other cat that possesses the same qualities in the same way. Consequently, in the case of the categorical imperative, the *moral* component seems to have to lie in the "will"part. Thus, the requirement of autonomy provides

133

the criterion of how the "will" through self-determination can become the moral law itself and can impose categorical obligations.

How does the categorical imperative help us to decide which "maxims" we are to choose? Kant advances several grounds, all turning on the issue of self-contradiction. The wider ground is that certain rules are not universalizable without self-contradiction. For instance, if everybody lied there would be no truth; if everybody stole there would be nothing left to be stolen, etc. But as Brentano's counterexample showed, such a "wider ground" can serve as a criterion only if it is supposed to regulate practices that are already accepted as "moral."[5] Brentano's point is made by means of the prescription "do not accept bribes." In the case of theft it is clear that if everybody stole this would lead to the abolition of property. Analogously, everybody's refusal to accept bribes would lead to the abolition of corruption. If we had only the formal criterion that Kant advances, refusing bribes would be wrong since it becomes "self-contradictory" in the sense that it ends the existence of a certain practice. The fact that we do not consider the abolition of bribery wrong clearly demonstrates that the criterion of the categorical imperative cannot tell us by itself what is right or wrong. Because of its formal nature it cannot decide between "right" practices (truth-telling, promising) and those judged *ab initio* to be wrong (bribery). Only if we already argue or know that bribery is wrong, Brentano's *reductio ad absurdum* does not hold.

Other grounds concern similarly the impossibility of willing something because it would involve the choosing agent in a self-contradiction. For example, nobody can will his own destruction as a general rule because this would entail the destruction of all life and thus the impossibility of a moral life for which the categorical imperative provides the criterion. Similarly, Kant claims that I cannot will *not* to help someone in distress, since this would imply that I would never want help even *in extremis*. This requirement, however, might prove too much. Should we conclude from Kant that we must always help everybody else who is in distress? At least in one passage Kant seems to draw precisely this conclusion from the fourth formulation of the categorical imperative, although a few pages later he modifies the argument significantly. The first version states:

> A fourth person, himself flourishing while seeing others (whom he could help) struggling thinks: "What does it matter to me? Let everyone be as happy as either heaven or he can make himself. I neither will take anything away from him nor will I envy him. Only I have no wish to contribute anything to his well being or to his support in distress!" Mankind could naturally exist if such a way of thinking

became a universal law of nature [*allgemeines Naturgesetz*] . . . never-theless, it is impossible to will that such a principle become univer-sally valid as a law of nature. For a will which decided this way would become contradictory, since it could imagine cases in which it needs the love and sympathy of others and in which it would have deprived itself from all hope to assistance by having adopted . . . such a law of nature.[6]

The "addition" inserted into the fourth version of the categorical imperative a few pages later, however, amounts to a considerable modification. It reads.

Now humanity could no doubt subsist if nobody contributed any-thing to the happiness of anybody else, without however taking away anything on purpose. However, if someone does not also further the ends of others, *as much as he is able to* [*so viel an ihm ist*], this represents only a negative and not a positive agreement to (treat) humanity as an end in itself. If the conception that a subject is an end in itself is supposed to have full effect on me, then its ends also must be my ends *as far as possible* [*so viel moeglich*].[7]

The obvious rub is a determination of what is meant by the term "can" or "could," which differs in the two versions. The first version is clearly the stricter one, since it imposes duties without a clear limi-tation derived from a substantive assessment of the chooser's abilities. Precisely because the "good will" in following the categorical impera-tive is supposed to be free of "inclinations" and calculating assess-ments,[8] it seems most accurately to convey the duty which is imposed. But in a way, such a construction leads to rather absurd consequences. For example, because someone's house burned down, do I have to help, and even if so, how much? Is it also true that all this can be decided by invoking my duty, which in turn results from the posibility that the same may happen to me? It does not seem to involve a simple self-contradiction to want "help" in abstracto, while not wanting to incur the general responsibility of helping everybody *in all conceivable* circumstances, precisely because the *scope* and *range* are at issue in such cases. This latter question, however, can no longer be settled by simple appeals to the formal characteristics of the categorical imperative, but depends upon a substantive assessment, as Kant himself realizes in introducing the "as far as possible" addition later.

No!

This limitation, however, introduces further puzzles. Kant assumes that limitations largely result from the negative attitude towards man as an end in itself, i.e., the limited generosity, or plain greed, character-istic of most. There are instances, however, in which the wish for such limitations results from eminently humanitarian considerations. Not only may I – as perhaps a morally obtuse person – discount the possibility of ever wanting to ask for the same type of help for which the other is now asking, but I could make sure (morally much less obtuse) that these circumstances do not arise and that I do not impose undue burden on others. Securing an insurance for one's house, procuring for one's own pension, etc., are all arrangements designed to lessen the burdens we would otherwise be inclined to put on others, such as children or other relatives.

A second puzzle arises, even if we accept the less rigoristic version of the fourth example of the categorical imperative as the authoritative interpretation. Consider the following case: I, as a poor swimmer, cannot discount the possibility of drowning; therefore I cannot "will" a rule not to save someone from drowning. Consequently, I have also to accept that I have to save someone whom I see drowning. But precisely because I am a poor swimmer, I know that not only might I *not* save the other person, I might drown myself. In that case my duties under one version of the categorical imperative are contradicted by those of the other version (preservation of life). Strangely enough, the two grounds of the categorical imperative appear to become self-contradictory under certain circumstances.

Weak!

The only way out, then, is to restrict the class of person to whom, for example, the "lifeguard" rule applies, i.e., to make it obligatory only for good swimmers. Although this seems sensible and unobjectionable, we should not be deceived about what happens in that case: the duty is derived neither from the good will itself nor from the deliberations of the actors themselves prescribing such a rule. Rather, duties are established by a complex assessment in which the needs of one party are weighed against not only the needs of others but also against their ability to contribute. On the basis of such considerations, excuses and exemption from categorical duties become possible and justifiable, although they may "heteronomously" impose duties on others (such as on good swimmers who might oppose a lifeguard rule on the basis of the principle that all truly autonomous persons ought to be able to swim).

In order to have some guidance in cases of conflicting duties, one solution is to fall back on some principle of utility. Although this would correct some of the rigorism, it does not satisfactorily deal with other issues thereby raised. Take the often-given example of lying to a criminal who threatens to kill my hidden friend. Since I know his hiding-place, am I justified in lying to the criminal who threatens my friend's life? Although virtually all of us would answer in the affirmative, the reason why such an action violating the precept "do not lie" appears acceptable is more complicated. Utilitarianism draws our attention to the relative weighing of the various "values" involved. But if such assessments were done consistently, valid rules would cease to exist and thus only idiosyncratic decisions, made *ad hoc*, would result.

Thus, both principles, that of the categorical imperative as well as that of utility, turn out to be questionable devices for reasoning and deciding issues of certain conflicts. I suspect that this at first rather counterintuitive result – i.e., that exactly opposite principles lead to similar dilemmas – is not so surprising after all. In both cases issues of the infliction of interpersonal harm are decided according to either the valuation or the self-imposed criteria *of the agent*. This leaves out important areas in which a different point of view is required. As Samuel Stoljar points out:

> it should then be evident that morality is not just a matter of oneself making a moral decision, or personally committing oneself to a moral act, or prescribing to oneself a moral view, or just a matter of personal sincerity and personal moral strength. It is pre-eminently a matter of being able to assess or judge somebody's action morally, that is, in terms of moral rules. If moral judgments were really self-prescriptive or self-commanding, as some moral theories strongly suggest, then moral fanaticism, or its opposite, moral weakness, would make morality as irrelevant as it would be imperative. Hence we need moral rules by which we can (no longer autonomously or personally but now heteronomously or, as it were, supra-personally) justify or judge our actions and, more particularly, those actions giving rise to complaints or grievances; and we need rules informed by arguable reasons, not simply action-ordering imperatives.[9]

In this context it was surprising that neither the deontological position nor utilitarianism made much of the conception of "rights." However, it is precisely through these devices that we limit duties, decide questions of rank order of duties, and provide some intersubjectively communicable criteria for a decision even if, under certain circumstances, such rights defeat established moral principles. It seems important, therefore, to pay more attention to two factors.

One is the *process* by which claims and counterclaims are advanced. Even if we make no special provisions for weighing of interests, the sequence in which alternatives are decided has tremendous bearing upon ultimate outcomes. There is no reason to believe that procedural rules, such as who is entitled to speak, when, or for how long, which assertions can be challenged, etc., are not of tremendous importance in discourses in which we decide competing claims. Two, we have to investigate further the bases on which claims can be defeated, or exceptions and exemptions from normative injunctions can attain assent. While the first set of norms deals with the constitutive rules of the discourse on grievances, the second assigns weights to claims which are based on competing assessments of the same "case," or on a different "description" of the issues involved. Consequently, not only may different rules become relevant, but different reasons for extending, modifying, or restricting the same rules and principles are suggested.

These brief remarks have two further implications. First, all of the above criteria attempted to provide an absolute foundation for the adherence to norms and rules. The logic of justification was thus essentially "monologic," i.e., its persuasiveness depended on the force of the logical criteria when applied to a rule in question. Kant's emphasis on noncontradiction is as important in this context as the utilitarian assumption that all actions or regimes can be unequivocally graded and thus be "rationally" assessed. Remember that in the latter case, a special form of noncontradiction, i.e., "transitivity," becomes an important yardstick. But consistency alone is hardly decisive, as the case of the sincere fanatic illustrated. Second, while the exceptions and exemptions to a rule or the preference of one prescription over another have to be justified, ultimately our substantive determinations cannot be grounded in an absolute Archimedean point. They depend for their validity on the assent they can marshal. What is a "cruel and unusual punishment," who deserves what type of assistance from his fellow man, are not decidable once and for all but depend upon shared practices and upon historical contexts.

But saying that no Archimedean point can be found is neither arguing that all moral questions are simple preferences nor suggesting that any factual agreement will do. The problem of the "sincere Nazi" is not alleviated the least bit by showing that this type of ideology was able to marshal substantial support. Thus, the process of arriving at decisions has to be guided by certain criteria, and in addition, assent to practical judgments must be gained in a noncapricious fashion. It is here that rules which constitute such a discourse and make non-idiosyncratic assent possible attain their great importance.

III   THE MORAL DISCOURSE AND PUFENDORF'S LAWS OF NATURE

If competing claims can no longer be decided either by reference to some cognitive yardstick (such as utility), or on the basis of purely formal criteria, how and on the basis of what principles can we

138

reason about our other-regarding choices? It is here that Pufendorf's teachings on natural law supply some answers. However, it is also clear from what was said that the term "reason" has then to be taken in a noncognitivist sense. Reason is, then, concerned with the pre-conditions (or "transcendental" conditions, we might say) of a "moral" discourse,[10] in which the effects of our actions on others can be assessed. Although not necessarily providing compelling solutions, it imparts at least a certain order and persuasiveness to the process of arguing and to its outcomes. In this conception a direct apperception of right and wrong on the basis of ontology is ruled out,[11] as is the derivation of the laws of nature in a teleological fashion (à la Grotius) from a "social appetite" or an overarching goal.[12]

Establishing the distinct domain of moral reasoning, Pufendorf rejects a religiously inspired system of deductions which derives the duties of man from man's creation by God, his intuition into eternal essences or ideas, or his fallen nature.[13] Reasoning about moral matters (the *entia moralia*) is characterized by its claim to universal validity among all human beings (Christians as well as "heathens"), by the recognition that actions arise out of the free determinations of the actors, and by the realization that their moral character cannot be derived from the perception of their physical characteristics.[14] Thus, long before Hume, Pufendorf espouses an approach to moral reason-ing which is opposed to scholasticism as well as to the physicalism of Hobbes. The moral quality of an action – Pufendorf still uses the somewhat traditional idiom of "moral entities" – results from the attitude people take towards the action, rather than in the act or its physical properties.[15] The attitudinal dimension is what Hume will later call the "generalized feeling of approbation," what Strawson terms "vicarious resentment,"[16] and what Durkheim meant by "collec-tive conscience."

But while the emphasis on feelings of approbation and resentment explains why we can marshal support even if our *personal* likes and dislikes are not at stake, it does not explain on the basis of what criteria we can sustain our claims and grievances. Here Pufendorf's teachings on the "law of nature" with regard to "other men" is helpful.[17] Pufendorf calls the applicable norms "precepts" and divides them into "absolute" and "hypothetical" ones. This distinction in turn depends on whether they are obligatory for "all men even before the formula-tion of any human institution,"[18] or whether "some public forms and civil methods of living have been already constituted."[19] He is furthermore careful to point out that the distinction made between the hypothetical laws of nature and positive law is not the same, since "the

139

reason of the former is drawn from the condition of mankind considered in general, but the reason of the latter is taken from the particular interest of any nation or state, or from the bare pleasure of the legislator."[20] This distinction is important since "our civil positive laws are not so many precepts of the natural hypothetical law, but do only borrow their force of obliging . . . from the virtue of some such hypothetical precept of nature."[21]

Pufendorf considers absolute laws of nature to be the principle that "No one should hurt another" (*neminem laedere*) and its corollary that "If he has caused another harm he should make it good."[22] Furthermore, that "Every man should esteem and treat another man as his equal by nature or as much a man as he himself."[23] These two principles concern largely the principles underlying common forbearances. But Pufendorf, unlike liberal "anarchists,"[24] sees that purely negative injunctions are not sufficient to provide rational grounds for dealing with grievances arising out of the indifference of other actors. Consequently, he postulates as the third law of nature that "A man should advance the interests of another man." "It is indeed a little thing," Pufendorf writes,

> not to have hurt another, or not to have taken from him his proper esteem, which things do but remove any just reason for hatred. But some benefit as well must be conferred upon another if the minds of men are to be united by a still firmer bond. A man has not paid his debt to the sociable attitude if he has not thrust me from him by some deed of malevolence or ingratitude, but some benefit should be done to me, so that I may be glad that there are also others of my nature to dwell on this earth.[25]

The *hypothetical* laws of nature, on the other hand, give rise to "adventitious obligations."[26] These concern the principle of good faith underlying human practices, which in turn create rights and duties on the basis of certain actions. The principle of veracity (telling the truth), of keeping one's promises, of fulfilling one's contractual obligations, and of taking an oath are then discussed in greater detail.

The capacity of actors to create their own rights and duties through practices is seen as necessary in order to avoid two common problems. On the one hand, the problem of indifference is thereby overcome, at least with regard to certain persons. On the other hand, practices are also designed to avert the embarrassment of imposing duties on others only because we ourselves might be willing to abide by a certain principle. (The latter issue was discussed in conjunction with the problem of the "sincere Nazi" above.) Pufendorf expounds:

The duties thus far set forth [absolute laws of nature] derive their force from that common relationship which nature establishes among all men even before any act was exchanged between them. But it is not enough to confine within such a circuit the duties which men owe to each other. For not all men are so constituted that they are willing to do everything, which they can, to help others, out of mere humanity and love, and without assuring themselves with some hope of receiving their equivalent; while it is often the case that the things which can come to us from others are of such a nature that we cannot have the boldness to ask that they be done for us gratis . . . Therefore, it had to be determined beforehand what one should do for another and what he should in his turn expect from another, and demand on his own right. This is indeed accomplished by promises and agreements.[27]

In this context an important further distinction between precepts of the most general nature and concrete practices can be made. While moral precepts such as "help thy neighbor" can embody a morality of aspirations (supererogation), practice-type rules and their resulting obligations are geared towards the "normal" conduct of affairs.[28] This is reflected not only in the well-known saying that "ought implies can" but in the view that the "can" itself is embedded in common understandings that, for instance, exempt an infirm swimmer from the duties of rescuing another man although he could do so. Furthermore, obligations incurred on the basis of common practices are more specific, precisely because there is usually a clear stipulation of what one has to do in reference to the person(s) to whom the obligation is owed. Although the duties contracted are "obligatory" only within the bounds of the practice itself, the prescriptive force of the practice in turn is placed within the wider understanding of the general duties of man, which flow from the absolute precepts of the laws of nature.[29] Thus, even decisions concerning the advantages and burdens resulting from contracts, which did not involve the "works of humanity or of love" but rather the duties required from "a right and . . . directed by actual justice,"[30] are in important ways tied to these most general notions.

These principles, or laws of nature, also supply standards for judging grievances when contractual issues can no longer be settled by appeals to unequivocal texts or precedents, or when the intentions of the parties are not clear, through unforseen circumstances. Similarly, these principles provide important guidance when considerations of equity suggest modifications of the strict application of the legal rules or contractual stipulations.

Three corollaries follow from this argument. First, it shows a sub-

141

stantial similarity between legal and moral reasoning insofar as both involve judgments on practical matters, and both have to be arrived at through a process of *principled argumentation*. Second, since both moral and legal reasoning are designed to lead to principled choices, the element of "heteronomy" that is involved in the decisions is different from the imposition of a superior will.[31] The heteronomy refers to general principles which are constitutive of the individual "self" as well as of the existence of society. To that extent their arbitrariness is sharply curtailed and Rousseau's paradox that the law will "force the lawbreaker to be free"[32] hereby attains a certain plausibility.

The principles Pufendorf calls "laws of nature" together neither form a set of purely formal criteria nor allow for the establishment of a structure of norms valid for all cases. In this type of naturalism, no timeless hierarchy of values or principles is available from which a decision could be derived simply by means of the normal deductive procedures. Most obviously, the laws of nature represent only certain "starting-points" for the discussion of value-claims.[33] They provide "contexts" and help with the selection of relevant facts; furthermore, they lead the actor in a certain sequence and order through the articulation of a claim. Precisely because these laws are in a way "transcendental" to a discourse on grievances, in that they provide for the possibility of a moral argument, they are not determinative of any particular decision that invokes them.[34]

Since no determination decision can be derived from these laws, it is clear that, as a consequence, *authoritative decisions* will be required if the problem of interference becomes serious and the parties cannot find a solution themselves. Not only, therefore, is such "naturalist thinking" compatible with the existence of positive law, but it is obvious that even positivistically inclined persons have to follow these naturalistic principles if they want to arrive at an intersubjectively valid decision. The next section will elaborate on this point.

IV   THE UNIVERSAL LAWS OF NATURE

For an argument concerning grievances, three conditions are necessary. First, the formal condition is that actors have depersonalized their reasons for complaints, i.e., allowed for the universalization of their claims. Second, the imperative of equality not only represents a principle of fairness in the claiming process, but it is the very obedience to this criterion that allows the parties to proceed to pleading *the merits* of their grievances. Finally, the parties must argue from a shared notion that there exists a "normal" state of affairs of which harm to others is not an intrinsic part. Consequently, harm that arises out of our actions – whether intentionally or not – occasions demands for making good the damages.

While the no-harm principle is a precept of highest generality and underlies all the more specific rules regulating our forbearances such as "do not steal," "do not kill," "do not bear false witness," etc., it is not purely formal in character as is, for example, the universalization criterion. Samuel Stoljar correctly points out:

> Important as universalisability is, it is still not enough for the forma-
> tion of moral rules, being only a first step, a necessary but still not a
> sufficient one. For, obviously, it is not enough to indicate, even if only
> in outline, what the rules are to be about: what sort of human actions,
> reciprocal commissions or omissions, moral rules are to comprise.
> Without this practical, action-specific, element . . . our moral rule
> would simply not do its job; it would remain not merely purely formal
> but vacuously formal, without even a hint as to what its content, let
> alone its moral content, might be. Indeed all formal principles must
> sooner or later connect with substantive phenomena, for unless they
> do they have nothing to be formal about. Formal principles are
> parasitic on, logical auxiliaries for, matters of substance, not sub-
> stitutes for them.[35]

It was exactly this problem of either leaving the substantive content of the rules to the individual actor or leaving it unspecified that created the problems with (rule-)utilitarianism and the categorical imperative in some of its formulations.[36]

Furthermore, Pufendorf's third law of nature concerning the obliga-
tion to help others is also highly general, but substantive in character. It thereby overcomes the problem of indifference which might be as legitimate a reason for a grievance as our complaints based on the infractions of rules of forbearance. Pufendorf's laws of nature are therefore quite different from the teachings of Grotius, and they differ also from the "minimal content of natural law" of Hart.[37] Similarly, unlike in Hobbes, the equality of men for Pufendorf is not rooted in the *fact* of near equal strength among human beings or, as Hobbes so graphically says, the ability of virtually everybody to "kill" every other person.[38] For Pufendorf equality is rather a postulate of reason which provides the preconditions for a rational discourse within which the merits of competing claims can be decided.

Although Hart (unlike Hobbes) includes the no-harm principle in his list of principles representing the rational core of the natural law doctrine, he, like Hobbes, derives the equality of standing of the parties in a conflict from the "approximate equality"[39] of men in terms of their physical and intellectual endowment. The "naturalistic fallacy" involved in such a procedure should be obvious.[40] Although transcendental arguments also imply some fundamental first principle, it is important to realize that their structure is quite different from the Hobbesian inference mentioned above. Transcendental arguments, whether cast in a Kantian form or in terms of a theory of communicative action, as is the case here, always concern issues *logically prior* to any assertion of natural "facts."

The true transcendental nature of the no-harm principle can best be grasped when we contrast it with Hobbes's argument. Hobbes derives the necessity of a social contract from the experience of the violence of the state of nature and from the incentives for "commodious living" in a society in which a division of labor and, therefore, arts and sciences can flourish. Since utility calculations are possible only after I can make reasonably accurate assessments of other people's actions in the pursuit of their self-interest – which in turn depend on *their* assessments about *my* actions, etc. – we have to postulate in initial state of *no harm*, otherwise our whole concept of rational action would break down. This is probably why Hobbes maintains that the "laws of nature" are, even in the natural state, obligatory "internally" (in *foro interno*), but goes on to say that they have no force in binding actual conduct.[41] Without the transcendental notion of such laws of nature the conception of a rational self-interest becomes impossible. Similarly, the binding character of the original contract is possible only if based on the prior notions that promises and contracts are binding even in the absence of enforcing institutions.

> While we can accept a hypothetical war by some against some, or even any against some, what seems impossible to accept is a situation of each fighting each since this would exclude any other expectation than pain or harm, a situation that would allow no room for harm-avoiding norms or standards to evolve; with maniac fighting maniac there would be no opportunity of learning what it is to have non-hostile expectations creative of shared standards or norms or, indeed, what it is to have non-violent relationships. Nor can we imagine that appropriate norms might nevertheless be introduced by our own enlightened self-interest or by a Leviathan who may be tyrannically cruel only to be benevolently kind: all these enlightened or benevolent intentions would end in nothing, unless there already existed some regular expectation or social norm of a reasonably regular immunity from harm.[42]

The last universal law of nature concerning the duty to advance others' interests is also a necessary principle in order to overcome the problem of indifference. It does not articulate, however, a general and comprehensive duty to help everybody under all circumstances, which creates the well-known difficulties with the fourth formulation of Kant's categorical imperative. Pufendorf's version has, at least in one instance, a limitation, i.e., the criterion of *innocent utility (innoxiae utilitatis)*. In this context Pufendorf cites Cicero, *De officiis* (I.14):

> All communities of men consist of things which are of that nature which, though placed by Ennius under one head, may be applied to many. "He (says that author) who kindly shows the bewildered traveller the right road, does, as it were light his lamp, by his own, which affords nonetheless light to himself after it lighted the other." By this single example he sufficiently enjoins on us to perform, even to a stranger, all the services we can do without detriment to ourselves. Of which service the following are common illustrations: "That we are to debar no man from a running stream," "That we are to suffer any who desire it to kindle fire at our fire"; That we are to give faithful counsel to a person who is in doubt . . ." all which are particulars to that are serviceable to the receiver without being detrimental to the bestower . . . As the means however of each particular person are very confined, and the number of the indigent are boundless, our distributive generosity ought still to be bounded by the principle of Ennius – it nevertheless gives light to oneself – that we may still be possessed of the means to be generous to our friends.[43]

While the idea of the works of *innoxiae utilitatis* is not in itself sufficient in providing a framework for distributive questions, or in enabling us to decide all disputes involving issues of indifference, its practical implications are far from negligible. Thus, Grotius already invoked this principle when he discussed the problem of "innocent passage."[44] In a very similar vein, Pufendorf's argument nearly anticipates the reasoning of the I.C.J. in its *Corfu Channel* decision[45] when he states that "passage should not be denied on the ground that it may be found in a more remote place and by a circuitous route."[46] Pufendorf adds two very important elaborations to this principle of innocent utility. One concerns the admission of foreigners to one's territory,[47] the other the restrictions one state might justifiably impose against the allegedly natural right of free trade, or the alleged duty of having to share universally one's resources.

These considerations allow, then, the introduction of "special" duties to those who are near to us: our families, friends, compatriots. Reasons such as these also provide the justification for using our liberty in entering "into roles and assuming obligations which constrain us to pursue goods more limited than the general good."[48] In this context, Pufendorf, although admitting to the advantages of a principle of free trade, suggests that

> such an assertion allows many restrictions, for we do not seem to be bound by any law to share with others things which are not absolutely essential to human life, or minister only to its pleasure. And if we ourselves are threatened with lack of such things, we are within our rights in keeping them from others for our own use.[49]

The duties mentioned above flow from the universal laws of nature and obtain between all persons, insofar as they are equal moral agents. Obligations arising out of the *hypothetical laws* of nature, on the other hand, concern certain duties owed to *particular* persons. They are obligations which result from our voluntary acts and they are connected with certain social practices such as promising and contracting. It is to these "institutional" obligations that we now turn our attention.

V THE HYPOTHETICAL LAWS OF NATURE

In establishing the obligatory character of promises and contracts, the modern discussion has often founded the obligation largely on the "reliance" of the promisee (i.e., his expectations).[50] If it took the deontological route, the duties of promise-keeping and contracting were usually derived from some fundamental principle. This in turn could be a principle governing speech in general[51] or from the conventions constituting the "speech act" of promising and contracting.[52] However, it has been pointed out against the latter position, espoused by Searle, that the institution can be called obligatory only to the extent that it has been accepted as such.[53]

Rooting the obligatory character of promises (and thereby contracts) in expectations creates, however, the embarrassment that it fails to distinguish adequately between threats and promises, although both create expectations. Since there is no obligation to make good one's threats, the clear implication of such a position seems to be that there is no obligation to keep one's promises either. But such an argument is clearly absurd.[54] One way of dealing with this last embarrassment is to draw the boundaries of promising narrower by insisting that promises, unlike threats, must concern some type of benefit to the promisee and/ or that promises have to be accepted by the promisee to be ogligatory.

Although this adjustment obviously takes care of some of the most disturbing implications, it is not sufficient to explain why the expectations which attend to promises are so different from those that result

146

from the announcement of "resolutions," i.e., unilateral declaration of intentions by an actor, a puzzle which Hume already pointed out.[55]

> For as regards statements of intent, the hearer may well expect the speaker's performance, yet such expectations are always tempered by the belief that he has a right to change his mind. In the promise case, however, the hearer's expectations, which expectations are supposedly the ground of the obligation, must be based on the belief that, *ceteris paribus*, the act will be performed even if the promiser does change his mind (i.e., his "inclinations," etc.). It is because this expectation is so strong, that people rightly come to rely on promises in a way that they don't on statements of intent.[56]

It is precisely this puzzle that speech-act theory appeared to solve. It was the utilization of the *institution* which created the obligation. Despite the fact that speech-act theory does not provide a satisfactory answer by itself, it *does* show that "reliance" (i.e., expectation in the hearer) and "promising" (i.e., the "uptake" of an obligation by the speaker) are only *contingently* related. This means, however, that expectations cannot be the sole reason (or even perhaps the main reason) for the obligation incurred.

From these distinctions it becomes clear why threats differ fundamentally from promises (i.e., not only in that the latter alone benefit the promisee). Threats are different simply because they alone are *necessarily* connected with the perlocutionary effect of the speech act. Thus, a threat is obviously in vain, has been ineffective, and/or misfired, if the addressee is not moved by it.[57] However, promises are not simply invalid if the promisee does not give too much credence to a promise. Someone unreliable, who promised to be at an appointed place at a given time, has surely made a promise even if everybody knows that he/she is kind of a deadbeat. Although we might prudently take precautions in order to minimize the damage, it is exactly the "uptake" of the obligation, i.e., its *ill*ocutionary force rather than the *per*locutionary effect, which is crucial in this respect. Unless we do not want to have anything to do with the other person, we cannot simply ignore or belittle the illocutionary effect of the promise. Doing so would mean that we do not take the person seriously, that we deny him/her the status of a moral agent by discounting his/her utterances, or that we imply he/she is like a child or an imbecile who does not know what he/she is doing.

These last remarks make it also doubtful whether the derivation of promissory obligations from the general requirement of veracity is useful. Although Warnock[58] (and before him Grotius[59]) treat a promise as a type of prediction for what I intend to do, this position creates a series of puzzles. True, promising is connected with indicating my intentions, and beyond that, with curtailing my liberty to change my mind in the future. Nevertheless, when we blame someone for not having made good on his/her promise, we do not usually argue that the person has not told us the truth, or spoke misleadingly, or incorrectly.

Consider the following case where Smith has no car and asks me whether I will be at the party tomorrow at Brown's house in the suburbs.[60] Indicating my intentions I can choose three different forms:

1. At the moment I intend to go.
2. Yes, I'll be there.
3. Yes, I promise you I'll be there.

It seems clear that differing degrees of commitment are implied by these statements: Case 1 is an indication of my present intentions, Case 2 is a resolution that may cause Smith to rely on it, but only 3 is a strict promise. If Warnock (or Grotius) were right there should not be any difference between Cases 2 and 3, since both concern "my being there." As long as I have the capability of doing so, no differentiation of the attending obligation appears possible. But while we might still be entitled to derive the "ought" for my presence in the second case from the requirement of not deceiving Smith, something else happens in Case 3.

> Certainly if I promise to go and then do not go then once again I will have misled Smith, but I am guilty of far more than that. This time I cannot eliminate my responsibility merely by warning Smith that I have changed my mind. For in promising I made it clear that Smith can rely not only on my words but *on me* [my italics]. I do not merely say that I will be there, realizing that Smith will rely on my presence; I give my word, so that what is at stake when it comes to doing as I promised is not so much the truth and reliability of what I said as the trustworthiness and reliability of me.[61]

In other words, what seems at issue in this respect is something more: it is our common conception of the freedom and responsibility of moral agents that *precedes*, and has to be logically prior to, any attainment or utility of goals that agents choose to undertake, singly or in conjunction.[62] It is our notion that there is a "self" which remains the same, despite a variety of changes in desires, moods, intentions, and circumstances, that is at stake as much as is the possible harm we do to others by misleading them or inducing their reliance on us. To that extent promising is constitutive of "agency" and of our ability to bind or commit ourselves by an act of will. Conversely, it is through the giving of reasons indicating the lack of free will or the impairment of an actor's

148

agency, or through the intervention of an unforseeable event, that we allow promisors to modify or abrogate their obligations. Precisely because the uptake of an obligation is so fundamental to our basic moral conceptions, promising is most probably paradigmatic for a wide variety of rule-bound actions, including the institution of asserting something (telling the truth).

Pufendorf's teachings on the hypothetical laws of nature appear to come close to the position outlined here. His treatment of promises and the requirement of veracity shows this most clearly. Rather than deriving the obligatory character from the hypothetical law which commands us to tell the truth, Pufendorf's position – largely developed in opposition to Grotius – views making assertions as an activity governed by *institutional rules*. This position in turn entails the rejection of attempts to construe some natural meanings of words as, for instance, Plato does in his *Cratylos*, a position Pufendorf criticizes extensively.[63]

> it is clear that the power which words have of bearing this or that meaning, that is, of giving rise to a certain idea in the mind, is theirs not by nature, or any intrinsic necessity, but arises from the mere judgement and institution of man. For otherwise no reason could be shown for the same thing being expressed in different languages.[64]

Therefore, Pufendorf concludes that the meanings of terms results from their *use*, a problem he discusses in conjunction with sub-cultural differences.

> It should be also noted . . . not only that many languages differ in dialects, but that words of the same language have different meanings in different places. The meaning, therefore, of such words will be judged according to the usage of the place where the business is being conducted.[65]

In a second step, Pufendorf establishes the rule-governed use of language and shows – very much as in the transcendental argument made above – that the conventions underlying assertions have to be understood in terms of the institutions of promise and contract. Beginning his discussion with the conventional character of signs – which he distinguishes from natural ones, i.e., those that signal[66] joy or pain – Pufendorf draws the analogy to speech:

> Now just as all signs, except natural ones, denote a certain thing from imposition, so this imposition is attended by a συνθήκη, συνάλλαγμα (consent, agreement), and pact, by reason of which such signs must be used to point out one and only one thing. And a pact of this sort must be understood in the case of all things used for signs, no matter what origin we posit for human speech.[67]

149

These remarks then set the stage for the discussion of truth-telling and lying. Pufendorf starts from the distinction that "every lie is an untruth but not every untruth" a lie. Only *intentionally saying* what is not true *to another* qualifies as a lie. On this basis Pufendorf investigates the special obligations of veracity that arise out of freely entered social relationships. He distinguishes these duties from those of a "general pact" underlying normal communication. Thus, "although we are bound by this general . . . convention to use words and other signs as agreed upon and according to general custom, we are not in the least obligated by that fact to disclose to everyone all our thoughts and ideas."[68] In other words, I am obliged to disclose to the other person "only those things as [sic] the other person has a full right to know."[69] Consequently, a lie can be defined as an assertion wherein the signs and words used "represent our thought as being something very different from what it really was, and yet the man to whom these signs are directed had a right to know and judge them, and obligation lay upon us to make them in such a way that he would understand our feeling."[70] It is this inviting of a belief which creates the special obligation to veracity in social relations, and not, as Grotius argued, the "faculty to know the truth" which would be hindered by lying. After all, Pufendorf argues,

> it does not follow that because a man can naturally understand something he therefore has a right to understand it; for a moral faculty is not without further ado to be inferred from a physical one.[71]

Thus, making assertions, telling the truth about my intentions, and inviting belief from others – not so much on the basis of independent evidence but on the *faith* of it – can be seen as following the same logic of speech acts for which promising was our paradigm. It is exactly this "uptake" by asserting something that distinguishes asserting from describing or frequently even recounting an event, although the two latter activities are governed by general speech conventions. As Charles Fried put it:

> A lie invites belief in an assertion which the speaker knows to be false. That is why my saying that it is raining outside when I know it is not, but when my sole purpose is to test my dictating machine, is not a lie. I am asserting nothing, and therefore I am asserting nothing false. What if my false utterance should be overheard? It is still not a lie. What if it is overheard and believed to be true? Once again it is not a lie, since I did not assert it to the hearer, believing it to be false. Indeed I *asserted* nothing.[72]

This analysis of lying shows that one can even lie other than by the use of words because "surely if a person nods assent to a proposition this should stand as an assertion of the truth of that proposition."[73]

Given these facts, Pufendorf also makes clear that in this sense the question of whether one deceived by omission or commission[74] is of minor importance as long as it is established that the interacting parties entered voluntarily into a special relationship and created rights and obligations through the institution of asserting. As a good lawyer, he argues, for example, against the duty of a defendant to tell the whole truth and incriminate himself instead of using evasive answers or keeping silent. He can do this without becoming inconsistent precisely because being cross-examined is in several respects quite dissimilar from entering by free volition into the "assertion game."[75] Nevertheless, if the defendant so chooses – especially by invoking an oath by which he hopes to strengthen the belief of others – he is bound by the rules governing the speech act.[76]

Pufendorf's other examples taken from the international arena attempt to illustrate this point further. For example, he allows "feigned speeches" by military commanders (to raise the drooping spirits of troops) and by heads of states.[77] While he very often comes close to a merely prudential stance, he *does* make some important conceptual distinctions which shows that he is not a simple utilitarian, as he is often depicted. Consider the following passage, which carefully distinguishes the absence of a veracity-requirement among enemies from the veracity-requirements of parties entering explicitly into the promising and contracting game. Furthermore, note the crucial distinctions between the obligations of the parties inter se and vis-à-vis third parties.

> It is clear that since the obligation to disclose our mind ceases between enemies, a man can, without censure of lying, make false statements to them, and terrify them or inflict some damage upon them by false reports, provided no undeserved damage arise therefrom to a third party who is our friend . . . But what is said about deceiving an enemy should in no wise be extended to any pacts entered into with the enemy about concluding peace, or about an armistice . . . And yet enemies cannot meet together again to make peace, unless there is a mutual obligation clearly to reveal their thoughts on the present matter, and consequently unless the necessity of their mutual suspicion is removed by an obligation to speak the truth in their negotiations for peace.[78]

With truth-telling conceptualized very much as an institutional practice for which promising served as the paradigm, it is not surprising that Pufendorf's hypothetical law of nature underlying the institu-

151

tion of contract, i.e., that commitments be kept in good faith, also stands in a close relationship to promising.[79] The distinction between promising and contracting, therefore, does not lie for him in the difference of the obligations they impose, but in fact that promises can be unilateral while contracts involve *mutual* promises.[80]

This purely formal distinction derived from the Roman Digests not only makes contractual obligations parasitic upon promissory obligations, but allows Pufendorf to deal systematically with a variety of other issues. For example, he points out that utilizing the institution of contracting severely limits the possible excuses and invalidating conditions that prudence might dictate. For instance, while fear may be a condition which makes a covenant void, i.e., when the promise was extorted, the fear "that men will break faith, based only on the general depravity of man's nature is not enough to justify refusal to fulfil a pact."[81] Neither will a general character defect of the other party do as an excusing condition, "for many vices have no relation to the matter of [good] faith."[82] The "moral" obligation flowing from contracts, although not independent of the purposes for which an undertaking is agreed upon, is nevertheless *independent* of the moral worth of the parties concerned. In other words, it is only the rules of the institution which circumscribe the conditions by which we as moral agents can choose, and incur and limit responsibility for our actions.[83]

Thus, while the obligation derives from the "hypothetical laws of nature," exemptions and excuses that might defeat such a *prima facie* obligation are increasingly regulated by positive law; it stipulates more clearly what "rights" the contracting parties acquire. Since the rights of one person impose duties on others, further positive regulations become necessary when rights conflict, or when the imposed obligation is defeated by general principles or policy considerations. For example, contracts *contra bonos mores* or to the detriment of third parties are held void.

VI

This chapter continued the discussion begun in chapter 3 of what is involved in rule-following and how norms and rules attain their prescriptive status. But while the reasons advanced in chapter 3 largely concerned the justifications of rule-following based on utilitarian and prudential grounds, chapter 4 was designed to probe deeper into Durkheim's and Freud's suggestions that social cohesion, guaranteed by rules, cannot be explained solely in terms of utilitarian calculations. In particular, practice-type rules and precepts could no longer be accommodated within the prudential paradigm.

The main thrust of this chapter was therefore devoted to the examination of the conditions of a discourse on grievances, i.e., the attempts to reason with rules in those cases when we are no longer concerned with the best choice of means in attaining our goals, but when we realize that our freely chosen goals conflict and when we decide that violence shall not become the arbiter. I argued in this context that grievances can only be aired in an intersubjectively meaningful fashion when a "moral point of view" emerges. In this context, the popular generalization argument, Kant's categorical imperative, and Pufendorf's laws of nature were examined as means for providing the conditions for such a meaningful discourse. Having shown that the categorical imperative often fares no better than the *ad hominem* argument of the generalization principle, I attempted to argue that the main reason for the failure lies in the formal character as well as the "autonomy" requirement of the categorical imperative. Insofar as utilitarianism too makes the individual the sole judge of his obligations, it also can be shown to be deficient.

In a second step I attempted to indicate why more substantive principles are required and I suggested that Pufendorf's absolute and hypothetical laws of nature provide an important way in which a discourse on grievances can be structured. This argument was intended to show several things. One, in giving structure to the discourse, the laws of nature are the constitutive principles for debates in which conflicting goals and priorities can be assessed. Two, it suggested not only that natural laws so conceived are compatible with positive law but that even positivistically inclined jurists have to invoke these principles in arriving at a decision. In addition, I indicated in what way this approach differs quite substantially from Hart's "minimal content" of natural law. Three, the example of Pufendorf, as well as the analytic arguments presented here, suggested reasons why attempts to draw the lines between morals and law in terms of taxonomic exclusive categories are bound to fail. Precisely because important legal institutions are parasitic on promises as well as on the substantive principle of no-harm, suggestions that legal rules can be distinguished easily from other rules and norms by some specific property appear to be of dubious validity. My presentation has, until now, avoided these difficulties by treating *all* rules and norms as if they were of one quality. This did not prevent me from distinguishing several rule-types, but these distinctions did not coincide with the normal distinction between morals, laws, and instructions based on instrumental or prudential considerations.

It will be the task of the following chapters to probe these distinctions more deeply. However, the notion of "right" has to be explicated first, a task taken up in the next chapter.

6 THE NOTION OF "RIGHT"

I INTRODUCTION

In our examination of different norm-types the notion of right was only cursorily treated as an example of impure norms of coordination.[1] Considering the importance of rights in our normal discourse, such silence appears strange indeed. Furthermore, as the discussion of Kant's rigorism in imposing duties on all of us shows, "rights" are different from duties. They are not simply prescriptions which demand something from us but are special entitlements, which at the same time may limit the range of persons who have a duty towards me as a right-holder. In a way, however, rights also seem to have the opposite function: they are sometimes claimed against "the world," as the argument for subsistence rights of all people everywhere shows. In addition, right-claims are often advanced *on behalf of* animals[2] and even inanimate objects of natural beauty or cultural importance. Thus, right-based arguments cover a wide field and put forward a variety of claims that cannot all have the same status for obvious reasons. Claims to subsistence are likely to deserve our attention more than appeals that our "species chauvinism" is misplaced, and that animals should not only be exempted from unnecessary cruelty and maltreatment but should be accorded full protection on the basis of rights.

In spite of all this diversity there is a common denominator. All arguments about rights stake out claims backed by reasons why these demands should be socially protected. Rights are, therefore, not only insistent claims, but are also claims imposing obligations on others, which, for instance, even the most persistent claims about "interests" cannot do. But precisely because right-claims are based on reasons, they can be defeated by certain other reasons. What *types* of reasons can serve as defeating ones in this context creates considerable difficulties. Conceptual distinctions among rights are therefore sometimes made in terms of the types of "duties" these rights impose. In this sense "negative" rights are then distinguished from "positive" ones.[3] The latter are said to impose specific positive burdens on others, while the duties of the former are said to be more or less "costless" and procured by mere nonactions. An example of such duties resulting from negative rights is the noninterference with someone else's right to movement, property, etc. Furthermore, negative rights are often considered primary, in that the enjoyment of every other right seems to be dependent upon them.[4] While this dichotomy focuses on one important aspect of the function of rights in society, the analysis below will demonstrate that it is of lesser help in understanding certain distinctive features of our rights-talk.

Similarly, other distinctions which revolve around substantive distinctions among the type of *entitlements* conferred by rights ("political" from "social" or "economic" rights[5]) suffer from the same shortcomings when primary is automatically given again to political rights.[6] The right to life, liberty, and the pursuit of happiness does not neatly coincide with the distinction of political and economic rights, since the enjoyment of happiness ("property," as originally phrased) is obviously not independent of constitutional guarantees of personal liberty, as well as of the protection of property. It is also of little help to understand rights in terms of property, precisely because the notion of property presupposes that of a right. Besides, the fundamental rights such as life and liberty are properties, or possessions of a very special character. They are rights that *cannot be alienated*, i.e., transferred to someone else, although their right-holder owns them. The distinction from conventional property rights, therefore, should be obvious.

Finally, a grading of importance among different right-claims could be based on arguments about the "natural" basis for certain rights. The fathers of the American Revolution argued for an original endowment of such rights by the Creator; other positions stress the intrinsic worth of persons, or the fundamental interests these rights protect.[7] The difficulty with these positions is again that, unless we assume that questions of rights can be decided solely on a cognitive basis, or through the acceptance of a certain revelation, there is no way in which we can derive the entitlement directly from the observation of certain facts of nature. Since in nature big fish eat little fish, observing natural facts and patterns provides us with precious little guidance how to decide which rights are to be protected[8] and what we are supposed to do in a conflict among such basic rights. In the same vein, attempts to bar challenges to right-claims through positing "absolute" rights are equally unsuccessful. Thus, the right to noninterference with one's activities and freedom from harm are as basic as we can imagine.

156

Nevertheless, coercion and the infliction of harm as punishment might not only be justified, but part of any meaningful concept of right.

Faced with such a bewildering variety of issues, it is best to take one step back and begin by asking the question of how the concept of right is used in different contexts. Through the introduction of various examples, we may be able to sharpen our awareness of conceptual differences that distinguish different *uses* of the term "right." In addition, the term "right" figures prominently in a variety of language-games, such as in the political discourse (through its connection with terms like "authority" and "power") and in the legal discourse (through the notions of fundamental rights, human agency, responsibility). It is therefore clear that no treatment of rights is satisfacory which focuses narrowly on only one of these dimensions.

These initial remarks provide the basis for the steps of my argument in the next few sections. In section II, a variety of uses of the term "right" are investigated by means of several examples. Furthermore, the problem of individual and collective rights is broached via the examination of the construct of a legal personality as a right-holder. Various examples from domestic and international law serve to illustrate the conceptual distinctions advanced in this context. Section III establishes rights as claims, i.e., as a particular *practice* of asserting claims. This practice, in turn, is illuminated by speech-act theory. The focus on the performative aspects allows us to distinguish rights from the more general concepts of duty and obligation. The conceptual elaboration is paralleled by a more historically oriented inquiry which traces the shift from the natural-law to a natural-rights discourse in the seventeenth century. Not surprisingly, a great deal of overlap between these discourses can be discovered, particuarly in the case of basic or fundamental rights. After all, the same basic interests were safeguarded by both the postulates of the "laws of nature" and natural rights. However, the distinctive contribution that rights-thinking made to the political and legal discourse comes to the fore when we consider the conceptualization of government powers and of personal liberties as special cases of rights pertaining to the "subjects." While the issue of powers and immunities and their connection with authority is then further investigated in the remainder of section III, the issue of liberties, fundamental and/or inalienable rights, and of "manifesto rights" is taken up in section IV. This discussion leads back to a fresh assessment of the positive/negative rights discussion with which this chapter began.

Some further conceptual refinements concerning the communitarian elements of rights are suggested in section V. These elaborations, in turn, allow for a critical evaluation of claims to subsistence rights against the community. Furthermore, the issue of inferring duties, and of determining a class of duty-holders from the assertion of human rights, is discussed. Finally, I contrast the function of manifesto (claim) rights with legal strategies to limit right-claims by stringent "standing" requirements and various judicial "avoidance techniques." Section VI, the conclusion, provides a short summary of the arguments made in this chapter.

II RIGHT AND RIGHT-HOLDERS

Let us begin our examination with an array of examples and focus first on an important aspect of rights: the discretion they provide for the right-holder and, therefore, the limitations of duties they entail. When Bill owes me ten dollars I have no right to ask George to pay me back, even if I know that George owes Bill the same amount. George not only is entitled to disregard my pleas but would violate Bill's rights if he paid me directly without the latter's consent. When Jane decides to throw the wrapping of her Big Mac out of the car, right in front of a sign which informs all of us that the fine for littering is 100 dollars, Joe, as a member of the community, may have reasons to be upset. He might even decide to call the cops, but he has no "right" vis-à-vis Jane.

On the other hand, in a certain context, rights seem to impose obligations on a virtually unlimited number of people, i.e., point in precisely the opposite direction. When, for example, Mr. Takada from Japan oversteps the fences of Dr. Brückner's property in Bavaria, in order to photograph the latter's children wearing *Lederhosen* while trying to bathe "Beau" their cat, he is remiss on fulfilling his duties which the property rights of Dr. Brückner impose upon him. Consequently, when "Bubu" the watchdog rips the pants of Mr. Takada, chasing him off the property, the latter cannot claim damages. Thus, rights of the type lawyers call *in rem* seem to impose duties on a potentially unlimited but vague group, including hypothetical people not yet even in existence.[9]

Further puzzles arise when we imagine that the policeman, mobilized by Joe, issues a ticket to Jane, after chasing her car for a few blocks. Having been pulled over, Jane defiantly claims that the officer had no right to stop her, as all the car's lights were on, and she was not speeding. While writing her the ticket for littering, the policeman tells her that he had "cause" and that his stopping her was, therefore, a proper exercise of his authority. Jane might plead (now in a much less assertive fashion) that the officer should just give her a warning since he obviously had discretion to exercise his right of issuing a ticket. The officer may be swayed by such arguments, and/or any flirtatious advances, but if Jane decides that more than an argument was needed to "persuade" the officer, she becomes eligible for arrest on a criminal charge.

Finally, we talk about rights in still another context, i.e., when we want to emphasize certain *desiderata* that we consider particularly important. The Universal Declaration of Human Rights reads in one of its provisions:

> Everyone has the right to a standard of living adequate for the health and well-being of himself and his family, including food, clothing, housing and medical care and necessary social services, and the right to security in the event of unemployment, sickness, disability, widowhood, old age or lack of livelihood in other circumstances beyond his control.[10]

What is striking in this formulation is the discrepancy between the specificity of the demands (care in the case of widowhood) and the total lack of a determination of who the duty-bearers are. While such a determination does not seem always necessary – *vide* the case of *in rem* rights – the difference between the claims advanced here and *in rem* rights is that the duties imposed on the not-specified group are merely negative in the latter case. In other words, these rights can be fulfilled by the duty-bearers without any particular efforts on their part. This distinction gave rise to the conceptualization of positive vs. negative rights. Although I shall argue below that it is less useful than usually assumed, it is nevertheless true that, when certain social structures are already in place, negative rights do not necessitate further organizational efforts.

The above examples, illustrating some of the major points in the present rights debate, are helpful in clarifying several issues. *First*, it should be clear that although rights impose duties, duty is the wider concept. The "no litter" ordinance, for example, clearly establishes duties without providing Joe with a right. As Joel Feinberg reminds us, "the word duty has come to be used for any action understood to be required, whether by the rights of others, or by law, or by higher authority, or by conscience, or whatever."[11] The *second* observation concerns the construal of rights from comprehensive duties. It creates the puzzles we observed in the fourth formulation of the Kantian categorical imperative. It seems that such a position misunderstands the distinctive nature and functioning of rights within the discourse on grievances. This leads me to a *third* important distinction, i.e., what *is* right vs. *having* a right. Claims that something *is* right, i.e., the right thing to do, make necessary the giving of reasons and invites challenges on the basis of intersubjectively shared standards. *Having a right* means that such challenges need not be entertained by the right-holder and, that in doing so, he/she is not committing a wrong. If some rightful owner of $10 decides to buy a racy magazine or a lottery ticket instead of saving the money or giving it to charity, we might criticize him on a variety of grounds, but he can quickly rebut our arguments by "standing on his rights." Having a right, therefore, means having discretion of how to exercise it, even when this entails doing "the wrong thing." Rights, therefore, not only confer entitlements belonging to the right-holder at his discretion, they are also "bars" to interferences and to arguments made against certain types of actions on moral and/or utilitarian grounds.

The latter point is of particular importance in the case of certain fundamental rights, such as our civil liberties, which bar the government from interfering with our exercise of free speech, for instance. The important thing is that the exercise of these rights cannot be abridged or defeated by simple consideration of the general benefit, or of "society's" right to order and predictability. As Ronald Dworkin points out:

> It is true that we speak of the right of a society to do what it wants, but this cannot be a competing right of the society that it might justify the invasion of a right against the Government. The existence of rights against the Government would be jeopardized if the Government were able to defeat such a right by appealing to the right of a democratic majority to work its will . . . We must distinguish the rights of the majority as such, and the personal rights of members of a majority, which may well count.[12]

Thus, although the issue of balancing rights might arise under certain circumstances, such an activity is not a simple weighing of competing goods, called individual freedom vs. social benefits, and of making sure that the greatest amount of overall utility is thereby safeguarded. The proper balance, according to Dworkin, involves rather complex assessments of competing *individual* rights. An example would be the freedom of association vs. that of equal protection under the law, which forbids exclusionary practices, for example, on the basis of race.[13]

While it is clear that individual rights cannot simply be defeated by invoking the right of the community, or the common weal (*salus publica*), it is also true that the rights of an artificial entity, be it a corporation or a state, cannot be conceptualized as the sum of

160

individual rights. Legal persons have rights *qua* subjects of law which are quite independent of those of the shareholders or citizens. Precisely because of the distinctiveness of the rights of the legal person, individual shareholders' claims that they have been wronged by actions against the corporation cannot be entertained by courts unless special circumstances, such as the demise of the legal person, allow for the lifting of the "corporate veil." Here, the decision of the I.C.J. in the *Barcelona Traction* case was only following the well-established practices in various domestic legal orders.[14] These considerations defeat, then, the often-made allegation that states cannot have distinct rights *qua* states, since states do not exist, but only people do. Aside from the fact that this inference seems to be based on the fallacy of misplaced concreteness, as far as the ascription of existential status to a phenomenon is concerned, it is also logically faulty. It assumes that attributes of a "whole" can only be those of the individual members, an error which amounts to a "fallacy of composition."[15] To that extent the controversy between Beitz and Walzer concerning the rights of states is somewhat of a red herring.[16] States have rights insofar as they are members of a practical association called the international community (legal order) which is based on the acceptance of common practices and the recognition of mutual rights. Furthermore, these rights, such as the right to carry on international relations, appoint ambassadors, make treaties, etc., cannot be construed as belonging to individuals who somehow have delegated these powers. Since nobody can delegate more rights or powers than he/she has, and since the rights mentioned are only part of the interactions of public legal bodies, such a construal of the rights of states in terms of rigorous individualism quickly runs into difficulties. To that extent, Justice Sutherland's dictum in *Curtiss Wright*, although stated in somewhat hyperbolic form and in regard to U.S. state-rights, rather than individual rights, makes the point eloquently:

> As a result of the separation from Great Britain by the Colonies, the powers of external sovereignty passed from the Crown not to the Colonies severally, but the colonies in their collective and corporate capacity as the United States of America . . . It results that the investment of the federal government with the powers of external sovereignty did not depend upon the affirmative grants of the Constitution. The powers to declare and wage war, to conclude peace, to make treaties, to maintain diplomatic relations with other sovereignties, if they had never been mentioned in the Constitution, would have been vested in the federal government as necessary concomitants of nationality.[17]

161

Similarly, the I.C.J. held in the *Western Sahara* advisory opinion that in order to establish the exercise of certain types of authority, proving thereby that the territory in question was not *terra nullius*, the display of activity need not resemble that of full-fledged states.[18] Thus, "peoples" (as here, nomadic tribes), may as collectivities be proper right-holders, at least in connection with issues of decolonization and self-determination. These rights, however, are neither those of a state nor those of individuals. The crucial criterion for judging whether an association has legal personality is therefore whether the "entity in question possesses in regard to its members rights which it is entitled to ask them to respect."[19]

III THE PRACTICE OF RIGHTS AND THE SHIFT FROM NATURAL LAW TO NATURAL RIGHTS

The upshot of the above discussion is that rights are very special devices for the creation and maintenance of social order. They are not simply prescriptions for regulating conduct by proscribing some actions. As H. L. A. Hart points out:

> The essential connection between the notion of right and the justified limitation of one person's freedom by another may be thrown into relief if we consider codes of behavior which do not purport to confer rights but only to prescribe what should be done . . . the Decalogue is perhaps the most important example . . . it would be a surprising interpretation of (the Ten Commandments) that treated them as conferring rights. In such an interpretation obedience to the Ten Commandments would have to be conceived as due to or owed to individuals, not merely God, and disobedience not merely as a wrong to (as well as harm to) individuals. The Commandments would cease to read like penal statutes designed only to rule out certain types of behavior and would have to be thought of as rules placed at the disposal of individuals and regulating the extent to which they may demand certain behavior from others.[20]

These observations have several corollaries. There is first, most obviously, the emphasis on *claiming* as the distinctive feature of rights. Rights are in this way typically conceived as possessed or owned by an individual or legal entity, and rights-thinking is often linked to the "possessive individualism" of modernity. However, even legal orders which do not have a term for a "right," such as the classical Greek tradition, nevertheless have the *notion*, or concept, of a right. After all, Greek law allowed suits to be brought by individuals against others and institutionalized explicitly the process of "claiming" through a

162

very explicit teaching of the "status," i.e., the procedural requirements in bringing claims.[21] Similarly, although the Digests of Roman law did not have our modern concepts of rights *in rem* or rights *in personam*, they carefully distinguished between *actiones*, i.e., legally valid causes for court action, in which suits *in rem* were treated differently from those which allowed for a claim *in personam*.[22] These examples show that in spite of the lack of a clear terminology the concept of a right which has to be "exercised," i.e., requires activation by the right-holder, is not unknown to these legal orders.

The emphasis on the process of claiming as a particularly significant dimension of rights also makes it clear why rights do not coincide with any of the normative types investigated in the previous chapters. Rights are not simply rules but complex composites which attain their meaning not from the concept of rule and norm alone, but rather from the *speech act* of claiming. The complex interaction between different types of rules in admitting and institutionalizing right-claims has been examined by Flathman. An argument for a legal right, he points out, not only

> presupposes and builds upon semantic rules that determine the generic features of the entity one is arguing for in a right . . . it also presupposes the concept of regulation-type rules that define the obligations, no-rights, and so on that correlate with rights. It . . . presupposes precept-type rules such as "Laws should be respected" as well as the possibility of defining constitutive rules that determine what counts as an exercise of the proposed right (voting!). Here the person who says I have a right to X is counting on the fact that this audience will be familiar with rules of these types and will understand what his contention implies, namely the addition of an authorization-type rule (decree) and the necessary regulations and constitutive rules. The sort of utterances we are considering is also used when a speaker believes that an authorization for X is established but in another realm or at another level of discourse . . . for example in a federal system where a right established at one level of government might be proposed at another.[23]

Although rights are intrinsically linked to a practice, they themselves cannot be understood as simple practice-type rules. Practice-type rules are, as we have seen, *constitutive* of a particular activity, such as a game. But while, for example, the rules of soccer regulate certain forbearances, such as not touching the ball with a hand, or not tackling another player unless he is in possession of the ball, they do not confer rights. If Smith fouls Jones and the referee does not see the foul or lets the game continue (because of the "advantage" rule), Jones may protest, but he has no claim against Smith, or the referee, which would allow him to appeal the latter's wrong decision. Moral or legal rights and duties, on the other hand, as Samuel Stoljar reminds us, do allow for

> questions as to their respective reasons, which is why we can treat them as *prima facie* or why they can be overridden or qualified. But rules of games cannot accommodate such qualifications precisely because questions of this sort would defeat the whole purpose of the games as they would interrupt, or at least inordinately delay, the very progress of the activity, including its being finalized in due course by one party winning, the other losing.[24]

In addition, we have to note that rights can be created by a variety of rule-types, such as decrees and practices. An example of the latter category, often taken as the paradigmatic case of rights *per se*, is a right acquired through a contract or promise. The conferral of rights through decree can be seen in the case where the public authority lowers or increases the age requirement for receiving social security benefits, thereby increasing or diminishing the number of eligible recipients.

With these points in mind, we can now return to the appraisal of the shift from a natural law to a natural rights discourse. Here, Hobbes provides us with a convenient starting-point. His work shows not only a curious mixture of natural right and natural law thinking, but also provides a good example for a further clarification of one special type of right: powers.

Hobbes's argument for the necessity of the establishment of public authority is intimately connected with the problem of the enforcement of individual rights. Particularly, the issue of sequential performance of contracts attracted Hobbes's attention, as we have seen. Strangely enough, the enforcing sovereign remains, however, in a state of war with the rest of society. In other words, no rights can be claimed against the sovereign.[25] This does not mean that the sovereign can do no wrong, as Hobbes is careful to point out; it only means that no right can be claimed against that sovereign. Relying on the biblical incident in which David, after killing Uriah, confesses to God, "To thee only I have sinned," Hobbes approves such a conception of law and order.[26] For superior–inferior relations, i.e., those between private persons and public authorities, only the old language of right and wrong is allowed, not that of *having a right*. Such a conceptualization of the role of the sovereign, very close to that of the umpire in a game, is all the more astonishing as, in accordance with the psychological tenets of Hobbes's theory, a sovereign in the state of nature is the least likely person or institution to possess the decisive qualifications of an umpire: impartiality, restraint, and fairness in the exercise of his/her powers.

In order to understand better the exercise of governmental powers, let us go back to the example of the policeman and his discretion in issuing a ticket. Both rights and authority (or power) give the holder an advance permission to interfere in certain ways with the plans of others. However, powers are different from rights in that they do not belong to the person but to the *office* or position.[27] This means that the power-holder is answerable to his/her superiors, to whom he/she also owes a duty. Thus, again differently from rights, where right-holder and duty-holder are different persons, rights which authorize, i.e. "powers," vest duties in the *same* person. Furthermore, a power-holder's duty is to enforce the performance of duties by the other duty-holders, or to prevent others from interfering with another person's rights.

The last-mentioned point has the following corollary: rights differ from powers also in that rights do not entitle their holders to issue commands or rules requiring third parties to behave in a certain way. However, it is this capacity that represents a particularly important dimension of power and authority. Finally, while both rights and powers confer discretion on the right-holder, the exercise of an official power-holder's right does not – or rather *must* not – depend upon his/her assessment that a particular action covered by his/her power is beneficial to him/her as a person. This requirement explains why attempts at influencing an official's exercise of discretion by means other than pleas is considered illegal. We not only expect office-holders to execute faithfully the laws which confer power upon them; in addition, we expect the exercise of the discretionary rights to be bounded by consideration of the common good. Office-holders have therefore to swear oaths of office, while nobody exercising his/her rights is bound by such communal considerations. The peculiar quality of "powers" becomes clear also when we think of circumstances which can defeat various claims. While it is not sufficient to defeat a right by demonstrating that the community would be better served if the action "X," protected by a right (such as, for instance, free speech), were to be disallowed, the discretion of an exercise of power given to an administrative official can sometimes be challenged on those grounds. Often the more specific authorizations are preceded by general formulas indicating the purposes and goals for which the power is conferred. To that extent an astute observer of American administrative law correctly pointed out that the function of administrative law is

165

increasingly not limited to the protection of private autonomy but concerns rather the establishment of a surrogate political process which ensures the fair representation of a wide range of affected interests in the process of administrative decisions.[28]

If the public official is not only a power-holder, but a power-holder of a special kind such as a judge, we expect, aside from impartiality and a commitment to the common good, a particularly strict observance of rules in arriving at a decision. To that extent, judicial "discretion" is bounded not only by the general requirements of fairness in respect to the parties' pleadings but also by a particular style in arriving at a decision.

There remains the discussion of the concepts of *immunities* within the conceptual boundaries drawn by rights. Although immunities are often likened to powers, it should be clear that the term "power" is used in this context rather metaphorically. Immunities are actually specific *exemptions* from otherwise well-established duties, such as the exemption of foreign diplomats and consuls (in differies degrees) from the *jurisdiction* of the host country. Immunities are therefore quite different from powers as discussed. Although notions such as extraterritoriality and inviolability have often been used in order to describe the status of foreign envoys and the off-limits character of foreign embassies,[29] something much more prosaic is involved: the exemption from the jurisdiction of the host country is established either *ratione materiae*, in the case of consuls, or *ratione personae*, in the case of envoys.[30] These distinctions are not of academic interest only, as the Iranian hostage case shows. If the embassy had been truly U.S. territory, then an attack on it would have justified measures of self-defense, rather than the remedies provided for in the Vienna Convention.[31] Although the United States finally *did* use force in order to rescue the hostages, such an operation was not, and could not have been, justified under the "inherent right of self defense" of the Charter.

IV LIBERTIES, INVIOLABLE RIGHTS, AND MANIFESTO CLAIMS

The discussion of the special character of governmental powers indicated to what extent the rights discourse differs significantly from previous conceptions. It is precisely the conferral of an explicit claiming capacity to individuals vis-à-vis their government which distinguishes modern (natural) rights-thinking from the older conception of natural law. Since the exercise of powers is subject to the consent of the governed, individuals can claim rights not only against others, but vis-à-vis the public authority. Such a theory fundamentally alters the conceptions of the role of government in a community. While the preservation of peace and justice had always been the traditional task of public authority, it is the embedding of these functions within a framework of rights that leads to constitutionalism. The *historical* transformation can be clearly seen in the shift away from the pre-occupation with the establishment of authority, characteristic of seventeenth-century theorists (Hobbes to Grotius and Pufendorf), to the liberal theories of Locke and other eighteenth-century writers. *Conceptually* this shift can be traced when we focus on the prominence of two important classes of rights during that period, i.e., on liberties, and on inalienable rights.

In order to clarify the concept of "liberties," consider the right to free speech, but also the, at first, somewhat ridiculous right to sing in the bathtub and the right of self-defense. One important peculiarity of this class of rights seems to be that technically, at least the last two do not seem to imply a duty on anybody's part. Nevertheless, even the right to sing in the bathtub, or the right to scratch my head, are

> rights which, though themselves unaccompanied by any duties or claims against, nevertheless presuppose correlative rights and duties; they presuppose prior normative relationships which dutiless rights can fasten on.[32]

Furthermore, although it has been customary to call these rights "liberties" in the Hohfeldian sense, the above remarks make it clear that they are not really dutiless since they impose even on governmental agencies positive obligations such as to insure that my right is not interfered with by any other member of society.

The right of self-defense provides still another peculiarity in that it seems to entitle the right-holder to protect him/herself, while not imposing a specific duty on those against whom this right is exercised. It provides, rather, a valid defense for a defendant in case the attacker is injured and raises an issue. "This right so attributed to B cannot be described as a normal claim against A, but it can be described as a claim in which B is affirming that, given the clear and present danger created by A, he (B) may do things he would be under a duty not to do otherwise."[33] The right to self-defense has been called "inherent"[34] because, like the Hobbesian right of nature, it establishes and protects the basic notion that individuals are to be free in their pursuit of satisfying their interests and to not interfere with, or harm, others in doing so. Flathman is right when he argues that

Hobbes' right of nature is not a right at all – whether in the Hohfeldian sense of a liberty or any other. It is a principle or precept that can be employed in reasoning about rights of the several kinds that have developed in our moral and legal practice.[35]

Here the similarity of Hobbes's rights of nature and Pufendorf's laws of nature become obvious. Both are *constitutive principles* of what we called above the discourse on grievances, establishing the practice in which the assertion of specific "rights" figures prominently.

It should not be surprising either why the assertion of rights becomes over time more important than the older and competing conceptualizations of natural law. Precisely because the latter was either wedded to a particular ontology or to revelation, it made sense only as long as reason was considered a *cognitive* source for the universal recognition of what *is* right (not *having* a right). As soon as it was shown that natural rights, like moral principles in general, are a matter neither of simple intuition nor cognition, the assertion of claims in terms of "it is right that" lost much of its persuasive power. Validity-claims had now to be backed by different "reasons," and it is in this context that the privilegization of certain claims through their recognition as positive rights attained importance. In other words, claims to validity were internalized by the legal order, as pointed out in chapter 1. The usual distaste of positivism for being drawn into a debate to what extent rights are founded on a conception of what *is* right attests to this fundamental shift.

In spite of the conceptual distinction between having a right and the assertions of what is right, much of the persuasiveness of manifesto rights, i.e., those claims not (yet) legally privileged and enforced, derives from a shared notion of what *is* right. Thus, the construal of certain welfare rights (human rights) of the have-nots against those who have is obviously connected with, and derives much of its force from, the argument that an unequal distribution of goods, for example, on the international level of 12:1, *is not* right.[36]

A second connection between conceptions of what is right and the rights-discourse can be seen in that the constitutive principles of this discourse have to be construed as "inalienable" rights. To the extent that these rights limit the freedom of the right-holders in exercising their rights at their pleasure, the concept of inalienable rights is therefore quite at odds with the voluntaristic conception of rights as discretionary "possessions." Originally, though, both the natural-law school and the early natural-rights theory stayed closer to the paradigmatic examples of doing the "right thing" or "possessing" a right. They begrudgingly allowed contracts such as selling oneself into

168

slavery in order to save one's life,[37] although the respective emphasis and justification are quite different in each case. For the natural-law argument, slavery is clearly the "lesser" evil and thus such contacts can be upheld on the basis of what is right. For liberal theorists, "having" a right also implied that the "owner" could dispose of his/her life and liberty according to his/her own preference.[38] It was only Rousseau who showed the incompatibility of the rights discourse with the notion of voluntary servitude. Precisely because the discourse on rights and grievances presupposes as a constitutive principle the equal freedom of the (contracting) subjects, the notion of selling one's liberty became conceptually an impossible construction:

> To renounce one's liberty is to renounce one's quality as a man, the rights and also the duties of humanity. For him who renounces everything, there is no possible compensation. Such a renunciation is incompatible with man's nature, for to take away all freedom from his will is to take away all morality from his actions. In short, a convention which stipulates absolute authority on the one side and unlimited obedience on the other is vain and contradictory. Is it not clear that we are under no obligation whatsoever towards a man from whom we have a right to demand everything? And does not this single condition, without equivalent, without exchange, involve the nullity of the act?[39]

Here we can see how the logic of the institution of rights led to the slow, but nevertheless total, revision of the Grotian or Spanish conception of natural law.

The evolution of the idea of inalienable rights which constrains the members' freedom of contract finally came to its logical conclusion only in the second half of this century, when the international legal order modified the conception of the absolute freedom of contract among states. The adoption of the notion of peremptory norms of international law (*ius cogens*)[40] in the Vienna convention on Treaties limits, in the same way as Rousseau's notion quoted above, a state's capacity to contract.[41] Strangely enough, these injunctions do not diminish a state's power to decide upon its dissolution or to be dismembered or extinguished.[42] But since, of course, states are not natural persons and our practice of claiming rights developed in the context of individual rights, the extension to other spheres via analogous reasoning cannot be perfect.

Given the success of "rights" as a means of securing recognition and respect for claims, it is only natural that a whole host of *desiderata* and interests are voiced as right-claims. Although interests alone are insufficient to create rights – precisely because rights are particularly well-protected demands which enjoy a social recognition that interests alone lack – the whole history of rights as a practice of claiming and establishing entitlements shows that neither the type nor the amount of rights is static. After the recognition of *in personam* and *in rem* rights came the struggle for the protection of basic liberties in the eighteenth century-political movements. To this extent, the emergence of claims for the redistribution of the global product in terms of minimum or basic rights proceeds according to a certain logic.[43] Nevertheless, the Universal Declaration's insistence on two weeks of paid vacation shows an overextension of right-claims.[44] Conventional rights-theorists resisted the expansion of the notion of rights to welfare claims on the basis of the distinction between positive and negative rights. Particularly in the case of guaranteeing certain "basic rights," such as a minimum level of nutrition worldwide, visions of staggering financial costs are invoked to justify the withholding of legal protection from these claims. Although it is quite clear that "manifesto rights," such as the right to food, are considerably less rooted in our practice of rights than traditional liberties, the conventional explanation suffers from several defects.

First, as the calculations of Wassily Leontieff have shown, even a worldwide guarantee of a right to subsistence (food) might be feasible and far from involving staggering costs.[45] Second, it is one of the most amazing myopias created by the liberal paradigm that "no-rights" corresponding to liberties, or even *in rem* rights, are viewed as "cost-less," i.e., their respective duties are supposed to be taken care of by nonaction of others. This is all the more astonishing in that anybody living in New York – or any American city for that matter – spends a considerable sum in reinforcing doors, procuring additional locks, and placing steel bars in front of his/her windows, in order to guarantee the "noninterference" of others. The costs of law enforcement, from police to jails and various correction programs, need not be belabored in this context. Similarly, the astronomical expense of national defense, which people apparently are quite willing to bear for their supposedly "costless" rights, stands in sharp contrast to the widely accepted allegations about the costliness of programs securing minimum standards by guaranteeing subsistence rights. Although the connection between hypertrophic defense costs and world poverty have not been overlooked, one has indeed to go rather far to the margins in international relations (and to a certain extent in rights) analysis[46] before one finds a challenge to these dominant assumptions.

While the argument about the costs and the nature of negative and positive rights is obviously faulty, providing for welfare rights *does* in a way differ from the guarantee of either liberties or *in rem* rights. The main difference is that the costs for the protection of the latter rights are directly connected with establishing and maintaining a functioning community. They involve, therefore, problems of providing *public goods*, which have at least a semblance to the nonrivalry criterion.[47] Welfare rights, on the other hand, are conceivable only *after* and *in addition to* the payments for the public goods. Nevertheless, there are obvious trade-offs possible which the conventional analysis neglects. Thus, as has been pointed out – tongue in cheek – sending someone to jail might be as expensive as sending him/her to Harvard or Yale.

V THE COMMUNITARIAN ASPECT OF RIGHTS

The discussion in the previous section of positive vs. negative rights as well as of manifesto claims brought to the fore two inter-related problems. One is the substantive extension of right-claims to areas not yet enjoying the protection accorded to rights; the other is the conferral of rights to new benefit-holders who are not claimants themselves. The last problem in turn raises the issue of the role of the "community" with respect to rights; it is ordered either not to interfere any further with the exercise of certain rights or to provide the means necessary in upholding such right-claims.

The thesis espoused here, that all right-claims have a communitarian dimension, might seem strange to those of us who are accustomed to view rights as something like a possession which individuals "bring" to society. But the notion that one leaves the state of nature with his/her rights, like people who come to a hotel with their suitcases in hand, is erroneous. This conception of rights has not only been criticized by Rousseau in his arguments against a natural right to a certain "pre-societally" acquired property,[48] but is also inconsistent with the notion of right itself. Even when we agree that certain rights are basic, natural or fundamental, and thus can be formulated as demands *against* society, the idea that this fundamental character has to be conceptu-alized as a presocietal right results from a myopia. A clarification of these issues will therefore be useful for understanding better certain aspects of welfare (basic or subsistence rights) and manifesto claims, particularly in the context of redistributive demands in the interna-tional arena. I shall begin the discussion with two extensions of right-claims to third parties not part of the claiming process, and then discuss manifesto claims which involve redistributive features in the name of "human rights."

Claiming rights on behalf of temporarily incapacitated or infirm members of a community who cannot actively participate in the claiming process is the least problematic extension of the practice of rights. In a similar vein, the extension of this beneficial protection of rights to children raises few issues save on the margins. Precisely because rights become operative only in a discursive community, defending the rights of future members of such a community can be construed as basic, or constitutive of the rights-practice itself. How far "back" this protection is to be extended has, however, been one of the most controversial issues, as evidenced by the abortion debate. Whatever conviction we might have on this point, it is important to remember that, even under the holding of *Roe* v. *Wade*, the right to have an abortion was not based on the conception of one's body as one's own "private property." Explicitly rejecting this latter argument, Justice Blackmun stated:

> In fact, it is not clear to us that the claim asserted by some amici that one has an unlimited right to do with one's body as one pleases bears a close relationship to the right of privacy previously articulated in the Court's decisions. The Court refused to recognize an unlimited right of this kind in the past.[49]

And in summarizing the holdings of the case, Blackmun writes for the majority:

> We repeat . . . that the State does have an important and legitimate interest in preserving and protecting the health of the pregnant woman . . . and that it still has *another* [italics in the original] important and legitimate interest in protecting the potentiality of human life. These interests are separate and distinct. Each grows in substantiality as the woman approaches term and, at a point during pregnancy, each becomes "compelling."[50]

What is important in this context is not only the explicit recognition of the duty to protect the potentiality of human life, but also the communitarian dimension of the *right to privacy* and to one's own body, which is quite at odds with the extreme libertarian or individualistic interpretation of the *amicus* brief.

This argument has important implications for the justification of subsistence rights. Since the surpluses in most societies are privately owned, the owners in all likelihood will be disinclined to share their wealth beyond some type of "charitable" contribution they might be ready to make. The poor, they might argue, have to be left to their own devices, as unfortunate as this might be, because to impose a duty on others diminishes the others' freedom. But, as Samuel Stoljar reminds us:

172

> What such views overlook . . . is that freedom does not belong to an individual in the same way as his eyes and ears belong to him; freedom rather is a right that appertains to a community-belonging individual since . . . it is only as an equal member of a community that he can argue to be let alone by other members of the same community . . . The poor man's claim thus comes from within the community which alone enables rights to exist at all – or more precisely, to be advanced as arguments – including the rights which attribute freedom or separateness to an individual. Outside a community an individual would be no more or no less free than his own physical capacities would guarantee him; only within a community as an equal individual amongst other such individuals can he make a claim, whether to freedom or to some assistance.[51]

It is precisely because rights as claims are not self-executory, but dependent upon a performance, that certain fundamental rights and obligations are generated by this *claiming process itself*. Not only are access and equality among the claimants necessary, but even "negative rights" such as rights of noninterference might require positive action on the part of the community so as to create an equal opportunity for right-claims.

It is on the basis of this "performance" requirement, intrinsic to the rights-practice, that the case for subsistence-rights can be made. Unless we are ready and willing to exclude certain people from the claims process and dissolve the notion of a community in which the pursuit of one's interests is guided and protected by law, all members of the community must be at least potentially effective participants in this practice. Without such an assumption there remains only repression since, as Rousseau pointed out in the quote above, we cannot expect rightless persons to honor the obligations imposed upon them by those enjoying the protection of rights. In return, the community can insist, however, that those receiving aid become, as soon as possible, fully autonomous members of the community, asserting their rights on their own and contributing their share to furthering mutual benefits. This does not entail altruistic actions, since as Adam Smith reminds us, "it is not from the benevolence of the builder, the brewer, or the baker that we expect our dinner but from their regard to their own interest."[52] Nevertheless such an attitude *does* entail an obligation to exercise one's abilities and make a contribution to the common life.

From the above argument it seems also to follow that further justifications become necessary when rights are vested in animals or inanimate objects which cannot become claimants *in principle* but whose protection we seek to assure. In the case of animals we can at

173

least still fasten on the concept of their "interests" such as that of not being subjected to cruel treatment.[53] The protection of natural beauty or of objects representing particular achievements of our cultural heritage, on the other hand, is assimilated to the practice of rights only with great difficulty. If rights are involved at all in these cases and not just invoked for propagandistic purposes, it is the protection of the rights of *those who want to lay claim to the enjoyment of unspoiled nature* or to the preservation of works of art rather than the rights of the objects themselves which is at issue.

The interpretation of rights stressing their communitarian aspect seems to be inconsistent with one very important function of our rights-talk: the assertion of fundamental rights irrespective of their recognition by any particular community. Claims to "human rights" not only stress rights against a community as an important aspect of the use of a right in making and justifying demands, but insist that particular communities have to give effect to, and institutionalize the protection of, these human rights. Thus, because of its independence from actual recognition, we can understand why the concept of "human rights" is often represented as a *presocietal* notion. Actually, there is no contradiction in arguing for the communitarian dimensions of rights while keeping in mind that part of the function of human rights is to serve as a particularly emphatic demand for the social (positive) recognition of certain claims. If the meaning of "community" is not taken in the sense of a concrete society but refers to the transcendental presuppositions of communication among independent actors engaged in a practice of claiming, the term "right" *is* independent of its actual recognition by any particular social order. This fact, however, does not warrant the conclusion of the presocietal nature of the rights claimed.

These considerations, in turn, throw into sharper relief the varying force of different manifesto claims. Insofar as the relevant community is "humanity" in general, very few right-claims can be made. However, these claims are decisive and strong. To that extent, human rights provide important yardsticks for the evaluation and criticism of concrete regimes. For example, denying someone access to the claiming process itself, on the basis of arbitrary criteria, is a fundamental violation of human rights; not fulfilling the obligations correlative to a right to paid vacations is not, although such a denial might violate municipal law.

From the above argument it also becomes clear that claims for human rights are first and foremost claims to and against *concretely established social entities*, since humanity itself is not constituted as a

174

concrete community. In other words, the participants who have established a society, and within it the social practice of claiming rights, can most properly use these manifesto claims.[54] If we grant this point then an important corollary follows: it does not seem contradictory to argue for universal human rights without deriving from such claims equally universal duties for definite persons beyond the actual community. Our discussion shows why this is so. Since rights are *prima facie* claims, the actual establishment of correlative duties is always mediated by some additional principles. Even within the moral discourse something like the principle of "subsidiarity" is needed in order to establish concrete duties as long as the existence of autonomous groups with their own rights is granted. This principle not only limits the correlative duties to certain identifiable duty-bearers, but is also an important way in which the autonomy of groups can be defended against paternalistic or even worse encroachments. Furthermore, it serves as an insurance that these groups become "responsible" – although thereby not necessarily responsive – right- and duty-bearers.

On a more concrete level, i.e., when the community or audience for right-claims is no longer humanity itself, but a concrete social group in which the claiming process has been institutionalized, issues of conflicting rights have to be settled through a variety of additional principles. Thus, it is usually not sufficient to jump from the assertion of even a recognized right to the conclusion that other bystanders are thereby necessarily duty-bearers. After all, not all rights function like *in rem* claims, and many additional principles and rules are necessary in order to decide concrete conflicts. Thus, my claims to property might be overridden by claims to eminent domain, and my right to be protected from bodily harm, by the duty to serve in the armed forces; my right of free movement might be restricted because of a protest march, or because fire-fighters block the passage through several streets.

Connected with these considerations is the following issue: every society must decide how various risks are to be allocated. Rights, because of their connection with the claiming process, provide, therefore, an ideal way of doing just this by restricting the number of potential claimants through providing only for certain actionable "causes." Even if manifesto or actual rights have been infringed upon, people cannot be protected from all injuries, and part of the legal proceeding is precisely to establish whether the *prima facie* claim shall stand or can be overriden.

Consider in this context the *caveat emptor* rule, which puts the

175

responsibility squarely on the side of the purchaser and significantly limits his "causes" and claims. Liability rules, although recognizing the infringement on the rights of others, do not leave the determination of the "corresponding duty" to the right-holder but to a neutral third party; here we have incidentally a clear instance of rights in search of correlative duty-bearers. Not only may the proof that the tortfeasor exercised "due care" establish his nonliability, but the "amount" of the duty and to how many duty-bearers it extends (insurance, the corporation, its officers) cannot simply be derived from the notion of a right. Similarly, different questions of "causality," for instance, who caused a particular accident, limit or expand the range of duty-bearers. Finally, policy considerations may be determinative of whether a claim can be brought, even when it is quite clear that a potential claimant's rights had been detrimentally affected. Issues of "standing" become decisive here.[55]

It is through such devices that right-claims which are inferred from a violation of duties are kept in check.[56] Consider in this context human rights-claims protected by international agreements. Here the "standing" issue is usually subject to an affirmative decision of whether the treaty is self-executing.[57] The history of the case *Fuji* v. *California*[58] is instructive. It concerned the racially discriminatory Alien Land Law of California. The plaintiff had challenged the law in question on the basis of its incompatibility with the U.N. Charter (Articles 55 & 56) to which the U.S. had become party and which, as a ratified treaty, had become the supreme law of the land. The holding for the plaintiff by the lower court caused a national uproar, gave impetus to efforts to pass a constitutional amendment (Bricker Amendment), and was overruled by the California Supreme Court. Significantly enough, the Appeals Court too struck down the Alien Land Law but did so on the basis of the equal protection clause of the Constitution, rather than on the basis of Articles 55 and 56 of the U.N. Charter. Noting that the U.N. Charter was not a self-executing treaty, Judge Gibson of the California Supreme Court held that "the fundamental provisions in the Charter pledging cooperation in promoting observance of fundamental freedoms lacks the mandatory quality and definiteness which would indicate an intent to create a justifiable right in private persons immediately upon ratification."[59]

Similarly, in the recent *Tel-Oren* decision,[60] the U.S. Court of Appeals (District of Columbia) narrowly circumscribed rights under international law, even if backed by domestic statutes. The plaintiffs in this case were the survivors and relatives of victims of a P.L.O. terrorist attack in Israel. They had sued under Section 1350 of the Alien Tort statute[61] for damages to be paid out of P.L.O. assets here in the U.S. The court took jurisdiction, but held that international law did not provide individuals with a "cause of action," i.e., did not directly vest individuals with rights that could serve as a basis for the plaintiffs' tort claims.

Even if we do not agree with the holding of the last case – particularly since different Appeals Courts have held in similar cases for the plaintiff[62] – several things are worth noting. There is, above all, again the recognition of the intimate connection between a right and a *cause for action* which transforms an inchoate (moral) claim into a socially recognized right. Second, it is clear that in deciding issues of rights, courts take into consideration a whole variety of factors, including the constitutive principles of the community and its constitutional order. Thus, contrary to Dworkin, private right-claims can be, and often are, defeated by general political considerations and not only by other private rights. In *U.S.* v. *Pink*[63] the Court overruled objections that the execution of the Litvinov assignment would deprive individuals of their rights under the Fifth Amendment and the special guarantees of the State of New York. The reasons given for this decision turned nearly exclusively on policy considerations concerning the overriding foreign relations powers of the Federal government (President).

However, such policy considerations are by no means limited to cases in which international legal questions play an important role. Consider, for instance, the whole problem of avoiding decisions because of "political questions."[64] Furthermore, let us also remember that the most convenient way for the Supreme Court to avoid hard choices in cases of conflicting rights is the simple denial of *certiorari*.[65] Even more vaguely articulated standards, such as "ripeness," can be invoked in order to justify a nondecision, and that means leaving the individual with no remedy. Justice Powell relied in his reasoning in *Goldwater* v. *Carter*[66] (concurring opinion) on this ripeness criterion in order to justify the refusal of the Court to decide the merits of the case. Senator Goldwater had claimed that his constitutional rights had been abridged by President Carter's renunciation of the U.S. defense treaty with Taiwan without the advice and consent of the senate.

There remain two further interrelated points concerning the functions of rights. The first is that many conventional rights-analyses are not sufficiently sensitive to capturing esssential dimensions of rights beyond the immediate claim process. Thus, the idea that rights simply "exist," and that we need only some additional principle of distribution according to which the enjoyment of a society's goods can be decided, is misconceived. Precisely because rights not only decide who

177

is to enjoy what types of freedoms and goods, but because they also create fundamental *incentive* systems for the *production* of societal goods, we cannot allocate all rights once and for all on the basis of a few basic distributive principles. To that extent the problem of "justice" in a society is somewhat more complicated than handing people the goods, as if the latter were readily available on a shelf and needed only to be distributed by philosophers or others armed with the veil of ignorance.

The second point is that we have to recognize the norm-generating capacity of fundamental rights, i.e., their role in spelling out in concrete detail the actual obligations. Thus fundamental, or human, rights not only work on the level of political rhetoric, where they serve as powerful arguments in favor of particular pieces of legislation, but they are generative in the adjudicative process as well. Obviously verbal and justificatory arguments within the public debates will differ depending on whether one wants to add a new right to a well-established set of claims, favors the establishment of a new practice, or considers fundamental changes in the ascription of rights. In the case where rights are well established, claims to rights can be built on the general precept that rights ought to be respected. "If a claimant succeeds in linking his particular claim with this general precept, he is well on his way to having his claim accepted, even if such a link is premature in terms of the actual practice of the society."[67] Similarly, the invocation of human rights in the adjudicative process provides powerful justification for changing well-entrenched precedents, an issue that will be addressed in chapter 8 below.

VI CONCLUSION

The examination of the notion of right in this chapter began with the discussion of various examples in which the term "right" played a crucial part. Fundamental to the argument was a distinction between the uses of "it is right that" vs. "having a right." Furthermore, the examples in section III provided a cursory treatment of various types of rights discussed throughout the chapter. My analysis of rights did not follow the standard conceptual distinctions between negative and positive rights, or a strict correlativity theory of rights and duties, precisely because these distinctions are often of dubious value. For this reason I focused the first discussion on the problem of who can be a right-holder. From there, the issue of correlative duties and its dependence on the type of right and of conditions of the defeasibility of right-claims was investigated further.

In section III, the fundamental distinction between "it is right that" and "having a right" was further elaborated, and its historical root was found in the shift from natural-law to a natural-rights discourse in the seventeenth century. While the rights discourse has clearly been in the ascendancy ever since, two important observations could be made. First, the original "natural rights" are of a peculiar nature in that their logic requires them to remain inalienable. This property sets them apart from the paradigmatic cases of rights, conceived as in personam- or in rem-claims. Natural rights, like the laws of nature, are, therefore, fundamental in that they are constitutive of a discourse in which claims can be examined and their validity can be established.

Second, these historical reflections also showed that legal orders which do not possess special terms for the notion of a right, such as, for example, ancient Greece, nevertheless possess the "concept" of rights since they allow for the assertion of claims on the basis of equality and noncoerciveness. Finally, on account of the fact that the assertion of a claim is paradigmatic for the concept of a right – exemplified by the different "causes" of action in Roman law – speech-act theory proved helpful for further analysis of this claiming practice. It showed why rights do not coincide with any particular rule-type, as developed in previous chapters, and why rights are only possible when a practice of claiming has been well established and secured by a variety of norms in a society.

Section IV investigated a particular set of rights: liberties, powers, and immunities. The first two in particular become important within the discourse of rights during the eighteenth century. Since the guarantee of basic liberties entails not only the regulation of certain forbearances but the positive duty of the government to enforce these rights, the distinction between negative and positive duties lost much of its explanatory utility. A brief discussion of basic or subsistence rights followed, which provided the conceptual bridge to the discussion of the "communitarian aspects" of right-claims taken up in section V. Unlike the conventional way of conceiving of rights as something akin to personal property, a concept of rights rooted in speech-act theory provided us with a more coherent account of the basis for human rights. Finally, by the placing of the concept of rights within the practice of claiming, the function of right-claims in the moral, political, and legal discourse could be analyzed and their mutual interconnection could be established. This conceptualization also pointed to the norm-generative capacity of these fundamental rights within positive legal institutions.

These last remarks lead us to the problems of the next two chapters.

i.e., first, the question of a criterion that would allow us to distinguish clearly between "legal' and other types of rules and norms, and second, the problem of how natural-law precepts or human rights claims enter into judicial decision-making and thus into the process of law-creation and the elaboration of legal institutions.

7 THE QUESTION OF "LAW"

I INTRODUCTION

The discussion in the preceeding chapter addressed the role of norms when the actors' goals collide and a solution is sought through non-coercive means. By granting equal standing and consideration of each other's interest, by limiting the dispute to identifiable issues, by utilizing norms that satisfy the universalizability criterion, and by adopting the no-harm standard as a substantive principle, the parties deliberately bound the conflict and agreed on a method to resolve their grievances. Although the final distributional outcome is still indefinite, much has been achieved thereby; now only results based on argument and persuasion are considered legitimate. To that extent the "discourse on grievances" shows important similarities and dissimilarities to normal bargaining. Appeals to norms, precedents, "salience," etc., naturally can be – and usually are – part of the conventional bargaining process. What gives "bargaining" its peculiar characteristic, however, is the latent presence of coercion. Moves therefore oscillate widely, ranging from coercive to noncoercive measures. In the latter case the breaking of the opponent's will rather than the solution of specific issues becomes the main objective. It is this relegation of the original goal to a secondary position and the substitution of coercion for the competition over the scarce original object that changes the nature of the dispute.

Conversely, we see that norms not only transform conflicts by providing "standard" solutions which the parties can utilize if they so desire, but also structure the antagonism between the parties and regulate the pursuit of their respective interests. It is this transformational capacity which makes Barkun's argument concerning norms as *"implicit" third parties*[1] so important. The role of *"explicit"* third parties can be treated analogously to our discussion above concerning the context of norm-use. Various modes of third-party intervention in

181

disputes can be distinguished according to the mode of involvement (along the loose–firm continuum). In addition, it might be useful to add the distinction of "interest" and "disinterestedness" in order to understand the role of the third party's involvement.[2]

Since it is the task of this chapter to clarify the concept of third-party law which is usually – although incorrectly – identified with judicial activity, my argument will proceed in the following fashion. The next section is devoted to a discussion of various modes of third-party involvement, and the conceptual connection that exists between "second-party" and "third-party" law. As we have seen, the second-party mode is characterized by *ad hoc* resort to norms and rules (bargaining). It is therefore important to distinguish two-party situations from situations in which the two parties explicitly accept the normative guidance of rules in resolving their dispute. Cases of the latter kind would be instances of "third-party context" even in the absence of a concrete third-party with judicial or mediative functions. Conversely, not every third-party involvement needs to be one of third-party law. A hegemonic power which settles a dispute among its clients by "fiat" is rather an example of "first-party" than of "third-party" law. The categorization attempted here is obviously based on *ideal types*. This means, however, that in the real world actual controversies can exhibit certain features of both second- and third-party law or that concrete conflict situations can oscillate between different ideal types.

The reason for the conceptualization of law in terms of norm-*use*, i.e., modes of reasoning, will become clearer in section VI. There I shall argue that attempts at formulating an essentialist demarcation might be useful for distinguishing "law" from other norms and rules. But in order to drive home this point sections III and IV are designd to prove the deficiencies of the conventional distinctions between law and other prescriptions. In particular, section III examines the systemic concept of law through an interpretation of Hans Kelsen's and H. L. A. Hart's theories. Section IV does the same with the McDouglian "law as process approach." Section V deals, once again, with the problem of "soft law" and demonstrates that neither a policy-oriented perspective nor the other systemic jurisprudential approaches provide an adequate understanding of these phenomena. The examination of "soft law" then sets the stage for the discussion of "law" as a "style" of practical reasoning which is taken up in section VI. A short summary of the most important points in this chapter is provided in section VII.

182

II IMPLICIT AND EXPLICIT THIRD PARTIES: THE VARIOUS MODES OF INVOLVEMENT OF RULES AND NORMS

Most of the time we conceive of an explicit third party as a mediator or an impartial judge who applies preexisting rules and norms to a "case and controversy." In the former instance the solutions need not invoke preexisting rules and norms but can be phrased solely in terms of a mutual adjustment of interests by proposing a particular point located on the "possibility boundary," or by limiting or expanding the contract-zone through a variety of packages.[3] We can even imagine an extreme case in which the mediator is simply entrusted with making a decision which the parties have bound themselves to accept. In that case the mediator's role amounts to little more than being a decision mechanism very much like flipping a coin or drawing lots. Real-life cases are probably hard to find for this logical possibility since they would be instances of pure "decisionism." Usually, third parties are entrusted with settling disputes only when the contestants, at least tacitly, agree that the decision has to have references to the facts, interests, or rights of the parties involved, and/ or when the mediator has acquired some reputation for impartiality, wisdom, or charismatic legitimacy. But even such charismatic authority and prestige is linked to widely accepted although diffuse value-orientations which provide the framing conditions for the mediational effort.[4] Conversely, in most instances the third party is unlikely to forgo the advantage of explicitly invoking rules, norms, and principles even if he/she has the power to disregard them. After all, invoking shared norms increases the persuasive power of the award as well as the adherence of the parties and bystanders to the settlement. Thus, important commonalities seem to exist between the function of implicit and explicit third parties, and between mediational and judicial efforts.

Nevertheless, there are also important dissimilarities. Unlike the judicial mode, mediational efforts usually entail some type of information function by the mediator to provide the parties with indices of their relative power positions vis-à-vis each other.[5] Since "power" matters in such cases and facilitates settlement, the latter function obviously violates the equality principle constitutive of the discourse on grievances, as well as of the *judicial* mode of settlement. In addition, since the mediator is often virtually the only person who knows the preference-schedules of the actors, he becomes indispensable and acquires considerable power which he can use for his own purposes.[6]

The last remark emphasizes an important dimension which distinguishes the judge from the mediator. While strict impartiality is one of the preconditions for the effectiveness of the judicial mode of settling disputes, the mediator's own interests need not be a disabling factor, even if they are recognized by the contending parties. Although no mediator can allow himself to be viewed as biased, i.e., in favor of one of the parties, his own effectiveness depends on several factors other than the perception of pure impartiality. As long as the parties have the hope that the mediator can resolve the deadlock, which both parties fear; as long as they view the proposals as still being within the range of the contract zone and as moving toward the possibility boundary; and as long as they can reasonably expect that the mediator can deliver the opponent after a tentative agreement has been reached, the recognition of the mediator's own interests need not impair his position.

Nevertheless, the perception of the mediator's interests is likely to complicate the negotiation efforts, because it will create incentives for both parties to align their particular interest with that of the mediator and thereby pressure the opponent. If such attempts become too obvious the party "on the out" might prefer to withdraw, or escalate, by making proposals which might find the approval of the mediator but have little chance of being accepted by the other. The danger of this strategy is that bargaining moves increasingly away from the effort of resolving the dispute at hand to attempts to gain side-payments, i.e., a propaganda-success, the approval of the mediator, etc.[7] To a certain extent the tables have then been turned: the original reason for bringing in a mediator was the willingness of the participants to have a third party manipulate their preferences and provide a solution. Now, the "meta-game" is about manipulating the preferences *of the mediator*.

The short discussion above shows that the context of the third-party law, i.e., the role of norms in contexts in which rules and norms are applied to an existing controversy, is much more varied than usually assumed. Furthermore, it is also clear that the distinctions between second- and third-party law are often fluid. Even in cases in which the third party has official authority to end the dispute by deciding the case, rule-application remains to a large extent nested in a wider setting of shared standards which make persuasion possible. Thus, the Hobbesian argument that authority and not truth makes the law (*auctoritas non veritas facit legem*) needs modification. The importance of common understandings buttressing norms is obvious because an authoritative decision backed by certain reasons is quite different from either the case of decisionism mentioned above, or the dictatorial fiat. Figure 13 summarizes our discussion.

184

TYPE OF THIRD PARTY

| | Disinterested | | | Interested | |
	Implicit	Explicit		Implicit	Explicit
	I	II	III	IV	V
Loose	"Fair" negotiated settlement (marginal class)	Decisionism third party serves as a "mechanism" for choice	Mediation (principles and norms play a role, but so do other factors such as position of mediator)	Empty set	Hegemonic arm-twisting
	VI	VII	VIII	IX	X
Firm	Acceptance of a strictly legal solution (end of controversy – limiting case)	Arbitration (rules and norms provide firm guidance as applied by third party, but choice of norms and arbitrator up to parties)	Adjudication (judicial settlement)	(Norms of inequality – limiting case)	Imposition of a solution upon the contenders on the basis of norms

MODE OF INVOLVEMENT OF NORMS

Figure 13

A few explanatory remarks in regard to figure 13 are in order. First, the figure encompasses part of the third-party as well as first-party context. What we called above the "discourse on grievances" finds here a place in cells I, III, VI–VIII. Conventional two-party bargaining, however, in which norms play only an episodic role, is largely excluded. Second, cell IV represents an empty set since an interested/implicit third party is difficult to imagine. In order to be classified as interested, the parties and/or the observer must notice the goals a third party pursues while trying to settle a dispute. Cell IX represents a marginal class because certain norms which could provide firm guidance might be those that have been "made" by a hegemonic power for its own benefit. The disputing parties might therefore prefer to ignore the relevance of such guidelines or even deny their existence. Similarly, cell VI defines a class of events that, although not conceptually impossible, is nevertheless practically unlikely. It presupposes the unequivocal correctness of a unique (legal) solution. Unless one assumes that the issues involved do not allow for conflicting legal interpretations, and that therefore the parties are willing to settle on

185

the "correct" solution as soon as it has been identified, the set is virtually empty.

Since cell V deals largely with cases of coercive moves by the third party and cell X with those situations resembling first-party law, the remainder of the investigation will focus largely on the cases which could be classified as third-party law under the rubrics of cells III, VII, and VIII. In this context the issue of the quality of the norms, i.e., their legal character which leads to firm rather than loose guidance, attains importance.

It is here that positivism in all its varieties appears to provide a simple answer. *Legal* norms are either those that share a particular characteristic, such as, for example, an attached sanction, or they are those norms which are part of a particular system of rules. In the first case each single rule can be independently examined and its legal character can be established by ascertaining the sanction as a component of the norm in question. The second approach makes such a determination dependent upon the existence of a "system," i.e., the (logical) interrelationship of various norms. Therefore, lower-level rules can be "derived" from, and retain their legal character through, higher-order norms.

These two approaches of positivism differ in significant respects. However, it should clear that they share *one* fundamental assumption, i.e., that the question of the "legal" validity of a norm can be largely reduced to a cognitive question of how one is to recognize a legal norm. Their "deontic" status is imputed on the basis of either their sanction or their membership within a system. The "system" as such is held to be obligatory for reasons which are usually no longer specified, or considered to lie outside the province of jurisprudence.

It is my thesis in this chapter that such attempts at defining a demarcation between legal and other norms is bound to fail becauses it fundamentally misconstrues the problem of arriving at a decision through the utilization of rules and norms. Although judges are bound by the "law" it can be shown that not all "legal" rules are characterized by sanctions, or form part of a deductive hierarchical system of norms. Consequently, legal rules and norms cannot be conceptualized as possessing one common characteristic, or by being treated merely as institutional rules. Our discussion of the complexities of contracting in chapter 4 has already shown why this is so. Even in cases when contracts are "valid," the decision a judge faces is usually quite different from merely ascertaining whether the parties were using the practice of contracting properly. All types of additional considerations, ranging from pre-contractual events (see the argument of the *culpa in contrahendo*) to questions of the effects on third parties, may become relevant.

In trying to understand the problem of rule-application as well as the issue of legal decision-making, I want to proceed in two steps. The first is largely negative. In criticizing the theories of Kelsen and Hart, I hope to demonstrate the problematic nature of the main tenets of positivism. I shall also argue aginst the goal-oriented jurisprudence of McDougal. In a second step I want to show that a demarcation criterion can be found that avoids most of these puzzles. By emphasizing the *stye* of reasoning with rules rather than either the intrinsic characteristics of the norms, or their membership in a system, or their contribution to an overarching goal, we can give a more realistic account of the legal enterprise. Furthermore, the problem of international law can be raised in a more fruitful way.

III SANCTION AND PEDIGREE AS CHARACTERISTICS OF LEGAL RULES

Conventionally, legal rules are distinguished from other norms by the type of obligation they impose on the actor. From our short discussion in the last chapter it should be clear, however, that the yardstick of seriousness of the psychological pressure is unsatisfactory. After all, "seriousness" has several dimensions. Moral precepts such as to keep one's promises not only impose a very serious obligation on the promisor, but this precept is also often advanced as the most basic legal principle of *pacta sunt servanda*. One of the recurring problems of this type of speculation is the difficulty in separating legal and other types of obligations and thus in distinguishing legal from other norms.

Positivism appears to avoid the embarrassment of such an insufficient demarcation by substituting an *external* characteristic as a criterion for that of the "internal" pressure by which actors experience the obligatory force of prescriptions. The *qualitative* test of "what counts as law"[8] recedes when a *formal* criterion is introduced. Law is now understood as the "command" of the sovereign and is thus clearly distinguishable from other prescriptions, be they morals, taste, or even edicts and statutes of private associations. Needless to say, international law cannot qualify in that case as true law and has to be downgraded to a status of international comity, morality, or convenience.

The disadvantage of such a conceptualization for the general understanding of law can easily be seen. While it might not have disturbed

187

many lawyers to deny the status of law to norms in the international arena, it was somewhat embarrassing to exclude by definition such systems as Roman law (during long periods of time) as well as customary orders that do not possess centralized institutions for law-creation. However, this is precisely what the command theory of law requires us to do when we are unable to establish the sovereign command as demarcation criterion.[9] The way out of *this* dilemma is to make "sanctions" the decisive characteristic of legal norms and thus to distinguish the "law" from other means of social control. But the clarity of the new conception, making criminal law the model of law in general, is bought at a heavy price. Thus, rules stipulating the validity of making a will – to use Hart's example – function quite differently from laws sanctioning criminal conduct, or from rules specifying the legal validity of customary rules.[10]

Only two strategies seem to be open now: First, one can show through various redefinitions that all law has a "sanctioning function" and that differences between, e.g., "nullity" and "punishment" are merely superficial.[11] Furthermore, allowance can be made for a variety of enforcement mechanisms (such as self-help) in addition to the historically late development of the monopoly of coercion by the sovereign. Second, a fundamental redefinition of law could be attempted by focusing on certain formalities that distinguish legal rules from other guidance devices. Pratically, this means that the "genesis," or the logical pedigree within a legal system, rather than the coercive character of the attached sanctions, becomes the decisive characteristic of a legal rule. While the first route is taken by Hans Kelsen – among others – the second conceptualization is most powerfully presented by H. L. A. Hart.

Kelsen's starting-point is the question of whether the social phenomena called "law" have a characteristic in common on the basis of which "we are able to differentiate . . . between a legal and a moral or religious order."[12] While law shares with other normative structures the "ought" characteristic, it is the *method* of bringing about the desired conduct that distinguishes law from other norms:

> A social order that attempts to bring about the desired conduct of individuals by sanctions we call a coercive order. It stands in sharpest contrast to all other social orders, which rest on voluntary obedience . . . Thus the antagonism of freedom and coercion fundamental to social life supplies the decisive criterion. It is the criterion of law, for law is a coercive order. It provides for socially organized sanctions and thus can be clearly distinguished from religious and moral order.[13]

188

Thus, legal prescriptions deal with behavior in terms of either a "right" or a "delict," and the question of whether international law can be truly called law pivots on whether delictual behavior is sanctioned in international relations. Needless to say, Kelsen, relying on the institution of *"self-help,"*[14] is able to "demonstrate" the legal character of international legal norms. In addition, Kelsen seems to utilize a second criterion, i.e., the *process of norm-creating* internal to the legal system in order to decide issues of validity. Thus, a norm is valid if created in accordance with a "higher" valid norm. The problem of obligation imposed by a specific rule can be answered by reference to its establishment. This argument obviously presupposes the logical closure of a system of norms because otherwise anything could be logically derived from higher norms or principles. Given these facts, the legal order is an "ideal construct" and the task of jurisprudence is not the elucidation of the workings of norms in social life – be they applied by courts, utilized by litigants, or misused by Holme's proverbial "bad man"[15] – but rather the patient explanation of its logical interrelationships and properties. The only precondition for the binding character of legal norms is then the obligatory nature of the highest norm (*Grundnorm*), which has to be justified in extra-legal terms.

As a further corollary Kelsen has to recast those norms that authorize – i.e., the "power-conferring rules" in Hart's terminology – and show that they fit the characterization of sanctioning prescriptions. Norms in this view are no longer addressed to the ordinary citizen, intending to guide his/her behavior, but are conditional orders to officials to apply sanctions under specified circumstances contained in the "if" clause of the rule. As Hart states in his criticism of Kelsen:

> by greater and greater elaboration of the antecedent or if-clauses, legal rules of every type, including the rules conferring and defining the manner of exercise of private or public powers, can be restated in this conditional form. Thus, the provisions of the Wills Act which require two witnesses would appear as a common part of many different directions [*sic!*] to courts to apply sanctions to an executor who, in breach of the provisions of the will, refuses to pay the legacies.[16]

Although through this recasting "the unity of all law" seems to have been preserved, the rescue creates considerable difficulties, particularly for international law, which Kelsen insists is part of his unified conception of law.

As is known, international legal arguments often do not go beyond the stage of *ex parte* contentions since authoritative decisions through adjudicatory procedures are – to say the least – underdeveloped. This creates some difficulty for the status of international law as genuine law. If norms no longer have as their defining characteristic simple sanctions addressed to the actors themselves, but are rather power-conferring, or command particular officials to *apply* certain sanctions, then international law is "true" law only if we can discover (analogously to the sanction/self-help parallel) a corresponding directive to some "international officials." What seems to be required now is – at a minimum – the incorporation of an authoritative norm-applying institution within the definition of law. But if "interpretation" becomes an intrinsic part of the legal enterprise, law is no longer simply analyzable in terms of an abstract logical system of norms. By definition, higher-level norms have to be more abstract and can therefore be logically compatible with a variety of more concrete regulations that might contradict each other. To that extent the question of whether lower-level norms were created in accordance with higher-level prescriptions does not dispose of the issue how the norm-applying party is supposed to find out which among the various possible and valid solutions is "the law."

The implausibility of some of Kelsen's positions leads H. L. A. Hart to his fundamental distinction of types of rules within a legal system. Aside from "primary rules" imposing obligations, "secondary rules" of recognition, change, and adjudication play, according to Hart, a decisive role within every legal system. While primary rules are concerned with the actions of individual subjects under the law, secondary rules are about (primary) rules, or better: "they specify the ways in which the primary rules may be conclusively ascertained, introduced, eliminated, varied and the fact of their violation conclusively determined."[17] Thus, power-conferring rules which were such an embarrassment to Kelsen's theory can now easily be amalgamated under the rubric "secondary rule." Furthermore, the rule of recognition finally creates the legal system in two senses: it allows for the test whether something is a rule of law as opposed to merely social rules, such as morals, etiquette, etc. The test is the "pedigree" which unequivocally shows the "character-tag" of a rule. In addition, the rule of recognition, by establishing a logical hierarchy among potentially conflicting "sources" of law, provides for the logical closure of the system. Thus, the question of what counts as a rule of law can be easily answered by tracing the pedigree of a particular rule until finally (at least in England), an act of parliament, the highest or ultimate rule of recognition, is reached. Since modern legal systems possess several "sources" – thus an act of parliament, custom, and precedent might lead to the identification of conflicting rules of law –

190

there exists a need to establish an arrangement of superiority. The traditional subordination of custom to statute is a case in point. Only in this way can we establish what counts as a rule of law and understand the various sets of rules as a closed system.

Conversely, a set of rules which does not possess such a supreme rule of recognition is not a genuine legal system but rather an agglomeration of (primary) rules.[18] Consequently, there is often a great deal of uncertainty as to which legal rule applies in a particular circumstance. According to Hart, international law fits this description and, at the same time, explains the indeterminacy of many international legal arguments. Nevertheless, since primary rules are duty-imposing prescriptions, the nature of the binding character of international law is now no longer dependent upon either sanctions, or the existence of a closed legal system. "It is a mistake," writes Hart,

> to suppose that a basic rule or rule of recognition is a generally necessary condition of the existence of rules or obligation or "binding rules." This is not a necessity, but a luxury, found in advanced social systems whose members not merely come to accept separate rules piecemeal, but are committed to the acceptance in advance of general classes of rule, marked out by general criteria of validity. In the simpler form of society we must wait and see whether a rule gets accepted as a rule or not; in a system with a basic rule of recognition we can say before a rule is actually made, that it will be valid if it conforms to the requirement of the rule of recognition.[19]

This quote brings out well Hart's emphasis on the "internal aspect" of rules which distinguishes him from "realists" as well as from "scientific" positivists. (The latter view legal rules as merely predictive statements of behavioral regularities.) Nevertheless Hart's emphasis on acceptance comes close to defeating his original purpose of distinguishing carefully between legal rules and other types of norms. After all, Hart spent a considerable amount of time and effort on the elaboration of the distinction between law and morals.[20] One of the main points he made in this context was that for the establishment of a *legal* rule one had to show the existence of a "pedigree," while no such proof is required for moral precepts. Thus, the systemic character of legal rules does not appear to be merely a luxury given Hart's approach. It is, rather, a necessity for an unequivocal identification of legal rules. After all, according to the "acceptance" view outlined in the quote above, any type of rule or precept can be "legal." On the other hand, according to the criteria of the rule of recognition, only those rules qualify as legal which are *part of a system* and *possess a pedigree*.

It is not difficult to fathom that in the second approach "legal" rules

191

are conceptualized largely analogously to institutional rules. However, as the discussion of the complexities of contracting in chapter 4 showed, even institutional rules establish only a *prima facie*, but not a conclusive, proof that a concrete controversy has to be decided solely in terms of the rules constitutive of the practice. This raises an important issue: if even in the case of well-developed institutional rules judges have often to go well beyond the institutional rules (see the discussion of *culpa in contrahendo*), then it appears problematic to take institutionalized practices as the model of law in general. Hart recognizes some of these difficulties in his criticism of "mechanical jurisprudence" without, however, drawing the conclusion that a "systemic" approach to law fosters such misconceptions.[21]

Some infelicities of expression as well as conceptual incongruencies strengthen further the suspicion that Hart's construct is fraught with more problems than at first appears. Consider, for example, his argument that a legal system comes into existence with the emergence of secondary rules. These secondary rules are conceptualized as power-conferring norms rather than directives in the sense of direct prohibitions or demands. Hart's identification of secondary rules with *rules* of recognition therefore appears justified. But somewhat surprisingly, Hart switches his terminology and suddenly talks about the *"rule* of recognition," which he likens to secondary rules. To emphasize this inconsistency between the singular and plural use of the term is not to engage in purely conceptual nitpicking since this distinction is of decisive importance for international law. While international law does not have a "rule" of recognition, it surely has *rules* of recognition or, to use the more common term, "sources of law."[22]

A further problem emerges when we consider the identification of *rules* of recognition with secondary rules. If the characteristic of a secondary rule is the conferral of public or private power, then it is difficult to see how the rule of recognition can be a secondary rule. While this rule establishes the hierarchy among sources of law and thus creates priorities, it is doubtful whether this capacity can be construed as conferring a "power" in the usual sense. In general, it appears unjustified to identify all secondary rules with a power-conferral. For example, all practice-type rules are secondary rules in the sense that they provide for the recognition of a legally relevant fact or action. However, it is *not* necessarily true that they are thereby power-conferring. Thus, to use Hart's own example of the will's act, the provision of intestate succession comes into operation by the mere

192

occurrence of an event, i.e., the death of the testator who failed to leave a valid will. As Neil McCormick has remarked,

> it would be decidedly odd to conceive of legislation about intestate succession as conferring powers upon property owners by dying to vest their property in others. Equally, . . . the constitution of an independent former colony might provide that all laws of the mother state in force on independence day should continue in force as valid laws of the new state until expressly or impliedly [sic] repealed by the new legislature. That would provide a criterion of validity of rules of law in the new state, but it would not imply that anyone in the other state had any legislative power in the new state after independence day.[23]

These conceptual puzzles, when added up, make it questionable whether the concept of law is indeed successfully explicated in terms of a system of rules. While Hart has considerably advanced our understanding of law, his analysis creates a series of new problems.

Two strategies are possible for dealing with the difficulties adumbrated above. On the one hand, one can continue to elaborate on the systemic character of law and thereby show that some of the problems disappear when more than two types of rules are admitted in constituting a legal system.[24] On the other hand, one can decide to forgo a clear demarcation criterion of law altogether and make law a matter of "degree" of influence that various norms have upon decision-making.

IV LAW AS AUTHORITATIVE DECISION, AND THE PROBLEM OF CUSTOM AND DISCRETION

According to the account of law as a system of rules, the set of primary and secondary rules is exhaustive of "the law." However, unless we assume that a legal system is a deductive system of norms, the process of deciding between two possible, although contradictory, *ex parte* contentions can obviously no longer be described in terms of purely logical operations. In order to substantiate this objection further one could, for example, show that not all devices invoked and applied by courts function like rules. In quoting several cases in which the decisions of courts could not be construed as the application of a rule, Ronald Dworkin elaborates the distinction between rules and legal "principles." While rules apply in an "all or nothing fashion," principles can be invoked in a discretionary way.[25] Furthermore, principles inherently have a dimension of "weight" or importance which needs to be considered in every case, whereas rules do not share this characteristic. True, rules which contain such standards as "unreasonable," "negligent," and "insignificant" seem to contradict this distinction. However, it is quite clear that these "standards" make the functioning of the rule dependent upon the application of a *principle* in Dworkin's sense. The application of principles requires, therefore, significantly different reasoning procedures.

This argument seems to demolish the conception of law as a static system of rules. Not only can judges in their decisions no longer simply defer to rules in reaching their decisions, but the wide variety of shifting and interacting standards apparently cannot be bolted together into a simple "rule of recognition." So the question of judicial discretion becomes all the more important. Lacking firm guidance from "all or nothing" rules, are judges free to import their personal preferences into the legal system, as the realists maintained, or are legal decisions fundamental policy choices whose essentially *political* character is disguised by the legalistic vocabulary? It is here that the radical reformulation of the legal problematique as expounded by McDougal and his New Haven school becomes important.[26]

While most legal theories take the domestic legal system as their point of departure, the McDougal–Lasswell approach avoids a premature identification of the concept of law with those institutions familiar from the domestic arena. This new departure has important implications not only for the treatment of international law but for the understanding and conceptualization of law in general. International law is no longer conceptualized via negatives, i.e., by showing what it is *not*, but is explicated in its own right. By focusing on the global *social process*, by identifying within it the process of *power*, and then in turn within that power process those decisions that are at the same time *authoritative and controlling*,[27] one sees a preliminary delineation of law emerge. Law is neither merely abstracted from the actual process of decision nor linked to a particular institutional design. In short, for McDougal and Lasswell, "the conjunction of common expectations concerning authority with a higher degree of corroboration in actual operation is what we understand by law." Law is thereby part of a "public order system" protecting the social processes of the community. Insofar as it can be demonstrated that "the globe as a whole is a public order system" we can speak of "universal international law."[28] To the degree that a public order system is composed of more than one national state but is less than universal in scope, "regional international law" exists.[29] Systems of public order thus can be distinguished according to their territorial inclusiveness and/or the functional specificity of the organs developed to carry on the decision-

194

making process. But since the present international arena is characterized by the absence of "authoritative and controlling arrangements
for minimal security," the entire world community at present cannot
be classified as a "complete legal system and hence . . . as a complete
public order."[30]

The "unsystematic character" of international law is, however, no
disabling characteristic for Lasswell and McDougal because the conception of a public order is oriented toward a *goal* which informs the
choices of the relevant decision-makers. While logical closure is
necessary for a static conception of law, Lasswell and McDougal call
attention "to the future-oriented nature of the challenge contained in
the idea of a universal legal order" and to the crucial fact that a "legal
order of inclusive scope can only come into existence in a process of
interaction in which every particular legal advance both strengthens a
world public order and is in turn itself supported and strengthened by
that order."[31]

This "international law" can be defined as "the process of authoritative decision insofar as it approximates a public order of human
dignity," and this process can then be further described as one "in
which the established decision makers of the world community seek to
clarify and implement the common, shared interests of the members of
that community as individuals and members of appropriate groups."[32]
The teleological orientation to law is deliberately chosen and the goal of
universal order of human dignity is left to "everyone . . . to justify . . .
in terms of his preferred theological or philosophical tradition."
Human dignity, in turn, "refers to a social process in which values are
widely and not narrowly shared and private choice rather than
coercion is emphasized as the predominant modality of power."[33]

The rest of McDougal's theoretical work is then devoted to the
specification of categories for the investigation of the power process
protected by law. It is not difficult to see that instead of a rule of
recognition, an overarching goal, called human dignity, functions in
McDougal's scheme as the criterion for the "legal" character of particular decisions. "Law" in this conception is no longer susceptible to a
clear statement in rules or precedents, but consists in an agglomeration
of shifting and interacting standards, policies, and preferences of the
various decision-makers. The legal character of a decision has to be
ascertained by means of an appraisal which includes the description of
past trends, factors affecting the decision, projection of future trends,
and evaluations of policy alternatives in terms of the overarching goal
of human dignity.

While I do not want to embark upon a comprehensive critique of

195

McDougal's exceedingly complex "theory" *about* law,[34] it is clear that the shift of focus away from rules to the decision process often makes a distinction between "law" and "politics" virtually impossible. After all, politics has been defined sometimes as the "authoritative allocation of values,"[35] and thus the distinctive character of law and its obligation is in danger of being lost. McDougal and Lasswell themselves seem to be rather ambiguous on this point, as one of their definitions of law simply refers to the making of "authoritative and controlling decisions"[36] while another includes a reference to the goal of "human dignity."[37] A third definition of law mentions "decisions sustained by effective sanctions taken in accordance with authority."[38]

It is clear that these three definitions embody rather different criteria, and they have different implications for the status of law in the international arena. While the first conceptualization is coextensive with the bargaining process of international politics, the second definition includes a qualitative yardstick by means of which the degree of legality of an action can be ascertained. The third definition is rather "Kelsenian" and need not coincide with either the first or the second.

Let us, however, assume *arguendo* that the second version is what McDougal and Lasswell really mean. In that case one could indeed speak of law by degree, a conception quite useful for the description as well as the appraisal of the "soft" areas of law. Such a conceptualization clearly devalues a single hard and fast demarcation criterion in favor of a more flexible set of considerations determining the varying degrees of authoritativeness of certain statements and pronouncements.

Most frequently the issue of quasi-legal norms is raised in connection with the assessment of General Assembly resolutions.[39] International courts have quoted from these documents in deciding cases without going so far as to argue that the General Assembly pronouncements have become a new "source" of international law. Furthermore, even practices of nonauthorized persons have been invoked as manifestations of legal relevance. As Oscar Schachter has noticed, "several . . . international arbitral decisions have recognized as authoritative the practices of private airlines and oil companies when their conduct was carried out in pursuance of international agreements."[40] The question nevertheless remains of how one is to ascertain the degree of legal force these quasi-authoritative pronouncements have. Traditional scholarship uses two tests: either one assesses the quality of the consensus underlying a purported norm, or one resorts to a teleological interpretation and appraises the contribution a given norm makes to the attainment of a predetermined goal. The first

196

strategy is most clearly represented in the *Texaco–Libyan* arbitration award,[41] which spells out a nearly "Calhounian" position on law creation.[42] Clearly resisting the tyranny of the majority in the General Assembly, this position nevertheless attributes legal relevance to resolutions passed by a majority which comprises members of all important power *groupings* within the U.N. The second strategy of determining the legal nature of a norm is to assess its alleged contribution to a goal; as we have seen, this is McDougal's approach.

However, neither of these strategies is entirely satisfactory. The quality-consensus view, while providing some reasonable standards for amassing the character of multilateral pronouncement, fails to take into account a wide variety of other such quasi-authoritative instruments. The teleological interpretation, on the other hand, is wider in scope but raises other difficulties, including those of utilising mistaken instrumentalist metaphors for ascertaining the legal validity of norms. A further discussion seems appropriate. Let us begin with the McDougalian position, then proceed to a critique of instrumentalism, and take up the question of other types of quasi-authoritative norms ("soft" law) in the next section.

Even if we agree that human dignity is of overarching importance, it is rather questionable whether such a teleological conception of human actions can provide us with standards sufficiently precise to come to a consensus of what is to count as law. The objections to such a form of "natural law" are legion and need not be rehearsed here. Lasswell's and McDougal's argument that everyone is free to justify the overarching goal of human dignity "in terms of his/her preferred philosophy, tradition, or religious conviction" is not particularly well suited to increase our confidence in the capacity of such a goal to guide choices. After all, one of the main functions of law is to mediate between adherents of fundamentally different conceptions of the good life, or of human dignity.

It is precisely for this reason that law, in the conventional understanding of the term, is primarily *not* concerned only with providing guidance towards predetermined ends but also with the legitimacy or illegitimacy of the *means*. It is this specificity which distinguishes law from policy as well as from moral principles. As Schachter pointed out correctly against a too policy-oriented jurisprudence: "In the Teheran hostage crisis . . . the specific rule against the arrest and detention of diplomats could not be disregarded on the ground that their behavior violated the fundamental policies in favor of sovereign rights and political independence (even if that could be proven)."[43] The clear and unequivocal rule on diplomatic immunity not only settles that issue, but also shows indirectly that much of law cannot be understood in simple instrumental terms. Three reasons militate against an instrumentalist approach.

One, even in the case of statutory law which has – unlike customary rules and norms – at least an author to whom some goal or objective can be imputed, the picture is often less than clear.[44] Only if we assume that statutes have a single unequivocal objective can the goal–means yardstick of rationality provide firm guidance. Consider, for example, the provisions of the U.S. statute concerning Occupational Safety which provides that due care has to be taken to prevent injury or the loss of life. Although this "purpose" appears clear enough, it is not so in practice. Since even with stringent safety regulations some risk of injury will persist, the question remains whether the "meaning" of the statute is to eliminate *any* risk, or to provide also some safeguards against costly safety precautions which are not necessary under normal conditions and which would impose undue costs on all of us. Even worse, most of the statutes are complex and attempt explicitly to mediate between a variety of legitimate purposes and goals.[45]

Two, many goals such as fairness, predictability, reliability, etc., are inherent in the legal process and have to be safeguarded as such; they neither fit the conception of a goal that a particular statute proclaims to serve (such as the "enhancement of highway safety" or the "prevention of the restraint of trade") nor the conception of a means. As Summers aptly remarks concerning the fallacies of "instrumentalism":

> instrumentalists think that means and goals are always separable and that it is therefore always appropriate to set goals first and then cast about for means. However true that might be of constructing houses or other artifacts, it is not always so in law. In law, when available means limit and in part define the goal, the means and the goal thus defined are to that extent not inseparable.[46]

The third objection to instrumentalism is of particular importance for international law. Not all rules are in fixed verbal form, as custom amply demonstrates.[47] In that case, the rules are not the intentional creation of a single person or institution, and the decision-maker applying the rule might have to infer it from the mischief it is supposed to alleviate. But as can readily be seen, the speculative nature of such attributions leads to doubt and indeterminacy.

McDougal attempts to deal with these problems in the following way. He focuses on the global process of claim and counter-claim in which the actors make diverse demands upon each other. These demands, McDougal observes, are appraised by the decision-makers external to the demanding state and then either accepted or rejected. Not only do state officials tolerate each other's claims, but they also accept the proposition that through this process expectations are created, that power is restrained, that certain uniform patterns of interaction emerge, and that common interests are perceived by people everywhere because of the universal striving for human dignity.

However, this conclusion follows only if we make the very heroic assumption that individual and collective interests coincide and that indeed something akin to the "unseen hand" of the ideal-typical market is also operating in international relations. Otherwise we are hardly justified in concluding that through the interaction of various self-interested actors the overarching goal of "human dignity" is served.[48] It was the merit of game- and public-choice theory to point out that there exists in many social situations an ineluctable contradiction between individual and collective interests, for which the "security dilemma" among states is the most obvious example.[49] From the fact that all states strive after security and that therefore "security" is a "shared purpose" in the international arena, we are not entitled to conclude that either security, mutual tolerance, or the enhancement of "human dignity" are bound to be the outcome of such interactions.

It is in analyzing this process of claim and counterclaim that McDougal expects at least some helpful clarification from the "scholar"[50] and, in particular, from the utilization of "policy science." Not only does the scholar's perspective provide a certain detachment through the elaboration of a very complex framework of inquiry, but the scholar also promises to provide a special expertise in resolving questions of policy if he/she is properly trained in the policy sciences. To that extent, the scholar becomes the silent legislator in international relations and, in the absence of effective institutional mechanisms, trust is placed in "science" for resolving the dilemmas the decision-makers encounter every day.

But there is something decisively odd in this position. Since science cannot resolve dilemmas among norms and values, it comes as no small surprise that McDougal's various stances seem more to be dictated by his particular point of view on U.S. policy – largely coinciding with the Cold War consensus – than by the method, or theory, of the applied policy sciences. Because he has eschewed traditional legal categories, personal preferences rather than norms provide the necessary decision-premises in his scheme. Thus, while

McDougal has liberated international law from the fetters of dogmatic legalism, he may have done so at the cost of dissolving law as a distinctive phenomenon altogether.

The above criticisms address largely the lack of a clear demarcation criterion which leads to the overinclusiveness of the category of legal norms and perhaps also the dissolution of distinctively "legal" phenomena. There is, however, a sense in which both McDougal's theory, as well as the Calhounian consensus as a criterion of law, could lead to underinclusiveness. This can best be seen in the area of "soft law" that contains – beside consensual bilateral or multilateral declarations of "principles," "guidelines," etc. – unilateral declarations and actions. A brief discussion seems in order. It will show that "soft law" can be identified and understood as a legal phenomenon without resort to the overarching goals of human dignity or the invention of a new source of law, or vesting international force with quasi-legislative powers. Our discusion of speech-act theory and of promising, as developed in the last chapter, will be helpful in this respect.

V THE ISSUE OF "SOFT LAW" RECONSIDERED

The problem of "soft law" arises usually in conjunction with the weight of General Assembly resolutions, as already mentioned. Particularly, scholars of the Third World, such as Bedjaoui,[51] insist on the law-creating force of such resolutions, viewing the General Assembly as an institution best expressing the newly emerging consensus on the purposes of international law. Other scholars, predominantly from developed countries, are fearful of the politicization of the world organization and object to the rather sweeping proposals for a reorientation of international law away from consent to consensus.[52] Inconsistencies abound in both positions. While it is difficult to make a straightforward case for the legislative competence of the General Assembly in the face of explicit Charter provisions to the contrary,[53] the developed countries have not consistently espoused such a purely legalistic stance, as the U.N. declarations concerning the Nuremberg principles and the injunctions against genocide show.

Furthermore, the problem of "soft law" not only surfaces in the often highly charged atmosphere of the General Assembly, but plays an increasingly important part in such technical areas as exchange arrangements within the regime of the International Monetary Fund.[54] In this context it is highly significant that the hardness or softness of the respective prescriptions can no longer be derived simply from the formality or genesis of the instrument. Concerning the various characteristics of soft law, Gold finds at a minimum four distinctive features:

> First, a common intent is implicit in the soft law as formulated, and it is this common intent . . . that is to be respected. Second, the legitimacy of the soft law as promulgated is not challenged. Third, soft law is not deprived of its quality as law [by non-compliance] because failure to observe it is not in itself a breach of obligation. Fourth, conduct that respects soft law cannot be deemed invalid.[55]

In general we can say that soft law imposes an obligation to seek a more specific and detailed solution to an issue without in itself imposing specific enforceable duties. Thus, we could say that soft law represents a weak institutionalization of the norm-creation process by prodding the parties to seek more specific law-solutions within the space laid out in the declarations of intent. Furthermore, by legitimizing conduct which might diverge from the existing practices, soft law provides an alternative which can become a legally relevant crystalization for newly emerging customs or more explicit norms.

This short discussion suggests that the normative force inherent in soft law is derived from the consensual nature of the instruments and/or the reliance or consideration they create. But there is still a type of obligation which cannot satisfactorily be explained in terms of consensual factors. Consider, for example, the famous Ihlen declaration, which played a pivotal role in the Permanent Court's decision in the *Eastern Greenland* case.[56] The declaration of Norway's foreign minister – that his country would not raise any issues in the settlement of Danish sovereign claims to all of Greenland – had been made in response to the Danish representative's question. Traditionally this "statement" has been treated as an informal international agreement – i.e., a *mutual* understanding. But such an interpretation overlooks the explicit statement by the Court that its holdings would have applied "even if this interdependence . . . is not held to have been established."[57] Since neither detrimental reliance nor acquiescence was shown – precisely because no affirmative duty to act resulted from the query – the Court correctly emphasized the obligation-creating nature of this declaration as falling outside the traditional framework of contractual or pre-contractual arrangements.

Furthermore, certain unilateral acts such as omissions (acquiescence) or "estoppel"[58] cannot be accommodated within either the bilateral or contractual paradigm. The I.C.J., however, has developed the idea further in that even unilateral acts might constitute a valid "uptake" of an obligation – very much along the lines of the explanation of speech-acts developed in chapter 5 – even when no reliance of the affected parties can be shown. In the *Nuclear Test Case*, the Court dealt with the French pronouncements, which had not been made vis-à-vis New Zealand. Besides, New Zealand had not accepted this declaration when it applied for interim measures of protection.

> An undertaking of this kind, if given publicly, and with an intent to be bound, even though not made within the context of international negotiations, is binding. In these circumstances, nothing in the nature of a *quid pro quo* nor any subsequent acceptance of the declaration, nor even any reply or reaction from other States, is required for the declaration to take effect, since such a requirement would be inconsistent with the strictly unilateral nature of the juridical act by which the pronouncement by the State was made.[59]

Three points are worth pondering in this context. There is, first, the issue of important similarities and dissimilarities between these decisions which construe "hard" legal obligations and our discussion of "soft law." Second, there is the question on what basis the Court decided that pronouncements made outside the framework of conventional obligation-creating practices (treaties) incur legal duties. In other words, what indications does the Court use in ascertaining the "intent to be bound" on the part of an actor? Third, and connected with the second point, there is the more general problem of interpretation by which the Court establishes the legal consequences of certain facts or actions. Since the second question is obviously the most crucial, let us begin with this issue and attempt to answer the other two from that vantage-point.

In deciding the issue of intent, the Court used two at first rather contradictory criteria. On the one hand, it requoted the rule enunciated in the *Lotus* case that "[w]hen States make statements by which their freedom of action is limited, a restrictive interpretation is called for."[60] On the other hand, citing the *Temple of Preah Vihear*[61] decision, which stated that international law does not impose any strict formal requirement as to the form of legally relevant governmental declarations, the Court declared:

> One of the basic principles governing the creation and performance of legal obligations, whatever their source, is the principle of good faith . . . Just as the very rule of *pacta sunt servanda* in the law of treaties is based on good faith, so also is the binding character of an international obligation assumed by the unilateral declaration.[62]

Both principles taken together enable us to clarify the two other issues mentioned above. Since *good faith* and the obligatory force of promising *rather than the formality of contracting* is seen as the reason for the binding nature of a statement, promising is taken as the paradigm. This means that not only consensual international obligations, captured in the rule of *pacta sunt servanda*, are brought under its penumbra, but so also is the anti-inconsistency rule in case of unilateral pronouncements. In other words, an actor who enters the assertion game indicates thereby that his declarations, irrespective of their informality, mean what they say, unless defeating circumstances can be adduced. It is consistent with my argument that the "restrictive" rule of interpretation is not applied by the courts to the form by which obligations are created, but only to their scope. These considerations help us understand why highly specific declarations referring to particular controversies are construed as obligations of "hard" law, even if made in unconventional contexts, while certain declarations of principle, or agreements on guidelines, only have a "soft" character, *even if made by formal instruments*. A *soft* construction suggests itself, in that case, precisely because principles and guidelines are of a higher order of abstraction. They might lead to far-reaching and often unforeseeable obligations, compatible with a variety of more specific and perhaps even mutually contradictory rules. In any case, which type of obligations result from particular acts and whether they are of "soft" or hard character is an issue that cannot be decided once and for all. Such a determination is rather the result of "interpretation" in which courts not only passively apply preexisting rules, but also enunciate standards and appraise certain factual features of a "case."

Consider in this context the *Nigerian Cultural Property Case*,[63] decided in 1972 by the German Federal Supreme Court in Civil Matters (B.G.H.Z.). The action concerned the collection of an insurance policy contracted in Hamburg for three crates of African artifacts which had been shipped from Port Harcourt to Hamburg. During the transport six bronze figures were lost. The insurance carrier refused payment on the ground – among others – that a lack of insurable interest existed since the transportation violated 138(1) of the German Civil Code (B.G.B.), which stipulates that contracts *contra bonos mores* are void. The Court decided, at first rather surprisingly, for the defendant (insurance carrier), upholding the *contra bonos mores* argument. Relevant in this context were two factors: one, the existence of a Nigerian law prohibiting the export of, or transfer of, ownership of cultural property; and two, the existence of a "soft law" instrument adopted as a recommendation by UNESCO in 1964. This recommendation concerned the "Means of Prohibiting and Preventing the Illicit

Export, Import, and Transfer of Ownership of Cultural Property." A multilateral convention with the same purpose had been adopted by the General Conference of UNESCO in 1970. At the time of the suit Nigeria had ratified the Convention, but West Germany *had not*.

Since the insurance was contracted under German law the export prohibition fell under the German private international law rule denying extraterritorial effect to foreign public law. Furthermore, since Germany had not ratified the Convention, no direct "hard" law could be adduced in denying the effects of the insurance contract. The Court had therefore to arrive at its conclusion by a more circuitous route. In citing the UNESCO declaration as well as the unratified Convention, it found that these instruments were the expression of certain "fundamental convictions" of the international community that each country had a right to the protection of its national heritage. Consequently, practices violating the principles enunciated in the Declaration were not entitled to the protection of private law rules. In the past, deprivations of cultural property might have been common and had been protected. Such practices could no longer be made the measure of what is compatible with "good morals" presently.[64] It was therefore in the "interest of preserving decency" in international trade with cultural objects to consider the insurance contract in violation of the *boni mores* rule.

In this case, the impact of "soft law" can be clearly seen. First, the declaration provided the German Court with some "evidence" of newly emerging law governing certain transactions. This evidence the Court could use in order to legitimize its decision. But since the declaration represented only "soft law" (in that it was permissive rather than demanding strict adherence), a contrary decision (i.e., enforcing the terms of the standard insurance contract under German law) would not have entailed a violation of an international obligation. Nevertheless, it is through the recognition of these quasi-authoritative statements that national courts develop new (binding) domestic case-law. Furthermore, through the use of soft instruments by domestic courts, these soft rules harden into proper international law via the building up of new customary practices.

Similar arguments can be made in conjunction with the various voluntary or non-binding codes of conduct for transnational enterprises,[65] which serve, in spite of their softness, as an important source of evidence in cases in which courts have to "fill gaps" in existing law, or when they must search for legitimizing norms that could be adduced for the creative development of law. All these points are quite at odds with the conventional view of law as a closed system of rules in which courts more or less automatically apply clearly specified rules to an existing controversy.

We seem to have arrived again at the same crucial point: if the law is not a fixed set of specific rules, having a common characteristic, are courts simply free to utilize standards and norms to their liking in deciding cases? The answer to this query is still no, because from the fact that not all rules that have legal import are of the same character it does *not* follow that anything goes. If the constraints for legal decision-making do not lie in the type of norms, such constraints can still lie in the way norms are *used*, i.e., in the decision-making *style* which distinguishes legal from other modes of decision-making. Therefore, I want to argue that the unity of law consists less in the special character of the norms involved, or in their systemic character, than in the norm-use. This skill is transmitted through a socialization process which people undergo when they become "rule handlers," i.e., either judges or advocates (lawyers). It is the task of the next section, and beyond that the next chapter, to expand on these issues.

VI LAW AS A "STYLE" OF REASONING

The hope of finding a demarcation criterion clearly distinguishing legal rules from other types of norms has been one of the main thrusts of positivism. Although, as our discussion showed, this search has not been successful, it should be obvious that for practical as well as epistemological reasons we cannot simply forgo such a criterion (or criteria) of demarcation. *Epistemologically* such a criterion is necessary for the delineation of a proper field of study without which our attention would be unfocused. The gigantic conceptual apparatus developed by McDougal pushes one already to the limits of human capacity of "data handling." Besides, it is never quite clear why all these intellectual operations in the McDougalian scheme are necessary, and what their relative importance is. *Practically*, the need for such a demarcation is obvious when we consider domestic legal problems which touch upon international legal questions. Thus, a suit concerning the legality of fishing a few tons of smack,[66] the legality of a federal statute in pursuance of a treaty protecting migratory birds,[67] the issue of ownership of assets located in the U.S.A.,[68] or the reach of U.S. law abroad all hinge upon questions of international law.[69] Similar problems also arise in nonadjudicatory contexts. In order to preserve living or nonliving resources of the sea, one may have to know the pertinent legal provisos of the respective regime. In order to manage one's macro-economic policy, successfully one must understand the "hard" and "soft" law of the various I.M.F. exchange arrangements.[70] In order to respond with a forceful reprisal[71] to unfriendly and illegal acts, one has to be familiar with a wide variety of legal prescriptions, since legal norms provide particularly powerful justifications for certain political choices.

Legal norms, therefore, figure prominently in defining issues and in legitimization and delegitimization attempts. Furthermore, with the increase of elements of horizontal ordering[72] even in hierarchically (vertically) ordered domestic systems, insights gained from the functioning of law in the international arena are no longer peripheral to domestic law or to the jurisprudential reflections on the concept of law in general. The importance of such a different perspective – called the "second concept of law" by Gottlieb – in the areas of constitutional law, civil rights, and labor laws has been noted.[73]

But how is one to conceptualize legal norms more adequately? Conventionally, theorists have been prone to identify the legal character of rules and norms either with the threat of deprivation (sanctions), i.e., their special "seriousness" to influence, or, conversely, with the lack thereof, as we have seen. The problem with such a delineation is not only that it is curiously contradictory, but also that it fails to provide an objective test for the existence or nonexistence of a legal obligation. After all, the most severe psychological pressures might, for example, in the international arena, result from unilateral but vague policy commitments which need not necessarily qualify as either a moral imperative or a direct legal obligation. The "intensity" test is therefore quite often indeterminate. Besides, no legal order can make private feelings the sole or ultimate test of legal obligation. Indeed, as strict liability incurred by ultra-hazardous activity shows, a legal obligation might exist even in cases of "no fault," i.e., when the feeling of responsibility might be quite low and the activity itself was not forbidden.

If the sanctioning as well as the pressure model of guidance is seriously deficient, then the guidance that rules provide has to be conceptualized differently. We have to focus less on the psychological impact than on the explicitness and contextual variation in the reasoning process. This point is well developed by Gottlieb's discussion of "policy" vs. "law." While policy, even if cast in rule form, is designed to guide inferences toward a goal, leaving the relevant decision-maker with a great deal of discretion as to the time, place, and mode of implementation, legal rules "provide relative firm guidance not only with respect to ends but also *to the means* to be adopted,"[74] to the contexts or settings of application, and to admissible and inadmissible exceptions. From these remarks follows the idea that reasoning with legal rules differs substantially from the type of reasoning appropriate for making policy decisions. The specificity of guidance of legal rules when contrasted with "policy" can be seen when we consider changes in decision-making which deviate from established rules. Thus, we speak of a "violation" of legal rules; policies, on the other hand, are not violated but changed, precisely because the discretion allowed makes implementation usually solely a matter of the unilateral calculus of the actor. Similarly, when a moral norm is transgressed, the justification for either condemning the conduct or excusing it will be substantially different from breaking a legal rule. *First* of all, moral arguments utilize mostly "principles" rather than specific rules. This, however, means that much of the argument will turn on the questions of applicability of a principle, since principles do not specify their range of application. It is the specificity of legal rules, most obvious in the cases of setting definite deadlines for legally relevant actions, or for specifying the conditions of the validity of an action, that leads often to divergent assessments of the "legality" versus the "morality" of an action.

Second, moral arguments often depend crucially upon the "intention" of the actor, especially in a Kantian type of ethics in which good will is the decisive criterion. Intention, on the other hand, is relevant in varying degrees in law according to specific provisos, starting from the requirement *mens rea* in criminal law to the neglect of intention in cases of strict liability.

Third, because of the specificity of contexts, the finding of the "truth" in legal proceedings is subordinate to provisos specifying what can count as a "proof" and which facts, although relevant to a "case," are inadmissible. Reference to legally relevant texts and documents limits the search for the factual delineation of a controversy considerably. Examples include the exclusionary rule of evidence, or the more common stipulations protecting relatives from testifying against one another. What is a relevant fact in a moral argument, on the other hand, is not so clearly specified and specifiable *ex ante*.

Fourth, moral arguments often exhibit a great deal of indeterminacy and the moral analysis of an issue often cannot but point out the existence of a "dilemma" and leave it at that. Legal decision-making, on the other hand, is characterized by the need to come to a final decision. No judge can refuse a decision, arguing that each party "has a point" and that an ineluctible dilemma exists.

The need for a decision often leads to "tragic choices."[75] Consider, for example, the issue of a bone marrow transplant that a U.S. court had to decide a few years ago.[76] A terminally ill patient could only be saved through the quick transplant of bone marrow, for which there was no available genetic match except that of a relative. Although the relative had a very good chance of leading a normal life after the donation, he refused to cooperate with the doctors. Morally, we could argue that the relative was obliged to donate the bone marrow, taking into account the special ties among relatives. Or we could argue, even more generally, that the urgency and need of the sick person might create some special entitlement. While most of us would probably not consider the need *per se* as a morally sufficient reason for demanding sacrifices on the part of those who are in a position to help,[77] the legal situation is clear: the judge had to refuse the request of a forced transplant. Standards of supererogation can supply the decision criteria for certain moral dilemmas; law, however, is geared toward the "normal" state of affairs that very narrowly circumscribes circumstances in which special efforts can be required[78] from people who have not chosen to enter into a special relationship with others.

Needless to say, despite significant differences, a considerable overlap also exists between law and morals; the discussion of precepts such as "one ought to keep one's promises" has shown this. Furthermore, the development of "equity" indicates that judges have often turned to moral principles for guidance when the strict application of rules led in particular instances to unjust results. Over time, "equitable relief" became part of the legal order itself, showing the emancipation of the law from purely moral precepts. The last remark also demonstrates one particularly important feature that legal norms share with moral norms, and which distinguishes both of them from policies: it is the *principled character of application*. Not only can one not make legal rules as one goes along, even if such decisions were to command substantial majoritarian support, but "legality" requires the evenhanded application of rules in "like" situations in the future.

This process of principled rule-application creates peculiar complexities, as already mentioned. It also suggests that third-party law is a wider concept than judicial decision-making. As a matter of fact, "judicial" reasoning is a narrower subset of rule-handling in this particular third-party mode. Judicial activity is significantly shaped by certain role-expectations which impose additional requirements upon a judge beyond the mere competency in reasoning with rules and norms in the third-party mode.

Most theories of law share a "judicial perspective" which explains the great attraction of legal realism to even the more pragmatically inclined theorists. But legal reasoning, if understood to comprise the formalization of, and the criteria appropriate for, judicial decision-making, is only one part of rule-handling and of "lawyering." As Twining and Miers point out:

> there is a certain artificiality in isolating reasoning on questions of law in their purest form: not only does this give a false sense of how such reasoning operates in practice but also there is a real danger that such a separation may also divert attention away from other aspects of lawyers' reasoning . . . and these might be at least as important in practice and at least as interesting from a theoretical point of view.[79]

This can easily be seen from the treatment of a "precedent" when viewed from the perspective of an advocate rather than the judge. Most often discussions of precedent assume the judge's perspective and quite incorrectly construe his task of finding the *ratio decidendi* as if the process of interpreting cases were like a treasure-hunt.[80] Such a mistaken perception is less likely to arise when we put ourselves in the shoes of an advocate. This shift in perspective is naturally of particular significance for the purposes of international law since "precedents" in the strict sense do not exist there.

The advocate in international law, like his partner in the domestic arena, faces either previous decisions or other pronouncements of varying authoritative quality. Typically, the opponent will also have a particular reading of the legal landscape. Consequently, the skill of the advocacy will consist in turning attention to the features of the case which, in a plausible fashion, buttress one's own side. Conversely, a variety of avoidance techniques are available to weaken authoritative decisions favoring the other side: faulty application of legal rules, fundamental incompatibility of the facts at hand, lack of clarity as to the scope of the rule enunciated in the decision, changed conditions, inconsistent subsequent practice, etc. These are some of the standard devices to inhibit adherence to the opponent's argument.[81] Note that this "reasoning" is strictly in the third-party mode and differs significantly from the invocation of rules and norms in bargaining situations (second-party law). Thus, good *ex parte* contentions are characterized by the same type of stringency of reasoning with rules as judicial pronouncements, although the task of the advocate is obviously to strengthen the case for his party. Quite different from such "legal" arguments are the freer negotiations in which advocates (and judges) engage, as, for example, in plea bargains, in custody/divorce cases, or in contract disputes when lawyers attempt to prepare a settlement which the court then ratifies. Although legal reasoning (third-party rule application) exhibits a certain stringency when compared with the freer forms of bargaining, its logical form is less than that of a deductive

209

entailment or an inductive procedure. On the contrary, legal reasoning exhibits features that are fundamentally rhetorical in character.

To call attention to the rhetorical features in legal arguments might offend many of us who have come to see rhetoric as a more or less clever manipulation of the symbolic universe, as a kind of skillful deception, or as a study of stylistic figures. The "rhetorical tradition," as exemplified by Aristotle[82] and revived by the legal philosopher Chaim Perelman,[83] however, understands its task to be the investigation of the ways in which *adherence or disavowal of a particular position* can be obtained. Rhetoric is concerned with the problem of praxis, i.e., with gaining adherence to an alternative in a situation in which no logically compelling solution is possible but a choice cannot be avoided. In investigating the logical form of such arguments, John Wisdom put the matter in the following words several years ago:

> In such cases we notice that the process of argument is not a chain a demonstrative reasoning. It is a presenting and representing of those features of the case which severally cooperate in favor of the conclusion . . . in favor of calling the situation by the name which he wishes to call it. The reasons are like legs of a chair, not the links of a chain.[84]

Thus, adherence to a decision is gained neither by demonstrative "proof" nor generalization arrived at inductively, but rather by the "cumulative effect of severally inconclusive premises."[85] Another metaphor which drives the same point home, and which is more familiar in the legal literature, is the notion of "weighing" and "balancing." Indeed, it is one of the distinctive features of legal reasoning that weights are assigned to particular factors or standards. It will be the task of the next chapter to examine this form of reasoning in greater detail.

VII

This chapter was concerned with the clarification of the concept of law, or more precisely, with the identification of those characteristics that distinguish legal prescriptions from other types of norms. Since "law" is usually identified with the application of existing norms to a controversy by a third party, the first step was to clarify the modality of norm-use in third-party contexts. The traditional techniques of mediation, arbitration, and judicial settlement of disputes were discussed and the linkages to second-party and first-party law were shown through the variation in the variables of strict/loose norm guidance, interested/disinterested third party, and explicit/implicit third party.

The next two sections were devoted to the examination of traditional legal theories which founded the distinctiveness of law on either a common characteristic of all legal norms, on the membership in a system, or on an instrumental link between norms and certain over-arching values. However, as the critical appraisal of the theories of Kelsen, Hart, and McDougal demonstrated, the respective "demarcation criteria" are either seriously under- or over-exclusive.

The discussion concerning the phenomenon of "soft law" in section IV set the stage for a different attempt to conceptualize "law" in section V. Instead of arguing that the distinct characteristics of law consist in the quality of the rules themselves, I maintained that law is better understood as a particular style of reasoning with rules. This norm-*use* obtains its coherence and characteristic as a distinct phenomenon from a peculiar style of arguing, which is transmitted through the "training" of the practitioners. I also maintained that this mode of decision-making through normative guidance satisfies the criteria neither of logical induction nor of deduction. While it will be the task of the next chapter to flesh out these ideas further, the discussion in section V showed that the identification of legal reasoning with judicial rule-handling is somewhat misleading since judicial activity is significantly shaped by certain role-expectations going well beyond the technical criteria of competency in reasoning with rules. These last remarks are particularly important for "international law," where adjudicative rule application represents the exception rather than the normal mode in which rules are applied in order to resolve controversies.

8 THE PATH OF LEGAL ARGUMENTS

I

According to the requirements of most, if not all legal systems, a judgment not only has to contain at a minimum the "decision" reached but has also to provide reasons in support of the particular choice made by the judges. Similarly, Article 56(1) of the I.C.J. statute stipulates that a statement of the "reasons on which the judgment is based" is necessary. Furthermore, in accordance with the ideals of formal justice and the separation of powers doctrine, judges are "bound" in their decisions by the "law," or as the German Basic Law elaborates, by *Recht und Gesetz*.[1] Similarly, the I.C.J. statute provides in Article 36 a list of primary and subsidiary "sources" of law by which the Court is directed in its search for applicable rules and norms.

Precisely because judicial decisions have to be based on certain relevant features of the factual setting, but also have to invoke general norms, the argument has been made that judicial reasoning is best understood in terms of the standard logical procedures of deduction (or induction).[2] As persuasive as these arguments appear, there are several problems with such comparisons. First, in spite of the tendencies of some courts (particularly in the French legal system) to make their decision resemble deductively derived conclusions,[3] legal reasoning differs in significant respects from the logical entailments familiar from traditional logic. Consider the following two examples:

  I. All men are mortal
     Socrates is a man
     Socrates is mortal
  II. All murderers are criminals to be punished by life imprisonment
     X is a murderer
     X is a criminal to be punished by life imprisonment.[4]

At first sight both arguments exhibit the same logical structure of entailment (*modus barbara*). Nevertheless, there is one significant difference. In the first case, it has always been noted that the "conclusion" does not contribute anything new to our knowledge. After all, the validity of the major premise depends upon the generalization backed by our experience that Mr. Mayer, Mrs. Smith, and Dupont are all mortal. The same is not true of the second case. In this instance, the major premise cannot be gained by generalizing the conclusion, but rather the premise's validity depends upon the existence of a norm which in turn is backed by certain ethical considerations. To that extent one can argue that juridical ratiocinations, although using the same modes of reasoning, are different in that their conclusions presuppose "something new."

In addition, one runs the risk of seriously distorting the legal reasoning if one focuses solely on the finished product as provided in the final judgment. The main issue in proceedings is usually concerned with the choice of alternative, but competing major premises, such as whether a particular action represents an instance of negligence, manslaughter, or murder. Such questions cannot be answered by formal logic, but the choice of a "narrative" is necessary before a judgment can be presented in a syllogistic form. When decisions are appealed, the appellant's objections focus largely on whether certain "facts" were properly evaluated and the fact-pattern had been appropriately characterized, rather than on problems of syllogistic procedures.

Similarly, the ordinary model of inductive reasoning is of limited help in understanding legal ratiocination. As W. T. Blackstone has pointed out, "Although both judicial decisions and empirical generalizations may share on occasion the predicate 'probable', the grounds for the former is not assimilable to empirical data."[5] Most obvious is the different meaning of "probable" in the types of hypothetical examples lawyers use in arriving at a decision, examples which do not claim overwhelming empirical evidence. Consider, for example, the "reasonable man" standard in deciding issues of liability, which often turn on questions of "foreseeability" of an action's consequences. The function of such assessments is not to indicate how a particular universe of persons is likely to act, but what can be expected from an individual in certain circumstances. In other words, the goal of such consideration is not to prove something, such as a "trend" or a "distribution," but rather to specify the conditions under which reasonable people will accept and share *certain value judgments*. This does not mean that statistical considerations cannot play a role in legal deliberations – indeed, the use of social science methods and findings has been one of the most striking features in recent times – but it *does* mean that the deliberative process of coming to a conclusion cannot simply be subsumed under the conventional patterns of statistical inference.

But how are we then to understand the nature of legal reasoning? Perhaps the model which comes closest to capturing the specific characteristics is the "good reasons" approach as developed by Toulmin,[6] although some of the "quasi-logical" proofs which provide the "backing" for its inferences need further development. In this respect, the teachings about "practical reasoning," as expounded in the rhetorical tradition, are helpful, especially[7] when read in conjunction with some of the modern attempts at developing a "rhetorical" legal theory.[8] Although such a theory is also concerned with the clarification of the logical properties of certain modes of inference, such as the reasoning from "case to case," its main task is to clarify the processes by which assent can be gained to value judgments on reasoned rather than idiosyncratic grounds. It is this problem that this chapter examines in greater detail.

In arguing that legal reasoning is best understood within the wider horizon of practical reasoning, my argument will evolve in the following way. In the next section, I discuss the distinctive features of practical reasoning as examined by the classical tradition. Section III focuses on legal reasoning. The argument there proceeds in two steps, one deconstructive, and one, I hope, constructive. By demonstrating the inadequacies of the traditional subsumption model of legal reasoning, I hope to clear the way for a model of reasoning that is mainly concerned with problem-solving in a concrete case.[9] Consequently, such a model has to pay particular attention to finding the right premises from which a reasoned decision can begin. The "topical" character of this type of proceeding becomes obvious and, consequently, section IV examines the influence of the commonplaces. Legal topoi, or "seats of arguments,"[10] are concerned with the appropriate characterization of actions. The analysis in this section is largely systematic but also provides some historical evidence in support of my thesis that legal reasoning exhibits fundamentally "topical" rather than systemic-deductive features. The latter point is of obvious importance for my concept of law since my thesis is that law is best understood as a particular *reasoning style*. Legal arguments are, in addition to their rhetorical character, "path dependent," i.e., influenced by the sequence of pleadings and rebuttals. Section V examines in greater detail the process by which courts arrive at a decision. Section VI summarizes briefly the main point of this chapter's argument.

II PRACTICAL REASONING AND RHETORIC

How is one to deliberate and come to conclusions about practical questions? After all, practical issues include evaluations which allow neither for the same type of certainty as matters of pure logic nor for the well-corroborated statements of science based on inexorable natural laws. The classical tradition discussed these problems in the context of the "persuasiveness" rather than stringency of arguments, and issues involved were held to require "dialectical" rather than "demonstrative" reasoning. In the first chapter of the *Topica* Aristotle briefly reviews the important conceptual distinctions:

> Reasoning is a discussion in which, certain things having been laid down, something other than these things necessarily results through them. Reasoning is demonstrative when it proceeds from premises which are true and primary, or of such a kind that we have derived our original knowledge of them through premises which are primary and true. Reasoning is dialectical when it reasons from generally accepted opinions. Things are true and primary which command belief through themselves and not through anything else; for regarding the first principles of science it is unnecessary to ask any further questions as to 'why', but each principle should of itself command belief. Generally accepted opinions, on the other hand, are those which commend themselves to all, or to the majority, or to the wise – that is, to all of the wise or to the majority, or to the most famous and distinguished of them.[11]

There are several themes here that deserve further elaboration. First, there is the issue of the nature of the premises from which one reasons. It is introduced as the chief characteristic distinguishing practical – or as Aristotle also calls it, "dialectical" – reasoning from that of formal logic or science. Second, the province of practical reasoning is that of "deliberation," which deals with contingent things which are judged to be in our control.[12] About things which either by necessity are the way they are, or are beyond our control, nobody deliberates. In this context, Aristotle focuses on three "speech acts" which constitute "deliberation." These are: (a) the giving of advice in regard to an action, i.e., persuasion or dissuasion,[13] (b) the defense or accusation of an actor, and (c) the attribution of praise or blame.[14]

But while some type of assent can be attained through the arousal of passions and prejudices, or through the standing and authority of the person making the argument,[15] Aristotle is not interested in dealing with the *psychological* epiphenomena of persuasion. He focuses rather on the nature of the logical inference, which is a type of "proof"

215

(*syllogismos*: συλλογισμός) as he points out.[16] Consequently, it is the task of "rhetoric" to explicate the nature of this type of proof, which is the *enthymeme* (᾽ενθυμήμη). Rhetoric can therefore be defined as

> the faculty of discovering the possible means of persuasion in reference to any subject whatever . . . But Rhetoric, so to say, appears to be able to discover the means of persuasion in reference to any given subject area.[17]

It is the nature of the "enthymeme," or the "rhetorical proof," which is the heart of the Rhetoric. Before we can examine the specific features of the enthymeme and its relationship to other forms of inferences, it might be useful to focus briefly on the fundamental distinctions between the "certain" and the "probable" which distinguish modes of formal logic, as well as the "sciences," from practical reasoning.

The problem of certainty–probability

If the confidence we can have in our conclusions depends upon the certainty, or upon the probability, of the first principles from which we reason,[18] then two extreme cases of transition are possible. In one case, the "probable" is transformed into certainty; in the other, certainty is shaken and what has been held to be true suddenly appears only as probable. Thus, we have two interrelated problems: the problem of the validity of the inference, and the necessary, or only probable, character of the indicators or signs which are used in the premises

> If one were to say that all wise men are just because Socrates was both wise and just, this is a sign, but even though the particular statement is true, it can be refuted, because it cannot be reduced to syllogistic form. But if one were to say that it is a sign that a man is ill, because he has fever, or that a woman has had a child because she has milk, this is a necessary sign . . . for only in this case, if the fact is true, is the argument irrefutable.[19]

The syllogism based on "necessary signs" falls therefore under the modus of strict reasoning, as exemplified in the first figure of the *Prior Analytics*, in which the "sign" serves as the crucial middle term.[20] Furthermore, this type of syllogism comes closest to the type of reasoning prevalent in the sciences. It exhibits the stringency of formal logical procedures while at the same time allowing for assertions about the real world. Conversely, it is true that when the sign is not necessary the conclusions of science are no longer compelling, precisely because the truth value of the premise is under attack. The communication among practitioners will therefore no longer be based on simple demonstration but will take on essentially "rhetorical" features, as pointed out in chapter 1.[21]

The formal characteristics of the enthymeme

At this point, it also might be useful to examine more closely the nature of the "rhetorical" proof and its place in practical reasoning. One traditional way of characterizing enthymemes is to view them as abbreviated syllogisms in which one premise is known but left out in the actual reasoning process. Although this interpretation squares well with one explicit example given by Aristotle,[22] it nevertheless indicates only a first, rather unsystematic, attempt of classification. The main characteristic, as we have seen, is the probabilistic character of the premises and their connections with certain assertions. Consequently, rhetorical proofs cannot start from mere assumptions which are *true by definition* (tethenton: τεθέντων) but have to start with "things as they really are" [tinon onton: τίνων ὄντων].[23] To that extent, logically valid inferences with only one premise, as well as simple conversions such as "no man is a horse, therefore no horse is a man," are excluded.[24] After all, the task of the orator is to point to new connections among "facts" which the audience has not grasped or understood. In this context Aristotle's proofs based on *examples* are instructive. They lead to conclusions by relating a single or few incidents via induction to an underlying generalization. The particular which is thereby derived is, however, less familiar to the audience than the example given.

> We have said that [reasoning by] example is a kind of induction . . . It is neither the relation of part to whole, nor of the whole to part, but of part to part, of like to like, when both come under the same genus, but one of them is better known than the other. For example, to prove that Dionysius is aiming at a tyranny, because he asks for a bodyguard, one might say that Pisistratos before him and Theagenes of Megara did the same, and when they obtained what they asked for, made themselves tyrants. All the other tyrants known may serve as an example of Dionysius whose reason, however, for asking for a bodyguard we do not yet know. All these examples are obtained under the same universal proposition that one who is aiming at a tyranny asks for bodyguards.[25]

From this example, we see that the enthymeme consists of two parts: the conclusion (Dionysius is aiming at tyranny) and the "backing" contained in the examples of Pisistratos and Theagenes of Megara.[26] By means of the examples, the (silent) second premise is gained which

217

consists in the generalization that anybody asking for a bodyguard is likely to aim at tyranny. This generalization provides the conditions for connecting the examples of the past with the present issue. Formally, the generalization serves as the middle term which is crucial in syllogistic modes of reasoning. Nevertheless, it should be obvious that the middle term here is not a *term* at all, but rather a commonplace, or topos. This topos expresses some shared interpretation of actions on the basis of certain practical experiences. Such a topos is therefore a *shared judgment* in a society that enables the respective actors to back their choices by means of accepted beliefs, rules of preference, or general classification schemes, such as Aristotle's own division in the *Topica* (accident, species, property, and sameness).[27]

The role of topoi

The above remarks indicate why the original characterization of the enthymeme as a dialectical proof which lacks stringency because of its *first premises* is somewhat misleading. What seems to be the case is rather that rhetorical syllogisms connect statements which are substantively based on only probable imputations expressed in the topos. In other words, *both the premises as well as the connection*, via the middle term, are only "likely." Precisely because not only the premises are not "necessary" but also because their *conjunction* is only probable, the persuasiveness of even a single case or a hypothetical example may suffice and persuade if it is properly chosen. The distinction of such a "proof" to inductive generalization is explicitly mentioned by Aristotle, and the importance of such inferences in law is recognized by pointing to the persuasive weight of a single trustworthy witness.[28] In this context even the use of fables has some force. Recounting Aesop's defense of a rich Samian demagogue, Aristotle provides us with the example the advocate used:

> A fox, while crossing a river, was driven into a ravine. Being unable to get out, she was for a long time in sore distress and a number of dog fleas clung to her skin. A hedgehog wandering about saw her and, moved with compassion, asked her if he could remove the fleas. The fox refused, and when the hedgehog asked the reason, she answered: They are already full of me and draw little blood; but if you take them away, others will come that are hungry and will drain what remains of me. You, in like manner, o Samians, will suffer no more harm from this man, for he is wealthy; but if you put him to death, others will come who are poor who will steal and squander your public funds.[29]

It is instructive to reflect a few moments on the reasons why this parable is persuasive, as it apparently was to the Samian audience. Formally, we have again a reasoning from the particular to the particular connected by a commonplace or topos. In this way the case of the demagogue is "linked" to the example of the fox by the implicit generalization that all of nature follows the same laws of behavior. As the fleas suck blood, so politicians fleece their constituency.

It is important to realize what has happened when we are ready to accept – or even apply only subconsciously – this topos in making the crucial connection: all questions of right and wrong are eliminated. The "case" is then simply presented as an instance of a universal natural phenomenon, i.e., "survival" or the pursuit of one's self-interest. There is, however, an additional unstated premise of "topical character" in this fable. It is the commonplace that "less is better than more," if faced with an evil. Given that all living beings act in a self-interested fashion, and given that this particular leader is likely to be satisfied by now (because he had his share), it is better to keep him around instead of being pestered by new and hungry fleas (politicians).

Attacks against such arguments can take a variety of courses. The most principled is the denial of the appropriateness of the topical analogy. Situating the problem in the *discourse of choice and responsibility* instead of that of "natural phenomena" dramatically alters the story. Other ways concern the nature of the generalizations which had been employed. For example: are animals which have smelled or licked blood likely to be satisfied, or does not this exposure, on the contrary, whet their appetites? Thus, the finding of an appropriate counter-topos, i.e., providing a different context, is more likely to be persuasive than arduous empirical proofs that the generalization upon which the above argument relies is not true most of the time. Consider in this context the skillful use of a countertopos upon which practically the whole persuasive weight of the following argument rests. When Austria was said to deliberate about making claims against Germany for Hitler's "rape," Adenauer responded, "If they make claims for compensation I'll send them back Adolf Hitler's corpse."[30] Since Hitler was born in Austria, using the topos of the "place" indicates that Hitler was situated in a society which was not "West German" only, and which could not simply absolve itself by ignoring its "place" in the chain of events. Adenauer thus made it impossible for Austria to disclaim all responsibility for the Nazi era.

Topoi, or commonplaces, thus not only establish "starting-points" for arguments, but locate the issues of a debate in a substantive set of common understandings that provide for the crucial connections within the structure of the argument. Precisely because topoi reflect our commonsense understandings, these general topoi are "persuasive" and can easily be resorted to when technical knowledge about an issue is lacking or has become problematic. It is through such a topical "ordering" that everyday language can mediate between different areas of knowledge.[31] Everyday language, therefore, also is able to bridge the gaps between various, more specialized "discourses" which have emancipated themselves from the "imprecision" of ordinary language through the creation of specialized systems of signs and meanings. However, commonplaces also play a part in more specialized discourses. They give structure and coherence to certain areas of practical reasoning. In this context, the *legal topoi* have to be mentioned. In order to establish the importance of such "topoi" in the finding of the "law" it is first necessary to correct some of the most egregious misconceptions about the process of law-application. The next section addresses this problem.

III THE FALLACIES OF THE SUBSUMPTION MODEL, AND THE NATURE OF ANALOGOUS REASONING

Subsumption: facts and norms

According to the common but naive view of the role of norms in "third-party" contexts, the judge has to apply a norm to a case by subsuming the relevant facts under the general norm. To that extent, "judging" has to be legitimated by the use of "the law" as it is legislatively set forth or customarily received. Consonant with this view is another tenet, derived from political theory and going back at least as far as Montesquieu. The adage suggests that the freer a form of government is, the more tightly should the judges be held to the mechanical application of the law.[32] This led in France to the absurd decree of 1790 which forbade judges to interpret the law and directed them in case of doubt to refer the matter to the legislature.[33] Similarly, the original function of the Cour de Cassation was conceived to be that of disciplining judicial liberties with *la loi*.[34] Needless to say, such attempts to curb judicial activity were bound to fail and, in a way, already the Code Napoléon reversed the gears by providing that a refusal to render judgment in a controversy was not available to judges even in the absence of explicit provisions.[35] Ironically, it was the fiction of the "completeness" of the code – originally intended to limit judicial creativity – that now provided the justification for judicial "law-making" even if it was limited to closing alleged "gaps" in the law.

Although common law systems have always accepted judge-made

220

law, similar difficulties of law application arise in these legal systems when courts have to apply the *ratio decidendi* of a precedent to a controversy.[36] The difficulties connected with "finding" the *ratio decidendi*, particularly in the case of concurring opinions, and of distinguishing the ratio from the *obiter dicta* are well known. In addition, the issue has to be faced on which level of generality the earlier "holding" of the court applies. Consider in this context the famous case of *Donoghue* v. *Stevenson*,[37] where the purchaser of a bottle of ginger beer found a dead snail in the opaque bottle and sued for damages after consumption of the drink. Does the decision of the Court for the plaintiff provide a precedent for "dead snails," or any snails, or any noxious or disgusting foreign body in objects made for human use, or only for those of consumption, or only for such objects which come in bottles? Or does it establish only liability for cases in which the noxious element is not discoverable by the consumer without destroying the saleability of the commodity, thereby restricting the scope of the general *caveat emptor* rule?[38] Thus, even when we accept Professor Goodhart's view that the "material facts" and not the verbal statement of the original Court's holding provides us with the *ratio decidendi*, subsequent courts still have to decide which of the various readings at which level of generality is the proper one.[39] This in turn will necessitate an interpretation which is derivable neither from the material facts themselves nor from the rules (such as the injunction against negligence) which are part of the *ratio decidendi*. Legal riddles, Roy Stone reminds us:

> are settled by comparing and contrasting instances, cases, hypothetical situations which fit and square and those that clash and jar until the cases, after reflection, produce what Wisdom calls a sharpened awareness . . . "Is it negligence?" To answer the question is seeing that the presence of a snail in a ginger beer bottle is like the spark from an engine . . . travelling on the London and South West Railway Line.[40]

One could now object to Stone's argument by claiming that the reasoning on both cases, i.e., the railway case and Donoghue, is not reasoning by analogy as Stone suggests, but rather that both cases can be subsumed under the no-harm principle, and that therefore the proper mode of reasoning is that of entailment rather than that of analogy. Although it is true that both cases can be represented as illustrations of the no-harm principle, it is important to see that the no-harm principle is not sufficient in establishing a legally valid claim. For that purpose the evaluation of the "relevant facts" on a certain level of generality becomes necessary. Thus, while all torts can be brought under the no-harm principle, not all cases of demonstrable harm provide for actionable tort cases. Imagine, for example, the hypothetical case of Mr. Biedermann, who suffers considerable damage because he did not show up for the closing of a real estate deal. The reason for his nonappearance is his getting stuck for two hours in traffic. Assume further the traffic jam was solely the result of a large demonstration by the International Movement to Free the Bound Periodicals which – unforeseeably – tied up traffic for miles. Attempts to recover damages from this group will not only be in all likelihood unsuccessful; it is even questionable whether Mr. Biedermann, who suffers the damages, has "a case."[41] Or consider the instance in which a plaintiff (Ultramares Corporation) brings a tort suit against professional defendants (accountants). By relying on the accuracy of the balances of another firm which the defendant had prepared, it suffered financial losses. The corporation bases its claim upon the *ratio decidendi* in McPherson v. *Buick.*[42] In the latter case, the purchaser of a defective automobile had suffered injury and had sued the Buick Motor Company, despite the fact that no privity of contract existed between him and Buick. Although the Buick precedent seems to "back" the Ultramares Corporations claim, Ultramares lost the case when the Court made a distinction between physical and economic harm, and required for a tort action against professional defendants privity of contract with them.[43] Again, a "different reading" of the factual circumstances defeat a clear "subsumption" of the case under the old McPherson rule.

This reflection upon the similar and dissimilar factual situations has led some legal theorists to claim not only that legal reasoning is analogous reasoning – *simila e similibus*, as Bracton has called it – but that no rules are at all necessary for analogous reasoning "from case to case." As Christie put it succinctly:

> The significant differences between cases that will justify differences in results will lie in the factual circumstances of the cases rather than in the rules or principles which they supposedly illustrate . . . any two cases will be considered similar if, according to whatever criterion of similarity is imposed, they are within a certain degree of proximity.[44]

Insofar as Christie wants to imply that general rules are not necessary, his claim is of dubious validity. The frequently only implicit character of the generalization utilized in the reasoning from case to case does not entitle us to conclude that general rules or norms are superfluous. Only by presupposing at least a latent premise does the conclusion *a similibus ad similia* become logically possible. However, to the extent that Christie calls attention to the problem of the indeterminate nature of the *type* as well as the *level* of generality of the similarities, his observation is important. The logical difficulties become most obvious in instances when one has to reason from "case" to "case," and that means in legal systems which rely on precedents. However, precisely the same logical difficulties are encountered by judges who apply a statutory norm or, for instance, in civil law systems, subsume a criminal or civil case under the applicable legal rules. In both cases an *interpretation* of the relevant facts becomes necessary. This involves decisions as to the similarities and dissimilarities of the "case" with the prescribed norm. Consequently, the persuasiveness of the decision depends on the validity of the analogies which link the present fact-pattern either to a precedent, or to the general norm contained in the code respectively. Since I claim analogies lie at the heart of legal reasoning and illuminate a wide variety of jurisprudential problems ranging from "interpretation" to "legal fictions," and "standards" (prudent man), a further discussion of the problem of analogy is relevant.

Analogies

Formally speaking, the task of analogies is to establish similarities among different cases or objects in the face of (striking) dissimilarities. The similarity established thereby concerns a (partial) equality among the compared objects or phenomena in regard to a relevant aspect. The importance of analogies for law and for the problem of justice is brought out in Aristotle's definition of justice. Justice is seen not as an absolute equality (identity) among like persons or cases, but as a "proportion" or mean which treats the "similarity" established by a relevant aspect as an analogy (*to gar analogon meson*: τὸ γὰρ ἀνάλογον μέσον).[45] However, what can serve as a "relevant" aspect and what establishes, therefore, the "equality," is no longer susceptible to formal determinations. Whether the prohibition of taking "dogs" on the train (with the exception of guide dogs (Seeing Eye dogs)) also "covers" the case of someone transporting a cat, a Boa constrictor (even after she has been fed), laboratory mice, or (contagious) amoeba cultures will depend on a variety of substantive considerations. The "relevant" aspect which, logically speaking, provides the *tertium comparationis* cannot be determined once and for all, although it is clear that not *any* aspect will do. What considerations can become "relevant aspects," and on the basis of what grounds we establish and judge that a characteristic represents a relevant or significant difference, has to be left for the discussion below. For the moment, let us return to the pervasiveness of analogies in law.

Consider in this respect the problem of legal "fictions." The conventional wisdom is to treat fictions *cognitively* as conceptual extensions.[46] The lack of "realism" in the conceptual apparatus is justified by pointing out the obviously "false" and therefore "fictitious" character of such extensions. Thus, the Canadian government is said to have ceded to the Netherlands the maternity ward in which the Dutch successor to the throne was born when the Queen was in exile during World War II (since Dutch law provided that only children born on Netherlands soil could become monarchs).[47] These extensions are useful for filling "gaps" in the system of rules without formal legislation.[48] Nevertheless, such an interpretation of fiction as cognitive or "unrealistic" conceptual extensions misrepresents the problem. Fictions are nothing more and nothing less than analogies. An adoption, for example, which establishes the membership of the adoptee in a family, does not pretend by extension that the child is now a natural child of the parents in question. It only provides for *legally* equal treatment of the siblings and the adoptee.[49] Furthermore, by endowing the *nasciturus* (or a corporation, for that matter) with legal personality, the law implies neither that they are "persons" in the common understanding nor even that they have all the same rights. In this respect, the words of the I.C.J. in the "Reparations for Injuries Suffered in the Service of the United Nations" are instructive.

> The subjects of law in any legal system are not necessarily identical in their nature or in the extent of their rights, and their nature depends upon the needs of the community . . . Accordingly the Court has come to the conclusion that the Organization is an international person. That is not the same thing as saying that it is a State, which it certainly is not, or that its legal personality and rights and duties are the same as those of a State . . . It does not imply that all its rights and duties must be on the international plane.[50]

In short, the analogous character of legal fictions is here clearly recognized.[51]

Analogies also play an important role in the normal characterizations of facts or fact-patterns. Even when legally relevant features appear in the form of *definitions*, such taxonomic exercises are hardly ever very successful. The valiant efforts to define for purposes of liability the "keeper" of animals has attained a certain notoriety in the German legal discussion, as have the efforts of the *Reichsgericht* to define a railway exhaustively. Similarly, the definition of a "weapon," in the sense of satisfying the provisos of a penal code dealing with an armed robbery[52] cannot be determined *ex ante* but depends on the function of an object in the concrete situation. Thus, while a gun, a knife, or an ice-pick are "weapons" in our common-sense understanding, a water-pistol when brandished in a hold-up attempt, or a bottle of acid, or an attack dog can serve the same purposes. But does it therefore also follow that a cream pie when shoved into the face of a store-owner, or a soda pop sprayed in his face in order to distract him from watching his cash register, is a "weapon" in the sense of the law?[53] Or does such use simply represent an (aggravated) assault and subsequent theft? While analogies are obviously very important for relating "similar" cases to the type of delict covered by the prescription, not all analogies will be successful.

Two corollaries follow from these observations. One, what is considered as a weapon does not depend on the classificatory definition or the common usage of the term but rather on the underlying "type" which characterizes the delict. Types, however, are different from classical definitions since the instances subsumed under them do not need to have all the defining characteristics as the *taxa* and *genera* of definitions in classical logic. (Thus, all "cats" must share certain characteristics in order go be "counted" as such.) Although modern logic has given us some means to go beyond the rigid definitional distinction of classical taxonomies,[54] there is no way by which we could once and for all decide on the basis of which "resemblances" we are entitled to treat a case as "similar" or, vice versa, as dissimilar.

This brings to mind the context of the famous legal controversy of how to treat the tapping of power lines which led in the 1930s to opposite decisions of French and German courts in spite of a virtually identical definition of theft as the "illegal taking of a movable thing." While the German Court decided that electricity is not a "thing" in the meaning of the law and that therefore no penalty could be attached to the tapping of power lines (*nullum crimen sine lege*), the French Cour de Cassation came to the contrary decision.[55] Modern codifications for these reasons seem to have given up on the futile hope of defining their subject-matter exhaustively. They use a variety of means, ranging from the omission of a definition in the case of "libel" (*Beleidigung*)[56] in German law to the casuistic circumscription as in the case of theft,[57] to a mere recitation of illustrative exemplars, as the U.C.C.[58]

Directly explicitly is the "exemplary" rather than the definitive character of certain norms in the case of "standards." Thus the paradigm of the *bonus pater familias* in Roman law, or the "prudent man" standard for assessing liability in common law, are cases in point. However, even in the most explicitly codified systems, analogous reasoning figures prominently.

Consider the following "case" in which the apparently unequivocal meaning of the legal concepts led nevertheless to considerable puzzlement and to an at first counterintuitive reformulation of the meaning of the legal rule. The Old Testamentarian formulation of the *lex talionis*, "an eye for an eye, a tooth for a tooth," is unequivocal and familiar to all of us. Although we might not share the attitude of retaliation in kind, no particular problem in the application of the rule appears to exist. Nevertheless, the historical records as to the meaning of the word "for" among the Talmudic scholars tells a different story. Only a minority interpreted the text literally in spite of the common rule for the exegesis of texts that no interpretation is necessary when the text is clear (*interpretatio cessat in claris*).[59] The majority, apparently in clear violation of the text, held that the "for" meant the *monetary value* for an eye, a tooth, or a hand, rather than the part of the body itself. The reasons given for this interpretation are instructive: the scholar pointed out that the literal application would lead to impasses and injustices when, for instance, a blind person were to cause damage to another's eye, or when a maimed perpetrator caused the loss of another's hand or foot. In neither case could the victim obtain redress if a literal interpretation prevailed. Therefore, the obvious "meaning" of the rule was the universal duty of all those who had harmed someone to make good as far as possible the damage, and this in turn amounted to monetary damages.

Here two observations are in order. The first concerns the shift from the "clear" literal meaning to another interpretation. It indicates that norm-application is never a mere subsumption, but always entails an evaluation on the basis of analogies which are held to be relevant. As long as the "for" is simply seen as a permission to retaliate, as long as the process of rule-application is widely dispersed and not necessarily oriented towards treating cases alike, the literal meaning serves largely as a "trigger" indicating that someone is entitled to take the law into his/her own hands. Questions of "formal" justice in treating similar cases alike are therefore subordinate to the simple idea of retaliation. However, as soon as the process of reasoning with rules is institutionalized, i.e., a special class of "rule-handlers" has developed, and the community has made retaliation increasingly dependent on antecedent authoritative determination as to what the "relevant" issues are, requirements of formal justice attain new importance. This means, however, that analogies as a special technique of reasoning with rules became an indispensable tool for arriving at a decision. Historically we notice the shift from a "second-party" law to a "third-party" law with the emergence of explicit third parties.[60] As I have pointed out, however, such a connection is only a historically contingent, but not a conceptually necessary, condition.

The second observation concerns the conditions of a clear meaning among the "consumers" of the law. Precisely because legal norms do not *refer* to objects existing irrespective of the understandings of the norm-addressees, a clear meaning of legal terms simply signifies that there is no doubt or disagreements among the members of an audience. Such doubts, however, can arise in connection with concrete "issues."[61] To that extent the controversy about the correct interpretation of the meaning of a norm is "the juridical-semantic parallel to the conflicts of interests in the social world: it is the way in which law represents these differences."[62] Judges therefore are usually not simply "applying" norms to a case but to a large extent select among the presented interpretations which are tendered by the parties to a controversy. For this selection judges have to provide reasons precisely because the literal meaning is no longer able to represent a social consensus.

This preliminary transformation of making out of an issue a "case," i.e., hammering it into legal shape through the pleas of the parties and through the decisions during the pre-trial procedures, has often been overlooked in its importance for the "final" decision. Thus, while the final decision of a court might be understood as a "subsumption" of a case under a norm, neither the selection of one alternative among the contending readings of "fact patterns" nor the original transformation of a set of events into a "plea" can be represented in this fashion. With this observation we have in a way returned to the question on the basis of what criteria we choose what fact description and apply which rule on which level of generality to a "case" at hand. The examination of this problem entails a more detailed discussion of two interrelated problems connected with the function of topoi in legal reasoning; it is taken up in the next section.

IV   TOPOI AS MEANS FOR APPRAISAL

Given that any action or event is susceptible to a variety of "descriptions," how do we choose among the various characterizations, and how can we defend the appropriateness of our choices? Since the characterization of an act stands in a close nexus to relevant norms governing a case, these issues are not merely of peripheral interest. Our discussion in the previous chapters is helpful in this

227

respect. I want to argue that the "typifications" which we use in characterizing actions – although not subject to rigid criteria specifiable once and for all – have to satisfy certain requirements which derive from the communicative situation of the practical discourse. In particular, the situation of a discourse on grievances as elaborated in chapter 5 excludes certain characterizations while not necessarily determining the choice of an appropriate typification.

I shall argue that a specific appraisal becomes possible only through the discursive application of more specialized (legal) "topoi" for which the laws of pleadings are a good example. Furthermore, the enumeration of legal topoi contained in procedural rules and settled practices provides not only instructions as to how a practitioner is to go about a case, but also assurances that in the process, a case is looked at from different angles. Finally, the "authoritative" decision which establishes the holding by either subsuming the case under a certain norm or by stating the applicability of rule of *stare decisis* (together with the relevant facts and *obiter dicta*) depends for its persuasiveness largely upon a careful weaving, into one strand of thought, of legal and common-sense arguments. They "back"[63] the decision and its characterization of the case. It is through this embeddedness of the specialized "legal" language in the practical discourse that the importance of topoi as backings or groundings for decisions becomes visible.

In this section I intend to analyze this process of characterization and decision in greater detail. The persuasive reasons in support of a decision, i.e., commonplace arguments rooted in the practical discourse, are taken up in the next section.

Characterizations

Let us begin with an example: why is it not permissible to decribe the action by a contractor of passing a stack of twenty dollar bills to a city official and saying, "this little help is a token for one hand washing the other" as an action which entails emptying one's pockets, handing over the contents to another person, and conducting thereby a conversation? From what we said above about the necessary conditions for distortion-free communication within a discourse on grievances it is clear that no description of an action is acceptable that hides or evades the effect our actions have on others' interests. These considerations provide the reasons for the privileged status of some accounts over others, as D'Arcy has noted:

> Certain kinds of acts are of such significance that the terms which denote them may not, special contexts apart, be elided into terms which (a) denote their consequences and (b) conceal, or even fail to reveal, the nature of the act itself . . . For instance "Macbeth stabbed Duncan, and as a consequence, killed him" may be redescribed simply as "Macbeth killed Duncan; but "Macbeth killed Duncan and as a consequence succeeded him," may not be redescribed simply as "Macbeth succeeded Duncan."[64]

Furthermore, as Christopher Stone reminds us, thinking like a lawyer is to share a categorical apparatus for interpreting the world in which

> People not only walk and punch, they trespass and commit battery. They are not persons simpliciter, but buyers and sellers. The legal language answers the fundamental question of jural ontology . . . The language too determines what attributes of the world are to be noticed: monetary value and certain mental states have gained a place as have pain and suffering and consent.[65]

While both quotes emphasize the cognitive dimension of typification, it should be clear from D'Arcy's remark – and this point is curiously obscured in Stone – that the characterization of actions whether in the legal or in the practical discourse is not a description at all, but rather an *appraisal*; it is an evaluation of "facts" in terms of some normative considerations. We might take issue with a specific characterization, bracket the implicit evaluation, or make it the explicit topic of our dispute; but what does not seem possible – unless we leave the practical discourse – is the reduction of the characterization to a description in a language of pure observation.[66] On the contrary, what acquires here the status of an "objective" fact is not the thing described but rather the intersubjective *validity* of a characterization upon which reasonable persons can agree.

True, no unanimity might actually be achieved. Nevertheless, this observation does not detract from the fact that it is only on the basis of the presumption that such intersubjective characterizations *are* possible and that they can, at least in principle, be reasonably debated, that we can communicate about practical matters and attribute praise or blame. The imperfections of reality, i.e., the actual unavailability of a consensus, can be overcome by three types of strategies. Either one restricts the type of participants one admits to the discourse, or one takes a "transcendental turn" by specifying the conditions under which consensus can be reached.[67] Finally, one can opt for the *authoritative* settlement of the issues involved.

229

The first strategy is advocated by Aristotle towards the end of his *Topica*, when he gives the following advice:

> You ought not to discuss with everybody . . . for with some people argument is sure to deteriorate; for with a man who appears to try every means to escape from the right (conclusion) you are justified in trying everything to come to such a conclusion; however, this is not a seemly proceeding. You should, therefore, not readily join issue with casual persons; this can only result in a debased sort of discussion; for those who are practicing cannot forbear from disputing contentiously.[68]

The second possibility is illustrated by Habermas's construction of an "ideal speech situation"[69] in which validity claims (and thereby also characterizations) can be discoursively decided. Finally, the last possibility consists in the resort to authoritative institutions in order to resolve the relevant issues.

In the last case, it is necessary to design procedures which allow for the nonidiosyncratic selections of characterizations. This means that criteria have to be specified which allow not only for the limitation of evidence in support of a characterization, but also for the "weighing" of the information buttressing one over the other characterizations. Here the law of pleadings and evidence becomes decisive. Its essentially rhetorical roots, shown in the specialized topoi catalogues of jurists and rhetors from Cicero[70] to Quintilian,[71] Bartolus,[72] and Mopha,[73] have been established by the investigations of Stroux,[74] Viehweg,[75] and Brugi.[76] The fact that even the common law, whose law of evidence is usually identified with the jury trial,[77] exhibits fundamentally "rhetorical" features suggests a more systematic root for these similarities. It is not the rather weak "diffusion" of Roman legal doctrine through universities and through the incorporation of principles of canon law in the Court of Chancery and the Star Chamber[78] but rather the requirements of the discoursive treatment of claims which accounts for such a coincidence.

Topoi and pleadings

The common rhetorical tradition which views a legal action as a contest between two *pleadings* leading to an authoritative judgment establishes the commonality between continental and common law.[79] Furthermore, it is the notion of proof as an *argumentum*, rather than as a more deductive entailment or inductive generalization which constitutes the judicial "style" of reasoning common to both legal cultures.[80] Consider first the nature of proofs in legal proceedings. As is known, inductive logic considers as a "proof" an inference from a known fact to the unknown fact on the basis of the broadest possible evidence. Legally relevant proofs, on the other hand, result from the application of a *series of exclusionary* rules that *prohibit* certain methods of inquiry. As Giuliani has pointed out:

> The concept of proof as *argumentum* rests on certain principles: a) the theory of the formation of the issue (status, constitutio, causae) . . . proofs are rigidly selected and subordinated to the issue "ad quem probationes partium referantur" [to which the proofs of the parties refer]; b) a theory of the probable and normal, formulated not in objective, statistical terms . . . but ethically biased. Not all probables have equal value: some are preferred to others for ethical reasons; c) a theory of relevancy of proof formulated in negative terms: certain methods of inquiry are excluded so that errors should be avoided.[81]

It cannot be my task here to examine in greater detail the law of evidence in both legal cultures. It is sufficient to say that in both cases evidence has to be related to the truth of *certain perceptions* and not to inferences from the "facts."[82] Thus, evidence may be discounted not only on the basis of the secondhand nature (hearsay, *ex auditu*) but also in accordance with the principle of interest disqualification (*cui bono*).[83]

The second important aspect in which juridical and rhetorical reasoning connect is in the teaching concerning the importance of the first formulation of the issues, through the "pleadings" of the parties. The "science of well pleading,"[84] as Littleton has called it, had precisely the same tasks as the "status" theory of a controversy developed by Greek and Roman rhetors.[85] It was designed to arrive at the issues (*quaestiones*) through the debate of the plaintiff and defendant. "Pleading began with the plaintiff's declaration (count) and it was the judge's duty to moderate this oral controversy in such a way that a specific matter was affirmed by one and denied by the other party. When the opponents reached that stage they were *ad placitum* (at issue)."[86] Consider in this context the close parallels between the dilatory pleas, perfunctory pleas,[87] and the status argument developed by the Greek "stasis" teachings which is recorded by Cicero and Quintilian.[88]

According to Cicero, each case is first hammered into shape by the assertion of one party (*accusatio, intentio*) and the response by the other (*defensio, depulsio*).[89] In the limiting case, in which the jurisdiction of the court is at issue, the accused need not provide a detailed refutation of the charges, but can rely on a formal defense by explaining his nonappearance in terms of lack of jurisdiction, wrong charge, etc. (*alter in iudicium vocat, alter recusat iudicium*). Although the concept of a

231

dilatory plea is wider in that it also includes other procedural defects (wrong defendant, etc.), the parallel is striking.[90] In case the defendant has to respond, his defense will focus on the definition of the issues, which in turn leads to the appropriate characterization and determines the type of "proofs" necessary for a successful refutation (or corroboration) of the charge. For example, the person accused of killing someone can defend himself by asserting that he either has not committed the crime (*feci–non feci*),[91] or that the act was done rightfully, i.e., in self-defense (*feci-sed iure feci*).[92] In the first instance, the "factual question" (*status conjecturalis*)[93] will require proofs such as an alibi; in the second, the "quality", i.e., the characterization, of the action is at issue (*status qualitatis*)[94] that will require more complicated "proofs." Many of the most important legal arguments will turn upon the interpretation of the various pertinent legal prescriptions. For example, has someone who took objects from a temple committed a sacrilege or a theft?[95] This last question was treated in the "status" doctrine as a problem of definitions and interpretation, for which a host of topoi were collected in order to provide an inventory for argumentation.[96]

Four main lists of topoi can then be distinguished. The first set of topoi revolved around the question whether the literal meaning or the ascertainable will of the legislator shall be decisive (*scriptum et voluntas*, or *sententia*).[97] The second set of topoi dealt with the possibility of inconsistent or contradictory legal prescriptions (*antinomia, leges contrariae*).[98] Third, laws might suffer from unclear or ambiguous formulations (*amphibolia, ambiguitas*),[99] and fourth, the incompleteness of the legal order (lacuna) might make the closing of "gaps" necessary for which, again, a variety of topical considerations becomes relevant.[100] While I do not want to enter into a detailed discussion of the respective catalogues,[101] it might be useful to examine briefly some of the topoi in the second and first set. In case the legal regulations contradict each other, a variety of topoi can be adduced to establish priorities. Thus, one topos regards chronology as the decisive criterion,[102] and another establishes priority according to the special–general distinction.[103] Other possible topoi concern the importance of the conflicting rules for the community, or their moral standing.

A short reflection drives home the fact that, while all these topoi provide the starting-point for arguments by emphasizing an important consideration as a criterion, there is no *system* which would accommodate all of the relevant topoi through a complete ordering among them. Thus, the main ordering device *among* topoi is the *pairing* of topoi, each taking a different starting-point and each having different implications. The topos of "more is better than less" can be paired with a topos starting from a different "commonplace" and pointing in the opposite direction: "quality is better than quantity."[104] Similarly, the loose organizational principle which establishes the set of topoi in the first category is the opposition between *voluntas* (will of legislator) and *lex scripta* (letter of the law). Since the same topoi attain importance in the interpretation of testaments, contracts and treaties, a brief discussion is appropriate.

The topoi buttressing a "strict" or literal construction emphasize the following: (1) The capacity of the legislator or disposing party to communicate their intentions clearly; (2) Since the *scriptor* expressed his will directly the intention has to be derived from the clear text and must not be imputed through subjective speculations of unexpressed purposes or motives; (3) To that extent those emphasizing the literal meaning are also closest to the scriptor's will; (4) Any other construction violates the principle of equal treatment before the law; (5) Consequently, justifications for a nonliteral reading for equity's sake are to be rejected; (6) All of law is concerned with creating equitable solutions and particular deviations from strict rules are therefore modified by the law itself through exceptions; (7) Exemption from the law through interpretation and the application of equitable principles is nothing but the subversion of the law; (8) Through such exemptions it is no longer the law that is supreme but rather the caprice of judges; (9) However, since judges and jurors are bound to uphold the laws, an interpretation leading to results *praeter* or *contra legem* is illegal; (10) Changes in the law are the exclusive task of the legislator (people), and, therefore, until such changes occur, the judge cannot deviate from the text even if it leads to some regrettable hardships; and (11) Aside from these general considerations, the care and competence with which this particular law (testament, contract) was drafted shows the deliberate nature of the regulation, which is not to be distributed by *ad hoc* measures.

The topoi on the other side organized around the *voluntas* argument are the following: (1) Since all laws need interpretation the question is not what the meaning of the words entails but rather what the "clear meaning" is, and how it applies to this particular case; (2) Such an "application" therefore requires a reconstruction of the intention of party in these particular circumstances (*voluntas scriptoris*); (3) Precisely because all law application requires interpretation it is the task of judges not to automatically subsume a case under a general norm but to do justice in a particular case; (4) Judges and lawyers are therefore not slaves of the literal meaning, but their constitutional duty is to "find" how the law applies; (5) Since nobody is omniscient, no legislator or promisor can foresee all possible circumstances which could give rise to exceptions or exemptions; therefore the argument that deviations from the literal meaning have to be sanctioned by the legal text directly is invalid; (6) No social interaction would be possible if people clung to the literal meanings instead of being guided by what the *scriptor* intended; (7) The reason and value of laws does not exist in their textual formulation but in the underlying purposes and in the realization and protection of values for which the laws are passed. This establishes the precedence of equity over literal readings; (8) Furthermore, even a literal interpretation of the text requires a reading which does not limit itself to particular passages. An inquiry has to take into account all of the relevant regulations including other "texts" which clarify what is "meant" by a particular passage. The contextual factors, however (might) buttress an equitable rather than a strict construction. The fact that in most cases a different reading of the text is possible shows that the text is usually *not* clear and that we need an authoritative decision before we know "what the law" is; (9) It is therefore wrong to identify the "law" with the texts, and judges are always involved in one way or another in legislation. The general argument against judge-made law is therefore invalid; (10) Judge-made law is also not a threat to the constitutional order since the judge's power is severely limited by the case. The judge neither has the power to decide *ex aequo et bono* nor to legislate in a general fashion. (11) The pleader ought to try having a definition of law accepted that does not identify "the law" with the written text (*lex scripta*) and/or should show that even in a strict reading of the text some facts speak for *his/her* interpretation.[105]

Topoi and interpretation

Anybody familiar with the discussion within the International Law Commission during the draft stage of what later became the Vienna Convention on the Law of Treaties will recognize the importance of these topoi in the discussion of the Draft Articles 69–71 (later 27 and 30–33). They dealt with the interpretation of treaties and were adopted (with modifications) as Articles 31 and 32 of the final Convention. Since international agreements largely rely on the self-interpretation of the parties the topoi concerning the "constitutional" side of the proper role of the judge were naturally absent. Discussion revolved, therefore, around the issue of the "text" (sens clair, ordinary language meaning, etc.) vs. the intention of the parties (preparatory works, purposes, etc.). Furthermore, contextual factors including the limitation of interpretation by principles of general international law and the topos that the literal reading must not lead "to absurdities" or "defeat the purposes of the treaty" (*res magis valeat quam pereat*) occupied a prominent place in the debates.

The debates within the International Law Commission also show very little consensus about how these different topical considerations could be systematized through establishing clear rules of priority among the principles of interpretation. The present articles, separating the "general rule of interpretation" (Art. 31) from the supplementary means of interpretation (Art. 32), and the even more technical details concerning the authenticity of texts in two or more languags (Art. 33) suggest a "hierarchy" that is misleading. Listing the "good faith" requirement (which obviously goes back to what the parties intended) together with the "ordinary meaning," the "context," and the "purposes" shows merely that several topoi have been bolted together without resolving the contradictory implications of such a listing. Matters are not much helped by the observation – discussed several times in the law commission – that the intention of the parties in case of a multilateral treaty are particularly difficult to ascertain. But even in the simpler case of a bilateral treaty, the "will" or the intention of the party is simply a "construct" of the interpreter which might or might not have much to do with the actual motives and intentions of the (negotiating, or ratifying?) party(ies). As Sir Eric Beckett pointed out, the attempts to establish a clear rule of interpretation for the simpler construction of statutes by invoking the will of the legislature are a

> cliché tending to obscure rather than illuminate the real task of the Tribunal . . . This is even more so in the case of interpretation of treaties. As a matter of experience it often occurs that the difference between the parties to the treaties arises out of something which the parties to the treaties never thought of when the treaty was concluded.[106]

Obviously what the intentions of the parties are is a matter for interpretation which, in turn, is a hermeneutic task. Consequently, it cannot be used as a "neutral" or objective rule as to the course, the limits, and the aims of interpretation.

Thus, we are once more thrown back to the importance of topoi for structuring arguments without, however, determining their outcomes. Two observations deserve our attention once more. One, while there does not seem to exist an *a priori* specifiable limit of challenges to arguments which use topoi and arrive at decisions through this mode of practical reasoning, there

> may be well-established grounds of reasoning which, even though

capable of abandonment or modification, deserve to be examined, acknowledged, and acted on. These grounds of reasoning can be rejected only if overriding reasons become available. Even though the universe of discourse in question is not governed by the requirements of self-consistency, independence, completeness . . . which are mandatory, and decidability, which is aimed at, in axiomatic systems, some general standards of organisation of thought should be observed here also. Thus the reasoner must take care that his grounds of reasoning are not unnecessarily overlapping, redundant, irrelevant to each other, or mutually defeating. If they prove to be conflicting, their opposition would not be such which [sic] amounts to contradiction but would tolerate their coexistence after appropriate limitation or qualification of each. It is indispensable for any disciplined reasoning to shun logical inconsistency; hence in rhetorical reasoning too, any step in reasoning must be logically consistent with the argumentative steps preceding it. In special universes of discourse operating with topoi, special rules have been developed which impose limits and restraints on argumentation through exclusion of certain arguments..[107]

To that extent, the rules of exclusion that define what counts as a legally relevant "proof" fit well in this argument.

The second observation is that interpretations and topical argumentation require attention to the reasonable expectation of others, to basic rather than transient interests, impartiality, and to stability of attitudes. Those qualities Tammelo considers "ethical"[108] rather than merely logical, even in the sense of "practical logic." It is precisely this ability which distinguishes great judges from good lawyers who have merely learned to present their client's interest in the most effective manner. In this context, some lawyers have talked about a juridical "art" for "which legal science is certainly indispensable but not sufficient."[109] If we accept this description, is this "art" susceptible to further specification, or do we have to stop here and be satisfied with the explanation of the *ignotum per ignotius*?[110] How do judges choose between competing characterizations of actions, and what criteria govern the process of their "interpretation" of the law, which is then adduced as the backing for their decision? It is to these questions that the next section is addressed.

V DECIDING AND PROVIDING REASONS

Our discussion has once more cast doubt upon the conception of law as a "system" of rules. First, the example of principles in any legal order showed that principles function quite differently from rules.[111] Second, the largely topical ordering of the law, even in codified systems, makes the image of a "deductive system" of norms inappropriate.[112] Third, the importance of procedural norms in admitting or rebutting "proofs" for the characterization of an action demonstrated that questions of evidence do not easily fit into the Hartian distinction between primary rules (largely regulating forbearances) and secondary, or power-conferring, rules. Rules of evidence try rather to regulate the appropriateness of the characterization of an action susceptible to a variety of readings.

In civil law systems, such prescriptions not only comprise the various rules specifying the burden of proof among the parties but also contain provisos which allow for an appeal if a "legal norm has not been applied, or has not *correctly* been applied."[113] What "correctly" (*richtig*) means here is obviously not decidable solely in terms of purely formal criteria but has something to do with the "fit" between the invoked norms and the relevant facts. If this argument holds, then not only does the conventional distinction between questions of fact and questions of law break down, but the distinction itself can be seen as a rhetorical strategy of enhancing support for a decision. It presents the problem of competing evaluations in a judicial decision as issuing largely from "factual" elements. Facts are, however, widely held to be susceptible to relatively easy verification. We can observe a similar "transformation" of a characterization into a factual question in the case of the *res ipsa loquitur* rule in American law. Where the rule applies (for example, in the cases of negligence), the evaluative characterization of an action can be inferred directly from the *fact* of an accident, if the character of the accident and the circumstances attending it lead

> reasonably to the belief that in the absence of negligence it would not have occurred and that the thing which caused the injury is shown to have been under the exclusive management of the alleged wrongdoer.[114]

Technically, the rule amounts to a shift in the burden of proof from the plaintiff to the defendant.[115] For our purposes it is important to notice that thereby the "characterization" of an act is decided and supported on the basis of common-sense judgments which marshal wide assent to such evaluations. While such strategies of transformation explain the selection of certain fact-descriptions over others by settling the normative issue through an appeal to the "facts," some cases may exhibit more complicated features. What, then, are the criteria for a selection in such cases?

237

Two interdependent points deserve attention in this context. One is the importance of the "technique" (*ars legis*) for arriving at a decision which has to be, according to legal standards, "acceptable" or "in conformity" with the law. Traditional jurisprudence has attempted to deal with this problem in terms of rules of interpretations or *canones*.[116] However, as we have seen, such collections of rules only list often incompatible topoi without being able to determine the relative "weight" of the principle of a "clear text" vs. the clear intention. In short, it is not the canons of interpretation that determine what the correct or "conform" interpretation is; rather the weight of various *canones* is determined by the *object* of interpretation, i.e., whether we deal with a will, a contract, or a statute,[117] and by the commonly accepted claims to protection.

This leads us to the second point of importance: the rootedness of claims to protection for particular interests in the value consensus of a society.[118] The latter consideration is as important as the invocation of abstract principles. This becomes clear when we realize that the norm that one is "obliged to restitute the damage done to another" is insufficient in establishing an actionable cause and that even the reference to settled rules or clear texts does not lead to a decision unless such invocations satisfy the conditions of legal arguing. The last point indicates the importance of having the case processed through a set of argumentative steps. It is this procedure that prepares the matter for the final decision. Through a series of "turning-points," competing interests and interpretations can be taken into account, and can then be either rebutted or accepted. Thus, the judicial decisions are path-dependent, and it is this characteristic that distinguishes them from mere random choices, or from an unsystematic subjection of the subject-matter to competing evaluations. Nevertheless, such paths are not the result of a strict logical algorithm for decisions.[119] Furthermore, the path, as established through the process of legal arguing, is additionally controlled by certain ethical principles that the participants have to heed – even the adversary attorneys are, after all, officers of the court. Both elements serve as a backdrop to understanding and as a "frame" for the practice of legal arguing.

Consider, for example, the path of a legal decision in the following case which Thomas Seibert has mapped.[120] In this case, a person (Mr. Biedermann) had booked a package tour (cruise) commencing in Venice with a travel agent in Munich. In addition, the customer purchased an air ticket from Munich to Venice from the same agent. Because of a delay in the flight, caused by a reported slowdown of air traffic controllers, Mr. Beidermann missed the departure of the ship

238

and thus the cruise. Refusing to pay the full amount of the cruise, he is sued by the travel agent. The relevant legal prescriptions are: (1) If someone ordered an "object" (*Werk*), he is liable to pay the agreed-upon price. Relevant in this context is now the question of whether a package tour is an object in the sense of the law (the meaning in this sense is regulated by Para. 651 B.G.B. a, ff) so that subordinate rule can be formulated: (2) If someone has booked a tour he has to pay the agreed-upon price to the organizer (or his agent). Again, a subsidiary question attains importance: is booking sufficient to make a customer liable for the full price, even if he does not participate in the tour?[121] If no liability is incurred for the full amount, what proportion is fair in order to indemnify the loss to the operator? In the present case, again a different rule appears to solve the problem by providing: (3) Who misses the departure of the ship is fully liable. While this rule interprets the case in terms of fault, the topos contained in (4) brings to bear on the facts a competing set of considerations: (4) Those liable for the timely arrival of the passengers are primarily the tour operator and his agents, particularly when they recommend and offer the booking of transportation to the cruise.

Here the legally relevant fact description no longer focuses on the missing of the boat and the fault but rather on the issue of *venire contra factum proprium*, i.e., a tour-operator is "estopped" from blaming the passenger when the delay was caused by the reliance of the passenger on the operator's arrangements. After all, the passenger booked a *package tour* in the belief that thereby the bother of making all the relevant arrangements was taken over by the tour operator and his agents.

Note that rules (3) and (4) are not "meta-rules" which would clearly prescribe how to apply the more abstract second (and thereby first) rule to the concrete case. While (1) and (2) could be said to stand in a relationship of logical entailment (3) and (4) "organize" the facts differently and make different rules relevant (fault vs. invalidation of the contract through possible *culpa in contrahendo*).

How is one to choose now between these possible interpretations? In order to get the court to adopt rule (3), the travel agent has to argue that the flight connection which was recommended to the customer (via Milan) left plenty of time for arriving in Venice. However, because of the work slowdown of the controllers, which was widely reported in the press, it was the customer's responsibility to secure a punctual arrival and change the booking. The topos which implicitly is invoked here for the selection of the relevant fact is "Act of God." If the defendant intends to rebut this claim, he will have to argue that precisely because the slowdown of controllers was of direct relevance to the organizers of package tours, the buyer of such a service can rely on the organizer to get him in time to the appointed place. The lack of action on the part of the organizer (no call, no change in the booking), therefore, indicated that the organizer did not think that special precautions were necessary. Consequently, the purchaser of the package deal was justified in relying on the bookings made and cannot be held to be at fault in missing the crucial connection.

The legally relevant topos is then "reliance," or "good faith," which again rebuts the construction in terms of fault. The German Supreme Court (B.G.H.), however, in its decision, short-circuited some of these considerations by counting additional offers, such as the trip to Venice, as falling under the provisos of "services." Such a characterization of the fact-pattern is justified, the Court held, if the organizer of a package tour in his advertisement and offering does not make significant distinctions between the package tour and the additional services.[122] Thus, liability is placed squarely on the organizer.

The above narrative of a "case" shows that the same results can be reached by different routes. Furthermore, while the paths can be traced, following them is not reducible to clear algorithms, or to subsumptions of the particular norms and rules under the more general principles or higher-level norms. Such an interpretation is faulty if for no other reason than the fact that at each turning-point a "practical judgment" is required as to how a certain factual situation is to be appraised. It is precisely this going back and forth between "facts" and norms[123] in which the "artfulness" of legal reasoning (*ars legis*) consists. If this argument is correct, it has an important corollary: it appears that "justice" is not so much an attribute of the formal principles contained in positive law as it is the result of reasonable and principled use of norms in making practical judgments about factual situations. Viewed from this angle, we can understand why "Law" and "Justice" stand in a certain relationship of tension, as it is only through the authoritative decision of a court that it can be established what is fair and reasonable in a particular case. Justice is therefore created only *arte legis*, or through the "judicial policy" of the court, although it is (contingently) related to (preexisting) legal prescriptions.[124] The contingent character of this relationship is visible not only in the case of legal systems where existing precedents can be "overruled," but also in codified systems where the wide variety of possible interpretations makes it problematic to view a court's decision as "prefigured" or "deduced" from the existing body of rules.

These considerations have two further implications. One, it appears to be insufficient to identify justice with the existence of a certain body of rules or a regime. Doing justice involves, above all, the exercise of practical judgments in which abstract norms and concrete circumstances are fitted to each other. It seems therefore that the specification of purely formal criteria, such as the yardstick that one has to treat similar cases alike,[125] is important but of limited utility as opposed to the appraisal of the more substantive criteria embodied in precedents and institutional history. Thus, in spite of the efforts of analytical philosophy to solve normative puzzles ranging from animal rights to nulear war through logical derivation from specified principles, our discussion suggests that there is a certain artificiality in these attempts.[126] The problem of justice lies not so much in the invariant principles for formal justice as in the *field-dependent criteria* of what counts, for instance, as a good faith effort, what is negligent in a certain set of activities, or what type of honesty and disclosures can be legitimately expected in simple economic transactions, partnerships, or in the intimacy of a marriage.[127]

This leads us to the discussion of the second implication. Given the fact that juridically relevant characterizations are the result of specific "paths" and of field-dependent substantive criteria of appraisal, can the process of choice and of judicial discretion be further illuminated? Furthermore, on the basis of what means can the choice resulting from judicial discretion be persuasive and marshal support? In a way the first corollary provides the most important clues for resolving the (second) puzzle of judicial discretion.[128] As we have seen, judges are always creatively forming the law, whether they simply "apply" rules in a codified system, or whether they find it and formulate it more explicitly, as in common law orders. We also saw that such law-creation is not, however, norm-creation *de novo*, but that it is path- and field-dependent in that dogmatic (systematic) considerations and/or precedential "starting-points" provide the context in which the decision has to be made. Thus, creativity is circumscribed by guidelines that specify what good legal arguing is.

While most "decisions" can be explained in terms of these constraints, there remains the problem of legal interpretation *praeter legem* and the "overruling" of the precedent. Neither problem seems to fit the pattern outlined above. It has been the merit of Josef Esser's comparative studies to show that judicial discretion even in these cases follows certain "paths."[129] This dispenses, on the one hand, with the argument of the arbitrariness of judicial discretion. On the

241

other hand, it also demonstrates that judicial law-making is not simply a matter of "courage" or social activism, as it has sometimes been depicted.[130]

As Esser has argued, four specific judicial topoi help the judge in these cases to arrive at a solution. The solution in turn is acceptable, i.e., falls within a range of plausibility, because it follows an intersubjectively traceable path within a "field" bounded by commonly accepted appraisals (value-judgments). The specific topoi are reason (natural reason), equity, the nature of things (*Natur der Sache*) and, finally, the implicit logic in the legal order. The latter topos relates various fields of law to each other.[131] The fields in turn are characterized by topical orderings and the acceptance of "standard-solutions" for various "law jobs."[132]

In this context, the wording of the famous Article 1 of the Swiss Civil Code is worth recalling. It stipulates somewhat fictitiously that the judge who is formulating a rule in the absence of a legal prescription shall "make a rule which the legislator would have passed." It furthermore instructs him/her to follow thereby the "well-proved legal teachings (doctrine) and tradition."[133] Consequently, the traditionally accepted values form the basis upon which the legal order rests, and judicial decisions attain their persuasiveness from this value-consensus or overlap. Nevertheless, against a naive version of naturalist thinking we have to remember that a "tradition" of values is already *legally* informed and differs from either pure ethics or simple commonsense considerations. This point clearly emerges from the reference to "legal teachings," or doctrine, in the above quote, but also from the observation that legal institutions have *their own* values and logic. Examples abound: see, for example, the elimination of intention from a wide variety of legal transactions leading to the proviso that a (malicious) motive cannot be made a cause of action in civil matters,[134] the tolerance of even illegally acquired property as in the Roman *usucapio*,[135] and the emphasis on "normal" standards (*quod plerumque fit*)[136] instead of standards of supererogation. All instances clearly show the separateness of the legal order from ethics. Although it is true that equity, reason, etc., imbue law with ethical traits, it is also true that thereby ethics is *juridified*, as Esser correctly remarks.[137] To that extent the traditional view of natural law as some sort of prescriptions "beyond," or standing "behind," positive law, giving positive law its validity, is misleading.[138] It pretends to establish a normative hierarchy at odds with reality, and it misdiagnoses the interaction of principles and their norm-generative force in the judicial decision.

Even if we grant these arguments about judicial law-making, one serious objection to my interpretation could be that the appraisal of the role of norm-generating principles only applies to legal "systems." After all, the fourth topos mentioned above is based on the implicit logic of a deductive system of rules. The argument of the "logic" of the system *does* seem to be extraneous to common law thinking. However, as Michael Moore has shown,[139] in at least some legal theories of precedent, systematic considerations are of decisive importance. For example, such considerations figure prominently in the minds of judges when they intend to overrule a previously established rule. In a similar fashion, when we talk about the "holding" of a case, we conventionally mean the historical event when a particular rule was enunciated. But actually the rule that got established made sense only in conjunction with all other rules of the common law. Consequently, the rule depends in its validity upon its coherence with other common law "truths" and not solely on its historical enunciation in a particular case. Moore concludes therefore:

> This leaves us with something like Llewellyn's dual theory of precedent. We find it helpful in casual discourse about cases to talk of their holdings in [a] historical way. Among other things, speaking this way is a good heuristic for teaching law to beginning law students who are not in any position to cohere an entire body of law into a systematic expression of morality and institutional facts. Yet when judges decide, or lawyers or scholars urge reasons for decisions, the historical/psychological view disappears. Here we assess each case not for its ability to establish a rule to decide some new case, but rather, for its impact on the totality of our common law.[140]

This change in perspective away from the case to the *logic of institutions*, i.e., how different rules of, for instance, contract law, torts, etc., fit together, provides important clues about the constraints of judicial law-making. We no longer focus simply on the case but on the decision process which develops out of the interplay of the parties' pleadings, out of the search for the precedent and out of the practice which locates the case within the context of contracts, torts, etc. As in a discourse where certain answers given at one time foreclose other responses or make them more or less persuasive, the historical decisions of courts exert their influence on later law-creation. But unlike purely historical considerations in which judges merely refer to the "will" of the legislator, a full account of law realizes that claims to the "intention of the legislator" are not simple-minded references to purely historical facts but "interpretative proposals," as Dworkin has called them, through which the *integrity* of law is safeguarded.

243

> Law as integrity, then begins in the present and pursues the past only so far as and in the way its contemporary focus dictates. It does not aim to recapture even for present law, the ideals or practical purposes of the politicians who first created it. It aims rather to justify what they did . . . in an overall story worth telling now, a story with a complex claim: that present practice can be organized by and justified in principles sufficiently attractive to provide an honorable future . . . [Law as integrity] commands a horizontal rather than vertical consistency of principle across the range of the legal standards the community now enforces.[141]

From our discussion, it also appears that the resort to purely "rhetorical" topoi is the more important the less well the legal institutions are elaborated, be it because of the newness of an institution, or be it because the legal order lacks established and accepted means of norm-creation. Under such circumstances, rhetorical figures such as the invocation of "authorities" (*argumentum ex auctoritate*), of ridicule (in order to refute a characterization of an opponent), and the argument distinguishing between (true) "reality" and "appearance" play a particular role.[142] Lyndell Prott[143] has shown in his careful study how these rhetorical techniques are of particular importance in international law where in the absence of "international legislation" and a reliable set of cases with precedential value, judges have to rely on such means of persuasion. For example, the reasoning of Judge van Wyk in the *South West Africa* case (1962) contained no fewer than twelve extracts from decisions and authors and thirteen other sources.[144] Van Wyk based his characterization of the case largely on the "subsidiary" source of international law which allows the adduction of decisions and of publicists in order to support his adherence to a particular interpretation of a fact-pattern. Needless to say, in the absence of additional arguments, the attempt to ground a claim basically in an *argumentum ex auctoritate* is not too persuasive.[145]

Even more significant in this context is Judge Wellington Koo's dictum in the *Barcelona Traction* case, which utilizes the disjunction of "appearance–reality" in order to back his choice of a legally relevant characterization:

> International law, being primarily based upon the general principles of law and justice, is unfettered by technicalities and formalistic considerations which are often given importance in municipal law . . . It is the reality which counts more than the appearance. It is the equitable interest which matters rather than the legal interest. In other words it is the substance which carries weight on the international plane rather than the form.[146]

244

Here the weakness of international law to provide for normatively elaborated "fields" is adduced as an explicit reason for utilizing the "rhetorical proof," i.e., that substance is more important than form in order to buttress a decision.

One step further removed from the practical or rhetorical figures of reasoning are attempts to gain assent to a characterization through the *power of metaphors*. Metaphors are sometimes treated as analogies, in that their power consists in the comparison of certain common traits of otherwise dissimilar facts. However, metaphors are different from analogies in that they do not require to make explicit the point or dimension according to which a similarity is asserted.[147] As a matter of fact, the power of metaphors, as exemplified in modern lyrics, often cannot be understood cognitively, or even in terms of a good reason approach, but has its roots in the evocation of certain emotions or moods.[148] Thus, assent to a valued position is gained directly by an appeal to emotions rather than through reasoning. To that extent we clearly transcend the boundaries of practical reasoning and "rhetorical proofs."[149] Nevertheless, there is no doubt that such emotional appeals are of importance in the practice of persuasion. Consider in this context the powerful effect of the term "sacred trust" which the I.C.J. chose in its advisory opinion in the *South West Africa* case, as Prott remarks:

> Throughout the whole of this advisory opinion the Court continues to use the almost mystical expression "sacred trust" as a means of justifying a particular interpretation of the perplexing mandate instrument. Using words this way enables a judge to exploit the evocative function of language in order to adumbrate and suggest what has come to him perhaps only by intuition.[150]

Other metaphors, less central for the respective argument, were nevertheless important in rallying support for particular characterizations in various cases.[151] Thus the Court urged the metaphor of a "toboggan down the slide";[152] "le carcan de l'étroite conception classique";[153] "cobwebs in the attics";[154] "the swamp in which the argument is bogged down";[155] "put the clock back';[156] "to dangle the carrot";[157] "the litmus test';[158] "to sift the wheat from the chaff";[159] "a sort of 'ostrich-act' – a hiding of the face in the sands . . ."[160]

While judges sometimes have to resort to such means, which are deeply ingrained in our techniques of arguing in everyday life, there is no doubt that there is a certain uneasiness among legal professionals about grounding a decision in such common-sense structures, rather than in the techniques and art of jurisprudential reasoning. Also typical for such an uneasiness is the problem of weighing when a judge has no other way than to argue that competing values have to be traded-off. Usually, judges try to enunciate some type of "test" in order to provide a more general criterion for their particular weighing. Nevertheless, as the example of the balancing-test, enunciated in First National City Bank[161] and subsequent decisions in other Circuit Courts show,[162] such tests are usually indeterminate. They also easily allow for interpretations which establish a virtually exclusive predominance of the values of the "forum" over other competing interests. Such an outcome is all the more likely because judges and courts are primarily institutions entrusted with the protection of interests funneled through the domestic legal order.

This difficulty leads to some peculiar tensions in transnational legal disputes when domestic courts have to wear two hats at the same time, i.e., that of a domestic institution and that of an international agency.[163] Principles like "comity" and "discretion" are then sometimes invoked in order to prevent the most foreseeable embarrassments. Part of the problem is, however, that these principles are invoked *ad hoc* precisely because the interaction of norm and more specific rules is only weakly articulated in the transnational arena. In the absence of a clearer identification of the international legal order's needs, interest adjustments rarely go beyond the *particular* weighing of the concrete interests in the *particular* case. It thus inhibits the growth of normative "solutions" or structures in the sense of Moore's or Esser's normatively structured fields. As Harold Meier has pointed out, the traditional balancing, as well as the comity argument, based on the distinction between authority (jurisdiction) and restraint,

> frees the court from weighing its decision in the light of its impact on the international law formation process and insulates it from the need to evaluate the impact of the assertion of jurisdiction on the development of reciprocal expectations about the legitimacy of the exercise of power in similar situations by other potential regulators in the international community . . . Since courts . . . are always operating under legislative language that on its face suggests that the statute is applicable to the foreign events . . . there is some anomaly in a court's finding that a regulation may be applied without violating international jurisdictional standards but that the congressional command will not be followed if the court determines that as a matter of policy the regulation is inappropriately applied . . . Furthermore, this judicial approach suggests that Congress should regard itself as being free of international legal constraints when drafting legislation, as long as it can identify an appropriate effect upon U.S. commerce within the context of objective territoriality.[164]

246

To that extent the characterization of the international arena as a primitive (social) system has some validity. The norm-generative capacity of principles and the logic of institutions do not point in a clear direction in an arena which does not provide for the many underpinnings found in the setting of domestic social orders.

VI CONCLUSION

The main objective of this chapter was a further clarification of rhetorical and practical reasoning, of which legal reasoning has been claimed as a subcategory. For showing the relevance of this thesis, it was necessary to take one step back and deal more systematically with the problem of practical reasoning as outlined in Aristotle's *Topica* and *Rhetoric* and contrast these figures of thought (or modes of reasoning) with the classical syllogisms and patterns of inference in inductive logic. By emphasizing the particular importance of *appraisals* I briefly discussed the context between communicative structures and the ability to rally support (assent) to practical judgments on the basis of commonly accepted value-positions.

In a second step, the logical structures of the two most important logical figures of practical reasoning, i.e., enthymeme and analogy, were examined in greater detail. This examination not only showed the context between the hidden-value premises for the normative assessments in enthymematic figures, but also provided a first cut at criticizing the naive rationalistic model of "subsumption" as a basis for understanding legal reasoning. Section III was therefore designed to show some of the most obvious shortcomings of this interpretation. This section also intended to demonstrate that a wide variety of specific legal techniques shaping the reasoning style of lawyers are based on *analogies* (fictions, interpretation, legal types, etc.). By showing, furthermore, that legal "definitions" do not function like taxonomic divisions, I marshalled another argument against the naive subsumption model.

The discussion in turn led to the recognition that not subsumption, but rather the appropriate *characterization* of actions, i.e., their attribution to a legal "type," makes for some of the most puzzling and interesting problems in legal reasoning. In this context the importance of topoi as "seats" of arguments became obvious. In particular, we found that the specialized topoi, which formed the basis of the classical "status" teachings, influenced the law of pleadings, as well as that of legal proofs in continental and common law systems. The role of the more specialized legal topoi in providing a path for judicial decisions was then examined further.

The next step consisted in demonstrating the essentially topical character of many important legal *principles*. This point then led back to a discussion of the context of norms and rules and the norm-generative components of certain legal principles through the structuring of "fields."

The observations made in this context helped us to deal finally in greater detail with the problem of the binding character of legal prescriptions and the issue of judicial discretion, both of which provided a rich set of puzzles for legal theory. While I cannot claim to have solved all or perhaps even the most important of these issues, my approach did advance our understanding in a variety of ways. It showed the close practical as well as conceptual connection between "law," traditional values, and institutions without making one merely an appendix of the other. Our discussion also suggested the artificiality of attempting to address the problem of justice from a purely analytical perspective. On the other hand, "law" was shown to be a distinct phenomenon not reducible to either purely idiosyncratic preferences, such as utility or even duty, or to purely ethical criteria. Its distinctive nature, it was argued, could be captured best by tracing the distinctive features of reasoning with rules and norms and their embeddedness in topical thinking.

CONCLUSION: THE INTERNATIONAL LEGAL ORDER, INTERNATIONAL SYSTEMS, AND THE COMPARATIVE ANALYSIS OF THE PRACTICE OF STATES

I

With the demonstration of the special nature of reasoning with rules employed in the third-party mode, the systematic exposition of my argument concerning rules and norms has come to an end. This exposition began in chapter 3, after the evaluation of the regime approach had shown certain shortcomings in the conventional treatment and understanding of the function of norms. By utilizing a rather unorthodox methodology which I justified in chapter 1, I began with the examination of the function of norms, i.e., their problem-solving capacity, and their emergence. The following chapters were then devoted to the clarification of the role of norms in various contexts and, in particular, to their capacity for resolving conflict in a nonviolent fashion by structuring a discourse on grievances.

A more refined conceptual apparatus derived from speech-act theory and the communicative action approach enabled us to transcend some of the conventional pitfalls of regime-analysis, which explains norm-following in terms of the "long-term" interest of the actors and in terms of the "injunctions" regimes provide. As the discussion in chapter 5 demonstrated, aside from the very special circumstances of iterative PD games in tournament approaches, the (rule-)utilitarian argument becomes inconsistent.

Furthermore, the emphasis on claims and claiming opened the way for the analysis of one particularly important set of norms: *rights*, by which we decide the appropriateness and priority of conflicting claims. The discussion of chapter 6 dealt with the concept of right in an historical as well an analytical fashion. It advanced a constructionist view on certain human or basic rights, an approach which has implications for the domestic as well as the international legal order. In addition, such a conceptualization enabled us to clarify some of the long-standing puzzles concerning the issues of state vs. individual rights.

Finally, the concept of constitutive, as distinguished from regulative rules, was helpful in assessing the reality status of the international *legal* order. Conventionally, the debate in international relations revolves around two competing ideas: that of an "anarchy" and that of a more communitarian conception, often called the Grotian perspective. While few analysts would go so far as to infer the existence of a community from the ever-increasing interdependencies of international life, few specialists are also inclined to subscribe to the conventional Hobbesian interpretation of international relations as a war of all against all. Therefore, the respective positions are very quickly redefined and become "structural realism" on the one hand and a "primitive" social system, community, or whatever, on the other.

Since this book was devoted – among other things – to a refutation of the "anarchy" argument, no further extensive discussion of its conceptual distortions seems necessary. However, it is fitting that I address briefly the shortcomings of the "societal" metaphor, in particular its "primitive-systems" analogy. Although it is obvious that my substantive understanding of international relations is in a way closer to this mode of analysis, I do not consider the primitive-systems analogy very helpful for understanding either the international system or the international legal order. A brief discussion seems in order.

II THE INTERNATIONAL LEGAL ORDER AS A REGULATIVE IDEA OR AS REALITY

Since the power of metaphors consists in their ability to evoke associations and thereby make the unknown understandable by means of the known, the primitive-systems conceptualization suffers from a variety of shortcomings. One is the implicit suggestion of a continuum between primitive and developed social systems. Two, by the suggestion of a course of development from a "primitive" customary order to a fully developed "positive" legal order – in the case of the international legal order – many of the distinctive features of the international legal order are misinterpreted. Thus, a particular view of legal development is imposed which is of questionable validity even for domestic legal systems. Though we might be willing to accept the view that the development of domestic law is from "custom to contract," international reality is more complex. The conception of multilateral treaties as indicators of emerging "custom" not only reverses this sequence by subordinating contract to custom but also shows that the international legal order has several important characteristics *sui generis*.

Third, another important correction should also be kept in mind. In a naive vision of law, legal prescriptions are often viewed as the "tip of the iceberg." They are the most visible and specific regulations, but they rest on a wide variety of other normative structures. Although this metaphor captures an important aspect of the interaction of law and society, it is misleading in other respects. As our discussion showed, legal norms are not different from other norms by some intrinsic characteristic (such as sanction, etc.), but become so only through the process of application. To that extent "the law" is not only the very visible "tip" but reaches also "down" into far greater depths by informing other societal norms. Thus again, attempts to delineate mutually exclusive sets of norms have failed.

Similar difficulties arise when we attempt to distinguish the wider and narrower concepts of "political system" vs. that of a legal order. While the concept of a political system seems wider than that of "law" – in that politics also includes law-making, bargaining, interest-articulation, etc. – the legal order is in another respect the wider concept. After all, it is through the constitutional provisions that law provides for the orderly *political process*. Precisely because the constitution is "constitutive" of the political system, the conventional taxonomy of "politics" and "law" hides rather than illuminates important conceptual dimensions.

Viewed from this vantage-point the concept of the international legal order becomes clearer. In following Coplin's argument about the constitutive nature of international legal prescriptions we can say that the international legal order exists simply by virtue of its role in defining the game of international relations.[1] It informs the respective decision-makers about the nature of the interaction and determines who is an actor; it sets the range of permissible goals which the actors can pursue; it specifies the steps necessary to insure the validity of their official acts and assigns weight and priority to different claims.

Nowhere does this constitutive function of law become clearer than in the concept of "sovereignty" and its norm-generative force. The term was originally developed as a construct for justifying internal hierarchy.[2] In opposition to the privileges and freedoms of feudal society, a supreme authority was created in the person of the sovereign who was "absolved" from all internal laws, though subject to natural law. Sovereignty thus ended the "anarchy" of medieval society by making all members "subjects" to a central authority. But "sovereignty," conceived as exclusive internal rule (*dominium*) made it also necessary to conceive of the relationships among "persons of sovereign authority." As I have pointed out, it was fortuitous that these were conceptualized as being *legal* in character, i.e., as owners or possessors of rights. It is here that sovereignty attained a new dimension: sovereign equality. From the understanding of sovereignty as a bundle of rights analogous to "property," the principle of non-intervention could easily be derived. Many analogies taken from Roman private law which found their belated recognition in the famous "principles recognized by civilized nations" then provided further conceptual tools for developing a full-fledged international *legal* order.[3]

The importance accorded to rights in this respect was of decisive importance for developing the *practice* of international law. The international legal order was therefore not simply a kind of regulative idea, such as the ideals of a good prince invoked in the various mirrors of princes, or of the heavenly Jerusalem on its earthly pilgrimage. While those ideas informed much of medieval political thought, international law became a *well-ingrained practice*, whose exceptional character was deeply appreciated among the participants. Although several European powers had various dealings with "outsiders," such as the Ottoman Empire, the High Porte never became a recognized member of this state system until after the Crimean War. The reason was precisely the nonrecognition by the Sultans of mutual rights and common legal practices[4] (such as immunity to diplomats), which prevented Istanbul from becoming a player with full status within the European system.

These brief remarks help us also to clear up some of the misunderstandings occasioned by the primitive-system, and the primitive-law, analogy. First, while systemic characteristics can be imputed to phenomena by outside observers, the importance of the "internal aspect" of rules and norms for social systems has been pointed out in chapter 1. This recognition not only imparts a peculiar type of reflexivity into the behavior of the participants of the system, but is also the reason why such systems do not disintegrate but reproduce themselves in spite of often important divergences of actual behavior and norms. The reason for maintaining these rules through practice is, however, quite different in international law than in customary legal orders or in primitive societies. "Primitive" law is not only customary, but comprises a wide variety of other prescriptions concerning the "right" way of life such as taboos, rites, mythical lore, etc., which depend in their effectiveness on the mutual reinforcement of face-to-face contacts. All these factors are quite alien to international law. International law is a purely secular construct and it is clearly distinguishable from religion, rituals, myths, or particular conceptions of morality. Here, our discussion of "it is right that" and having "rights" in chapter 6 provided the appropriate distinctions. After all, it was no accident that a *legal* conceptualization of international relations attained importance when attempts to use the "right way of life" as an organizing principle of political life had to be abandoned. The wars of religion had demonstrated that neither the old orthodoxy nor the new religious forces could organize the old *res publica Christiana*. On the contrary, each day of continued warfare over questions of rectitude led to new savageries without these ultimate issues being decided; the creation of a legal conceptualization on the basis of the ascription of rights appeared to be the only possibility of creating the normative framework necessary for social coexistence.

The characterization of international law as a largely customary system of law needs further important modifications. One of the peculiarities of the international legal order is that it presupposes the distinction between a public and a private legal sphere, a division usually undeveloped or absent in primitive customary systems. The last point has important repercussions for the role of public officials as "agencies" of the international legal order.[5] Thus, unlike a primitive order, where law is the set of customary norms everybody follows, international law is *applied* to problems by a special class of public officials. In this sense international law exhibits some features of a developed legal system and it possesses at the same time traits of a customary order characterized by horizontal patterns of authority.[6] Finally, there is the special feature of the prescriptions of transnational law, which regulate the conduct of private associations, such as multinational corporations, in their interaction with states.[7]

Now that it has been stated to what extent the term "primitive" is misleading, it is easier to analyze the weaknesses of international law without subscribing to the implications of the "domestic analogy." One of the decisive shortcomings of the international legal order is most obviously its lack of compulsory jurisdiction. Nevertheless, as experiences from the domestic order show, even subjecting members of a community to the compulsory settlement of disputes might not prove very effective. As soon as well-organized groups are involved the contribution of law to conflict resolution even in domestic systems consists more in bounding the conflict than in resolving it through authorititative decisions. This bounding is achieved by the definition of a bargaining zone and by the availability of (legal) precedents to which the bargaining parties can resort. On the other hand, attempts to deal with demonstrations and strikes through the issuance of injunctions and the strict application of "the law" very quickly leads to the realization of the limits of law for resolving conflict. To the extent that the subjects of international law are for the most part nations, i.e., well-organized groups, similar problems would have to be expected even if the unlikely situation arose and all nations were to accept the compulsory jurisdiction of the I.C.J. or some other international tribunal(s). The separation of the legal process from the political process in the domestic arena is possible because *both* processes are well institutionalized. However, since the world political process lacks institutionalization, a more effective utilization of the international legal process is considerably hampered.

Although international law provides for a rudimentary informal organization of social life among independent actors, there are no effective formal organizations that can translate interest and issues into policy. Collective goods on the international level are thus not provided or achieved suboptimally through hegemonic leadership and, infrequently, through some type of voluntary contributions. The world political process remains *sporadic*, in spite of all communications. It is often characterized by bargaining and coercive moves rather than by persuasion and by appeals to common standards, shared values, and accepted solutions. Thus, not only can the legal process not be separated from the political process, but the impartiality of legal reasoning is crucially impaired by the lack of authoritative decisions concerning the applicability and scope of legal norms.

International adjudicative institutions are more often than not quite limited in their ability to determine what the law *is*. Quite apart from the hoary institutional problem of how authoritative decisions of international tribunals can be enforced, the problem of determining the applicable legal principle is often made impossible by the narrow limits to the jurisdictional domain of such tribunals.[8] These considerations have two corollaries: first, if the relevant legal rules or principles cannot be authoritatively established, many issues remain unclear. An unknown rule can neither be followed nor violated. In this way, one of the major advantages of a legal settlement is diminished, i.e., that future quarrels can be avoided by taking the authoritatively established rule into account. The second corollary is that substitutes have to be found so that such impasses do not become totally disabling characteristics of the legal order. In this context advisory opinions,

254

decisions by national institutions, and scholarly expositions have to be mentioned. Their weight, however, will largely depend upon their persuasive power rather than their institutional authority since the rule of *stare decisis* is not accepted. Only in this sense does the importance of advisory opinions by the I.C.J. become understandable. This also explains why the writings of legal scholars are considered a "subsidiary source" of international law.[9]

National institutions, however, often fail in establishing "the law" persuasively because of their partisan nature. The observer is then confronted with practices varying from state to state. The most obvious example of the partisan nature of decision-making is provided by the regulations of administrative agencies, whose rulings are bound by national policy. But even the independent courts have considerable difficulty in acting in a detached fashion. They might have to defer to the executive agencies because of constitutional considerations, or they are bound by national legislative interpretations or by precedents. Thus, while a decision of a national court settles a particular dispute which may have international legal ramifications, and while its decision might be authoritative as a precedent *within* a given domestic legal system, it will often fail to be considered as an authoritative decision on the level of international law.[10]

The lack of international credibility of domestic decisions has important implications for an assessment of international law as an instrument that impartially protects the interests of all claimants. It is clear that those parties which have the most developed domestic organizational structures as well as the most far-reaching interests can adjudicate the largest number of disputes. Although no modern nation is currently in the same privileged position as England was in the nineteenth century, differentials of development and power still matter, and the calls for a New International Economic Order are not simply appeals for a greater share in the world's products. They largely concern the imbalance of power resulting from the unequal distribution of resources and know-how that is supposed to be corrected by a regime-change. An even-handed assessment must admit, however, that national courts occasionally deviate from established national policies and try to come to terms with the changing structure of international society, thereby providing important new crystallization points for the development of international law. The reasoning in the famous Sabbatino case in the U.S. and the decision of the B.G.H. in Germany in the Nigerian Cultural Properties case mentioned above are cases in point.

Finally, the lack of effective channels for an authoritative determination of what the law is and how it can be modified, changed, or rescinded sheds new light on the problem of compliance and legal change. Noncompliance is usually conceived as a transgression in which an actor works for his/her advantage by violating the prescriptions in the hope of not being discovered. Even in the domestic arena, however, there are cases of noncompliance in defense of a valued position and with the explicit purpose of changing an objectionable rule. Cynical acts of rascality, therefore, are different from actions of civil disobedience. Nothing in the nature of the international legal order allows us to neglect such crucial differences. Precisely because the means of peaceful change in the international arena are few and, by and large, ineffective, the violation of a legal norm is often not a pure act of lawlessness but rather part of a larger bargaining game for change. It would be a legalism of the worst kind to reduce the problem of compliance to the technical problem of ensuring norm conformity at the least cost through the elaboration of repressive techniques, while leaving the issue of justifying actions in terms of broader principles, demands for justice, and pleas for peaceful change to history and philosophy.

The above considerations also make it clear that the hopes for increasing compliance with international law through its criminalization are likely to be disappointed. Traditional international law has understood itself not as a primarily punitive order – at least since Kant,[11] who stressed its unique character, which is well captured by Oakshott's and Nardin's terms of a "practical association."[12] Such an association is united by the recognition of rights and practices but is not organized for the pursuit of a common vision of the good life. This means, however, that the social preconditions for the emergence of central enforcement mechanisms are presently simply not given. Such an assertion, however, obviously does *not* entail that certain deeds cannot also become international crimes, which various states can choose, or are even bound, to prosecute.[13] It only means that we had better think of alternatives in enhancing compliance rather than rely once more on the well-worn and misleading domestic analogy. Many of Roger Fisher's[14] and Norton Moore's[15] suggestions seem to have better chances than the plans for a proliferation of formal international institutions which are likely to be condemned to inactivity, ineffectiveness, or both.

256

III THE RESEARCH PROGRAM

The particular conceptualization advanced in this book is obviously at odds with the present fashion of characterizing the international arena as "anarchic," or of "systems" as being constituted by the distribution of capabilities. There is no need to rehearse the objections to this perspective once more. Nevertheless, the mere fact that the "balance of power" emerged only once in history should caution us in maintaining that such a system is the natural outcome of an anarchical realm. Former "anarchies," be they those of Chinese history before Ch'in's conquest, or of classical antiquity after the Peloponnesian War, or of the multiplicity of states in the Mediterranean which were incorporated into the Roman Empire, were all overthrown and ended with the emergence of an empire.

Thus, what needs explanation is precisely the system of a balance of power, which is the exception. Besides, if the analogy of the market as the prototype of "anarchy" is to hold, we had better accept that markets also are not natural outcomes but can come into existence after a whole host of conventions – such as the acceptance of money, to name only a minor issue – have attained widespread adherence. Similarly, the conception of a system of states is dependent – and here the historical record unearthed by Martin Wight[16] is unambiguous – upon the emergence of norms which regulate practices and guarantee the mutual recognition of rights. Is it really conceivable that a system in which the participants carry on their business through the assassinations of leaders, through spies and acts of terror against civilian populations, is identical with one in which diplomatic intercourse, sovereign immunity, and non-intervention are the guiding principles? However, precisely such a conclusion would be necessary if only the distribution of capabilities mattered and we had established that it is the same in both systems.

Similarly, attempts to derive the stability or instability of an international system solely from its structure without any reference to the motivating beliefs and conception of legitimacy of the actors has largely failed, as the discussions of the 1960s showed.[17] Aside from the difficulty of giving "pole" or "polarity" an unequivocal meaning – did, for example, an alliance count as one pole, or as many countries? – it soon became painfully obvious that the model was indeterminate on this high level of abstraction. Furthermore, different empirical referents for stability (avoidance of war vs. maintenance of structure) led to opposite conclusions about the way in which configurations of

257

"power" influence outcomes.[18] Besides, some of the most interesting questions could not be asked within this framework, such as: Under what circumstances do nations go to war? Under what circumstances will they pass the buck? When is bandwagoning likely?[19] All these questions arise only within a "world of intentional facts," as pointed out in chapter 1. Although intentional explanations are supposedly "reductionist" (if we follow Waltz's strange usage), they are nevertheless necessary, otherwise nothing can be derived from structure alone. To say that states "balance" is not saying much if this balancing includes everything from war to alliances, to buck-passing, to rolling over and playing dead, to verbal protests, or to negotiating a settlement.

These remarks are not merely of academic interest and they do not concern solely the relative advantages of modes of analysis. What is at stake is rather the understanding of social reality and, through practice, its reproduction. Every now and then, when our diplomats get assassinated or imprisoned, when innocent persons are gunned down at airports, when atrocities are committed in war and whole populations are exterminated, or when true believers are crusading against Satan, we begin to realize that a capability approach to politics à la Genghis Khan is – thank God – the exception. What these examples show is how much we take for granted and how much we depend on conventions for conceiving and formulating rational policies, even if they are cast in terms of the pursuit of power. The discussion of countervailing strategy showed that an analysis which is largely capability-driven loses track of essentially political elements. These concerns appear only when we cast the net wider and deliberate on a wider range of issues. Instead of focusing on such niceties as "ethnic targeting"[20] or on particular mixes of strikes designed to eliminate the opponent's leadership – implausibly claiming to enhance deterrence thereby – we realize then that we ought to pay more attention to the problem of *war termination* and to issues connected with the credibility of promises and commitments. It is these factors which are absolutely essential if the flexibility which we allegedly acquire through the purchase of new weapons systems is to lead to the limitation rather than to the boundless escalation of conflict. The problem with approaches which define "structure" largely in terms of capability is not only that they are ahistorical and that they prevent us from understanding the fundamental transformations of world politics, as Ruggie has pointed out;[21] the more serious issue is that they misstate the problem of politics in general. When conflict is no longer normatively bounded, violence becomes the first and foremost concern instead of the *ultima ratio* of politics, as von Clausewitz still conceived it.

Several areas for further research flow from the perspective outlined here. Since it is most obviously closer to a decision-making focus than to conventional structural analysis, the empirical investigation of the factors making for compliance with, or deviance from, norms is clearly of importance. Here again the Hobbesian heritage limits our research agenda rather than expands it. By focusing mainly on threats, social interactions are reduced to one type of communication, i.e., that of the *per*locutionary force of certain speech acts. What is left out is not only the effects of illocution but also a more detailed investigation of why actors comply. As Oran Young has pointed out, there are several parts to (non)compliance, and, consequently, compliance is best understood as a *system* or context in which various trade-offs are possible.[22] Thus, increased capabilities for discovering violations might be more useful than an increase in threats, particularly when violations cannot easily be established and/or the ambiguity and the lack of authoritative decisions concerning the relevant facts make the threatened punishment unlikely and/or impossible. The implications for a rational strategy of deterrence and arms control are obvious and need not be elaborated further.

There is a second reason why the Hobbesian framework is misleading. In focusing on the potentially unlimited desires of actors which are kept in check by constraining norms, it suggests that deviance immediately leads to "regime decay" or, worse, to anarchy in the sense of anomic interaction. However, as studies of deviance have shown, noncompliant behavior usually exhibits quite distinct patterns depending upon the institutional settings.[23] The idea that somehow the "unrestrained desires" and/or instincts lead to chaos is not only empirically false but prevents us from understanding the phenomenon of deviance. Although much of the more ethnomethodologically oriented approaches[24] to deviance have been carried out in domestic institutional settings,[25] such an approach appears to be promising even for international relations analysis. This methodology treats people's actions as "enactments" rather than as simple choices under constraints. The metaphor of a drama stresses the production of reality and allows for adaptation, improvisation, and departure from the underlying script which has to be enacted in order to become real. The metaphor of a choice under constraints, on the other hand, evokes the mechanical imagery of a force trying to break through, but which is kept in bounds by (normative) ramparts. Machiavelli's image of the dams and canals holding back the flood,[26] or the Newtonian conception that bodies will move unless restrained, is much closer to the latter imagery than the idea of a drama which tells a story and which through interaction and a possible *katharsis* leads us to the realization of our predicament.[27]

The last point has important repercussions for our conception of institutions and of formal organizations in general. While the present regime approach conceives of norms largely in instrumental terms, exemplified by the "demand" for regimes, our discussion above showed that certain functions of norms cannot be analyzed in terms of merely instrumental rationality. Norms in the third-party mode especially present complexities in their application which gives rise to the famous saying that the law is what the court says the law is. But this means that such decisions are quite different from instrumentally rational solutions. Even more inappropriate is the conception of formal organization as simply instruments for the "implementation" of regimes. Although we are accustomed to view organizations from the standpoint of instrumental rationality, complex organizations are not simply devices like hammers or egg-beaters.[28] Much of the organization literature from Simon,[29] Cyert and March,[30] and March and Olson[31] to Pfeffer[32] has shown why the instrumental perspective is faulty. At a minimum, instrumental rationality is dependent upon a static environment and complete and costless information. It also assumes that organizational goals are operational and are not part of an internal bargain among the participants. Under conditions of bounded rationality, time-pressures, nonoperational goals (such as, for instance, "national security"), internal dissent and "turbulent environments,"[33] none of the preconditions for instrumental analysis are given. Modern organization analysis has therefore increasingly stressed the symbolic dimension of organizational structures and the negotiated nature of the reality that defines organizational activity.[34] It seems therefore that the approach developed here fits these new theories of formal institutions better than the rational choice perspective or the old Weberian and largely instrumental orientation to formal organization. How informal social organization, i.e., normative components of interactions, mesh with formal organizational structures remains to be investigated. The present lack of concern with formal institutions in the field of international organization is perhaps one of its most serious shortcomings.

Finally, the approach developed here should be useful for international relations theory in still two further respects. On the one hand, it is likely to free the analysis from the restrictive underlying assumptions of logical positivism without, however, sacrificing rigor or parsimony in explanations. While the traditional model of explanation, taken largely from physics, is no longer the only or even the foremost paradigm, it should be clear that certain aspects of international interactions can nevertheless be analyzed well by positivistic methodologies. When specialized institutions make interpretations of actions unproblematic, the positivistic methodology provides elegant and powerful explanations. Thus, when in a market the problem of rights and contract have been solved and when all participants have agreed to a medium of exchange, the conventional microeconomic tools are of obvious help. It needs no further elaboration that such happy circumstances do not usually prevail in politics and that social interactions therefore raise many more complicated issues for which the problem of intersubjective understanding and of gaining assent become paradigmatic.

On the other hand, the approach developed here focusing on the existence or absence of conventions explaining patterns of interactions should open the way for a more comparative and empirical analysis of international relations. The emphasis on the need for a comparative analysis might seem strange since the international system seems synchronically all-encompassing. Nevertheless, it can be studied comparatively in a *diachronic* dimension. In this way important historical data become relevant that are otherwise eliminated if we begin the analysis with the postulation of a *homo oeconomicus* (or *politicus*). The utilization of the comparative method should allow for important insights into some enduring as well as differing features of international interactions. Instead of assuming that the international political game always exhibits the same features captured in a "systems" model (with or without a feedback loop), we notice that the actions within a system, and therefore the reproduction of the system through practice, are not independent of the conventions constituting the system. Thus, in a previous study[35] I was able to demonstrate that the emergence of a notion of "national interest" in the European state system resulted in fundamentally different interactions than in the allegedly universal pattern of "power politics" familiar from the Melian Dialogue and the description of the Corcyrean revolution.[36] The lack of a common conception of the state's "interest" in Greece led to interventions and counterinterventions, and prevented the emergence of a Balance of Power and of a common legitimacy in which the management of international relations could be grounded.

The investigation of crucial cases within this comparative perspective should allow us to examine more critically the conventional wisdom that system-wide wars are the fundamental reordering device of international relations (Gilpin).[37] Although wars are obviously the most salient factors for fundamental alterations, changes within systems and the differentiation of types among systems are probably more related to perceptual shifts that, in turn, are influenced as much by the emergence and decay of norms as by particular wars. This is so because wars decide some issues, such as the defeat of challengers (e.g., Athens, France, or Germany/Japan) but not others (such as what the pattern of interaction will be after the challenge has been met). If the hegemonic-war theory were correct, then the emergence and/or decay of the respective systems would have to be accounted for by the preceding military conflict. However, the demise of the Greek system because of internal exhaustion and the emergence of an imperial external balancer (Persia) can be contrasted with the successsful management of the European system by an *internal* balancer which shared the conventions of the state system (England after the War of the Spanish Succession). These two cases, then, can be compared with the problems that arise in a system that has neither such a balancer nor many shared conventions for the management of international affairs and has to evolve them through iterative bargaining and crises (the modern system).

Similarly, a system that is largely organized in terms of personal associations (*politeiai*, for example, the conception of *politeia ton Athenaion* (πολιτεία τῶν ᾿Αυηναίων) rather than the abstract concept of "Athens"), as well as the phenomenon of cities "without territory," can be set against a territorially organized system in terms of a "negative community" that shares no common purpose but mutually recognized rights and common practices. Again, these two cases are different from the modern system in which nonstate actors (international organizations, M.N.C.s, organized ideologies, etc.) play an important role and in which the bundling of exclusive rights inherent in the conception of territorial sovereignty is modified by tacitly established spheres of influence. Although the groundwork has been laid for such an investigation in this book – and the discussion of tacit rules and spheres of influence above are cases in point – such a comparative analysis of international systems will have to be taken up on another occasion.

262

NOTES

Introduction: The resort to norms

1. See, e.g., Stephen Krasner (ed.), *International Regimes*, special issues of *International Organization*, 36 (Spring 1982).
2. Friedrich Kratochwil and John Ruggie, "International Organization: The State of the Art on an Art of the State," *International Organization*, 40 (Fall 1986), 753–775.
3. See, e.g., H. L. A. Hart, *The Concept of Law* (New York: Oxford University Press, 1961) .
4. See, e.g., Hans Kelsen, *Principles of International Law*, 2nd edn., edited by Robert W. Tucker (New York: Holt, Rinehart & Winston, 1966).
5. Although it is virtually impossible to give an adequate account of McDougal's prolific writings, the main features of his legal theory can be gathered from two articles: see Myres McDougal and Harold Lasswell, "The Identification and Appraisal of Diverse Systems of Public Order," and Myres McDougal, "Some Basic Concepts about International Law: A Policy Oriented Framework," both reprinted in Richard Falk and Saul Mendlovitz (eds.), *The Strategy of World Order*, vol. 2, *International Law* (New York: World Law Fund, 1966), pp. 45–75 and 116–134.
6. For a discussion of the problems of soft law, see Joseph Gold, "Strengthening the Soft International Law of Exchange Arrangements," *American Journal of International Law*, 77 (July 1983), 443–489. For a contrary view, see Prosper Weil, "Toward Relative Normativity in International Law?", *American Journal of International Law*, 77 (July 1983), 413–442.
7. For a general and thoughtful discussion of the issues involved, see Oscar Schachter, "International Law in Theory and Practice," *Recueil de cours*, 178 (1982–V).
8. For a discussion of the "anarchy" debate in international relations, see the contributions of Richard Ashley, Hayward Alker, Robert Jervis, John Ruggie, Ken Oye, Nicholas Onuf, and Friedrich Kratochwil in Hayward Alker and Richard Ashley (eds.), *Anarchy, Power and Community: Understanding International Collaboration* (New York: Columbia University Press, forthcoming).
9. This point is well made in Richard Ashley's contribution, "Hedley Bull and the Anarchy Problematique," in Alker and Ashley (eds.), *Anarchy, Power and Community*.
10. Charles Taylor, "Philosophy and History," in Richard Rorty, et al. (eds.),

Philosophy and History (Cambridge: Cambridge University Press, 1984), pp. 17–30, at p. 21.

11. For a further discussion of this point, see Inis L. Claude, *Power and International Relations* (New York: Random House, 1962).

12. See, e.g., Hobbes remarks in ch. 13 of *Leviathan*:
    But though there had never been any time, wherein particular men were in a condition of warre one against another yet in all times, Kings, and Persons of Sovereigne authority, because of their Independency, are in continuall jelousies, and in the state and posture of Gladiators, having their weapons pointing, and their eyes fixed on one another; that is their Forts, Garrisons, and Guns upon the Frontiers of their Kingdomes . . .
    Thomas Hobbes, *Leviathan*, ed. C. B. Macpherson (Baltimore: Penguin, 1968), p. 187.

13. See Hobbes's cryptic remark in the same chapter: "But because they [states] uphold thereby the Industry of their Subjects; there does not follow from it [staying in the state of nature] that misery, which accompanies the Liberties of Particular Men"; ibid., p. 188.

14. See his remark in the same chapter that "Out of Civil States there is always warre of everyone against every one," but this state of war need not coincide with actual fights: "So the nature of War, consisteth not in actual fighting, but in the known disposition thereto, during all the time there is no assurance to the contrary"; ibid., pp. 185–186.

15. Ibid., ch. 15, p. 215.

16. Samuel Pufendorf, *De jure naturae et gentium* (Oxford: Clarendon Press, 1934).

17. Christian Wolf, *Jus gentium methodo scientifica pertractatum* (Oxford: Clarendon Press, 1934).

18. The term "genesis amnesia" was used by Richard Ashley to convey the flaw of structural international relations theory that did not take into account its own presuppositions either historically or pragmatically See his criticism against structuralism in Ashley, "The Poverty of Neorealism," *International Organization*, 38 (1984), 225–286.

19. See, e.g., Robert Keohane's argument in his "Theory of World Politics: Structural Realism and Beyond," in Ada W. Finifter (ed.), *Political Science: The State of the Discipline* (Washington: American Political Science Association, 1983), 503–540.

20. Hugo Grotius, *De jure belli ac pacis libri tres* (Oxford: Clarendon Press, 1925).

21. Emmerich Vattel, *Principes de la loi naturelle appliquées à la conduite et aux affaires des nations et des soverains* (Washington: Carnegie, 1966).

22. Heinrich Triepel, *Völkerrecht und Landesrecht* (Leipzig: C. L. Hirschfeld, 1899).

23. For a further discussion of the impact which the shift away from scholars to bureaucrats had for the development of international law, see Nicholas Onuf, "Law-Making and Legal Thought," in Nicholas Onuf (ed.), *Law-Making in the Global Community* (Durham: Academic Press, 1982), ch. 1.

24. See, e.g., the interesting observations on the functions of teachers of

international law in Oscar Schachter, "The Invisible College of International Lawyers," *Northwestern Law Review*, 72 (1977), and the practical problems arising from the specialization of litigating attorneys in Detlev Vagt's "Are There No International Lawyers Anymore?", *American Journal of International Law*, 75 (January 1981), 134–137.

25. For a modern version of this argument, see Arnold Gehlen, *Der Mensch*, 2nd edn. (Bonn, 1950).

26. See Aristotle, *Politics*, transl. by T. A. Sinclair (Baltimore, Md.: Penguin, 1962), bk. 1, ch. 2, 1253a9–12:

    It follows that the state belongs to a class of objects which exist in nature, and that man is by nature a political animal; it is his nature to live in a state. He who by his nature and not simply by ill-luck has no city, no state, is either too bad or too good, either sub-human or super-human – sub-human like the war-mad man condemned in Homer's words "having no family, no morals, no home"; for such a person is by his nature mad on war, he is a non-cooperator like an isolated piece in a game of draughts. But it is not simply a matter of cooperation, for obviously man is a political animal in a sense in which a bee is not, or any gregarious animal. Nature, as we say, does nothing without some purpose; and for the purpose of making man a political animal she has endowed him alone among the animals with the power of reasoned speech. Speech is something different from voice, which is possessed by other animals also and used by them to express pain or pleasure; for the natural powers of some animals do indeed enable them both to feel pleasure and pain and to communicate these to each other. Speech on the other hand serves to indicate what is right and what is wrong. For the real difference between man and other animals is that humans alone have perception of good and evil, right and wrong, just and unjust. And it is the sharing of a common view in these matters that makes a household or a city.

27. I use here "communicative acts" in a wider sense than speech acts since "indirect speech acts" are not well accounted for by traditional speech-act theory and need a more socio-linguistic approach to be comprehensible. For a further discussion of these points, see below, chapter 1.

28. J. L. Austin, *How to Do Things with Words* (Cambridge, Mass.: Harvard University Press, 1962).

29. Jürgen Habermas, *Theorie des kommunikativen Handelns*, 2 vols. (Frankfurt: Suhrkamp, 1981). Habermas's theory includes speech-act theory but provides a more generalized argument based on the analysis of discourses rather than particular speech acts.

30. See, e.g., the discussion in John Searle, *Speech Acts* (Cambridge: Cambridge University Press, 1969), ch. 7.

31. For a discussion of the differences between threats and promises which do not allow us to understand one as the flip side of the other, see the analysis in chapters 2 and 5. See also the discerning articles by David Baldwin, "The Power of Positive Sanctions," *World Politics*, 24 (October 1971), 19–38, and "Thinking about Threats," *Journal of Conflict Resolution*, 15 (1971), 71–78.

32. See below, chapter 2.

33. See the discussion by Richard Falk, "The Interplay of Westphalia and Charter Conceptions of the International Legal Order," in Cyril Black and Richard Falk (eds.), *The Future of the International Legal Order*, vol. 1. (Princeton: Princeton University Press, 1969), ch. 2.

34. For a more extensive discussion of the differences, see my "Rules, Norms, Values, and the Limits of 'Rationality,' " *Archiv für Rechts- und Sozialphilosophie*, 73 (1987), 301–329.

35. To that extent, my definition of practical reasoning differs from at least one version of Aristotle's argument as presented in the *Nicomachean Ethics* and from the "actionist" perspective of Georg Henrik von Wright, which argues for a particular understanding of "causality" in explaining actions but does not explicitly deal with the problem of deliberation. See, e.g., Georg Henrik von Wright, *Explanation and Understanding* (Ithaca: Cornell University Press, 1971). For a further discussion of the epistemological problems entailed in such an action perspective, see Jürgen Mittelstrass and Manfred Riedel (eds.), *Vernünftiges Denken* (Berlin–New York: Walter de Gruyter, 1978). For a more extensive discussion of my approach, see below, chapter 1.

36. See Thomas Franck, *The Structure of Impartiality* (New York: Macmillan, 1968), ch. 1.

37. See Kratochwil and Ruggie, "International Organization: A State of the Art on an Art of the State."

38. On the issue of "soft law," see Ignaz Seidl-Hohenfeldern, "International Economic Soft Law," *Recueil de cours*, 163 (1979), 169ff.

39. See, e.g., the arguments of Robert Jervis and Charles Lipson; Robert Jervis, "Security Regimes," in Stephen Krasner (ed.), *International Regimes*, special issue of *International Organization*, 36 (1982), 352–378; Charles Lipson, "International Cooperation in Economic and Security Affairs," *World Politics*, 37 (October 1984), 1–23.

40. John Ruggie shared with me the arguments which were made during the conferences predating the "International Regime" issue of *International Organization*. On the basis of the example taken from (Keynesian) economics, the conceptual distinctions evolved.

41. On the notion of contestable concepts, see William E. Connolly, *The Terms of Political Discourse*, 2nd edn. (Princeton: Princeton University Press, 1984).

42. This term is used by Philip Heymann to describe norms in "The Problem of Coordination: Bargaining with Rules," *Harvard Law Review*, 86 (March 1973), 787–878.

43. For a more extensive treatment, see my "Rules, Norms, Values, and the Limits of 'Rationality.'"

44. For a discussion of the problems involved in this position, see Ilmar Tammelo and Lyndell Prott, "Legal and Extra Legal Education," *Journal of Legal Education*, 17 (1965), 412–422. See also the contributions by Rommen, Danto, Friedmann, Abelson, and Frankena in Sidney Hook (ed.), *Law and Philosophy* (New York: New York University Press, 1964).

45. For a general discussion of these problems, see Chaim Perelman and L.

Olbrechts-Tyteca, *The New Rhetoric: A Treatise on Argumentation* (Notre Dame: University of Notre Dame Press, 1969), especially paras. 21–26.
46. See Ken Oye (ed.), *Cooperation and Anarchy*, special issue of *World Politics* 38 (October 1985).

1 Rules, norms, and actions: laying the conceptual foundations

1 The idea that science concerned with the objective world had to forgo metaphysical stances and be concerned solely with "positive" facts was the original position of "positivism" as espoused by Comte. Bentham – quite different from Comte – was an extreme empiricist and is said to have left to the London School of Economics numerous books of notes in which he had recorded "facts" which are – needless to say – useless for any science.

   Logical positivism shares with Bentham neither the inductivist bias nor the idea that "facts" are theory-independent. To that extent, the term "positivism" used in much of the contemporary epistemological discussion is ambiguous, as it is used for empiricism *and* logical positivism.

2. On the importance of an unproblematic background knowledge, see Karl Popper, *Conjectures and Refutations* (New York: Harper & Row, 1965), ch. 10.

3. On the importance of a refutability criterion (rather than a verification criterion) and the only "corroborated" (rather than verified) nature of our scientific knowledge, see Karl Popper, *The Logic of Scientific Discovery* (New York: Harper & Row, 1960).

4. James Coleman, *Introduction to Mathematical Sociology* (New York: Free Press, 1964).

5. On this point, i.e., that modern science has largely dispensed with the notion of cause in favor of functional relationships, see Ernst Cassirer, *Substance and Function and Einstein's Theory of Relativity*, translated by Curtis Swabey and Mary Collins (New York: Dover, 1953).

6. Coleman, *Introduction to Mathematical Sociology*, p. 63.

7. Max Weber, *Wirtschaft und Gesellschaft*, ch. 1., sec. 10, translation by H. P. Secher, *Basic Concepts in Sociology by Max Weber* (Secaucus: Citadel Press, 1962), p. 49.

8. Ibid., p. 39.

9. Ibid., p. 56.

10. Ibid., p. 56.

11. On finalistic explanation schemes, see two seminal works: Donald Davidson, "Actions, Reasons and Causes," *Journal of Philosophy* 60 (1963), 685–700, and G. Henrik von Wright, *Explanation and Understanding* (London: Routledge & Kegan Paul, 1971).

12. A special case could naturally be that this person never attains what he intends; thus a "causal" psychological explanation might be required if certain unconscious factors defeat the person's conscious purposes.

13. Searle, *Speech Acts*, p. 51.

14. Ibid., p. 37.

15. For a further discussion of this mistaken notion, see below, ch. 7. The remark obviously refers to the nineteenth-century legal philosopher and not to Austin the language philosopher.

16. H. L. A. Hart, *The Concept of Law* (New York: Oxford University Press, 1961), chs. 1 and 2.

17. Hans Kelsen, *General Theory of Law and State*, translated by Andreas Wedberg (Cambridge, Mass.: Harvard University Press, 1945).

18. Searle, *Speech Acts*, p. 35.

19. Ibid., p. 52.

20. Ibid., p. 46.

21. See the discussion below in chs. 4 and 5.

22. Kenneth Waltz, *Theory of International Politics* (Reading, Mass.: Addison-Wesley, 1979), ch. 5.

23. Ibid., pp. 76–77 and ch. 9.

24. For a good nontechnical discussion of the importance of pragmatic factors in communication, see Michael Stubbs, *Discourse Analysis* (Chicago: University of Chicago Press, 1983), example at p. 97.

25. Ibid., pp. 97–98.

26. Classical linguistic analysis leaves out two problems: (a) the problem of the syntagmatic chaining of clauses to larger exchanges or sequences since the largest unit analyzed is the sentence; (b) the pragmatic dimension of language.

27. For a short discussion of the various conceptions of "truth," see Waldemar Schreckenberger, "Über den Zugang der modernen Logik zur Rechtsdogmatik," in Ottmar Ballweg and Thomas-Michael Seibert (eds.), *Rhetorische Rechtstheorie* (Freiburg: Alber, 1982), pp. 151–180.

28. R. M. Hare, *The Language of Morals* (Oxford: Oxford University Press, 1974), p. 18.

29. See, e.g., Niklas Luhmann, *Ausdifferenzierung des Rechts* (Frankfurt: Suhrkamp, 1981), chs. 2–4, and 10 and 12. For a discussion of Kelsen, *General Theory of Law and the State*, see below, ch. 7. Another possibility in dealing with this problem of validity is to treat normative statements similarly to assertions, as, e.g., ethical descriptivism does. On this problem, see Ulrich Klug, *Juristische Logik*, 3rd edn. (Berlin–New York: Springer, 1966), and R. Schreiber, *Die Geltung von Rechtsnormen* (Berlin: Springer, 1966).

30. Thomas Franck, *The Structure of Impartiality* (New York: Macmillan, 1968), ch. 1.

31. I. William Zartman and Maureen Berman, *The Practical Negotiator* (New Haven, Conn.: Yale University Press, 1982), especially ch. 4.

32. Michael Barkun, *Law without Sanctions* (New Haven, Conn.: Yale University Press, 1968).

33. Immanuel Kant, *The Groundworks of the Metaphysics of Morals*, translated by H. J. Paton (New York: Harper, 1953), p. 125 (Akademie-Ausgabe, p. 117).

34. For a good picture of the inadequacy of the instrumental model in solving practical-choice problems in its version found in Aristotle and (in a different form) in Maimonides and Vico, see Jaakko Hintikka, "Practical

vs. Theoretical Reason: an Ambiguous Legacy," in Stephan Körner (ed.), *Practical Reason* (Oxford: Basil Blackwell, 1974), ch. III.

35. This was the point eloquently made by Bachrach and Baratz against theories of pluralism and decision-making, precisely because focusing on decisions leaves out the "power" that comes from setting an agenda and preparing something for a decision, or preventing it from being voiced and decided upon. See Peter Bachrach and Morton Baratz, "Two Faces of Power," *American Political Science Review*, 56 (December 1962), 947–962.

36. See, e.g., René Descartes's rejection of everything only "probable" in *Discourse on Method*, translated and edited by Donald Cress (Indianapolis: Hackett, 1981), p. 1 (part 2) and p. 17 (part 4). For a biography and characterization of Pierre de la Rameé's work, see F. P. Graves, *Peter Ramus and the Educational Reformation of the Sixteenth Century* (New York: Macmillan, 1912) and the indispensable study by Walter J. Ong, *Ramus, Method and the Decay of Dialogue* (Cambridge, Mass.: Harvard University Press, 1983).

37. For an extensive discussion of the changes in the function and meaning of rhetoric, see the excellent study by Wilbur Samuel Howell, *Logic and Rhetoric in England 1000–1700* (Princeton, NJ: Princeton University Press, 1971). See also Wilbur S. Howell, "Sources of the Elocutionary Movement in England, 1700–1748," in E. F. Howell (ed.), *Historical Studies of Rhetoric and Rhetoricians* (Ithaca, NY: Cornell University Press, 1961), p. 139.

38. Paul Corcoran, *Political Language and Rhetoric* (Austin: University of Texas Press, 1979), p. 124.

39. Hans-Georg Gadamer, *Truth and Method* (New York: Crossroad, 1975), appendix I, pp. 449–452.

40. Perelman and Olbrechts-Tyteca, *The New Rhetoric*.

41. For a good overview of the classical context between rhetoric and practical reasoning, see Corcoran, *Political Language and Rhetoric*, passim.

42. Marcus Tullius Cicero, *Topica*, translated by H. M. Hubbell (Cambridge, Mass.: Harvard University Press, 1960), chs. 2, 7: "sedes e quibus argumenta promuntur."

43. See Alessandro Giuliani, "The Influence of Rhetoric on the Law of Evidence and Pleading," *Juridical Review*, 3 (1962), 216–251.

44. Theodor Viehweg, *Topik und Jurisprudenz* (München: C. H. Beck, 1963), and Ernest Meyer, "Die Questionen der Rhetorik und die Anfänge der Juristischen Methodenlehre," *Zeitschrift der Savigny-Stiftung* (Romanistische Abteilung), 68 (1951), 30–73.

45. See the argument below in ch. 6.

46. See, e.g., the studies on crises and international law, such as Abraham Chayes, *The Cuban Missile Crisis* (New York: Oxford University Press, 1974) and Robert Bowie, *Suez* (New York: Oxford University Press, 1964).

2 Anarchy and the state of nature: the issue of regimes in international relations

1. For a good discussion of the "idealist" position in international relations, see F. H. Hinsley, *Power and the Pursuit of Peace* (Cambridge: Cambridge University Press, 1967).
2. See, e.g., the once rather influential book by Grenville Clark and Louis Sohn, *World Peace Through World Law*, 3rd edn. (Cambridge, Mass.: Harvard University Press, 1966).
3. This was John Austin's position as expounded in his *The Province of Jurisprudence Determined*, ed. H. L. A. Hart (London: Weidenfeld and Nicolson, 1954).
4. This point has been eloquently made by Claude, *Power and International Relations*.
5. On this point, see my discusion in "The Force of Prescriptions," *International Organization* 38 (1984), 685–708.
6. Jervis, "Security Regimes," in Krasner (ed.), *International Regimes*, pp. 352–378. See also Lipson, "International Cooperation in Economic and Security Affairs," *World Politics*, 37 (October 1984), 1–23.
7. Terry Nardin, *Law, Morality and the Relations of States* (Princeton: Princeton University Press, 1983), ch. 1.
8. Such a conceptualization was provided by Stoic natural law. For a discussion of the historical development of international law see Artur Nussbaum, *A Concise History of the Law of Nations* (New York: Macmillan, 1947).
9. Waltz, *Theory of International Politics*, chs. 3–5.
10. For a critique of Waltz's argument of reductionism, see my "Errors have their Advantage," *International Organization*, 38 (1984), 305–320.
11. For a further discussion of the various rule-types, see Max Black, *Models and Metaphors* (Ithaca: Cornell University Press, 1962), pp. 261–285.
12. David Baldwin, "Money and Power," *Journal of Politics*, 33 (1971), 578–614; and David Baldwin, "Power Analysis and World Politics," *World Politics*, 31 (January 1979), 161–194.
13. Jervis, "Security Regimes," in Krasner (ed.), *International Regimes*, p. 359.
14. Ibid., p. 357.
15. For a careful study of deterrence failures, see Alexander George and Richard Smoke, *Deterrence in American Foreign Policy* (New York: Columbia University Press, 1974).
16. See Thomas Schelling, *Arms and Influence* (New Haven, Conn.: Yale University Press, 1966), chs. 2 and 3.
17. Robert Jervis, "Why Nuclear Superiority Does not Matter," *Political Science Quarterly*, 94 (Winter 1979/80), 617–633; also Robert Jervis, *The Illogic of American Nuclear Strategy* (Ithaca: Cornell University Press, 1984).
18. Jack Snyder, "New Methods and Old Virtues in the Study of Soviet Foreign Policy" (Columbia University, 1986), (mimeo).
19. Roger Fisher and William Ury, *Getting to Yes* (New York: Penguin, 1981), p. 10.
20. Walter La Feber, *Eastern Europe and the Soviet Union*, vol. 2 of the collection

of documents by Arthur Schlesinger (ed.), *The Dynamics of World Power* (New York: Chelsea House and McGraw Hill, 1973), p. 700.

21. Edward Weintal and Charles Bartlett, *Facing the Brink* (New York: Scribner, 1967), p. 68.

22. Jervis, *The Illogic of American Nuclear Strategy*, pp. 84–85.

23. See, e.g., Hans Morgenthau's argument in his *Politics Among Nations*, 4th edn. (New York: Knopf, 1967), ch. 6.

24. On the importance of a common understanding of legitimacy for a moderate system, see Henry Kissinger, *A World Restored* (New York: Grosset & Dunlap, 1964).

25. On the notion of a Great Power see ch. 5 by Martin Wight, in *Systems of States*, ed. Hedley Bull and Carsten Holbraad (Leicester: Leicester University Press, 1977). In this context, see also my "On the Notion of Interest in International Relations," *International Organization*, 36 (1982), 1–30.

26. See, for example, Richard Falk's treatment of the rules of the game in his "The Interplay of Westphalia and Charter Conceptions of the International Legal Order," in Cyril Black and Richard Falk (eds.), *The Future of the International Legal Order* (Princeton: Princeton University Press, 1969), vol. 1, ch. 2.

27. For a good discussion, see Thomas Mayberry, "Laws, Moral Laws and God's Commands," *The Journal of Value Inquiry*, 4 (Winter 1970), 287–292.

28. Alf Ross, *Directives and Norms* (London: Routledge & Kegan Paul, 1968).

29. Hart, *The Concept of Law*, chs. 2 and 3.

30. Gidon Gottlieb, *The Logic of Choice* (London: George Allen & Unwin, 1968).

31. For a discussion of the gunman example, see Hart, *The Concept of Law*, ch. 2.

32. Morton Kaplan and Nicholas de B. Katzenbach, *The Political Foundation of International Law* (New York: Wiley, 1969), p. 4.

33. Schelling, *Arms and Influence*, ch. 4.

34. The problems of "soft law" are ably discussed in Ignaz Seidl-Hohenfeldern, "International Economic Soft Law," *Recueil de cours*, 163 (1979), 169ff; see also Joseph Gold, "Strengthening the Soft International Law of Exchange Arrangements," 443–489.

35. *Coumbia* v. *Peru* (1950), I.C.J. 266; *Federal Republic of Germany* v. *Denmark*, and *Federal Republic of Germany* v. *Netherlands* (1969), I. C. J. 4.

36. Paul Keal, *Unspoken Rules and Super-Power Dominance* (London: Macmillan, 1984).

37. Ibid., p. 50.

38. David Hume, *Treatise of Human Nature*, part II, section 2, "Of the Origins of Justice and Property," in Henry Aiken (ed.), *Hume's Moral and Political Philosophy* (Darien: Hafner, 1970), pp. 59–60; the explicit reference to common interest is on p. 59.

39. For a thorough discussion of the problems associated with compliance with norms, correcting the mistake that only "sanctions" (as opposed to "discovery" and authoritative decision) count, see Oran Young, *Compliance and Public Authority* (Baltimore: Johns Hopkins University Press, 1979).

40. This is the reason why modern comprehensive codifications of regimes such as the Vienna Convention on Treaties or the UNCLOS III Draft Treaty provide for comprehensive dispute-settling machineries, even if the "choice of means" is preserved.

41. For a brief discussion of the functions of the "Standing Consultative Commission" in Geneva within the SALT I framework, see Strobe Talbott, *End Game* (New York: Harper & Row, 1980), passim, and the report by the Carnegie Panel on *U.S. Security and the Future of Arms Control: Challenges for U.S. National Security* (Washington, DC: Carnegie Endowment, 1983).

42. Susan Strange, "Cave, hic dragones," in Krasner (ed.), *International Regimes*, pp. 479–496, at p. 479.

43. Stephen Krasner, "Structural Causes and Regime Consequences: Regimes as Intervening Variables," in Krasner (ed.), *International Regimes*, p. 186.

44. This point is powerfully made by Waltz, *Theory of International Politics*, p. 105; see also Robert Gilpin, *U.S. Power and the Multinational Corporation* (New York: Basic Books, 1975), p. 34.

45. See, e.g., Robert Axelrod, "The Emergence of Cooperation among Egotists," *American Political Science Review*, 75 (1981), 306–318; and Harrison Wagner, "The Theory of Games and the Problem of International Cooperation," *American Political Science Review*, 77 (1983), 330–341. In this context, it is important that a tit-for-tat strategy works only if the first round is played cooperatively.

46. See, e.g., Dulles's remark to that effect in Townsend Hoopes, *The Devil and John Foster Dulles* (Boston: Little, Brown, 1973), p. 180.

47. These issues are further discussed in connection with the Soviet–American "thaw" after Stalin's death in Deborah Welch Larson, "The Austrian State Treaty," *International Organization*, 41 (Winter 1987), 27–60.

48. For a further discussion of this point see Richard Flathman, *Political Obligation* (New York: Atheneum, 1972), ch. 5.

49. According to the utilitarian calculus we should be (marginally) happy about small gifts and should be interested neither in what gifts others receive nor in what "costs" these gifts represent to the donor.

50. Krasner, "Structural Causes," in Krasner (ed.), *International Regimes*, p. 186.

51. I owe this thought to John Ruggie, who shared with me some of the background which led to the regime special issue of *International Organization*. Thus, free trade provided the principle, nondiscrimination the higher-order norm, and most-favored-nation treatment the specific "rule" within the regime.

52. For an extensive discussion of the difficulties in statutory interpretation that arise from the construal of a "will" of the legislator, see the special issue on statutory interpretation of the *Vanderbilt Law Review*, 3 (1950).

53. See, e.g., R. S. Summers, "Naive Instrumentalism and the Law," in P. S. Hacker and J. Raz (eds.), *Law, Morality and Society* (Oxford: Clarendon Press, 1977), ch. 6.

54. For a good discussion of the issues involved, see Gold, "Strengthening the Soft International Law of Exchange Arrangements," 443–489.

55. See Krasner, "Structural Causes," in Krasner (ed.), *International Regimes*, p. 187.

56. It has been pointed out by Luhmann that legal systems and therefore also regimes (particularly when codified) are *self-referential* systems, i.e., their changes can be understood as change "within" the system itself. For a further discussion of the issues that arise in the context of auto-poietic or self-referential systems, see Niklas Luhmann, *Rechtssoziologie*, 2nd edn. (Opladen: Westdeutscher Verlag, 1983).

57. Usually the question of what are the appropriate boundaries for historical phenomena (historical individuals) is raised in the context of the old "individualistic" vs. "holistic" mode of explanation. Phrasing the question in these terms overlooks the fact that the definition of boundaries also fundamentally influences the assessment of "causality" and, therefore, also of the question of who is to blame or to praise for a particular event. The controversy between Taylor and his opponents concerning the "causes" and responsibility for the Second World War hinges to a large extent on the question of whether the Second World War is one event of a series of independent decisions (e.g., the wars against Poland, France, Norway, the Balkans, Russia, etc.), which can no longer be considered the consequences of the initial decision to invade Poland. For an illuminating discussion of the issues involved, see William Dray, *Perspectives on History* (London: Routledge & Kegan Paul, 1980), chs, 3 and 4 respectively.

58. On the contestability of most political concepts, see William Connolly, *The Terms of Political Discourse*, 2nd edn. (Princeton: Princeton University Press, 1983).

59. For a critique along these lines, see Robert Keohane and Joseph Nye, *Power and Interdependence* (Boston: Little, Brown, 1977).

60. On the point of "enabling" rather than "constraining" rules, see Hart, *The Concept of Law*, ch. 3.

61. For a sociological critique of the "blueprint-model of society," see Judith Blake and Kingsley Davis, "Norms, Values and Sanctions," in Robert Haris (ed.), *Handbook of Modern Sociology* (Chicago: Rand McNally, 1964).

62. Ernst Haas, "Regime Decay: Conflict Management since 1945," *International Organization*, 37 (1983), 189–256.

63. Ibid., 225ff.

64. John Ruggie, "International Regimes, Transactions and Change: Embedded Liberalism in the Post-War Economic Order," in Krasner (ed.), *International Regimes*, pp. 379–416.

65. See, e.g., Art. 60 of the Vienna Convention on Treaties (defining "material breach"). For a further discussion of the legal remedies involving unilateral countermeasures, see Elisabeth Zoller, *Peacetime Unilateral Remedies* (Dobbs Ferry: Transnational Publishers, 1984).

66. On this point, see my "Rules, Norms and Limits of Rationality."

67. On this point, see Nicole Fermon, "The Politics of Sentiment: Rousseau's

Teachings on the Family and the State," dissertation, Columbia University, 1987.

68. For a good discussion of Rousseau's political teachings, see Stanley Hoffmann, "Rousseau on War and Peace," in Stanley Hoffmann, *The State of War* (New York: Praeger, 1965), ch. 3.

69. See, e.g., Karl Marx's remarks on "die vergesellschafte Menscheit" in his *Theses on Feuerbach*, and his comments on the "new man" who is to emerge from the abolition of alienation in the *German Ideology*, both reprinted in Robert C. Tucker (ed.), *The Marx–Engels Reader* (New York: Norton, 1972), pp. 107–162.

70. For a discussion of utopianism and its failures to admit and deal with conflict, see Frank Manuel (ed.), *Utopias and Utopian Thought* (Boston: Houghton Mifflin, 1966).

71. See, e.g., Emile Durkheim, *The Division of Labor in Society* (New York: Free Press, 1964); on the importance of face-to-face contacts in primitive society, see Max Gluckman, *Politics, Law and Ritual in Tribal Society* (New York: Mentor, 1965).

72. For a further discussion along these lines, see Max Weber, *Economy and Society* (Berkeley: University of California Press, 1978).

73. On the importance of stabilized "love-objects" for social interaction, see Francesco Alberoni, *Movement and Institution* (New York: Columbia University Press, 1984), ch. 4. See also the discussion below in ch. 4.

74. The solution of both problems is crucial for the establishment of a collective identity, as Rousseau realized in his teachings on the general will (vs. the sum total of individual wills – "volonté de tous"), and in his educational projects such as *Emile*. See also his remarks that "a child opening his eyes should see nothing but his fatherland [patrie]," and that it should "imbibe with the mother's milk the love of the fatherland," *Rousseau's Political Writings*, ed. C. E. Vaughan, 2 vols. (Oxford: Basil Blackwell, 1962), vol. II, p. 437.

75. To that extent, reformist activists attempt to propagate the idea of a "global citizenship" as an alternative to the identification with only "national interests." See a critique of U.S. foreign policy along these lines by Robert Johansen, *The National and the Human Interest* (Princeton: Princeton University Press, 1980).

76. See, e.g., Stanley Hoffmann, *Duties Beyond Borders* (Syracuse: Syracuse University Press, 1981).

77. See the various official certification procedures and evaluations of the human rights record of foreign governments, particularly during the Carter administration, as well as the "watch" of such private organizations as Amnesty International, The Commission of Jurists, etc.

78. This can be seen even in advertising in American television, where in one advertisement a young boy accuses an older person in front of a jury of minors of having squandered the resources and left the children with nothing but debts.

79. For an extensive evaluation of such judicial pronouncements, see Oscar

Schachter, "Towards a Theory of International Obligation," *Virginia Journal of International Law*, 8 (1968), 300–310.

80. This was, e.g., one of the goals of the World Order Models Project. For a short description of this project, see Saul Mendlovitz, *On the Creation of a Just World Order* (New York: Free Press, 1975).

3 The emergence and types of norms

1. These and other problems of interference are imaginatively discussed in Philip Heymann, "The Problem of Coordination: Bargaining and Rules," *Harvard Law Review*, 86 (1973), 787–878.
2. For a good treatment of the distinction between inducement and sanctions see Baldwin, "The Power of Positive Sanctions," 19–31.
3. Pufendorf, *De jure naturae et gentium*.
4. On Hume, see my *The Humean Perspective on International Relations* (Princeton: Princeton University, Center of International Studies, Occasional Paper no. 9, 1981).
5. Hedley Bull, *The Anarchical Society* (New York: Columbia University Press, 1977).
6. Duncan Snidal, "Coordination vs. Prisoners' Dilemma, Implications for International Cooperation and Regimes," *American Political Science Review*, 79 (1985), 923–942.
7. Ullman-Margalit, *The Emergence of Norms*, p. 7.
8. See, e.g., Robert Axelrod, "The Emergence of Cooperation among Egotists," *American Political Science Review*, 75 (1981), 306–318 and Harrison Wagner, "The Theory of Games and the Problem of International Cooperation," *American Political Science Review*, 77 (1983), 330–346. See also Robert Axelrod, *The Evolution of Cooperation* (New York: Basic Books, 1984) and Glenn Snyder and Paul Diesing, *Conflict Among Nations* (Princeton, NJ: Princeton University Press, 1977), especially ch. 2.
9. Harold H. Kelley, John W. Thibaut, and O. Mundy, "The Development of Cooperation in the Minimal Social Situation," *Psychological Monographs*, 76, no. 19; H. H. Kelley and John W. Thibaut, "Group Problem Solving," in Gardner Lindzey and Elliot Aronson (eds.), *The Handbook of Social Psychology*, 2nd edn. (Reading, Mass.: Addison Wesley), pp. 1–101.
10. This is the description of the minimal social situation mentioned in figure 14. (see p. 276).
11. Robert Axelrod, *The Evolution of Cooperation*.
12. Thomas Schelling, *The Strategy of Conflict* (Oxford: Oxford University Press).
13. Salience refers in this context to the "uniqueness of a coordination equilibrium in a preeminently conspicuous respect." David K. Lewis, *Convention: A Philosophical Study* (Cambridge, Mass.: Harvard University Press, 1969), p. 38.
14. Ullman-Margalit, *The Emergence of Norms*, p. 115.
15. Ibid., p. 81.
16. See notes 12 and 13 above.
17. Ullman-Margalit, *The Emergence of Norms*, p. 87.

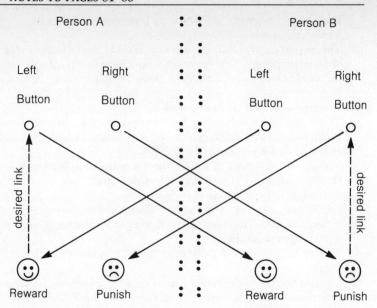

Figure 14. Source: Karl Weick, *The Social Psychology of Organizing*, 2nd edn. (Reading, Mass.: Addison Wesley, 1978)

18. In a way this game resembles Snyder and Diesing's discussion of "Bluff." There are, however, certain differences in that my formulation here has three choices (allowing for an explicit "strategic move") and that my pay-offs are not meant to be merely ordinal preferences. For a further illuminating discussion of "Bluff," "Bully," and other asymmetric, mixed-motive games, see Snyder and Diesing, *Conflict Among Nations*, ch. 2.
19. For an extensive treatment of "tacit" or "unspoken" rules, see Keal, *Unspoken Rules and Superpower Dominance* (London: Macmillan, 1984).
20. Thomas Schelling, *Arms and Influence* (New Haven: Yale University Press, 1966).
21. For a more extensive discussion of the "rules of the game" in the post-war era, see my *International Order and Foreign Policy* (Boulder: Westview, 1978), and Coral Bell, *The Conventions of Crisis* (Oxford: Oxford University Press, 1971). See also Richard Falk, "The Interplay of Westphalia and Charter Conceptions of International Legal Order," in Cyril Black and Richard Falk (eds.), *The Future of International Legal Order*, vol. 1 (Princeton: Princeton International Press, 1969), ch. 2, Falk is, incidentally, one of the very few "process-oriented" international lawyers who would be inclined to grant "rules of the game" some quasi-authoritative status.
22. For a further discussion, see my "On Systems and Boundaries," *World Politics*, 39 (October 1986), 27–52.
23. See my case study "Arctic and Antarctica," in Friedrich Kratochwil, Paul

Rohrlich, and Harpreet Mahajan, *Peace and Disputes Sovereignty* (Lanham, Md: University Press of America, 1981).

24. See Henry Kissinger, *A World Restored* (New York: Grosset & Dunlap, 1964), ch. 15.

25. On this point, see my "On the Notion of Interest in International Relations," *International Organization*, 36 (Winter 1981–1982), 1–30.

26. For a discussion of F.D.R.'s plans for a world organization after the war, see Willard Range, *Franklin Delano Roosevelt's World Order* (Athens: University of Georgia Press, 1959). For the various incompatible conceptions emerging from the interactions before and during the San Francisco conference, see Thomas Campbell, *Masquerade Peace* (Tallahassee: Florida State University Press, 1973).

27. This point is further elaborated in Thomas Franck, "Who Killed Article 2, 4?", *American Journal of International Law*, 71 (April 1977), 224–247; see also the response by Louis Henkin, "The Reports of the Death of Article 2,4 Are Greatly Exaggerated," *American Journal of International Law*, 65 (1971), 544–548.

28. For an extensive treatment of Churchill's proposal, see Herbert Feis, *Churchill, Roosevelt, Stalin* (Princeton: Princeton University Press, 1966), pp. 447–451.

29. For an extensive discussion of Stalinist policies in Eastern Europe, see Zbigniew Brzezinski, *The Soviet Bloc* (Cambridge, Mass.: Harvard University Press, 1971).

30. For a discussion of the European Concert, see Richard Rosecrance, *Action and Reaction in World Politics* (Boston: Little, Brown 1963).

31. Thomas Franck and Edward Weisband, *Word Politics: Verbal Strategy Among the Superpowers* (New York: Oxford University Press, 1972).

32. For a good discussion of this technique, see Inis Claude, *Swords into Ploughshares*, 4th edn. (New York: Random House, 1984), ch. 14.

33. For an extensive discussion of the détente and the reasons for its failures, see Coral Bell, *The Diplomacy of Detente: The Kissinger Era* (London: Martin Robertson, 1977). See also Alexander L. George, *Managing US–Soviet Rivalry: Problems of Crisis Prevention* (Boulder: Westview, 1983).

34. For a good brief discussion of the U.S.–Soviet conflict in the Middle East, see George W. Breslauer, "Soviet Policy in the Middle East, 1967–72," in George (ed.), *U.S.–Soviet Rivalry*, and Alexander George, "The Arab–Israeli War of October 1973, in *US–Soviet Rivalry*, pp. 139–154.

35. Luhmann makes the point that rights are means by which conflicts can be limited and resolved without endangering the overall relationship. See *Soziologie der Aufklärung*, vol. 2, pp. 29–33.

36. Pufendorf, *De jure naturae et gentium*, pp. 227 ff.

37. Ibid., p. 226.

38. This point is well made by Anthony d'Amato, *The Concept of Custom in International Law* (Ithaca, New York: Cornell University Press, 1971).

39. I.C.J. Statute, art. 38.

40. *North Sea Continental Shelf Cases* [1969] I.C.J. 4.

41. See Ullmann-Margalit, *The Emergence of Norms*, sec. 3.

42. This is, e.g., the solution of the "assurance" game espoused by Amartya Sen in "Choice Orderings and Morality," in Körner (ed.), *Practical Reason*, pp. 54–67.
43. J. L. Austin, *How to Do Things with Words*, p. 63.
44.

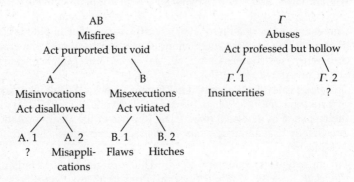

Infelicities

```
                         AB                                    Γ
                       Misfires                              Abuses
                 Act purported but void              Act professed but hollow
                  /              \                      /              \
                 A                B                   Γ. 1             Γ. 2
           Misinvocations    Misexecutions        Insincerities         ?
           Act disallowed     Act vitiated
             /      \          /      \
          A. 1     A. 2     B. 1     B. 2
            ?     Misappli-  Flaws   Hitches
                  cations
```

Figure 15. Source: J. L. Austin, *How to Do Things with Words*, p. 18.

45. See the new codification of this clause in Art. 62 of the Vienna Convention on Treaties.
46. For the distinction between rules and principles, see Ronald Dworkin, "Is Law a System of Rules?", in Ronald Dworkin (ed.), *The Philosophy of Law* (Oxford: Oxford University Press, 1977), ch. 2.

4   The force of prescriptions: Hume, Hobbes, Durkheim, and Freud on compliance with norms

1. See Hume's remarks concerning the problem of "willing" which is common to both promises and resolutions. But while the former oblige, the latter do not; consequently, it cannot be the "willing" or the pursuit of one's self-interest that adds obligatory force to promises. David Hume, *A Treatise of Human Nature*, ed. L. A. Selby-Bigge (Oxford: Clarendon Press, 1888), pp. 516–525.
2. See the discussion in section III below.
3. Samuel Stoljar, *Moral and Legal Reasoning* (New York: Barnes and Noble, 1981), p. 121.
4. For a discussion of the character of sociological facts, see Emile Durkheim, *The Rules of Sociological Method* (New York: Free Press, 1964).
5. On the conditions of such a discourse deciding in a nondictatorial fashion on validity claims, see Jürgen Habermas, "What is Universal Pragmatics?", in Jürgen Habermas, *Communication and the Evolution of Society*, translated by Thomas McCarthy (Boston: Beacon Press, 1979), ch. 1.
6. For an extensive treatment of the revival of "practical philosophy," see Manfred Riedel (ed.), *Rehabilitierung der Praktischen Philosophie*, 2 vols. (Freiburg: Rombach, 1972–1974).

7. For a critique of such a conceptualization, see my "Errors have their Advantage," *International Organization,* 38 (1984), 305–320.

8. Hempel, "Scientific Explanation," and Karl Popper, *Conjectures and Reductations* (New York: Harper, 1965), especially chs. 3 and 10.

9. On the criterion of "refutability" as a criterion for "science" see Karl Popper, *The Logic of Scientific Discovery* (New York: Harper and Row, 1960). For a critique of the adequacy of this criterion in the social sciences, see Jürgen Habermas, *Zur Logik der Sozialwissenschaften* (Frankfurt: Suhrkamp, 1970), and Habermas, *Theorie des kommunikativen Handelns,* especially chs. 1 and 5.

10. Imre Lakatos, "Falsification and the Methodology of Scientific Research Programmes," in Imre Lakatos and Alan Musgrave (eds.), *Criticism and the Growth of Knowledge* (Cambridge: Cambridge University Press, 1970), pp. 118ff.

11. See, e.g., Paul Feyerabend, *Against Method* (London: Verso, 1978).

12. Lakatos, "Falsification and the Methodology."

13. On these points see Popper, *The Logic of Scientific Discovery,* especially ch. 8.

14. Hart, *The Concept of Law,* pp. 55 and 56.

15. See the argument against empathy above in chapter 1, based on Max Weber.

16. This is borne out by the invalidity of a "reservatio mentalis" in canon law.

17. For the distinction between constitutive rules and other types of rules, see John Rawls, "Two Concepts of Rules," *Philosophical Review,* 64 (1955), 3–32. For the discussion of the implications of the Wittgensteinian arguments about forms of life for social science, see Peter Winch, *The Idea of a Social Science* (London: Routledge & Kegan Paul, 1963).

18. Hume, *The Philosophial Works,* ed. Thomas H. Green and Thomas H. Grose (reprinted from the 1886 edn, Aalen: Scientica, 1964), vol. 2, p. 105.

19. Frederick Whelan, "Property as Artifice, Hume and Blackstone," in J. Roland Pennock and John Chapman (eds.), *Property* (New York: New York University Press, 1980), p. 112.

20. Hume, *The Philosophical Works,* vol. 2, p. 280.

21. This is naturally the standard economic argument. For a twist of the argument in favor of inequality in international relations (i.e., greater equality would lead to a "disjunction between power and order and justice"), see Robert W. Tucker, *The Inequality of Nations* (New York: Basic Books, 1977).

22. John Rawls, *A Theory of Justice* (Cambridge, Mass.: Harvard University Press, 1971), ch. 2.

23. This is, of course, the contribution Marxian analysis makes to the study of society. For a careful analysis of the role of property-regimes, class-structure, and conflict in a society, see Ralf Dahrendorf, *Class and Class Conflict in Industrial Society* (Stanford: Stanford University Press, 1959).

24. This point has been eloquently made by Brian Barry, *The Liberal Theory of Justice* (Oxford: Clarendon Press, 1973), ch. 11, in connection with the Rawlsian choice of constitutional principles. Arguing against the assump-

tion that a rational person would necessarily choose to have more of some things rather than less (the primary goods of Rawls), Barry states:

The point which I wish to make here is that, even if it is accepted that primary goods are things each person would (other things being equal) sooner have more of than less of, it does not follow that it is rational to choose, in the original position, principles of general application for the distribution of as much as possible of these primary goods . . . The standard liberal fallacy says, in effect, that if something is a collective good it is *ipso facto* an individual good: the Rawlsian fallacy says in effect that if something is an individual good it is *ipso facto* a collective good. It is an illicit move to go from 'I would prefer more of X to less of X, all else remaining the same' to 'I should like society . . .' (pp. 116–118).

To the extent that McDougal and Lasswell's approach is also based on the assumption that "human dignity" as a goal of the legal order refers to "a social process in which values are widely and not narrowly shared and in which private choice rather than coercion is emphasized," it is open to the same type of criticism. See Myres McDougal and Harold Lasswell, "The Identification and Appraisal of Diverse Systems of Public Order," in Richard Falk and Saul Mendlovitz (eds.), *The Strategy of World Order*, vol. 2, *International Law* (New York: World Law Fund, 1966), p. 55.

25. I use the term "common good" here rather than "collective good," since for the latter not only nonexclusivity but also "joint supply," i.e., nonrivalry of consumption, has to be given. Although many problems of international relations have been treated as public-goods problems, both Snidal and Conybeare show that such analyses might be misleading when the nonrivalry of consumption criterion is not met and/or the commonly perceived good provides methods for exclusion. See Duncan Snidal, "Coordination versus Prisoners' Dilemma: Implications for International Cooperation and Regimes," *American Political Science Review*, 79 (1985), 923–942; John Conybeare, "Public Goods, Prisoners' Dilemmas and the International Political Economy," *International Studies Quarterly*, 28 (1984), 5–22.

26. I owe this example to Deborah W. Larson.

27. Thomas Schelling, "Hockey, Helmets, Concealed Weapons and Daylight Savings," *Journal of Conflict Resolution*, 17 (1973), 381–428.

28. Garrett Hardin, "The Tragedy of the Commons," *Science*, 162 (1968), 1243–1248.

29. In this context, see the discussion in Toshio Yamagishi and Kaori Sato, "Motivational Bases of the Public Goods Problem," *Journal of Personality and Social Psychology*, 50 (1986), 67–73, which indicates that experimentally these two motivations correlate with the provision of the good, i.e., fear with conjunctive supply and greed with disjunctive supply. See also R. M. Dawes, J. McTavish, and H. Shaklee, "Behavior, Communication and Assumptions About Other People's Behavior in Common Dilemma Situations," *Journal of Personality and Social Psychology*, 35 (1977), 1–11.

30. Ibid., 1–11.

31. See Robert Axelrod, *The Evolution of Cooperation*. For a discussion of different solutions to general PD see the classic work on collective goods,

Mancur Olson, *The Logic of Collective Action* (New York: Schocken, 1969). For a recent critical evaluation of the collective good argument, see Richard Kimber, "Collective Action and the Fallacy of the Liberal Fallacy," *World Politics*, 33 (January 1981), 178–196.

32. Heymann, "The Problem of Coordination: Bargaining and Rules."

33. John Harsanyi, "Basic Moral Decisions and Alternative Concepts of Rationality," *Social Theory and Practice*, 9 (Summer–Fall, 1983), 231–244.

34. Note that this is quite a different issue than that of altruism or empathy with someone else's feelings. In both of these cases, the actor acts on the basis of his *own* desires, feelings of pleasure, etc., even if they are "caused" by observing someone else's satisfaction, happiness, grief, etc.

35. For an extensive discussion of the problems involved, see Reiner Wimmer, *Universalisierung in der Ethik* (Frankfurt: Suhrkamp, 1980).

36. This point has already been made forcefully by Leibniz in his "Noveaux essais sur l'entendement," in C. I. Gerhardt (ed.), *Die Philosophischen Schriften von G. W. Leibniz*, vol. 5 (Hildesheim: Georg Olm, 1960), pp. 39–509.

37. Joseph Heller, *Catch 22* (New York: Dell, 1955), p. 107; also quoted in Ullmann-Margalit, *The Emergence of Norms*, pp. 56–57.

38. I owe these thoughts to Jon Elster, who presented the "bunching" problem, i.e., aggregating states of the world, in a talk entitled "Weakness of Will and the Free Rider Problem" to the Baruch Colloquium for Philosophy, Politics and the Social Sciences, New York City, 5 November 1984.

39. David Hume, *An Inquiry Concerning the Principles of Morals*, ed. Charles Hendel (Indianapolis: Bobbs-Merrill, 1957), pp. 102ff.

40. Thomas Hobbes, *Leviathan*, ed. C. B. Macpherson (Baltimore: Penguin, 1968), ch. 14, p. 196.

41. See, e.g., Hobbes's discussion on the importance of language and the common meanings of terms, and his argument about religion and the need of authoritative regulation of both areas by the sovereign: *Leviathan*, part I, ch. 4 (speech); part III, ch. 42 (religion); and part II, ch. 18 (right of the sovereign to regulate).

42. For a fundamental discussion about rights within a constitutional order, see Bruce Ackerman, *Private Property and the Constitution* (New Haven, Yale University Press, 1977). For a good selection from the enormous literature generated by the economic analysis of rights, see Erik Furnbotn and Svetozar Pejovich, *The Economics of Property Rights* (Cambridge, Mass.: Ballinger, 1974). For a critical assessment of the economic analysis of rights and law, see A. Mitchell Polinsky, "Economic Analysis as a Politically Defective Product: A Buyer's Guide to Posner's Economic Analysis of Law," *Harvard Law Review*, 87 (1974), 1655–1681; and C. Edwin Baker, "The Ideology of the Economic Analysis of Law," *Philosophy and Public Affairs*, 5 (1975), 3–48.

43. See the interesting argument by John Conybeare, "International Organization and the Theory of Property Rights," *International Organization*, 34 (Summer 1980), 307–334.

44. See, e.g., the creation of the Exclusive Economic Zone. For a summary and evaluation of the UNCLOS III regime, see Bernard Oxman, "Summary of the Law of the Sea Convention" and Per Magnus Wijkman, "UNCLOS and the Redistribution of Ocean Wealth," both in Richard Falk, Friedrich Kratochwil, and Saul Mendlovitz (eds.), *International Law: A Contemporary Perspective* (Boulder: Westview, 1986), chs. 33 and 35.

45. Fundamental for this discussion is the perspective developed by Guido Calabresi and Douglas Melamed, "Property Rules, Liability Rules, and Inalienability, One View of the Cathedral," *Harvard Law Review*, 85 (1982), 1089–1128. For an excellent discussion of the problem of inalienable rights, see Susan Rose-Ackerman, "Inalienability and the Theory of Property Rights," *Columbia Law Review*, 85 (1985), 931–969.

46. *Norrington* v. *Wright* 115 US 188 (1885).

47. *Helgar Corp.* v. *Warner Features Inc.* 222 NY 449 N.E. 113 (Ct. of App. 1918). On this point and its implication for legal theory, see also Peter Gabel, "Intentional Structure in Contractual Conditions, Outline of a Method for Critical Legal Theory," *Minnesota Law Review*, 61 (1977), 601–643. For a fundamental discussion of the influence of ideas of distributive justice, even in contract law, aiming at a redistribution of wealth in a less "obtrusive fashion" than though taxation, see Anthony T. Kronman, "Contract Law and Distributive Justice," *Yale Law Journal*, 89 (1980), 472–511.

48. While in the American legal practice since Holmes's influential teachings some type of "objective" theory of contract prevails, most civil law countries still hold a "subjective theory" that presupposes the meetings of the minds (*concours de deux volontés*). For a brief discussion of the American practice, see Grant Gilmore, *The Death of Contract* (Columbus, Ohio: University of Ohio Press, 1974), ch. 1. For a comparative discussion of the civil law on contracts, see Arthur von Mehren, *The Civil Law System* (Englewood Cliffs, NJ: Prentice-Hall, 1957), chs. 11–15.

49. This is the famous case of *Stees* v. *Leonard* 20 Minn. 494 (1874) discussed by Gilmore, *The Death of Contract*, pp. 44–46. Under the "strict" construction rule of the contract, a court (at that time) would not grant relief from the contractual obligation.

50. In this case, the nonfulfillment of the contract does not involve a material breach and thus the contractor would have to be paid for all work done up to the point. See also Charles Fried, *Contract as Promise* (Cambridge, Mass.: Harvard University Press, 1981), ch. 8.

51. Under the "perfect tender" rule as developed by American courts, the buyer was absolutely privileged to reject the goods purchased if they deviated in the slightest degree as to quality, appearance, shipment, etc. Only the Sales Article of the Uniform Commercial Code has modified this doctrine. For a discussion of this problem and cases, see Gilmore, *The Death of Contract*, pp. 80ff.

52. This is the notorious case of *Raffles* v. *Wichelhaus* decided in 1864 by an English court. 2 Hurl and C 906, 159 Eng. Rep. 375 (Ex. 1864) as discussed by Gilmore, *Death of Contract*, pp. 35–42.

53. According to the holding in *Wadsworth* v. *New York Life Insurance Co* 349 Mich. 240, 84 N.W. 2d 513 (1957), the court would decide for plaintiff, since the insurance company was guilty of an unreasonably long delay in processing the application. These and similar issues dealing with "pre-contractual" duties and the protection afforded to parties which seek relief in cases when through blameworthy conduct of the other party a contract became invalid or was prevented from being perfected are analyzed from a comparative perspective by Friedrich Kessler and Edith Fine, "Culpa in contrahendo, Bargaining in Good Faith, and Freedom of Contract: A Comparative Study," *Harvard Law Review*, 77 (1964), 401–448.

54. *Obde* v. *Schlemeyer* 56 Wash. 2d 449, 353 P. 2d 672 (1960). The case is discussed by Anthony Kronman, "Mistake, Disclosure Information and the Law of Contract," *Journal of Legal Studies*, 7 (1978), 1–35 at pp. 24ff.

55. For an excellent treatment of the courts' refusal to enforce such liability limitations imposed through standard form contracts, see George Gluck, "Standard Form Contracts: The Contract Theory Reconsidered," *International and Comparative Law Quarterly*, 28 (1979), 72–90.

56. *Wood* v. *Boynton* 64 Wis. 265. 25 N.W. 42 (1885).

57. *Sherwood* v. *Walker*, 66 Mich. 568, 33 N.W. 919 (1887). In this case, the "court found that the seller had not transferred nor had the buyer paid for the chance that an apparently barren prize cow was in fact pregnant." Fried, *Contract as Promise*, p. 59.

58. "Consideration" as an "initial" necessary condition for the enforceability of a contract is defined as "something of value given in return for a performance or a promise of performance by another, for the purpose of forming a contract," Steven Gifis, *Law Dictionary* (New York: Barron's Ed. Series, 1975).

59. *Hamer* v. *Sidway* 124 N.Y. 538, 27 N.E. 413 (1891). Decided for plaintiff (against executor).

60. *Harris* v. *Watson* Peake 102 (170 Eng. Rep. 94) (1791).

61. This is the problem of third-party beneficiaries. For a short discussion of the problems involved, see Fried, *Contract as Promise*, pp. 44–45. See also *Copeland* v. *Beard* 217 Ala 215, 115 So. 389 (1928), which is a leading case holding that the mere assent by the third party abolishes the promisee's power of discharge.

62. According to British law, the money would probably go to the innkeeper, while U.S. law gives the finder the right to the money. See for a further discussion Fried, *Contract as Promise*, ch. 5.

63. According to the Law of Admiralty, the loss should be totaled and distributed among shipowners and shippers. See Grant Gilmore and Charles Black, *The Law of Admiralty*, 2nd. edn. (Mineola, NY; Foundation Press, 1975), ch. 5.

64. Oliver W. Holmes, "The Path of Law," *Harvard Law Review*, 10 (1897), 458–478.

65. As a "seal" was construed to impart a "consideration."

66. See Gilmore, *Death of Contract*, p. 111. For a more general discussion, see

Patrick Atiyah, *Promises, Morals and Law* (Oxford: Clarendon Press, 1981).

67. This is the problem of the "Good Samaritan," who has been rewarded in American courts less often than in civil law countries. For a discussion, see Dean Wade, "Restitution for Benefits Conferred without Request," *Vanderbilt Law Review*, 19 (1966), 1183ff. See also John Dawson, "Negotiorum Gesti: The Altruistic Intermeddler," *Harvard Law Review*, 74 (1961), 817–865.

68. Gilmore, *Death of Contract*, p. 77.

69. As quoted ibid., p. 25.

70. See Fried, *Contract as Promise*, p. 59.

71. The doctrine itself goes back to von Jhering's article published in 1861 in *Jahrbücher für die Dogmatik des heutigen Römischen und Deutschen Privatrechts*; for a discussion of von Jhering's influence, see Kessler and Fine, "Culpa in contrahendo."

72. See William Prosser, *Law of Torts*, 4th edn. (Minneapolis–St. Paul: West, 1971), p. 699. "The law appears to be working toward the ultimate conclusion that full disclosure of all material facts must be made."

73. See Stanley Henderson, "Promissory Estoppel and Traditional Contract Doctrine," *Yale Law Journal*, 46 (1936), 52–96 and 373–420. See also, e.g., the demand of "good faith" of the U.C.C., which it defines as "honesty in fact" U.C.C., paras. 1–201. For a discussion, see E. Allan Farnsworth, "Good Faith Performance and Commercial Reasonableness under the Uniform Commercial Code," *University of Chicago Law Review*, 30 (1963), 666–679, and Russell Eisenberg, "Good Faith under the Code," *Marquette Law Review*, 54 (1971), 1–18.

74. 2 Hurl & C 906, 159 Eng. Rep. 375 (Ex 1864).

75. On this point, see Fried, *Contract as Promise*, ch. 5, and Richard Posner and Andrew Rosenfield, "Impossibility and Related Doctrines in Contract Law," *Journal of Legal Studies*, 6 (1977), 83–118.

76. Aside from the works of Atiyah, Fried, Gilmore, and Horowitz, see also in this context Duncan Kennedy, "Form and Substance in Private Law Adjudication," *Harvard Law Review*, 89 (1976), 1685–1778. For the complex problems associated with the allocation of risks which courts are often called upon to decide, see the discussion of the notorious Westinghouse Uranium Case by Paul Joskow, "Commercial Impossibility, the Uranium Market and the Westinghouse Case," *Journal of Legal Studies*, 6 (1977), 119–176.

77. See Roger Fisher, *Improving Compliance with International Law* (Charlottesville: University of Virginia Press, 1981), part II.,

78. See, e.g., Kurt Baier, *The Moral Point of View* (Ithaca: Cornell University Press, 1958). What we understand as the "core meaning" of morality entails, according to Gewirth, "a set of categorically obligatory requirements for action that are addressed at least in part to every actual or prospective agent, and that are concerned with further the interests of persons or recipients other than, or in addition to, the agent or speaker." Alan Gewirth, *Reason and Morality* (Chicago: University of Chicago Press, 1978), p. 1.

79. Ibid., p. 69.
80. Jürgen Habermas, *Theorie des kommunikativen Handelns*, vol. 2 (Frankfurt: Suhrkamp, 1981), p. 79 (my translation).
81. Ibid., p. 79.
82. Durkheim, *Sociology and Philosophy*, p. 45.
83. The program for such an investigation has been outlined by Habermas in his "What is Universal Pragmatics?", in Jürgen Habermas, *Communication and the Evolution of Society*, translated by Thomas McCarthy (Boston: Beacon Press, 1979), ch. 1. The fundamental distinction between rules and principles is that rules "apply in all or nothing fashion," while principles "have the dimension of weight and importance." Thus, their application usually requires trade-offs between competing values. For a further elaboration see Dworkin, *Taking Rights Seriously*, chs. 2 and 3.
84. For a more extended discussion of this point, see Thomas Mayberry, "Laws, Moral Laws and God's Commands," *Journal of Value Inquiry*, 4 (Winter 1970), 287–292.
85. Francesco Alberoni, *Movement and Institution* (New York: Columbia University Press, 1984), p. 87.
86. Ibid., p. 87.
87. Sigmund Freud, *Civilization and its Discontents*, translated by James Strachey (New York: Norton, 1962), pp. 59 and 69 respectively.
88. Alberoni, *Movement and Institution*, 91.
89. Aeschylus, *The Eumenides*, translated and edited by Philip Vellacott, in *The Orestian Trilogy* (Baltimore, Md.: Penguin, 1959).

5 **The discourse on grievances: Pufendorf and the "laws of nature" as constitutive principles for the discursive settlement of disputes**

1. I follow here the distinctions of William Frankena, who sees in prudentialism an insufficient basis for moral reasoning. See, e.g., "Prudentialism, or living wholly by the principle of self love, is just not a kind of morality," *Ethics*, 2nd edn. (Englewood Cliffs: Prentice Hall, 1973), p. 19.
2. Stoljar, *Moral and Legal Reasoning*, pp. 24–25.
3. Theory in this sense would imply some type of deductive scheme which would allow for the derivation of particular judgments via a logical algorithm.
4. Immanuel Kant, *Kritik der praktischen Vernunft*, A 54, in Immanuel Kant, *Werke in zwölf Bänden* (Frankfurt: Suhrkamp, n.d.), vol. 7, *Schriften zur Ethik und Religionsphilosophie*, p. 140.
5. This example is discussed in Marcus Singer, *Generalization in Ethics* (London: Eyre and Spottiswoode, 1963), pp. 278–280.
6. Immanuel Kant, *Groundwork of the Metaphysics of Morals*, translated by H. J. Paton (New York: Harper, 1956), pp. 90–91, BA 57.
7. Ibid., p. 98, BA 69.
8. Ibid., p. 99, BA 71.
9. Stoljar, *Moral and Legal Reasoning*, p. 44.
10. Pufendorf himself stressed the "systematic" character of the modern conception of natural law, which he traced to Grotius. In spite of such an

assertion by Pufendorf, I am not convinced that an interpretation of his thought in terms of a closed system comparable to that of astronomy is correct. Although he is clearly more systematic than the seventeenth-century jurists, as Heckel has shown, an interpretation along mechanistic lines seems problematic since his "system" appears to come very close to the "topical ordering" of the traditional Roman lawyers. For the discussion of the seventeenth-century background, see Martin Heckel, "Staat und Kirche nach den Lehren der evangelischen Juristen Deutschlands in der ersten Hälfte des 17. Jahrhunderts," in *Jus ecclesiasticum*, vol. 6 (München: Claudius-Verlag, 1968), ch. 10.

11. For a good discussion of Pufendorf's teachings, and in particular his differences with the medieval speculation on an ontologically founded moral order, see Horst Denzer, *Moralphilosophie und Naturrecht bei Samuel Pufendorf* (München: C. H. Beck, 1972), especially pp. 35–59.

12. On this point, see Hans Welzel, *Naturrecht und Materiale Gerechtigkeit* (Göttingen: Vendenhoek and Ruprecht, 1951), dritter Teil, Abschnitt 6.

13. See Pufendorf's biting criticism of the Lutheran Theologian Valentin Alberti, who espoused the doctrine of a "Christian" natural law. Pufendorf, *Eris Scandica* (Mascovius edn. of 1744), p. 288. Also quoted in Welzel, *Naturrecht*, p. 150.

14. Pufendorf, *De jure naturae et gentium*, bk. I, ch. 1, sections 2 and 3, concerning his teachings about the "entia moralia," which are sharply distinguished from the "entia physica." To that extent, Pufendorf decisively differs from either Hobbes or Spinoza, who dissolves his "law of nature" as a science of norms into a causal natural science. See, e.g., Spinoza, *Tractatus theologico-politicus*, ch. 16, and Pufendorf's argument about "attribution" rather than causal interpretation as the proper province of jurisprudential thinking (*De jure naturae*, bk. I, chs. 5 and 9).

15. See Pufendorf's harangue against "perseitas," i.e., the attempt to found the moral qualities of an act by arguing that it is "good" (or bad) *per se* or by its nature (*sua natura*). *Eris Scandica*, p. 251.

16. P. F. Strawson, *Freedom and Resentment* (London: Methuen, 1974), p. 1.

17. Pufendorf distinguishes three types of duties flowing the law of nature, i.e., the duties vis-à-vis God, vis-à-vis oneself, and vis-à-vis other men. *De jure naturae*, bk. II, ch. 3 passim.

18. Pufendorf, *De jure naturae*, bk. III, ch. 1, section 1, p. 313.

19. Ibid., bk. II, ch. 2, section 23, p. 230.

20. Ibid., bk. II, ch. 2, section 23, p. 230.

21. Ibid., bk. I, ch. 2, section 23, p. 230.

22. Ibid., bk. III, ch. 1, section 1, p. 313.

23. Ibid., bk. III, ch. 2, section 1, p. 330.

24. See, e.g., Robert Nozick, *Anarchy, State and Utopia* (New York: Basic Books, 1974).

25. *De jure naturae*, bk. III, ch. 3, section 1, p. 346.

26. Ibid., bk. III, ch. 4, section 3, p. 381.

27. Ibid., bk. III, ch. 4, section 1, p. 379.

28. On the distinction between a normal state of affairs and the problem of

"supererogation," see Joel Feinberg, *Doing and Deserving* (Princeton: Princeton University Press, 1978), chs. 1 and 2.

29. This is similar to Rawls's position that the obligations resulting from promises have to be assessed in terms of the principle of justice which the institution as such has to satisfy, and from the voluntary uptake of the particular obligation. See Rawls, *A Theory of Justice*, section 18. For a critical comment on this Rawlsian position, see A. I. Melden, *Rights and Persons* (Berkeley: University of California Press, 1977), ch. 4.

30. *De jure naturae*, bk. III, ch. 4., section 1, p. 379.

31. Here Pufendorf seems to go much further by nearly defining, like Austin after him, law as an imposition of the "sovereign." See, e.g., the following passage:

> 1. Because human actions depend upon the will, but the wills of individuals are not always consistent, and those of different men generally tend toward different things, therefore, in order to establish order and seemliness among the human race, it was necessary that some norm should come into being, to which actions might be conformed. For otherwise, if with such freedom of the will, and such diversity of inclinations and tastes, each should do whatever came into his head, without reference to a fixed norm, nothing but the greatest confusion could arise among men.
>
> 2. That norm is called law, that is, a decree by which a superior obliges a subject to conform his acts to his own prescription.
>
> Pufendorf, *De officio hominis et civis libri duo* (New York: Oxford University Press, 1927), bk. I, ch. 2., p. 12.

32. Jean-Jacques Rousseau, *The Social Contract*, bk. I, ch. 7, in Jean-Jacques Rousseau, *The Social Contract and the Discourse on the Origins and the Foundation of Inequality among Mankind*, ed. Lester Crocker (New York: Washington Square Press, 1967), p. 22.

33. This argument is developed further in chapter 8 below.

34. I am following here the argument of Michael Robins, "The Primacy of Promising," *Mind*, 85 (1976), 323–340. On the general issue of "transcendental arguments," see Barry Stroud, "Transcendental Arguments," *Journal of Philosophy*, 65 (1968) 241–256. See also Jaakko Hintikka, "Transcendental Arguments: Genuine and Spurious," *Nous* 61(1972), 274–281.

35. Stoljar, *Moral and Legal Reasoning*, p. 54.

36. On this point see above, chapter 4 and section II of this chapter.

37. Hart, *The Concept of Law*, p. 194.

38. Hobbes: "For as to strength of the body, the weakest has strength enough to kill the strongest . . . From this equality of ability ariseth equality of hope in attaining ends." *Leviathan*, edited by C. B. Macpherson (Baltimore: Penguin, 1968), part I, ch. 8, pp. 183–184.

39. Hart, *The Concept of Law*, p. 190.

40. For a discussion of this fallacy, see G. E. Moore, *Principia Ethica* (Cambridge: Cambridge University Press, 1959).

41. Hobbes, *Leviathan*, ch. 15, p. 215.

42. Stoljar, *Moral and Legal Reasoning*, p. 63.

43. *De jure naturae*, bk. III, ch. 3, section 1, p. 346.

44. Grotius, *De jure belli ac pacis*, bk. II, ch. 2, section 15.
45. *United Kingdom* v. *Albania* 1949 I.C.J. 4.
46. *De jure naturae*, bk. III, ch. 3, section 5, p. 355.
47. Ibid., bk. III, ch. 3, section 9, pp. 365–366.
48. Charles Fried, *Right and Wrong* (Cambridge, Mass.: Harvard University Press, 1978), p. 168.
49. *De jure naturae*, bk. III, ch. 3, p. 369.
50. See, e.g., Patrick Atiyah, *The Rise and Fall of Freedom of Contract* (Oxford: Clarendon Press, 1979); Gilmore, *The Death of Contract*; Morton Horowitz, *The Transformation of American Law* (Cambridge, Mass.: Harvard University Press, 1977), ch. 6. For the opposite position, see Fried, *Contract as Promise*.
51. See, e.g. G. J. Warnock, *The Object of Morality*, (London: Methuen, 1971), ch. 7.
52. John Searle, "What is a Speech Act?", in John Searle (ed.), *The Philosophy of Language* (Oxford: Oxford University Press, 1971). See also John Rawls, "Two Concepts of Rules," *Philosophical Review*, 64 (1955), 3–32.
53. See, e.g., the critique by Alan Gewirth, "Obligation: Political, Legal, Moral," in Roland Pennock and John Chapman (eds.), *Political and Legal Obligation* (New York: Atherton, 1970), ch. 4. See also a useful collection of articles that were written in regard to institutional obligations in W. D. Hudson (ed.), *The Is–Ought Question* (London: Macmillan, 1969).
54. On this point see Pall S. Ardal, "And that's a Promise," *Philosophical Quarterly*, 118 (1968), 232–233.
55. See Hume, *A Treatise of Human Nature*, part II, section 5 in Aiken (ed.), *Hume's Moral and Political Philosophy*, pp. 82f.
56. Robins, "The Primacy of Promising," 323–334.
57. This analysis cuts against the formal "identity" argument between promises and threats such as expounded by Searle, *Speech Acts*, pp. 58ff. Searle conceptualizes the difference between promise and threat in terms of the prospective "benefits" to the promisee.
58. Warnock, *The Object of Morality*, passim.
59. See Grotius. For a short critical discussion of the problem of promise in the natural law tradition, see Atiyah, *Promises, Morals and Law*,. ch. 2.
60. These examples are given by Don Locke, "The Object of Morality and the Obligation to Keep a Promise," *Canadian Journal of Philosophy*, 2 (1972), 135–143.
61. Ibid., 141.
62. This point is powerfully made by Fried, *Right and Wrong*, chs. 1 and 2.
63. *De jure naturae*, bk. IV, ch. 1, section 5, pp. 465–466.
64. Ibid., bk. IV, ch. 1, section 4, p. 461.
65. Ibid., bk IV, ch. 1, section 7, pp. 468–469.
66. This is the traditional distinction dating back to Aristotle's distinction between "voice" and "language" in his *Politics*, 1253a9–11. See also the discussion of this passage in the introduction above.
67. *De jure naturae*, bk. IV, ch. 1, section 5, pp. 465–466.
68. Ibid., bk. IV, ch. 1, section 7, pp. 468–469.

69. Ibid., bk. IV, ch. 1, section 7, p. 469.
70. Ibid., bk. IV, ch. 1, section 8, p. 470.
71. Ibid., bk. IV, ch. 1, section 10, p. 473.
72. Fried, *Right and Wrong*, p. 57.
73. Ibid., p. 57.
74. *De jure naturae*, bk. IV, ch. 1, sections 11 and 13, pp. 475–476.
75. Ibid., bk. IV, ch. 1, section 20, p. 485.
76. Ibid., bk. IV, ch. 1, section 20, pp. 485–490 and bk. IV, ch. 2, section 6.
77. Ibid., bk. IV, ch. 1, sections 16 and 17, pp. 479–481.
78. Ibid., bk. IV, ch. 1, section 19, pp. 484–485.
79. Ibid., bk. III, ch. 6, section 15, pp. 402–427.
80. Ibid., bk. III, ch. 6, section 15, p. 424.
81. Ibid., bk. III, ch. 6, section 8, p. 413.
82. Ibid., bk. III, ch. 6, section 8, p. 414.
83. Ibid., bk. III, ch. 6, section 1, p. 402.

6 The notion of "right"

1. See above, chapter 4.
2. See, e.g., Peter Singer, *Animal Liberation* (New York: New York Review, 1975); see also Joel Feinberg, "The Rights of Animals and Unborn Generations," in Joel Feinberg, *Rights, Justice and the Bounds of Liberty* (Princeton, NJ: Princeton University Press, 1980), ch. 8; Joel Feinberg, "Human Duties and Animal Rights," ibid., ch. 9. For a counter-argument see R. G. Frey, *Interests and Rights: The Case Against Animal Rights* (Oxford: Clarendon Press, 1980).
3. See, e.g., David Lyons, "Rights, Claimants and Beneficiaries," in David Lyons (ed.), *Rights* (Belmont, Calif.: Wadsworth Publishing Co., 1979), pp. 58–77.
4. This argument is further elaborated in U.S. Foreign Policy Statements and in the philosophy of dividing "social" from the "political" human rights. For a further discussion and critique see Henry Shue, *Basic Rights* (Princeton, NJ: Princeton University Press, 1980), introduction. For the traditional conceptual distinction see Samuel Stoljar, *An Analysis of Rights* (New York: St. Martin's Press, 1984), chs. 7–9.
5. See the division of an "International Covenant on Civil and Political Rights," annex to G.A. Res. 2200, 21 GAOR Supp. 16 (A/6316) at 52, and "International Covenant on Economic, Social and Cultural Rights," annex to G.A. Res. 2200, 21 GAOR Supp. (A/6316) at 49.
6. See Maurice Cranston's and Robert Nozick's argument that there are no "human rights" or social and economic rights to well being; Maurice Cranston, *What are Human Rights* (London: Bodley Head, 1973), pp. 63ff; Robert Nozick, *Anarchy, State and Utopia* (New York: Basic Books, 1974), pp. 30–34.
7. See for an overview of various arguments along these lines Alan Gewirth, *Human Rights, Essays on Justification and Application* (Chicago: University of Chicago Press, 1982), introduction. See also H. L. A. Hart's well-known

essay, "Are there any Natural Rights?" *Philosophical Review*, 64 (1955), 175–191.

8. On this point see Stoljar, *An Analysis of Rights*, ch. 7.
9. Joel Feinberg, "Duties, Rights and Claims" and "The Nature and Value of Rights," in Feinberg, *Rights, Justice and the Bounds of Liberty*, chs. 6 and 7.
10. Art. 25, 1 of the Universal Declaration of Human Rights, G.A. Res. 217 GAOR (A/810) at 71.
11. Feinberg, "The Nature and Value of Rights," p. 143.
12. Ronald Dworkin, *Taking Rights Seriously* (Cambridge, Mass.: Harvard University Press, 1978), p. 194.
13. Ibid., p. 199.
14. *Case Concerning The Barcelona Traction Light and Power Co., Ltd.* (Belgium v. Spain), Second Phase (1970), I.C.J., 3ff.
15. A fallacy of composition is committed when attributes of the parts are also predicated of the whole, as: chocolate pudding is good; cucumber salad is good; therefore, chocolate pudding with cucumber salad is "good."
16. See the controversy between Michael Walzer, Charles Beitz, Gerald Doppelt, David Leben, and others in *Philosophy and Public Affairs*, 9 (Summer 1980), 384–403. See also Michael Walzer, "The Moral Standing of States: A Response to Four Critics," *Philosophy and Public Affairs*, 9 (Spring 1980), 209–229 and Gerald Doppelt, "Walzer's theory of Morality in International Relations," *Philosophy and Public Affairs*, 8 (Fall 1978), 3–26. Symptomatic for this debate is the assertion that a state's right would be a "collective right" and that this furnishes a rhetoric of morality in international relations which places the rights of states *de facto* above those of individuals. See Doppelt, "Walzer's Theory of Morality." 26. From the argument above it should be obvious that there is neither anything mysterious about the rights of states, nor that Doppelt's conclusion follows.
17. *US v. Curtiss Wright* 299 US 304 (1936) 316, at 318.
18. 1975 I.C.J. 12, especially 785–789 and 150–152.
19. Ibid., especially 785–789 and 150–152.
20. H. L. A. Hart, "Are There Any Natural Rights?", in David Lyons, *Rights*, pp. 14–26, at p. 19.
21. The Greek term *dikaios* and its opposite *adikos* mean the "just" or "unjust" or the "right" or "wrong" thing to do rather than having a right. For the importance of the "status" doctrines underlying the legal proceedings in Greek law which had a decisive influence on Roman law see below, chapter 8, with sources.
22. See, e.g., Richard Tuck, *Natural Rights Theories* (Cambridge: Cambridge University Press, 1976), p. 116.
23. Richard Flathman, *The Practice of Rights* (Cambridge: Cambridge University Press, 1976), p. 116.
24. Stoljar, *An Analysis of Rights*, p. 37.
25. Thomas Hobbes, *Leviathan*, part II, ch. 20.
26. Samuel II. 11, cited with approval by Hobbes ibid., part II, ch. 21.
27. That powers belong to offices is most characteristic of "rational" legal

orders, but even in "patrimonial systems," in which offices reflect the functional specialization of the ruler's household, we can see the rudimentary notion of the powers of an office. For a further discussion of these points see Max Weber, *Economy and Society* (Berkeley: California University Press, 1978).

28. Richard B. Stewart, "The Reformation of American Administrative Law," *Harvard Law Review*, 88 (1975), 1679–1715.

29. The classical historical study on the development of diplomacy and its privileges is Garrett Mattingly, *Renaissance Diplomacy* (Boston: Houghton Mifflin, 1971); For the modern regulations concerning diplomats and consular personnel, see the two Vienna Conventions (*Vienna Convention on Diplomatic Relations* (1961), and *Vienna Convention on Consular Relations* (1963).

30. Yoram Dinstein, "Diplomatic Immunity from Jurisdiction Ratione Materiae," *International and Comparative Law Quarterly*, 15 (1966), 76–89.

31. Since Iran had signed the Optional Protocol concerning the Compulsory Settlement of Disputes accompanying the Vienna Conventions, the I.C.J. had jurisdiction; the U.S. also could apply for interim measures of protection under Art. 41 of the I.C.J. statute. Furthermore, the Court could proceed with a judgment on the merits in spite of Iran's nonappearance. Although the Court termed the takeover by Iranian "students" twice an "armed attack," it is doubtful whether such a usage of the term was intended to convey the "armed attack" requirement of Art. 51 of the U.N. Charter, since other characterizations of the takeover can be found too – such as "attack" in sections 17, 24 and 25 and "assault" in section 18.

32. Stoljar, *An Analysis of Rights*, p. 40.

33. Ibid., p. 14.

34. See Art. 51 of the U.N. Charter, protecting the "inherent right of individual or collective self-defense."

35. Flathman, *The Practice of Rights*, p. 44.

36. This shocking disparity is mentioned by Henry Shue, *Basic Rights*, p. 107f.

37. See, e.g., the argument of Locke, *Second Treatise on Government*, p. 85. For a critique of this position in Lockian terms, see A. I. Melden, *Rights and Persons* (Berkeley, Calif.: University of California Press, 1977), ch. VII, "Changing Conceptions of Human Rights."

38 See, e.g., the argument of Grotius, *De jure belli ac pacis*, bk. I, ch. 3, para. 7.

39. Jean Jacques Rousseau, *Social Contract*, bk I, ch. 4, pp. 12f.

40. Art. 53 of the Vienna Convention on Treaties defines *ius cogens* as "peremptory" norms. According to the Convention, a norm is peremptory when it is "accepted and recognized by the international community of states as a whole as a norm from which no derogation is permitted and which can be modified only by a subsequent norm of general international law having the same character."

41. The notion of *ius cogens* was particularly eloquently advocated by Alfred Verdross throughout his long career. See his "Forbidden Treaties in International Law," *American Journal of International Law*, 31 (1937), 571–577; for a critical discussion of the notion of *ius cogens* in international law

see Georg Schwarzenberger, "International Jus Cogens?", *Texas Law Review*, 43 (1965), 455–478; see also Jerzy Sztucki, *Jus Cogens and the Vienna Convention on the Law of Treaties: A Critical Appraisal* (Vienna–New York: Springer Verlag, 1974), denying the existence of a *ius cogens* in international law based on very detailed investigations.

42. See, e.g., the draft conventions on state succession, "Convention on the Succession of States in Respect of Matters Other than Treaties" and "Vienna Convention on Succession of States in Respect to Treaties."

43. See the argument about a variety of "generations" of human rights in Stephen Marks, "Emerging Human Rights, A New Generation for the 1980s," *Rutgers Law Review*, 33 (Winter 1981), 435–452. For example, the Universal Declaration of Human Rights reads in one of its provisions:

> Everyone has the right to a standard of living adequate for the health and well-being of himself and his family, including food, clothing, housing and medical care and necessary social services, and the right to security in the event of unemployment, sickness, disability, widowhood, old age or lack of livelihood in other circumstances beyond his control.

> Art. 25, 1 of the Universal Declaration of Human rights, G.A. Res 217 GAOR (A/ 810) at 71.

44. Even such a sympathetic advocate of rights as Henry Shue criticizes the "rather ethereal quality" of many of these pronouncements. See Shue, *Basic Rights*, p. 93.

45. Wassily Leontieff, Ann P. Carter, and Peter A. Petri, *The Future of the World Economy: A United Nations Study* (New York: Oxford University Press, 1977).

46. See, as a notable exception to standard international relations analysis, the World Order Models Project. For an introduction to these modeling exercises see Saul Mendlovitz (ed.), *On the Creation of a Just World Order* (New York: Free Press, 1975).

47. See the remarks above concerning the problem of collective goods in chapter 3.

48. See his remarks in the *Second Discourse* and *The Social Contract*.

49. *Roe* v. *Wade* 410 US 155 (1973).

50. Ibid., at 163.

51. Stoljar, *An Analysis of Rights*, p. 109.

52. Adam Smith, *The Wealth of Nations*, ed. B. Mazlish (Indianapolis, Ind.: Bobbs Merrill, 1961), bk. I, ch. 2, p. 15.

53. See Joel Feinberg, "Human Duties and Animal Rights" and "The Rights of Animals and Unborn Generations," in Feinberg, *Rights, Justice, and the Bounds of Liberty*, chs. 8 and 9.

54. On a discussion of the subsidiary principle, see Cletus Dirksen's *Catholic Social Principles* (St. Louis: Herder, 1961). However, I do *not* want to argue that human rights proper only insofar as the "right is the claim *as* recognized in law and maintained by governmental action," as Rex Martin asserts. See Rex Martin, "Human Rights and Civil Rights," *Philosophical Studies*, 37 (1980), 391–403, at p.396. For a thoughtful critique

of the latter argument which at the same time admits the "self-liquidating"' quality of human rights-claims, see Jack Donnelly, *The Concept of Human Rights* (London: Croom Helm, 1985), ch. 2.

55. For the "test" used by U.S. courts in ascertaining "standing" see *Flast* v. *Cohen* 392 US 166 (1974).

56. The attempts of U.S. citizens to challenge the secrecy of potentially illegal intelligence operations conducted by the U.S. in violation of international law, on the basis of their status as U.S. taxpayers, have been routinely dismissed by the Supreme Court. See, e.g., *US* v. *Richardson* 416 US 166 (1974).

57. For a discussion of the issues involved in self-executing vs. non-self-executing treaties see Henkin, *Foreign Affairs and the Constitution*, ch. V, and my "The Role of Domestic Courts as Agencies of the International Legal Order," in Richard Falk, Friedrich Kratochwil and Saul Mendlovitz (eds.), *International Law: A Contemporary Perspective* (Boulder, Colo.: Westview, 1985), ch. 13.

58. *Supreme Court of California* 242 P. 2d 617 (1952).

59. Ibid., at 621f.

60. *Tel-Oren* v. *Libyan Arab Republic* 726 F. 2d 774 (D.C. Circuit, 1984).

61. Sec. 1350 provides: "The district courts shall have original jurisdiction of any civil actions by an alien for a tort only, committed in violation of the law of nations or a treaty of the United States," 62 Stat. 9343.

62. See, e.g., *Filartiga* v. *Peña-Irala*, 630 F. 2d 876, in which the tort claim of the plaintiffs for the death of their brother and son through torture in a Paraguayan prison was upheld. For a further discussion, see my "Domestic Courts."

63. *US* v. *Pink* 315 US 203 (1942).

64. For the elaboration of the political questions doctrine, see *Baker* v. *Carr* 369 US 186 (1962).

65. This was the usual response of the Supreme Court in dealing with draft-registers during the Vietnam War. See, e.g., *Mora* v. *McNamara* 389 US 934 (1967).

66. *Goldwater* v. *Carter* 444 US 996 (1979).

67. Flathman, *The Practice of Rights*, p. 117.

7 The question of "law"

1. I follow here the conceptualization developed by Michael Barkun in his *Law Without Sanctions* (New Haven: Yale University Press, 1968).

2. For a further discussion of these various modes, see Kratochwil, Rohrlich, and Mahajan, *Peace and Disputed Sovereignty*.

3. For the common two-party bargaining problem the usual representation is as shown in figure 16 (see p. 294).

4. The term *auctoritas* clearly emphasizes this factor. In its original meaning *auctoritas* referred to some informal, although important, influence, and was clearly differentiated from official power as *imperium* or *potestas*. *Auctoritas* derived from *augere*, i.e., enhancing the standing of a decision through either personal prestige (of the *princeps*) or particular competence

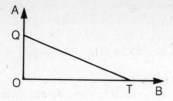

Figure 16. Anything north of point O will be to the advantage of A, while anything east will be to the advantage of B. Q–T describes the possibility boundary which says that everything within the triangular area Q–T–O is suboptimal while anything outside is impossible.

For a discussion of the conditions for a "package" deal vs. unpacking the issues, see James Sebenius, "Negotiation Arithmetic: Adding and Subtracting Issues and Parties," *International Organization*, 37 (Spring 1983), 281–316.

or knowledge in a given area, e.g., among the jurisconsults. See Theodor Eschenburg, *Über Autorität* (Frankfurt: Suhrkamp 1965).

5. For a fundamental discussion of mediation see Oran Young, *The Intermediaries* (Princeton: Princeton University Press, 1967).

6. For a good discussion of the mediator's own interest in the case of Middle East disengagement following the Yom Kippur War, see Matti Golan, *The Secret Conversations of Henry Kissinger* (New York: Quadrangle Books, 1976).

7. For a further elaboration see Fred Jklé, *How Nations Negotiate* (New York: Praeger, 1964), ch. 4.

8. For a further discussion of Anthony D'Amato, "What 'Counts' as Law," in Nicholas Onuf (ed.), *Law Making in the Global Community* (Durham, NC: North Carolina Academic Press, 1983), ch. 2.

9. Much of Roman law was created by the magistrates, i.e., praetores, aediles, etc., who developed the law case by case but without the doctrine of binding precedent. For a short discussion see Wolfgang Kunkel, *Römische Rechtsgeschichte* (Köln: Böhlau Verlag, 1956).

10. See Hart, *The Concept of Law*, ch. 5.

11. This leads to Kelsen's attempt to "recast" empowering rules as sanctioning rules. For a discussion of this problematic procedure, see Hart, *The Concept of Law*, pp. 35–36.

12. Hans Kelsen, *Principles of International Law*, 2nd rev. edn., ed. Robert W. Tucker (New York: Holt, Rinehart, and Winston, 1966), p. 31.

13. Ibid., p. 4.

14. Ibid., part A, ch. 1; part B, pp. 16–87.

15. Oliver Wendell Holmes, "The Path of Law," *Harvard Law Review*, 10 (1897), 458–478.

16. Hart, *The Concept of Law*, pp. 35–36.

17. Ibid., pp. 92f.

18. Ibid., ch. 10.

19. Ibid., p. 229.

20. Ibid., ch. 9.

21. See, for example, Hart's remarks:

> Even when verbally formulated general rules are used, uncertainties as to the form of behaviour required by them may break out in particular concrete cases. Particular fact-situations do not await us already marked off from each other, and labelled as instances of the general rule, the application of which is in question; nor can the rule itself step forward to claim its own instances . . . If the world in which we live were characterized only by a finite number of features, and these together with all the modes in which they could combine were known to us, then provision could be made in advance for every possibility. We could make rules, the application of which to particular cases never called for a further choice. Everything could be known, and for everything, since it could be known, something could be done and specified in advance by rule. This would be a world fit for "mechanical" jurisprudence.

Hart, *The Concept of Law*, pp. 123 and 125, respectively.

22. I owe this thought to Nicholas Onuf.

23. Neil McCormick, "Law as Institutional Fact," *The Law Quarterly Review*, 90 (1974), 102–129 at p. 120.

24. See, e.g., Joseph Raz, *The Concept of a Legal System* (Oxford: Clarendon, 1979).

25. Ronald Dworkin, "Is Law a System of Rules?", in Ronald Dworkin (ed.), *The Philosophy of Law* (Oxford: Oxford University Press, 1977), ch. 2.

26. It is virtually impossible to provide a comprehensive account even of only the major works of McDougal and his associates because of their prolific publications. Nevertheless, the main conceptual tenets of this approach can be gathered from two articles: Myres McDougal, "Some Basic Theoretical Concepts about International Law: A Policy Oriented Framework of Inquiry," in Richard Falk and Saul Mendlovitz (eds.), *The Strategy of World Order*, vol. II, *International Law* (New York: World Law Fund, 1966), pp. 116–133; and Myres McDougal and Harold Lasswell, "The Identification and Appraisal of Diverse Systems of Public Order," *ibid.*, pp. 45–74.

27. McDougal and Lasswell, "The Identification," p. 53.

28. Ibid., p. 53.

29. Ibid., p. 53.

30. Ibid., p. 44.

31. Ibid., p. 47.

32. Myres McDougal, "Some Basic Theoretical Concepts" p. 129.

33. McDougal and Lasswell, "The Identification," p. 129.

34. See McDougal's remarks in this respect concerning the difference between theories about law and theories of law in Myres McDougal, "Some Basic Theoretical Concepts," p. 116.

35. See, e.g., David Easton's definition in *A Systems-Analysis of Political Life* (New York: Wiley, 1965).

36. McDougal and Lasswell, "The Identification," p. 53.

37. Ibid., p. 50.

295

38. McDougal, "Some Basic Theoretical Concepts," p. 119.
39. See, e.g., Jorge Castañeda, *Legal Effects of United Nations Resolutions* (New York: Columbia University Press, 1969); Richard Falk, "On the Quasi-Legislative Competence of the UN General Assembly," *American Journal of International Law*, 60 (October 1966), 782–791.
40. Oscar Schachter, "Towards a Theory of International Obligation," *Virginia Journal of International Law*, 8 (1968), 300–320 at p. 310.
41. *Texaco Overseas Petroleum et al.* v. *Libyan Arab Republic, International Legal Materials*, 17 (1978), 1–37.
42. Like the American political theorist who stressed the importance of a consensus by the different segments of a society, René Jean Dupuy (appointed sole arbitrator) espoused a similar position in his award; see especially sec. 84–91.
43. Oscar Schachter, "International Law in Theory and Practice," *Receuil de cours*, 178 (1982–V), 50.
44. This leads to considerable puzzles in statutory interpretation. For·a good discussion of some of the most striking issues involved see the Symposium on Statutory Construction, *Vanderbilt Law Review*, vol. 3 (1949–50), no. 3, with contributions by Felix Frankfurter, John McDonald, Karl Llewelyn, Frank Horack, Wolfgang Friedmann, Charles Clark, John Quarles, Charles Curtis, Nathaniel Nathanson, et al.
45. See, e.g., the conflicting goals and purposes in the Clean Air and Water Act which are hardly papered over by "notwithstanding" clauses.
46. R. S. Summers, "Naive Instrumentalism and the Law," in P. M. S. Hacker and J. Raz (eds.), *Law, Morality, and Society* (Oxford: Clarendon Press, 1977), ch. 6, at p. 124.
47. For the problem of rules which are not in fixed verbal form see David Miers and William Twining, *How To Do Things With Rules* (London: Widenfeld and Nicolson, 1976), chs. 4–7.
48. A good case can be made that very often the "unseen hand" is not benign. For an account of the dysfunctional aspects, which he calls the "back of the invisible hand," see Russell Hardin, *Collective Action* (Baltimore, Md.: Johns Hopkins University Press, 1982), ch. 1.
49. For a further discussion of this problem see Robert Jervis, "Cooperation Under the Security Dilemma," *World Politics*, vol. 30, no. 2 (1978), 167–186.
50. McDougal and Lasswell, "The Identification," 49. See in this context the critique by Oran Young, "International Law and Social Science: The Contribution of Myres McDougal," *American Journal of International Law*, 66 (1972), 60–76.
51. Mohammed Bedjaoui, *Towards a New International Order* (Paris: UNESCO and New York–London: Holmes and Meier, 1979).
52. See, e.g., Schwebel, "The Effects of Resolutions of the UN General Assembly," in *Proceedings of the American Society of International Law*, 1979, 302–309.
53. See the explicit provisos of Art. 11 in conjunction with Art. 12 as well as the *travaux préparatoirs* to these articles.

54. For an interesting account see Gold, "Strengthening the Soft International Law of Exchange Arrangements," 443–489. For a more general theoretical discussion see Ignaz Seidl-Hohenveldern, "International Economic Soft Law," *Receuil des cours*, vol. 169 (1979–II).

55. Gold, "Strengthening the Soft International Law," 443.

56. The Ihlen Declaration is mentioned in *Legal Status of Eastern Greenland*, case P.C.I.J. Series A/B, 1933, no. 53 at 71.

57. Ibid., at 267 and 473.

58. On the problem of estoppel in international law, see Ian Brownlie, *Principles of Public International Law*, 2nd edn. (Oxford: Oxford University Press, 1973), pp. 617–619.

59. *Nuclear Tests Case* (New Zealand v. France), I.C.J. Reports 1974, 22 at p. 477.

60. Ibid., at pp. 267 and 473.

61. *Temple of Preah Vihear* case, preliminary objections, I.C.J. Reports 1961, 17 at p. 31.

62. *Nuclear Tests Case*, 268 and 473.

63. Entscheidungen des Bundesgerichtshofs in Zivilsachen (B.G.H.Z.) 59, 82 (1972).

64. Ibid., at p. 85.

65. For an extensive discussion see Hans Baade, "The Legal Effects of Codes of Conduct for Multinational Enterprises," *German Yearbook of International Law*, 22 (1979), 11–52.

66. *The Paquete Habana* 175 US 677 (1900).

67. The validity of a statute in pursuance of a treaty which would have otherwise been invalid since it violated the 10th amendment was litigated in *Missouri* v. *Holland* 252 US 416.

68. See the issues concerning the U.S. assets of a nationalized Cuban firm in *Banco Nacional de Cuba* v. *Sabbatino* 376 US 398.

69. The issues in *US* v. *First National City Bank*, US Court of Appeals 2nd Cic. 1968, 396 F. 2d 887 concerned the compliance with a Grand Jury subpoena in an anti-trust case by a branch office of a U.S. bank in Germany in spite of the civil liabilities which the German branch might be subject to because of the secrecy requirements of German law.

70. For a detailed examination of the obligations under the old par value system and the new rules that developed since the 1970s, see Joseph Gold, *Legal and Institutional Aspects of the International Monetary System*, selected essays ed. Jane B. Evenson (Washington, D.C.: International Monetary Fund, 1979).

71. See, e.g., the careful analysis of the Security Council decisions on reprisals in Derek Bowett, "Reprisals Involving the Recourse to Armed Force," *American Journal of International Law*, 66 (1972), 1–36; see also Oscar Schachter, "The Right of States to use Armed Forces," *Michigan Law Review*, 82 (1984), 1620–1646.

72. The term "horizontal ordering" was introduced by Richard Falk, "International Jurisdiction: Horizontal and Vertical Conceptions of Legal Order," *Temple Law Quarterly*, 32 (1959), 295–320.

73. Gidon Gottlieb, "The Nature of International Law: Toward a Second Concept of Law," in Cyril Black and Richard Falk (eds.), *The Future of the International Legal Order*, vol. 4 (Princeton: Princeton University Press, 1972), ch. 9, at p. 332.

74. Ibid., at p. 370.

75. For a general discussion of "tragic choices" in a society, see Guido Calabresi and Philip Bobbitt, *Tragic Choices* (New York: Norton, 1978).

76. *McFall* v. *Shimp* 10 DJC 3d 90 (1978).

77. On the problem of need as an insufficient basis of a right-claim, see Stoljar, *An Analysis of Rights*, ch. 9 – although "vital needs" probably ought to be treated differently.

78. One such example is the requirement to help seriously injured persons in acute danger even if one simply happens to come to the place where the injury occurred; or *vide* the requirement in some states to help a stranded motorist in a snowstorm because otherwise he/she might freeze to death.

79. Miers and Twining, *How to Do Things With Rules*, p. 159.

80. Ibid., p. 176.

81. Ibid., pp. 166f.

82. Aristotle, *Rhetoric* and *Topica*, trans. by E. S. Forster (Cambridge, Mass.: Harvard University Press, 1966).

83. Chaim Perelman, *Logique juridique* (Paris: Dalloz, 1976), and Chaim Perelman and L. Olbrechts-Tyteca, *The New Rhetoric: A Treatise on Argumentation* (Notre Dame, Ind.: Notre Dame University Press, 1969).

84. John Wisdom, "Gods," *Proceedings of the Aristotelian Society*, 45 (1944/45), 185–206 at p. 194.

85. Ibid., at p. 194.

8 The path of legal arguments

1. Grundgesetz der Bundesrepublik Deutschland, Art. 20, sec. 3.

2. For a general discussion of the logical issues involved in legal reasoning, see (out of a wide variety of works) the standard treatises: Julius Stone, *Legal Systems and Legal Reasoning* (Stanford: Stanford University Press, 1964); Edward Levi, *An Introduction to Legal Reasoning* (Chicago: University of Chicago Press, 1949); and also Hubert Hubien (ed.), *Le Raisonnement juridique* (Bruxelles: Emile Bruylant, 1971) and Sidney Hook (ed.), *Law and Philosophy* (New York: New York University Press, 1963).

3. See the discussion in Julius Stone, *The Province and Function of Law* (Cambridge, Mass.: Harvard University Press, 1950), ch. 7, "Fallacies of Logical Form in Legal Reasoning."

4. Ilmar Tammelo, *Rechtslogik und materiale Gerechtigkeit* (Frankfurt: Athaeneum Verlag, 1971), pp. 28ff.

5. W. T. Blackstone, "Criteria of Adequacy for Judicial Reasoning," in Hubert Hubien (ed.), *Le Raisonnement juridique*, pp. 233–242, at p. 234.

6. See, e.g., Stephen Toulmin, *Reason in Ethics* (Cambridge: Cambridge University Press, 1970).

7. For an extensive discussion of the revival of practical reason and its

distinctive mode of thinking, see Manfred Riedel (ed.), *Rehabilitierung der praktischen Philosophie*, 2 vols. (Freiburg: Rombach, 1972–1974).

8. See, e.g., Fritjof Haft, *Juristische Rhetorik* (Freiburg: Alber, 1978) and Otmar Ballweg and Thomas Michael Seibert (eds.), *Rhetorische Rechtstheorie* (Freiburg–München: Alber, 1982).

9. For a fundamental discussion of the issues involved in this "zetetic" thought, see Joseph Esser, *Vorverständnis und Methodenwahl in der Rechtsfindung* (Frankfurt: Athaeneum, 1970).

10. This definition of "topos" as "sedes e quibus argumenta promuntur" is taken from Cicero, *Topica* II.8, trans. Hubbell, p. 386.

11. Ibid., 100a25–100b24.

12. Aristotle, *Rhetoric* 1357a12–13.

13. Ibid., 1398a21.

14. Ibid., 1358b5.

15. Ibid., 1356a5 and 1357a12.

16. Ibid., 1554a3; also 1355.

17. Ibid., 1355b2.

18. Aristotle, *Topica* 100b18.

19. Aristotle, *Rhetoric* 1357b18.

20. Aristotle, *Analytica priora* 24b20–22.

21. See, e.g., 'Aristotle's argument in the *Topica* 101a25–101b1, that the "first principles" of each science must be subjected to a "dialectic" inquiry.

22. See the example given by Aristotle in his *Rhetoric* 1399a11–18 (taken from Euripides' *Medea*).

23. Ibid., 1356b9.

24. For a further discussion of the logical properties of enthymemes, see Markus Woerner, "Enthymeme – ein Rückgriff auf Aristoteles in systematischer Absicht," in Ballweg and Seibert (eds.), *Rhetorische Rechtstheorie*, pp. 73–98; see also Jürgen Sprute, "Topos und Enthymem in der Aristotelischen Rhetorik," *Hermes*, 103 (1975), 68–90.

25. Aristotle, *Rhetoric* 1357b19.

26. Ibid., 1357b19.

27. Aristotle, *Topica* 101b36–102b26.

28. Aristotle, *Rhetoric* 1394a9ff.

29. Ibid., 1393b6ff.

30. As quoted by Andreas Spira, "Topik und Ordnung," in Ballweg and Seibert (eds.), *Rhetorische Rechtstheorie*, pp. 125–140, at p. 139.

31. For a more extensive treatment of this thought, see Peter Berger and Thomas Luckmann, *The Social Construction of Reality* (Garden City, NY: Anchor, 1966).

32. Montesquieu, *The Spirit of the Laws*, trans. Thomas Nugent, (New York: Hafner, 1966), bk. VI, ch. iii, p. 75.

33. Organic Decree of 16–24 August 1790, as quoted in Stone, *The Province and Function of Law*, p. 150 (n. 4).

34. Stone, *The Province and Function of Law*, p. 150.

35. See Chaim Perelman, "Recht und Rhetorik," in Ballweg and Seibert (eds.), *Rhetorische Rechtstheorie*, pp. 237–245, at p. 244.

36. See, e.g., the argument by J. L. Montrose, "The Ratio Decidendi of a Case," *Modern Law Review*, 20 (1957), 578–595, which stresses what the Court *said*, as opposed to Herman Oliphant's theory that views the precedent as being contained in what the Court *did* on the "facts." H. Oliphant, "A Return to State Decisis," *American Bar Association Journal*, 14 (1928), 71–76 and 159–162. See also in this context Arthur Goodhart's modification of the Oliphant position restricting the precedent to those facts described *as material* by the Court in reaching its decision. Arthur Goodhart, "The Ratio Decidendi of a Case," *Modern Law Review*, 22 (1959), 117–124.
37. *M'Alister* (or *Donoghue*) (*Pauper*) v. *Stevenson*, House of Lords Privy Council Cases, *Law Reports* (1932), pp. 562–623.
38. These points are eloquently made in Julius Stone, "The Ratio of the Ratio Decidendi," *Modern Law Review*, 22 (1959), 579–620.
39. See Goodhart, "The Ratio Decidendi"; on the point that the relevant aspect is the evaluation of the fact by the subsequent (rather than the original court), see Edward Levi, "The Nature of Judicial Reasoning," in Sidney Hook (ed.), *Law and Philosophy* (New York: New York University Press, 1964), at p. 276.
40. Roy Stone, "Ratiocination not Rationalization," *Mind*, 74 (1965), 463–482, at p. 470.
41. For a critical examination of an alleged constitutional "right" to demonstration in the German legal order, see Ralf Brückner, "Zur Problematik des Individualbereichs in der Meinungsfreiheit," J.D. dissertation (Munich), 1974.
42. *McPherson* v. *Buick Motor Company* 217 N.Y. 382 (1916). *Ultramares Corporation* v. *Touche* 255 N.Y. 170 (1931).
43. Ultramares Corp. had sustained a considerable loss when it had granted a substantial loan to a firm on the basis of a balance sheet certified by the accountant. The balance showed the firm solvent. Ultramares sought recovery from the accounting firm because of negligence in their auditing practices. Deciding against Ultramares, Benjamin Cordozo, speaking for the Court, held that this decision

> does not relieve them [defendants] if their audit has been so negligent as to justify a finding that had no genuine belief in its adequacy, for this again is fraud. It does no more than to say that if less than this is proved, if there has been neither reckless misstatement nor insincere profession of an opinion, but only an honest blunder, the ensuing liability for negligence is one that is bounded by the contract and is to be enforced between the parties by whom the contract has been made.

A. L. Sainer, *Law is Justice: Notable Opinions of Justice Cardozo* (New York: AD Press, 1938), pp. 263–276, at p. 273.

44. George Christie, "Objectivity in the Law," *Yale Law Journal*, 78 (1969), 1311–1350, at p. 1337.
45. Aristotle, *Nicomachean Ethics*, bk. V, 1131a1ff.
46. See, e.g., Vahinger, *Die Philosophie des Als Ob*, 3rd edn. (Leipzig, 1918). For a more appropriate treatment based on a detailed study of fictions in

Roman law, see N. Demelius, "Über fingierte Persönlichkeit," *Iherings Jahrbücher*, 4 (1861), 133ff.

47. I owe this example to Thomas Franck.

48. See in this context particularly the problem of "extending" the scope of the law by the fiction of a legal personality. For a discussion of this problem, see Luc Silance, "La Personalité juridique, realité et fiction?", both in Chaim Perelman and P. Forier, *Les Présomptions et les fictions en droit*, pp. 48.278–317 and 317–338.

49. For a well-presented argument treating fictions differently, i.e., as a generative principle, see Joseph Esser, *Wert und Bedeuteung der Rechtsfiktionen*, 2nd edn. (Frankfurt: Vittorio Klostermann, 1969).

50. Henkin et al., *International Law*, p. 220.

51. The problem with fictions is that they are devices by which unfamiliar or alien matters can be regulated through existing rules without explicit law-making efforts. Thus, by analogizing e.g. a corporation to a "person" a new reference class is created which then allows for further developments. However, the more the new "fictitious" entities of a class are accepted, the more they loose their fictitious character and simple become shorthands for a class of phenomena.

52. Arthur Kaufmann, *Analogie und Natur der Sache* (Heidelberg: Decker und Müller, 1982), p. 51.

53. In recent times some lawyers have held that persons infected by AIDS who engage in sexual activity or are attempting to transmit the disease, e.g. through baiting, are committing "assaults with a deadly weapon."

54. See Carl Hempel and Felix Oppenheimer, *Der Typusbegriff im Licht der Neuen Logik* (Leiden: Sijthoff, 1936). See also Egbert Gerken, "Der Typusbegriff in seiner deskriptiven Verwendung," *Archiv für Rechts- und Sozialphilosophie*, 50 (1964), 367–385.

55. For a further discussion of this problem, see Kaufmann, *Analogie und Natur der Sache*, p. 27.

56. See para. 185 StGB (German Penal Code).

57. See par. 250 StGB (schwerer Raub).

58. See, e.g., the examples given in the commentary to sec. 1–201:12 of the Uniform Commercial Code (U.C.C.) of what is an "agreement shown by conduct," or who is a "merchant" in the sense of sec. 2–104 of the same code. Thus, a "lawyer buying fishing tackle for his own use" is not a merchant. Similarly a farmer who is a simple "tiller of the soil" does not qualify as a merchant even if he sells his surplus. However, a farmer (even of the same size) who sells futures to a broker is probably a "merchant" within the meaning of the code. For a further discussion see Richard M. Alderman, *A Transactional Guide to the Uniform Commercial Code*, 2nd edn. (Philadelphia, Pa.: American Bar Association, 1983), pp. 36ff.

59. See, e.g., Vattel's argument in *Droit des gens*, ch. XVII. See also R. D. Klinger, "The Vattelian Armory and the Logical Status of its Canons," in Ilmar Tammelo, *Treaty Interpretation and Practical Reason*, (Sydney: The Law Book Co., 1967), pp. 89–101.

60. See in this context the importance of the emergency of a class of "jurists"

for the development of law and, depending on their social organization, the different directions the development of law may take, as Weber pointed out. See Max Weber, *Economy and Society* (Berkeley, Cal.: University of California Press, 1978), pp. 973–980 and 875–794, 814, 889–892 (Rechtssoziologie).

61. See, e.g., in recent times the debate concerning the "wide" or "narrow" interpretation of the A.B.M. treaty which turns precisely on this issue. See, e.g., Kevin Kennedy, "Treaty Interpretation by the Executive Branch: The ABM Treaty and 'Star Wars' Testing and Development," *American Journal of International Law*, 80 (October 1980), 854–872.

62. Wolfgang Gast, "Recht als ius argumentandi," in Otmar Ballwey and Thomas Seibert (eds.), *Rhetorische Rechtstheorie* (Freiburg: Alber, 1982), p. 304.

63. On the importance of "backing" and warrants for claims within the context of arguments, see Stephen Toulmin, *The Uses of Argument* (Cambridge: Cambridge University Press, 1964).

64. Eric D'Arcy, *Human Acts* (Oxford: Clarendon Press, 1970), pp. 18–19.

65. Christopher Stone, "From a Language Perspective," *Yale Law Journal*, 90 (1981), 1149–1192, at p. 1158.

66. Legal phenomenology tries to do exactly that (though quite unsuccessfully). For an interesting attempt along these lines, see, e.g., David Kennedy, "Spring Brake," *Texas Law Review*, 63 (May 1985), 1377–1423.

67. The term "transcendental" is used here in the Kantian sense, referring to the conditions of the possibility of a discursive understanding of normative questions, rather than in the scholastic sense, which would imply some type of objectively "true," ontologically grounded, insight.

68. Aristotle, *Topica* 165b8–10.

69. See Jürgen Habermas, *Theorie des kommunikativen Handelns*, 2 vols. (Frankfurt: Suhrkamp, 1981).

70. Marcus Tullius Cicero, *De inventione, De optimo genere oratorum, Topica* trans. H. M. Hubbell, (Cambridge, Mass.: Harvard University Press, 1960).

71. Quintilian, *Institutio oratoria*, trans. H. E. Butler, 4 vols. (Cambridge, Mass.: Harvard University Press, 1979). For an extensive discussion of the relevance of Cicero and Quintilian to juridical thinking, see Rolf Gröschner, *Dialogik und Jurisprudenz, Die Philosophie des Dialogs als Philosophie der Rechtspraxis* (Tübingen: J. C. B. Mohr, 1982).

72. Bartolus (Bartolo de Sassoferrato) was one of the main exponents of the *mos Italicus*, which took the "unsystematic" topical thinking as the characteristic of legal thought and taught Roman law in terms of a problem-solving case method. Against this *mos Italicus*, French lawyers insisted on a more systematic instruction and thus became the exponents of a *mos Gallicus* which by the eighteenth century had won out over the Italian version. For a historical discussion, see Franz Wieacker, *Privatrechtsgeschichte der Neuzeit* (Göttingen: Vanderhoek and Ruprecht, 1967), pp. 26ff., and Paul Koschaker, *Europa und das Römische Recht* (München: C. H. Beck, 1966). For Bartolus' commentaries on Roman law,

see his *Bartoli Commentaria in Primam Partem Digesti Novi* (Lugundi: Georgius Renault, 1538).

73. Gribaldus Mopha, *De methodo a ratione studendi libri tres* (1541). For a historical discussion of Mopha's importance, see Roderich Stintzing, *Geschichte der deutschen Rechtswissenschaft*, vol. I (München–Leipzig: R. Oldenburg, 1880–1910), ch. IV.

74. Johannes Stroux, *Römische Rechtswissenschaft und Rhetorik* (Potsdam: Stichnote, 1949).

75. Theodor Viehweg, *Topik und Jurisprudenz*, 2nd edn (München: C. H. Beck, 1963).

76. Biago Brugi, *Il metodo dei Glossatori Bolognesi, Studi Riccobono*, vol. 1 (Palermo: Castiglia, 1936), pp. 23–31.

77. See Robert W. Baker, *The Hearsay Rule* (London: Pitman, 1950).

78. See, e.g., Theodore Plucknett, *A Concise History of the Common Law*, 5th edn. (Boston: Little, Brown, 1956), p. 407. See also R. W. Millar, "The Mechanism of Fact Discovery: A Study in Comparative Civil Procedure," *Illinois Law Review*, 32 (1937), pp. 261–294.

79. See, e.g., Wilbur Samuel Howell, *Logic and Rhetoric in England 1500–1700* (Princeton, NJ, Princeton University Press, 1956). See also D. S. Bland, "Rhetoric and the Law Student in Sixteenth Century England," *Studies in Philology*, 54 (1957), 498–508.

80. On this point, see Alessandro Giuliani, "The Influence of Rhetoric on the Law of Evidence and Pleading," *Juridical Review*, 3 (1962), 216–251.

81. Ibid., 221.

82. "If a witness were allowed to draw inferences from his own perceptions he would be substituting himself for the judge. The art of conjecturing is very difficult and requires much study of logic. One cannot ask, therefore, whether Titius is the owner of a certain thing because a reply would require an inference from certain facts. The witness can be questioned with regard to *causa scientiae*, as it is on this that the force of the evidence lies. As Cinus declared: *si non reddit causam sui dicti rationabiliter, non valet (testimonium)* . . ." Only "when direct evidence is notoriously difficult to obtain may the judge admit evidence based on hearsay." Guiliani, "The Influence of Rhetoric on the Law of Evidence and Pleading," 236. In this distrust of evidence *ex auditu* can be seen an anticipation of the hearsay rule.

83. This is not to say that certain exclusionary rules do not have directly to do with probity. See, e.g., *Mapp v. Ohio* 367 US 643 (1961), in which states were enjoined from using evidence obtained in violation of the 4th amendment.

84. Sir Thomas Littleton, *Tenures* (London: Hastings, 1846), sec. 534.

85. For a discussion of influence of rhetoric upon the *ius civile*, see Viehweg, *Topik und Jurisprudenz*, ch. 4.

86. See Plucknett, *Concise History of the Common Law*, pp. 399ff.

87. Steven Gifis, *Law Dictionary* (Woodbury, NY: Barron's Educ. Series, 1975), defines both pleas in the following way:
DILATORY PLEAS: those which tend to defeat the actions to which they

refer by contesting grounds other than the merits of plaintiffs case. Hence, they go to issues such as improper jurisdictions, wrong defendant, or other procedural defects.

PEREMPTORY PLEA, on the other hand, is one which answers the plaintiff's material contention.

88. For a discussion of the influence of Greek rhetoric on the Roman law of pleading as tradited by Cicero and Quintilian, see Stroux, *Römische Rechtswissenschaft und Rhetorik*.

89. See in this context Cicero, *De inventione* I.11 and II.14–15 and Quintilian, *Institutio oratoria* VII.1.4 and VII.2.8–57.

90. See also Cicero's argument in *De inventione* I. 8.10 concerning the following issues:

> But if it appears that the right person does not bring the suit, or that he brings it against the wrong person, or before the wrong tribunal, or at a wrong time, under the wrong statue, or the wrong charge, or with a wrong penalty, the issue is called translative because the action seems to require a transfer to another court or alternation in the form of pleading.

Also I.11.16.

91. Cicero, *De inventione* I.11, I.13.18.

92. Ibid., I.8.

93. Ibid. See also Stroux, *Römische Rechtswissenschaft*, p. 24.

94. Quintilian, *Institutio oratoria*, III.6.21: "Hemagoras statum vocat per quem subjecta res intelligitur et ad quem probationes etiam partium referuntur."

95. According to the Greek status doctrine these difficulties have to be dealt with in terms of defining the delicts more clearly. But as Aristotle already pointed out, such legal definitions are not definitions in the strict sense but means of appraisal, i.e., are "types" which include a complex fact and evaluative criteria. See, for example, his argument in his *Rhetoric*, trans. Lane Cooper (Englewood Cliffs, N.J.: Prentice-Hall, 1932), 1374a1ff.:

> Now it often happens that the accused will admit the fact, but will deny the legal name the prosecutor gives it, or deny what is assumed under this name. For example, they will admit they have taken something, but will deny that they stole it; will admit having struck the first blow, but will deny having committed outrage; will admit intercourse, but will deny adultery; will admit theft, but will deny sacrilege (saying that the property stolen was not consecrated); will admit having encroached in [by] cultivating land, but will deny that the land belonged to the state; or will admit having communicated with the enemy, but will deny that the communication was treasonable. Accordingly it would seem necessary to define these terms also – "theft," "outrage," "adultery," – in order that, whether we wish to prove the existence or the non-existence of the crime, we may put the case in a clear light. In all such cases the question is whether the accused is criminal and vicious, or the reverse; for the wickedness and injustice of an act lie in the purpose of the agent, and *terms like outrage and theft connote, in addition to the acts themselves, this purpose* [my italics].

See also Quintilian VII.3.21–22.

96. Cicero, *De inventione* II.116ff.

97. The topos of *scriptum et voluntas* vs. *sententia* goes back to the Greek distinction between *rheton* and *dianoia*. See, e.g., Aristotle, *Rhetoric* 1374a1ff:

> Let us begin by discussing the way in which the speaker should make use of laws in exhortation or dissuasion, and in accusation or defense. It is clear that, if the written law is adverse to our case, he must appeal to the universal law, and to the principles of equity as representing a higher order of justice. [He must say] that [the judge's obligation to decide] "according to my best judgment" means that the judge will be not guided simply and solely by the letter of the statute. The speaker will contend, too, that equity is permanent and unchanging, and the universal law likewise – for it is the law of nature; whereas the written laws are subject to frequent change. Hence the speech in *Antigone* . . .
>
> On the other hand, if the written law favors his case, the speaker must say that [the judge's obligation to decide] "according to my best judgment" is not intended to produce verdicts in opposition to the law, but to save the judge from perjury if he does not know what the law means . . . Or he may say that, if a law is not to be enforced, it might as well not have been enacted. Or he may say that in law, as in other arts – medicine, for example – it does not pay to be wiser than the doctor, as the doctor's mistake will do less harm than getting into the habit of disobeying authority. Or [lastly] he may say that the effort to be wiser than the law is precisely what the most approved codes forbid.

98. For a further discussion see Stroux, *Römische Rechswissenschaft*, pp. 33ff.

99. Cicero, *De inventione* II.116–121. *Topica* 25.95.

100. Cicero, *De inventione* II.116–121. *Topica* 25.95.

101. Stroux, *Römische Rechtwissenschaft*, pp. 39ff.

102. See, e.g., the principle *lex posterior derogat anteriorem*.

103. This is the reason for giving the *lex specialis* priority over the *lex generalis*.

104. For a discussion of various common topoi and their persuasive character, see Spira, "Topik und Ordnung," in Ballweg and Seibert (eds.), *Rhetorische Rechtstheorie*.

105. This catalogue of topoi is a modified version of those enumerated in Stroux, *Römische Rechtswissenschaft*, pp. 30–40.

106. Institut de Droit International, *Annuaire*, 43 (1950), 435–444.

107. Ilmar Tammelo, *Treaty Interpretation and Practical Reason* (Sydney: The Law Book Co., 1967), pp. 45ff.

108. Ibid., pp. 45–108.

109. Ibid., pp. 45–108; see also Quintilian's argument that the good rhetor has also to be a person of ethical qualities such as honesty and fairness. To that extent the appropriateness of speech (*bene dicere*) is rooted in the moral qualities of the person ("bene dicere non possit nisi bonus"), II.15.43:

> For my part, I have undertaken the task of moulding the ideal orator, and as my first desire is that he should be a good man, I will return to those who have sounder opinions on the subject . . . The definition which best suits its real character is that which makes rhetoric the *science of speaking well* for this definition includes all the virtues of oratory and the character of the orator as well, since no man can speak well who is not good himself.

110. See, e.g., the remarks by Jules Basdevant at the Siena Conference of the International Law Commission in 1952, *Annuaire*, 44.II (1952), at p. 375.
111. For a critique along these lines, see Dworkin, "Is Law a System of Rules?", in Dworkin (ed.), *The Philosophy of Law*.
112. For an early critique of this Kelsenian argument, see Alf Ross, *Theorie der Rechtsquellen* (Leipzig–Berlin: Franz Duticke, 1929), *passim*.
113. See, e.g., the German Code on Civil Procedure (Z.P.O.), para. 550.
114. Gifis, *Law Dictionary*.
115. See William Prosser, *Law of Torts*, 4th edn. (Minneapolis–St. Paul: West, 1971), p. 212.
116. For one of the first systematic attempts to bring the various *canones* into some kind of order, see Carl V. Savigny, *System des heutigen Römischen Rechts*, 2 vols. (Berlin: Veit, 1849), pp. 212ff.
117. See, e.g., the differences among the considerations in interpreting wills (*favor testamenti*), *Rechtsgeschäft* (para. 133 B.G.B.) and Contract (para. 157 B.G.B.) in German law. On this point also see Josef Esser, *Grundsatz und Norm in der Richterlichen Fortbildung des Privatrechts* (Tübingen: J. C. B. Mohr, 1956), ch. 7.
118. This is not to argue that there has to be a "core" of uncontested and universally held beliefs in a society. Rather, what seems sufficient is that a certain "value overlap" exists among various group positions. Thus, while the core might be very small, the various intersecting circles of value positions espoused by diverse groups may provide sufficient support for the persuasive arguments espoused in legal arguments. For a further discussion of this point see John Rawls, "The Priority of Right and Ideas of the Good" (mimeo) (August 1987).
119. The difference between a path and an algorithm seems to be that an algorithm establishes an unequivocal structure for choices while "paths" allow for chance elements at turning-points as well as the influence of past decisions upon future ones (through changes in probabilities) without fully determining future choices. "Paths" are traceable but not necessarily predictable. In addition to their probabilistic character, a further complicating feature of the logic underlying law is that it is not limited to the conventional two-valued logic familiar from assertoric logic but allows for a third possibility e.g., when something that is not forbidden may be demanded or simply be allowed. Precisely the last two possibilities create difficulties for the conventional attempts to understand legal prescriptions as "probabilistic" predictions.
120. Thomas Seibert, "Fall, Regel, Topos," in Ballweg and Seibert (eds.), *Rhetorische Rechtstheorie*, pp. 321–335.
121. Taking this route naturally does not preclude Mr. Bidermann from suing the airline and/or the air traffic controllers.
122. See the 1979 revised formulation of para. 651 a sec. 2, which came after the Supreme Court's decision (B.G.H. in Zivilsachen) in 1974. For further discussion, see Seibert, 'Fall, Regel, Topos," p. 332.
123. On this point, see particularly Karl Larenz's discussion of the various theories of norm-application in Karl Larenz, *Methodenlehrer der Rechtswissenschaft*, 5th edn. (Berlin–Heidelberg: Springer, 1983), chs. 1 and 2.

124. See in this context Esser's discussion in his *Grundsatz und Norm*, ch. 7.
125. See in this context Chaim Perelman's discussion in his *The Idea of Justice and the Problem of Argument* (London: Routledge & Kegan Paul, 1963), chs. 1 and 2.
126. To a certain extent, one could make this argument against John Rawls's *Theory of Justice*, but even more so against theorists who derive from "just" principles of all types of conclusions about the "just" or rather unjust character of our social arrangements. See, e.g., Charles Beitz's argument in his *Political Theory and International Relations* (Princeton, NJ: Princeton University Press, 1979). Beitz examines the "unjust" character of the principle of sovereignty over natural resources located in one's territory.
127. See, e.g., Cardozo's argument in *Meinhard* v. *Salmon* 247 NY 458 (1928): "Joint adventurers, like co-partners, owe to one another while the enterprise continues, the duty of finest loyalty . . . Many forms of conduct permissible in a workaday world for those acting at arms' length, are forbidden to those by fiduciary ties."
128. Thus, the problem of law-creation through judicial activity is not simply a matter of "policy" or of the "courage" judges "ought" to show. If such attempts are to be persuasive they have to be tied to a particular context of accepted norms.
129. In this context, see Josef Esser's important study, *Vorverständnis und Methodenweahl in der Rechtsfindung, passim*.
130. For a further discussion, see Esser, *Grundsatz und Norm*, chs. 9–12. For an interesting counterposition to the view espoused here calling for a more activist bench in the case of the I.C.J. and explicitly deemphasizing the common "judicial culture" as a restraint of judicial law-making, see Richard Falk, *Reviving the World Court* (Charlottesville, Va.: University of Virginia Press, 1984), *passim*.
131. The concept of law jobs was introduced by Karl Llewellyn in his "The Normative, the Legal and the Law Jobs: The Problem of Juristic Method," *Yale Law Journal*, 49 (1940), 1355–1400.
132. For a fascinating discussion along these lines, but going beyond Llewellyn's categorization, see Nicholas Onuf, "Global Law Making and Legal Thought," in Nicholas Onuf (ed.), *Law Making in the Global Community* (Durham, NC: Carolina Academic Press, 1982), pp. 1–82, especially pp. 36–44.
133. "Er folgt dabei bewährter Lehre und Überlieferung."
134. See, e.g., 1 *American Jurisprudence* 421, Actions, para. 25, note 20:

> Malicious motives make a bad case worse, but they cannot make wrong that, which is in its own essence [i.e., legal essence!], lawful. When a creditor has a just debt and brings a suit or issues execution, though he does it out of pure enmity to the debtor, he is safe. In slander, if the defendant proves the words spoken to be true, his intention to injure the plaintiff by proclaiming his infamy will not defeat justification. One who prosecutes another for a crime may not show that he was actuated by correct feelings if he can prove that there was good reason to believe the charge well-founded.

135. See, e.g., Gaius D 41.3.1: "Bono publico usucapio introducta est."

135. See, e.g., Gaius D 41.3.1: "Bono publico usucapio introducta est."
136. This is naturally a common topos since Aristotle; for its importance in law, see the discussion of supererogation above in ch. 5.
137. Esser, *Grundsatz und Norm*, p. 155.
138. See in this context the misguided discussion of whether an "unjust" law can be a law. For a clarification of this problem, see Ilmar Tammelo and Lyndel Prott, "Legal and Extralegal Justification," *Journal of Legal Education*, 17 (1965), 412–422.
139. Michael Moore, "A Natural Law Theory of Precedent," in L. Goldstein, *Precedent in Law* (Oxford: Oxford University Press, 1986), quoted from the mimeo version circulated in the Legal Workshop, Columbia University, 18 November 1985.
140. Ibid., p. 99. Esser speaks in this context of a "logic of institutions" rather than rules and principles (quoting Puchta). See Esser, *Grundsatz und Norm*, p. 102.
141. Ronald Dworkin, *Law's Empire* (Cambridge, Mass.: Harvard University Press, 1968), p. 227. In addition, there are the pressures resulting from charts and the community of judges and its appellate hierarchy. They too have a "centrist" effect since nobody wants to be – barring extraordinary circumstances – a lone dissenter and/or have his/her decisions reversed.
142. For the detailed examination of these "quasi-logical" arguments, see Chaim Perelman and L. Olbrechts-Tyteca, *The New Rhetoric*, part III.
143. Lyndell V. Prott, *The Latent Power of Culture and the International Judge* (Abingdon: Professional Books, 1979).
144. Ibid., p. 127.
145. For a more extensive discusion of the legal issues involved in the South-West Africa/Namibia issue see John Dugard, *The South West Africa/Nambia Dispute* (Berkeley, California.: University of California Press, 1973).
146. Wellington Koo, *Barcelona Traction* (Preliminary Objections) Case Sep. Op. 62–63, as quoted in Prott, *The Latent Power*, p. 126.
147. For further discussion of metaphors, see Donald Davidson, "What Metaphors Mean," *Critical Inquiry*, 5 (1978), 31–47, and George Lakoff and Mark Johnson, *Metaphors We Live By* (Chicago: University of Chicago Press, 1980).
148. For a good treatment of the role of evocative symbols in political life, see Murray Edelman, *The Symbolic Uses of Politics* (Urbana, Ill.: University of Illinois Press, 1965).
149. See the crucial distinction in Aristotle, *Rhetoric* 1354a4: "for the arousing of prejudice, compassion, anger, and similar emotions has no connexion with the matter in hand."
150. Prott, *The Latent Power*, p. 126. However, one has to keep in mind that the expression "sacred trust" is taken directly from Art. 73 of the U.N. Charter, in which the members administering non-self-governing territories accept the obligation to "further to the utmost . . . the well-being of the inhabitants of these territories" as a "sacred trust."
151. The following sets of metaphors has been compiled by Prott, *The Latent Power*, p. 140.

152. Jessup, *Barcelona Traction*, Sep. Op., p. 166.
153. Forster, *South West Africa Case* (1966), Diss. Opinion, p. 435.
154. Jessup, *Barcelona Traction*, Sep. Op., p. 166.
155. Jessup, *South West Africa Case*, Diss. Op., p. 432.
156. Spender and Fitzmaurice, *South West Africa Case*, Joint Diss. Op., p. 540.
157. Fitzmaurice, *Barcelona Traction*, Sep. Op., p. 78, para. 25.
158. Jessup, *South West Africa Case* (1966), Diss. Op., p. 435.
159. Spender, *Temple of Preah Vihear Case*, Diss. Op., p. 101.
160. Fitzmaurice, *Barcelona Traction*, Sep. Op., p. 78, para. 25.
161. 369 F. 2d 897 (Second Circuit, 1968); in this case the interests of U.S. anti-trust law forced an official of a New York-based bank to divulge information concening its branch office in Germany. This information was privileged under German law and disclosure incurred penalties.
162. See, e.g., *Arthur Andersen and Co.* v. *Finesilver* (570 F. 2d 388, Tenth Circuit, 1976), and *Ohio* v. *Andersen and Co.* (570 F. 2d 1370 Tenth Circuit, 1978), where the Court held that for all intents and purposes, local law always has to take precedence over foreign law.
163. See my discussion in "The Role of Domestic Courts as Agencies of the International Legal Order," in Richard Falk, Friedrich Kratochwil, and Saul Mendlovitz (eds.), *International Law. A Contemporary Perspective* (Boulder: Westview, 1985), ch. 13.
164. Harold Meier, "Extraterritorial Jurisdiction at a Crossroad: An Intersection between Public and Private International Law," *American Journal of International Law*, 76 (1982), 280–320, at p. 299.

Conclusion: The international legal order, international systems, and the comparative analysis of the practice of states

1. This point was eloquently made by William Coplin, "International Law and Assumptions about the State System," *World Politics* 17 (October 1964), 615–635.
2. See, e.g., Jean Bodin, *The Six Books on a Commonwealth*, ed. Kenneth Douglas McRae (Cambridge, Mass.: Harvard University Press, 1962); see also Julian Franklin, *Jean Bodin and the 16th Century Revolution in the Methodology of Law and History* (New York: Columbia University Press, 1963).
3. For a fundamental discussion of the importance of private law for the development of international law, see Sir Hersch Lauterpacht, *Private Law Sources and Analogies of International Law* (Hamden: Archon Books, 1970).
4. See, e.g., Jay C. Hurewitz, "Ottoman Diplomacy and the European State System," *The Middle East Journal*, 15 (Spring 1961), 141–52.
5. Georges Scelle, *Droit international public* (Paris: Donat Montchrestien, 1970).
6. Richard Falk, "International Jurisdiction: Horizontal and Vertical Conception of Legal Order," *Temple Law Quarterly*, 32 (1959), 295–320.
7. On a clarification of the concept of "transational law" see Friedman, *The Changing Structure of International Law* (New York: Columbia University Press, 1964).

309

8. Oscar Schachter, "The Enforcement of International Judicial and Arbitral Decisions," *American Journal of International Law*, 54 (1960), 1–24.

9. See Art. 38 of the I.C.J. statute.

10. Thus decisions of national courts concerning the expropriation of foreign property are notorious for not having established clear rules in spite of a considerable amount of case-law. Even worse is the situation in such gray areas as "creeping expropriations" by means of fiscal laws and health or labor regulations.

11. See, e.g., Kant's remarks in his *Rechtslehre* (sec. 57), in which a punitive war is excluded. Immanuel Kant, *Werke*, ed. Benzion Kellerman (Berlin: Bruno Cassirer, 1916), pp. 154–155. See also the argument of Elisabeth Zoller that countermeasures have no punitive function but are designed solely to force an opponent to desist from further illegal conduct. Zoller, *Peacetime Unilateral Remedies*.

12. Michael Oakshott, *On Human Conduct* (Oxford: Clarendon Press, 1975). Terry Nardin, *Law, Morality and the Relations of States* (Princeton, NJ: Princeton University Press, 1983).

13. Such duties either can arise under customary international law, such as the customary injunction against slavery, or might be the result of (multilateral) treaty obligations, such as to extradite or prosecute terrorists who have violated the rights of internationally protected persons, etc.

14. Roger Fisher, *Improving Compliance with International Law* (Charlottesville, Va.: University of Virginia Press, 1981).

15. Moore suggests the institutionalization of legal advice in the national security decision-making process in his "Law and National Security," in Falk, Kratochwil, and Mendlovitz (eds.), *International Law*, ch. 3.

16. Martin Wight, *Systems of States* (Leicester University Press, 1977).

17. See, e.g., the discussion of various models of "polarity" and stability of the international system: Kenneth Waltz, "International Structure, National Force and the Balance of Power"; Morton Kaplan, "Variants on Six Models of the International System"; Karl Deutsch and J. David Singer, "Multipolar Power Systems and International Stability"; and Richard Rosecrance, "Bipolarity, Multipolarity and the Future"; all reprinted in James Rosenau (ed.), *International Politics and Foreign Policy* (New York: Free Press, 1969), chs. 27–30.

18. See the important discussion of Joseph Nogee, "Polarity, An Ambiguous Concept," *Orbis*, 18 (Winter 1979), 1193–1224.

19. These questions are systematically raised by Jack Snyder, *The Ideology of the Offensive: Military Decision Making and the Disasters of 1914* (Ithaca: Cornell University Press, 1984), and in his paper "Strategy Among the Few" (mimeo) (Columbia University, 1985).

20. The idea that we enhance our options by targeting the Russian population in the case of a war while sparing the ethnic minorities is criticized by George Quester, "Ethnic Targeting: A Bad Idea Whose Time Has Come," *Journal of Strategic Studies*, 5 (June 1982), 228–235. See also Robert Jervis, *The Illogic of American Nuclear Strategy* (Ithaca: Cornell University Press, 1984), ch. 3.

21. John Gerard Ruggie, "Continuity and Transformation in the World Polity," *World Politics*, 35 (January 1983), 261–285.
22. Oran Young, *Compliance and Public Authority* (Baltimore: Johns Hopkins University Press, 1979).
23. See, e.g., the study of a half-way house for narcotics offenders by D. L. Wieder, *Language and Social Reality* (The Hague: Mouton, 1974).
24. For an excellent introduction to ethnomethodology and Harold Garfinkel's work see John Heritage, *Garfinkel and Ethnomethodology* (Cambridge: Polity Press, 1984).
25. See, e.g., Erving Goffman, *Relations in Public: Micro Studies of the Public Order* (New York: Harper, 1971).
26. Although the imagery of a river is invoked by Machiavelli in regard to the force of *fortuna,* his argument about the need of restraining the passions on the one hand and, on the other, diverting the rapacious private urges to a public purpose (glory) shows that very much the same metaphor applies. Thus, the topos that "all men are wicked and always will give vent to malignity . . . when opportunity offers" and that they are made "good" only by laws that restrain their ambition is a recurrent theme in Machiavelli's *Discourses.* See, e.g., bk. I, ch. 3 or bk. I, ch. 37. Niccolò Machiavelli, *The Discourses*, ed. Bernard Crick (Baltimore: Penguin, 1970), pp. 111–112 and 200 respectively. The metaphor of the flood and its canalization can be found in Niccolò Machiavelli, *The Prince*, trans. George Bull (Baltimore: Penguin, 1972), ch. XXV.
27. The idea of *katharsis* as one of the main functions of drama goes back to Aristotle's *Poetics*; for a mor contemporary analysis of the problem of mutual role-taking as a means for achieving common understandings in interactions, which, in turn, are the precondition of conflict resolution, see the various papers by Alfred Schutz, *Collected Papers* (The Hague: Matinus Nijhoff, 1962).
28. See, e.g., the criticism of this simplistic mode of technological thinking in Langdon Winner, *Autonomous Technology: Technics out of Control as a Theme in Political Thought* (Cambridge, Mass.: M.I.T. Press, 1977).
29. Herbert Simon, *Administrative Behavior*, 2nd edn. (New York: Macmillan, 1968).
30. James March and Richard Cyert, *A Behavioral Theory of the Firm* (Englewood Cliffs: Prentice Hall, 1963).
31. James March and Johan Olsen (eds.), *Ambiguity and Choice in Organizations* (Bergen, Norway: Universitets Forlaget, 1976).
32. Jeffrey Pfeffer, *The External Control of Organizations: A Resource Dependence Approach* (New York: Harper and Row, 1978).
33. See, e.g., the important argument in F. E. Emery and E. L. Trist, "The Causal Texture of Organizational Enviroments," *Human Relations*, 18 (1965), 21–32.
34. John Meyer and Brian Rowan, "Institutionalized Organizations: Formal Structure as Myth and Ceremony," *American Journal of Sociology*, 83 (1977), 4–63; Marshall Meyer, "Organizational Structure as Signaling," *Pacific Sociological Review*, 22 (October 1979), 481–500.

35. See my "On the Notion of Interest in International Relations," *International Organization*, 36 (Winter 1982), 1–30.
36. Thucydides, V.84–116 and III.69–66.
37. Robert Gilpin, *War as Change, in World Politics* (Cambridge: Cambridge University Press, 1981).

INDEX

action (social), 5, 7, 23ff., 63, 123
  appraisal of, 11, 25, 238, 240
  communicative, *see* communication
  characterization of, 228–230, 237
  of "innocent utility," 24f.
  and meaning, 24f.
  reasons for, 9, 23, 69, 97, 145
Adenauer, Konrad, 219
Aeschylus, 127
Aesop, 218
Alien Tort statute, 176–177
analogies, *see* reasoning, analogous
anarchy, 2, 19, 45, 47, 140, 250
Antarctica, 83
argument, 12, 99, 125, 142, 207, 219, 238;
    see also reasoning
  legal, 12, 18, 232–247
  logical, 31
  moral, 101; *see also* morality
  persuasiveness of, 32, 33, 38, 215, 21
Aristotle, 6, 40, 41, 210, 215, 216, 217,
    218, 230
Asylum case, 55
Austin, John, 26, 91, 92
Austria, 84, 85, 219
authority, 116, 124, 158, 165
Axelrod, Robert, 75, 109

Balance of Power, 83, 257, 261f
Baldwin, David, 47
Barcelona Traction case, 161
bargaining, 35, 48, 71, 114, 117, 181, 184,
    185
Barkun, Michael, 36, 181
Bartolus of Sassoferrato, 230
Beckett, Eric, Sir, 235
Bedjaoui, Mohammed, 200
Bentham, Jeremy, 21, 110
Beitz, Charles, 161
Blackmun, Harry, 172
Blackstone, W. T., 213
Brentano, Franz, 34
Bricker, Amendment, *see* United States,
    Constitution of

Brugi, Biagio, 230
Bull, Headley, 71
bunching, *see* games
Bundesgerichtshof (B.G.H.), 203f., 240

categorical imperative, *see* Kant,
    categorical imperative
cause, 22, 24, 25, 98
  actionable 162, 163, 175; *see also*
    reasons
certiorari, 177
Christie, George, 222, 223
Churchill, Sir Winston, 84
Cicero, Marcus Tullius, 145, 230, 231
Code Napoléon, 220
codes of conduct, *see* law, "soft law"
Cold War, 85, 199
Coleman, James, 23
comity, 246
common heritage, 115
communication, 5–8, 29, 30–34, 125, 174
  communicative action, 15, 16, 34, 123,
    144, 146
  discourse, 16, 17, 18, 33, 125, 131, 137,
    157, 179, 183, 219, 228, 229; on
    grievances, 16, 56, 70, 124, 130–152,
    153, 168, 185
  see also language, signals
compliance, 96, 102ff., 123, 255ff., 259;
    see also norms
Comte, Auguste, 21
Concert of Europe, 83, 85
Congress of Vienna, 83
Congress of Verona, 83
consensual knowledge, *see* knowledge,
    consensual
consideration, 119, 120, 126; *see also* law,
    contract
contract, *see* law, contract
cooperation, 58, 104, 106ff., 109
Coplin, William, 251
Corfu Channel case, 145
conventions, *see* norms; games
crisis, Bosnian, 84

313